DIVIDED BY THE WORD

RECONSIDERATIONS IN SOUTHERN AFRICAN HISTORY
Richard Elphick and Benedict Carton, Editors

Divided by the Word

*Colonial Encounters and the
Remaking of Zulu and Xhosa Identities*

Jochen S. Arndt

UNIVERSITY OF VIRGINIA PRESS

Charlottesville and London

University of Virginia Press
© 2022 by the Rector and Visitors of the University of Virginia
All rights reserved
Printed in the United States of America on acid-free paper

First published 2022

9 8 7 6 5 4 3 2 1

Library of Congress Cataloging-in-Publication Data

Names: Arndt, Jochen S., author.
Title: Divided by the word : colonial encounters and the remaking of Zulu
    and Xhosa identities / Jochen S. Arndt.
Other titles: Reconsiderations in southern African history.
Description: Charlottesville : University of Virginia Press, 2022. | Series:
    Reconsiderations in southern African history | Includes bibliographical
    references and index.
Identifiers: LCCN 2021041553 (print) | LCCN 2021041554 (ebook) |
    ISBN 9780813947358 (hardcover) | ISBN 9780813947365 (ebook)
Subjects: LCSH: Language and culture—South Africa—History. | Zulu
    language—History. | Zulu (African people)—Ethnic identity. | Xhosa
    language—History. | Xhosa (African people)—Ethnic identity. |
    Missionaries—South Africa—History—19th century. | South Africa—
    Ethnic relations—History.
Classification: LCC DT1754 .A76 2022 (print) | LCC DT1754 (ebook) |
    DDC 305.800968—dc23
LC record available at https://lccn.loc.gov/2021041553
LC ebook record available at https://lccn.loc.gov/2021041554

All maps by Nat Case, INCase, LLC

Cover art: Hlubi schoolgirl in Dengwane, near Tinana. Photograph by Bishop Johannes Vogt.
(Moravian Archives, Herrnhut, Germany, call no. LBS. 12343.)

• CONTENTS •

ACKNOWLEDGMENTS

When asked how I got interested in African history, I usually recount two episodes from my life. The first takes me back to the Côte d'Azur, France, where I spent time as a high school student at the Lycée Antoine de Saint-Exupéry in the city of Saint-Raphaël during the late 1980s. Saint-Raphaël melts almost imperceptibly into the neighboring city of Fréjus, which served as an important base of France's colonial army for much of its history, and especially for *L'Armée Noire* (the Black Army) during World War I. Even to a young student, this history was perceptible still in the 1980s, as Africans formed an integral part of both cities' cultural DNA. It also raised questions about Africa and its relationship with Europe that lingered in my mind until they surfaced again in the 1990s, when I lived and worked for almost a decade in Portugal. Portugal's historic ties with Africa likewise were detectable everywhere—the people, the food, the news—but they became especially noticeable when I conversed with older colleagues who had fought in the wars that brought the Portuguese empire in Africa to an end in 1974. As they shared memories of their experiences in Angola, Mozambique, and Guiné-Bissau, my desire to find out more about Africa and its historical relationship with Europe increased.

I decided to find some of the answers by embarking on a PhD program in history at the University of Illinois at Chicago (UIC) in 2008. I was determined to pursue a research project related to Lusophone Africa. In the second semester, however, I participated in a seminar, taught by my then-advisor Jim Searing, in which we discussed Richard Price's fascinating book *Making Empire: Colonial Encounters and the Making of Imperial Rule in Nineteenth-Century Africa* (2008). The book focuses on the encounters between South Africa's Xhosa chiefdoms and British missionaries, officials, and settlers during the first half of the nineteenth century. Price's argument grabbed my attention, inspired a research paper on the Cape Colony's frontier wars (published by the *Journal of Military History* in 2010), and moved me to focus on the history of South Africa's coastal belt. When Jim subsequently encouraged me to pursue the topic of colonial encounters and the remaking of ethnic identities in the coastal belt as part of my dissertation research, I embarked on a ten-year journey that comes to completion with this monograph.

During this decade I received generous support, encouragement, and guidance from mentors, colleagues, friends, and family members. From my time at UIC, I owe a big thank you to the late Jim Searing, as well as to Kirk Hoppe, Sunil Agnani, and Lynette Jackson, who stepped in as my mentors and dissertation readers when Jim unexpectedly passed away in 2012. UIC also supported my initial research financially with several fellowships and grants, including the Marion S. Miller Dissertation Fellowship and a Dean's Scholar Award.

Some of this research funding allowed me to do preliminary research at the Moravian and Berlin missionary archives in Germany, and to test some of my early conclusions at the "Jenseits von Afrika" workshop organized by Adam Jones of the University of Leipzig in 2011. Even though my ideas changed over time, these first steps were important; they led to a Title VI Foreign Language and Area Studies (FLAS) fellowship to study isiXhosa, a Social Sciences Research Council International Dissertation Research Fellowship, and to an American Historical Association Bernadotte E. Schmitt Research Grant.

Equipped with these skills and funds, I embarked on a year of focused research in South Africa and the United Kingdom. During this time, a tremendous number of people gave me encouragement and support, notably Jeff Peires who, while I was engaged in research at Rhodes University's Cory Library, took the time to introduce me to Grahamstown (Makhanda) and alerted me to an important debate among nineteenth-century missionaries about the geographic reach of the "Caffre" language community that now forms an important aspect of this book's argument. I am also thankful to Natasha Erlank who commented on my ideas about the history of language, religion, and ethnic identity while "doing lunch" at Wits University's Origins Centre in Johannesburg. She also kindly shared some of her research notes on nineteenth-century Scottish missionaries, which allowed me to flesh out the latter's attitude toward the coastal belt's language situation.

My thinking about the American Board missionaries' assessment of language and dependence on African intermediaries benefitted tremendously from conversations with Ben Carton, Robert Houle, Norman Etherington, and Scott Couper over the years. They all have showed me enormous generosity in other ways as well. Scott hosted me at the Inanda Seminary in 2017; Norman and Robert gave me access to some of their research notes on the American missionaries; and Ben, though he is not aware of this yet, has become an important mentor to me since Jim's passing in 2012. He has not only sharpened my understanding of Zuluness but also of the world of the professional historian and academic.

My ideas on the history of Zuluness have also benefited from conversations with John Wright and Carolyn Hamilton, notably during the 2015 Izithunguthu conference organized by the Archive and Public Culture Research Initiative, University of Cape Town. At this conference, I had particularly fruitful exchanges with Paul Landau, Jill Kelly, Gavin Whitelaw, and Rachel King, all of whom helped sharpen many of the key arguments of this book.

Other conferences have been important testing grounds for these arguments as well. The Northeastern Workshop on Southern Africa, the annual meetings of the African Studies Association and the Association for the Study of the Middle East and Africa, and the biennial conference of the Southern African Historical Society have all offered opportunities for conversations with a long list of colleagues whose comments and suggestions have helped make this book better. Special thanks are due to Robert Edgar, Stephen Volz, Thomas McClendon, Diana Jeater, Dingani Mthethwa, and George Simpson for their time, comments, and feedback over the years.

The Virginia Military Institute (VMI) has been my professional home since 2016. I have found my colleagues in the history department and the wider VMI community to be extraordinarily helpful and supportive of my work on this book. A heartfelt thank you goes to Tim Dowling who has not only provided valuable comments and suggestions on early drafts of the monograph but accompanied other important steps of the publishing process as well. Together with Geoff Jensen, Tim kindly provided feedback on my book proposal and, along with Qingfei Yin, helped me craft the book's title during long weekend walks. I am also indebted to the staff of VMI's Preston Library, especially Tonya Moore, who possesses a special genius for obtaining even the most obscure books on South African history via interlibrary loan, and to VMI's Faculty Development Committee for approving several grants that allowed me to do additional research in South Africa and the United States.

The research for this book took me to numerous archives whose staff members have always been welcoming and supportive. Special thanks go to Zamanguni Gumede of the KwaZulu-Natal Archives and Records service in Pietermaritzburg, Onesimus Ngundu of the Bible Society Archives at the University of Cambridge, Lucy McCann at the University of Oxford's Bodleian Library of Commonwealth and African Studies, Cornelius Thomas and Liz de Wet at Rhodes University's Cory Library for Historical Research in Grahamstown, Erika LeRoux at the Western Archive and Records Service in Cape Town, and Hanlie Rossouw at the South African Bible Society Archive in Bellville. I am also indebted to the staffs of the National Library of Scotland and the New College Library at the University of Edinburgh, the Killie-Campbell Africana Library in Durban, the Historical Papers division of the University of Witwatersrand Library in Johannesburg, the Manuscript Division of the School of Oriental and African Studies Library in London, the Special Collections at the University of Cape Town's Jagger Library, and the Manuscript Archive at Harvard University's Houghton Library.

I am particularly grateful to Claudia Mai and Olaf Nippe of the Moravian Archives in Herrnhut, Germany, who helped secure the photo on the book cover, which portrays an anonymous Hlubi girl. I thank her, and I thank all the other amaHlubi who helped me get a better understanding of how language and belonging intersect in post-apartheid South Africa. This includes Jobe Radebe, Sanele Godlo, the late Bandile Nodada, and Buyiswa Mini. I am especially indebted to Buyiswa for patiently teaching me isiXhosa during my Foreign Language and Area Studies fellowship. *Enkosi Kakhulu!*

An earlier version of chapter 2 was published as "What's in a Word: Historicizing the Word 'Caffre' in European Discourses about Southern Africa, 1500–1800," *Journal of Southern African Studies* 44, no. 1 (2018): 59–75. Chapter 7 and the epilogue also draw on earlier publications, notably "Engineered Zuluness: Language, Education, and Ethnic Identity in South Africa, 1835–1990," *Journal of the Middle East and Africa* 10, no. 3 (Sep., 2019): 211–235, and "Struggles of Land, Language, and Identity in Post-Apartheid South Africa: The Case of the Hlubi," *Journal of the Middle East and Africa* 9, no. 1 (Jul., 2018): 1–26. I thank both journals for permission to reuse some of these materials in this book.

The publication would have been impossible without the support of the University of Virginia Press. I owe immense gratitude to Nadine Zimmerli, the Editor for History and Social Sciences. Nadine's enthusiasm for my book's argument and scope energized my writing, and her editorial suggestions improved the final product immensely. The editors of the Reconsiderations in Southern African History series, Rick Elphick and Ben Carton, and the anonymous readers, deserve similar gratitude for their unwavering support and insightful comments. Thanks also to Morgan Myers, George Roupe, and Kate Mertes for helping me move the book through production.

Endless thanks also go to my parents, Günther and Gisela, and to my wife Sheri for their love and support. Sheri has accompanied me on all of my research trips to South Africa and has toured with me all the corners of the Western Cape, Eastern Cape, and KwaZulu-Natal Provinces. Her adventurous spirit, generous heart, and sharp mind have made her my true north in this endeavor and in life.

Finally, although the book is the product of collective effort and wisdom, all errors are entirely my own.

• ABBREVIATIONS •

ABC	American Board of Commissioners for Foreign Missions Archives
ABM	American Board of Commissioners for Foreign Missions in Natal-Zululand
ABMC	American Board Mission Collection
BFBS	British and Foreign Bible Society
BMS	Berlin Missionary Society
BSA	Bible Society Archives
CL	Cory Library for Historical Research
CWM	Council for World Mission
HFMR	*Home and Foreign Missionary Record for the Free Church of Scotland*
JAG	*Journal of Aldin Grout*
JJL	*Journals of James Laing*
JSA	*James Stuart Archive*
LMS	*London Missionary Society*
MH	*Missionary Herald*
MMS	*Methodist Missionary Archives*
MS	*Manuscript*
NLSA	*National Library of South Africa, Cape Town Campus*
QIGMS	*Quarterly Intelligence of the Glasgow Missionary Society*
PKM	*Presbytery of Kaffraria Minutes*
PMB	*Natal Archives, Pietermaritzburg*
RGMS	*Report of the Glasgow Missionary Society*
WMM	*Wesleyan Missionary Magazine*

• NOTES ON TERMINOLOGY •

The meanings and spellings of words can change over time. In general, I deal with this phenomenon by foregrounding the meanings and spellings used in the primary sources.

The most significant exception to this practice is that I usually omit Bantu language prefixes. Thus, I write of the "Zulu language" and the "Xhosa language" rather than of *isiZulu* and *isiXhosa*. And rather than referring to *amaZulu* and *amaXhosa*, I write of "Zulu" and "Xhosa" clans, polities, and ethnicities (terms that both languages can express with a single word—*izizwe*). The exception to the exception occurs in direct quotations and where words are better known with prefixes such as in *amantungwa* and *amalala, ukukhuluma* and *ukutekeza.*

The word "Caffre" ("Cafre," "Caffer," "Kafir," and "Kaffir") poses special problems because it acquired extremely derogatory connotations in recent history. I retain it in the book only because it is crucial to my argument, notably for the period between 1500 and 1850 CE, when it had very different meanings. To ensure uniformity and highlight the word's more recent derogatory implications, I use "Caffre" (in quotation marks) throughout the book except when it occurs in direct quotes.

Finally, the book frequently refers to the "eastern Cape" and "Natal-Zululand" regions. I use these terms in a geographic sense; they demarcate areas that are roughly coterminous with post-apartheid South Africa's Eastern Cape and KwaZulu-Natal provinces. Alternatively, one can think of the eastern Cape region as extending from the Gamtoos River to the Mzimkhulu River and of the Natal-Zululand region as stretching from the Mzimkhulu River to the Phongolo River.

DIVIDED BY THE WORD

Introduction

South Africa's transition from apartheid rule to nonracial democracy took place between 1990 and 1994. This transition is often portrayed as a miracle because it was not accompanied by an all-out race war. But while white and Black politicians negotiated the peaceful ending of the apartheid regime, a civil war raged in the African townships of the Witwatersrand (Rand). This conflict turned the Rand townships of Katlehong, Thokoza, Vosloorus, Soweto, Kagiso, Bekkersdal, Sebokeng, and Tembisa into war zones, killing some three thousand people and injuring many thousands more. It even threatened to derail the transition process and bury the new South Africa before its birth.[1]

The Rand conflict had complex causes. The unraveling of the apartheid regime caused South Africa's urban poor to compete for decreasing resources, while the accelerating rivalry between African-owned taxi businesses provoked a rift between migrant workers and township residents. Both dynamics contributed to the conflict, as did the use of "dirty tricks" by the apartheid state's police and security forces and the growing competition between Mangosuthu (Gatsha) Buthelezi's Inkatha Freedom Party (IFP) and Nelson Mandela's African National Congress (ANC). Once the conflict got underway, moreover, it developed its own logics of violence, notably endless cycles of revenge killings.

The people committing the killings held complicated identities. Those linked to the IFP, for instance, were often African male migrant workers from rural KwaZulu-Natal who lived in the Rand's dormitory-style complexes called hostels. Many of the combatants associated with the ANC, in contrast, were younger African men who resided permanently in the Rand townships. But even these descriptions are simplifications, because some IFP supporters lived in the townships, while some ANC followers dwelled in the hostels. Moreover, the conflict involved people of both genders, different age groups, and varied backgrounds. Veterans of the ANC's armed wing, *Umkhonto weSizwe* (the Spear of the Nation) and members of criminal gangs, such as the "Russians," joined in the fighting. The conflict also gave birth to new organizations, including township-based self-defense units, hostel-based self-protection units, and "revenge" gangs such as the "Germans." The violence, therefore, had complex causes and involved people with similarly complex identities.

As interviews conducted with combatants make clear, however, many people who experienced the Rand conflict firsthand understood it primarily as a Zulu-Xhosa war. "We are the Zulus and we are fighting the Xhosas" or "We are the Xhosas and are fighting the Zulus" were common statements uttered by those engaged in the township fighting.[2] Even when combatants acknowledged that the violence occurred within the context of a wider IFP-ANC power struggle, they usually linked the brutal acts themselves to the Zuluness and Xhosaness of each party's dominant membership base. One Zulu migrant who attended an IFP meeting at Kwesine hostel in Katlehong in 1990 explained, "The speakers . . . insist[ed] that they were not going to be ruled by a Xhosa" and "A few days later . . . the Xhosa in the hostels were attacked by the Zulu."[3] Another hostel dweller who self-identified as Zulu confirmed this logic: "When it was said Mandela was coming out, the Xhosas changed . . . which really created the tension amongst the Zulus and the Xhosas. . . . [The Xhosas] attacked us. . . . After that, as Zulus we organised ourselves and . . . we attacked them."[4] ANC supporters also suspected a much deeper Zulu-Xhosa animosity behind the IFP-ANC rivalry. "I think that because Mr Mandela is a Xhosa and Gatsha Buthelezi is a Zulu, so the Zulus say they are not going to be ruled by a Xhosa member," one of them argued, "so they start attacking the Xhosas."[5]

Township residents who were neither Zulus nor Xhosas viewed the conflict through the same bifurcated lens. A Sotho man who lived in Thokoza explained, "The Zulus would pass here crying saying the Xhosas are killing them and the Xhosas would say the same thing."[6] Township police, whose official task was to ensure security and peace, joined in the fray according to their Zulu or Xhosa identities. Thus, when during the night of 13–14 December 1990, township residents attacked a Thokoza hostel, one of the hostel defenders noticed "Xhosa-speaking policemen . . . fighting shoulder to shoulder with the Xhosa blanket men, gunning down the hostel residents in the yard."[7] In the early morning, the tide turned. "When we saw our police, that is, Zulu police, we got courage," another hostel defender claimed, adding, "We went straight to where the Xhosas were and we killed 25 of them. We were stabbing them with spears and our police brought some of the guns."[8] As Zulu policemen aligned with Zulu combatants against Xhosa policemen supporting Xhosa fighters, it is perhaps of little surprise that some participants believed that the Zulu-Xhosa divide superseded all other considerations, especially the political. "I don't think it was a political thing," one migrant worker explained. "They burned our house and we were not IFP or ANC, just Zulus."[9] Another migrant laborer confirmed, "It wasn't political violence to us. It was Zulu and Xhosa violence. . . . In Thokoza we [Zulus] are fighting with the Xhosas."[10] Although the causes of the Rand violence were complex and the identities of the agents of violence were complicated, it is striking how many of them subjectively experienced the conflict in terms of a Zulu-Xhosa divide.

But what exactly did they mean by claiming to be "Zulu" or "Xhosa"? Outside observers and even some insider participants were quick to characterize Zulu and Xhosa as "tribal" identities organically tied to South Africa's historical Zulu and Xhosa polities and clans.[11] Following a particularly bloody encounter between "Zulus" and "hundreds of Xhosa-speakers" in Thokoza in August 1990, the *Chicago Tribune*, following the lead of the *New York Times* news service, used as its headline, "Tribal Strife Widens in S. Africa; 140 Dead."[12] Embracing the same logic, one Kwesine hostel dweller referred to the Rand conflict as "the fighting among tribes."[13] However, there is good reason to question the "tribal" label and its static conception of Zuluness and Xhosaness. As Zulu historian Jabulani Sithole notes, "*ubuZulu bethu,* a phrase which can be roughly translated as 'our Zuluness,' . . . is not a sealed vernacular idea, but a phrase that encompasses competing views held by different actors for different reasons."[14] Change over time (rather than timelessness) is also crucial, as John Wright indicates when he asserts that identities such as Zulu and Xhosa "were constantly being made and remade, contested and negotiated, according to specific political circumstances."[15]

Despite the complex nature of these identities, however, by the 1990s, those who self-identified as Zulus or Xhosas on the Rand and elsewhere in South Africa had the striking tendency to define these identities first and foremost on the basis of language. One person involved in the Rand violence explained that the Xhosa "violence was directed to the Zulu-speaking people."[16] Another individual reasoned similarly. "The Xhosas were only looking for a Zulu-speaking person," he claimed. "They were just looking for your tongue, which language you were."[17] This is not to say that all so-called Zulus spoke Zulu and all so-called Xhosas spoke Xhosa in exactly the same manner. There existed subtle differences between urban and rural forms of speech, for instance. "We [from the township] are amaZulu B because we speak a different isiZulu"; another person from the Rand explained, "It is different from that of a person who [is amaZulu A and] comes from Durban, Umlazi or Natal."[18] However, as the statement shows, even when people noticed subtle differences between speech forms, they nevertheless labeled these forms Zulu or Xhosa and used them to identify the speakers as Zulus or Xhosas.

Subsequent interviews with Africans outside the Rand confirmed that language functioned as the most important marker of the Zuluness and Xhosaness in the 1990s. In 1994, Mary de Haas and Paulus Zulu commented on this phenomenon in KwaZulu-Natal Province, noting that "many people . . . describe themselves as Zulu, and explain this identity primarily in terms of the language they speak."[19] Catherine Campbell, Gerhard Maré, and Cherryl Walker reached a similar conclusion based on interviews conducted among the residents of a Durban township at about the same time. "Everyone expressed a great personal commitment to language as the cornerstone of Zuluness," they explained. "This was in fact the only feature consistently associated with Zulu identity across the interviews."[20]

Perhaps the most extreme form of this Zulu language-equals-Zuluness paradigm emerges from Sibusisiwe Nombuso Dlamini's interviews with high school students living in Durban's Umlazi and KwaMashu townships in the early 1990s. The students' language and identity politics were complicated, and they occasionally distinguished between real Zulus (*uZulu woqobo*) and other Zulus, as well as between various forms of Zulu speech, notably "Johannesburg Zulu" and "rural Zulu" (*isiZulu saseNkandla*). In spite of this complexity, the students saw all these forms of speech as part of *the* Zulu language and indicative of a speaker's Zuluness in ways that superseded other identity markers such as place of origin, genealogical descent, or political allegiance.[21] Indeed, as Dlamini notes, some of the youth even claimed that "there was often no difference between speaking a language and becoming that language"—"A person was most likely to 'become' Zulu (*wuZulu*) by merely using Zulu."[22]

A very similar language-equals-identity paradigm applied to Xhosaness, although the evidence is not as prolific. In 1992, for instance, the Ciskei homeland ruler Joshua Oupa Gqozo explained forcefully that "we consider all the Xhosa-speaking tribes to be Xhosas," a statement that illustrates the importance of a language-based Xhosa identity.[23] Similarly the Mpondo mineshaft steward Mlamli Botha explained about the same time, "When I say Xhosa, I mean the Xhosa-speaking people. It might be Pondos, Bacas, Bomvanas, Xhosas, but they are [all] Xhosas."[24]

One of the most publicized accounts of this Xhosa language-equals-Xhosaness paradigm comes from Trevor Noah, the South African comedian and now host of the US TV program *The Daily Show*. In the first part of his autobiography, *Born a Crime*, Noah recounts an episode from his childhood in Johannesburg in the early 1990s. On one particular Sunday, Noah, his younger brother, and his single mother were trying to hitchhike from the city's northern suburb of Rosebank to their home in the Eden Park neighborhood. Eventually a male African driver stopped but a minibus taxi driven by two Zulu men arrived at the same time. The Zulu men immediately got out of their vehicle and began to verbally assault the driver, accusing him of stealing their paying customers. To appease the situation, the Noah family entered the Zulu men's minibus. At this point of the episode, Noah describes his mother as a strong Xhosa women whose ancestral roots extended to the Transkei and who "didn't suffer lectures from strange men."[25] Thus, when the Zulu driver turned to berating her next for almost entering a male stranger's car, she told him to mind his own business. The Zulu driver's response to this verbal censure was as immediate as it was violent: "Oh, you're a *Xhosa*," he said. "That explains it. . . . That is the problem with you Xhosa women. You're all sluts—and tonight you're going to learn your lesson."[26] Thankfully, the Noah family escaped the dangerous situation by jumping out of the driving taxi and running for their lives. The event is a testimony to the power of the Xhosa-language-equals-Xhosaness paradigm; the Zulu driver identified Noah's mother as Xhosa as soon as she spoke to him in Xhosa. Evidently, by the 1990s, a language-based Zulu-Xhosa divide had enormous explanatory power in the Rand townships and the wider South Africa.

Divided by the Word offers a historical explanation for this phenomenon. Using sources from three continents and in multiple languages, the book argues that a single historical process, which involved the long and complex interplay of African and non-African actors and ideologies, produced both Zulu and Xhosa as distinct languages and language-based identities between circa 1500 and 1990. By recovering this long history, *Divided by the Word* provides a new understanding of the making and meaning of Zuluness and Xhosaness while fostering a novel awareness of the historical relationship between language and collective identity in South Africa.

Having this awareness has several benefits. First, when the battle lines in a conflict are drawn according to identities, it is important to problematize the violence by problematizing these identities. This is especially useful in situations where outside observers and even some inside actors characterize the conflict as a "tribal" war to suggest that the violence is timeless, irrational, and unexplainable. Historicizing the conflicting identities provides an important antidote to this mischaracterization and, in so doing, opens up opportunities for a better understanding of the conflict and its causes.

Second, South Africa's language-based Zulu and Xhosa identities have survived the era of transition and remain part of the country's post-apartheid political and cultural landscape. To some the post-apartheid era represents an opportunity to challenge these identities, however. "The current political context," writes Mbongiseni Buthelezi, "is an appropriate time for isiZulu-speaking Africans . . . to interrogate their long-held views of pure Zuluness."[27] One group engaged in this sort of post-apartheid interrogation are people who self-identify as Hlubi and who, in an attempt to shed their Zuluness and Xhosaness and assert their Hlubiness, have invested time and effort in developing and codifying their own distinct "isiHlubi" language.[28] The people who pursue these agendas have complex motivations, but it is nevertheless striking how concerned they are with renegotiating the established language-identity nexus in their favor. Moreover, these efforts have produced new antagonisms, especially between those who seek to assert new language-based identities and the defenders of the older language-based notions of Zuluness and Xhosaness. As Jabulani Sithole notes, there has been "'war talk,' which was last witnessed during the peak of violence in the 1980s and early 1990s."[29] To better understand why languages have become a battleground in post-apartheid power and identity politics, I provide a critical, historical engagement with South Africa's language-based notions of identity in general and those of Zuluness and Xhosaness in particular.

This engagement must begin with challenging the widespread assumption that language and collective identity—whether in the sense of nation, ethnicity, or "tribe"—are by nature coterminous. This assumption has some of its historical and ideological roots in eighteenth-century European thought, notably Gottfried W. Leibnitz's claim that languages reveal the true origins of peoples (nations, *Völker*) because "languages in general, being the oldest monuments of peoples, earlier than writing and the arts, best indicate the origin of their thinking and movements," and Johann Gottfried von Herder's idea that language is the defining characteristic of a people because "language embodies a people's . . . heart and soul."[30] The argument that a people's primordial essence can be found in their language influenced subsequent thinkers throughout the world. It especially influenced missionary societies, particularly Protestants, who interpreted the Pentecost to mean that the Bible should be taught to all the nations of the world, each in its own language.[31] It also shaped the thinking of linguists such as Jakob Grimm and Wilhelm Bleek, ethnologists and anthropologists such as Adolf Bastian and Franz Boas, and nationalist thinkers including the architects of the apartheid regime.[32] It is partly through this lineage of intellectual thought that the language-equals-group paradigm has become normalized in the modern world to the extent that it successfully masks a much more complicated history.[33]

Take Germany's language-based identity. In the early medieval period, the region now known as Germany consisted of a patchwork of local and regional vernaculars with limited mutually intelligibility, especially on a north-south axis. This prompted a thirteenth-century "German" author, Hugo von Trimburg, to explain, "Whoever wants to write German [*tiutsch*] must give his attention to various different languages [*sprâche*]."[34] Medieval "Germans," thus, had a hard time anchoring their sense of Germanness (to the extent that they even had one) in a common German language.

The problem of vernacular diversity persisted beyond the Middle Ages and explains the perhaps apocryphal story of nineteenth-century Protestant "German"-speaking missionaries who met in Switzerland and decided that each should tell a story in his vernacular. When they finished, they had to admit that they had not understood much at all and that the only language they possessed in common was the written language of Martin Luther's Bible. Although Luther's written language may have given the missionaries a sense of common Germanness, it could hardly reflect their common, primordial "heart and soul," to use Herder's words, because its creation can be dated to particular moments in time—1522 for the first edition of the New Testament and 1534 for the first edition of the complete Bible. Moreover, Luther did not create this written language by recovering the putative primordial core of that language but rather by forging it out of the vernacular of his home district, Meissen-Upper Saxony, and the very restricted, written language of the imperial government—*Kanzleideutsch* ("Chancery German").[35]

Once made available by way of the printing press to thousands of readers, however, Luther's written language gradually transformed a patchwork of local and regional vernaculars into "a supraregional language" that gave a growing number of literati a sense of linguistic unity.[36] Feeling threatened by Napoleon's France in the early nineteenth century, German Romanticists such as Johann Gottlieb Fichte used this sense of linguistic unity to advocate for the creation of a unified German nation-state. Crucially, they claimed that this unified state would give political life to a primordial German nation bounded by a common culture and language since time immemorial.[37]

When this political project came to fruition in 1870–71, the newly created German nation-state began to use school education to reinforce this language-based ideology of primordial German nationhood by teaching successive generations that their local vernaculars were but regional variants of the standard German language.[38] This explains why by the early twentieth century a majority of Germans came to accept the German language as an important marker of their Germanness, a sentiment that is captured by Adolf Bach, a leading figure of German studies, who wrote in 1938: "The German language . . . creates the strongest connection that holds the German folk together as a unity."[39] However, while this language-based sense of German nationhood has become widespread in the twentieth and twenty-first centuries, it is clearly not primordial but historical; it is the product of a long historical process that arguably began with Luther's creation of the German translation of the Bible between 1522 and 1534.

Similar historical processes of language and identity formation played out across the world in the modern period, and *Divided by the Word* historicizes South Africa's language-based Zulu and Xhosa identities. It uses a far-reaching approach to demonstrate when, how, and why language-based notions of Zuluness and Xhosaness first emerged and then entrenched themselves in the consciousness of the region's population. This approach is inspired by several recent works that have shown convincingly that by widening our temporal lens dramatically, we can gain new insights into the dynamic processes by which South African communities negotiated and renegotiated, constructed and reworked their collective identities in response to the region's changing political contexts.[40]

Paul Landau's work is particularly noteworthy because he showed that African notions of belonging, notably in South Africa's southern highveld, changed between circa 1400 and 1948 from predominantly political ones (chiefdoms) centered on "authority-building practices" such as amalgamations (*métissage*), alliances, and rankings, to more overtly ethnic ones (tribes) circumscribed by cultural traits such as religious beliefs and customary practices. He identified as the fulcrum of this transformation the nineteenth century when the arrival of Christian missionaries and European colonial expansion placed the old ways of organizing authority and community "under sustained discursive *and* material attack," causing the names of African communities—Barolong, Basuto, Bahurutshe—to remain intact even as their meaning shifted in radical ways toward the ethnic (tribal).[41] Landau summed up the entire history in a pithy phrase "At first South Africa was not a place of tribes. . . . Then it became so."[42]

Divided by the Word asks and answers how the history of language intersects with this transformation, while shifting the emphasis of inquiry from South Africa's highveld to the coastal belt and from the Tswana, Sotho, and Ndebele to the Zulu and Xhosa. As it does so it follows in the footsteps of another major work—Leroy Vail's 1989 pathbreaking edited collection of essays, *The Creation of Tribalism in Southern Africa*.[43] This collection derived inspiration from the disillusionment many academics experienced when, following independence from colonial rule, Africa's "tribal" (ethnic) identities did not simply give way to modern national identities but evolved into power bases of postcolonial national politics. The contributors were particularly disappointed with the ahistorical explanation of this phenomenon, notably the idea that these strong ethnic identities continued in the postcolonial era because Africans "are naturally 'tribal.'"[44] The collection challenged this assumption by carefully historicizing some of southern Africa's dominant ethnic identities. Its overarching conclusion was that these identities were "very much a new phenomenon, an ideological construct, usually of the twentieth century, and not an anachronistic cultural artifact from the past."[45] The collection's individual case studies suggested, moreover, that ethnic identities were the products of the complex interplay of European intellectuals (notably missionaries), who first formulated "the ethnic message" as part of their early engagement with Africans; colonial administrators and African intermediaries, who subsequently used this message to administer African subject peoples; and, finally, ordinary Africans, who assimilated it because its

"traditional values" offered comfort at a time when colonialism and capitalism changed their social world.[46]

The collection's most significant contribution was its attempt to historicize the relationship between language and identity. Vail's introduction
and several case studies placed missionaries at the center of the action.
"Missionaries themselves were often instrumental," Vail wrote, "[because]
they had the skills to reduce hitherto unwritten languages to written
forms. . . . [They] chose what the 'proper' form of the language would be,
thus serving both to further unity and to produce divisions by establishing
firm boundaries."[47] This argument had the virtue of drawing attention to
the intimate relationship between the missionaries' proselytizing endeav-
ors and their Bible translation work on the one hand and the process of
language standardization and the formation of language-based collective
identities on the other. It also challenged the romanticist and positivist
assumptions that undergirded these activities. Nineteenth-century missionaries commonly assumed that by recording and classifying linguistic "facts," they "discovered" not only primordial African languages but
also primordial language-based African communities.[48] The case studies
in Vail's collection showed, however, that the missionaries' language and
ethnic classifications were discursive constructs that reflected not linguistic facts but each mission society's unique history, ambitions, procedures,
and personalities.[49]

Terence Ranger's and Patrick Harries's essays in the collection produced
particularly important insights in this regard.[50] The latter, for instance,
explained that the Swiss-Romande missionaries began to work in the
region between the northern Transvaal and southern, coastal Mozambique
in the 1870s, when they established a base of operations in the Transvaal
Spelonken. While there, the mission's leading linguist, Paul Bertoud, and
his African intermediaries developed a written *lingua franca* for the mission field as a whole, which they called "Gwamba." When the Swiss mission opened a second base of operations on the coast at Lourenço Marques
in the 1880s, however, the missionaries and African intermediaries who
worked at this second location argued that the coastal community did not
speak a local dialect of "Gwamba" but a distinct language called "Ronga."
Led by another missionary linguist, Henri-Alexandre Junod, the coastal
faction brought about the bifurcation of "Gwamba" into separate "Gwamba"
(later renamed "Tsonga") and "Ronga" languages and language-based ethnic labels between 1894 and 1904.[51]

Vail's collection of essays in general and Harries's work in particular successfully challenged the primordialist paradigm by offering a more complicated understanding of the history of languages and language-based ethnic identities in southern Africa. But this understanding still remains incomplete, especially for South Africa.

The collection included two essays that dealt specifically with the history of South Africa and its Zulu and Xhosa identities. Jeffrey Peires's essay (written anonymously) argued that, while Xhosa polities had a long history in the region, the attempts of the government of the Ciskei homeland to create a narrow Ciskeian (-Xhosa) ethnic identity in the second half of the twentieth century represented an act of historical invention.[52] Shula Marks reached a similar conclusion for Zuluness. She acknowledged that the nineteenth-century Zulu kingdom, which had its center of gravity north of the Thukela River, provided some precolonial antecedents for South Africa's modern Zulu ethnicity. But she emphasized that the origins of this latter identity, which combined populations north *and* south of the Thukela, had to be ascribed to the work of Black and white intellectuals in the twentieth century.[53]

While these conclusions were significant, both essays avoided a critical engagement with the history of language and its relationship with ethnic identity. Marks's essay, for instance, argued that "the black intelligentsia of Natal and the white ideologues of South Africa" together forged a trans-Thukela Zulu consciousness in the twentieth century out of "the building blocks of past history, language and 'custom.'"[54] Readers were left to wonder what exactly the term "language" meant in this context. If it stood for the idea of a "Zulu" language, it was unclear who had decided that Africans north and south of Thukela River shared this language. And if, as Vail's model suggested, missionaries had made this decision, readers were told neither when nor why they had done so. Peires's work raised similar questions. His essay suggested that the inhabitants of the Ciskei and the Transkei homelands were all Xhosa speakers and most of them regarded one another as "one people."[55] The essay did not explain why and when the Xhosa language that seemingly helped underwrite this sense of unity had been created or by whom. If the history of language was important to understanding South Africa's Zulu and Xhosa identities, then a crucial blind spot existed in both essays.

One explanation for this analytical blind spot is that modern linguistics has normalized the Zulu-Xhosa language divide even in the face of contradictions. The discipline argues that Africa's contemporary speech communities can be divided into four language families—Afro-Asiatic, Nilo-Saharan, Khoesan (Khoisan), and Niger-Congo.[56] The Niger-Congo family includes distinct language branches, one of which is called Niger-Congo "B" for "Bantu," which covers much of subequatorial Africa and is said to include some 240 million speakers divided into more than five hundred languages.[57] Linguists include in this number modern-day South Africa's nine official Bantu languages—Zulu, Xhosa, Ndebele, Pedi, Sotho, Tswana, Venda, Swati, and Tsonga. Of South Africa's 40 million African Bantu speakers, some 11.5 million are said to speak Zulu, and 8 million are said to speak Xhosa as their home (i.e., first) language.[58]

Modern linguistics establishes these classifications by *recording* and *comparing* as objectively as possible the linguistic features—lexical (words and their meanings), phonological (sounds), morphological (word structures), syntactical (structure of sentences)—of contemporary speech communities. One classificatory rule of thumb, for instance, is that speech forms that have a lot of (core) features in common and have a high degree of mutual intelligibility not only belong to the same language family but are dialects of a *single* language.[59]

One key feature of the Bantu language family is that all languages within it build words by adding prefixes to word stems according to noun classes—for instance in modern Zulu, the prefix *umu* and the stem *ntu* gives *umuntu* ("person") while the prefix *aba* added to the stem *ntu* is *abantu* ("people"). Even though all Bantu languages build words in this manner, they are not all mutually intelligible because of important differences in words, sounds, grammar, and meaning between them. This can make it difficult for Zulu speakers, for instance, to communicate with Tswana or Tsonga speakers. This is not the case for Zulu and Xhosa speakers, however. These two languages share a lot of features in common. For instance, the admittedly simple Zulu sentence *Umuntu uthanda, kodwa abantu bathanda* ("A person loves, but people love") becomes the Xhosa sentence *Umntu uthanda, kodwa abantu bathanda*. There are some differences, of course. A Zulu speaker is likely to say *khuluma* ("to speak") whereas a Xhosa speaker uses *thetha* ("to speak"). But Zulu and Xhosa have a very high degree of mutual intelligibility in spite of their idiomatic and grammatical differences.[60] Nevertheless, in contradiction of its own classification rules, modern linguistics has for some time classified Zulu and Xhosa as distinct languages, thereby normalizing these language categories.[61] As Sinfree Makoni recently explained, this normalizing extends into the post-apartheid era because scholars and policy makers continue to portray "the existence of separate indigenous languages" such as Zulu and Xhosa "as self-evident, unproblematic, and an uncontested sociolinguistic fact."[62]

What reinforced the Zulu-Xhosa language dichotomy further is that historians have long divided the entire coastal belt region into similarly convenient binaries—Zulu and Xhosa peoples, Cape and Natal missionaries, Cape and Natal colonies, Eastern Cape and KwaZulu-Natal provinces— that are useful for their specific research objectives but tend to elide the historical connections, including the linguistic ones, across the region as a whole. The practice began with some of the early historical writings on the region.[63] It continued in Vail's edited collection with Marks's and Peires's essays, and it remains the dominant approach to historicizing Zulus and Xhosas and their languages to this day.[64]

This binary approach also informs and arguably weakens Rachel Gilmour's important pioneering work on the history of Zulu and Xhosa as languages. In the introduction to *Grammars of Colonialism* (2007), she explained the bifurcated structure of her work, noting, "In the eastern Cape, I map the development of Xhosa language study by Europeans. . . . In Natal and the Zulu kingdom, I trace key themes in the development of Zulu language study by Western writers."[65] As the quote suggests, Gilmour accepted from the beginning that there *are* two distinct Zulu and Xhosa languages with distinct histories. Consequently, her work reinforced rather than explained the divide. To historicize the language-based Zulu-Xhosa divide properly, however, I refrain from imposing the divide on the past. Rather, I use the past to explain the emergence of the divide.

Divided by the Word shows that the Zulu-Xhosa divide emerged from the long and complex interplay of indigenous stakeholders, foreign actors, and their respective ambitions and ways of knowing. This process began with the movement of Bantu speakers into southern Africa and their encounters with South Africa's Khoesan-speaking firstcomers in the first fifteen centuries of the Common Era. I argue that while these encounters helped create important lexical, phonological, morphological, and syntactical differences between South Africa's speech communities, these differences were not particularly meaningful to the speakers themselves at the time. In the habit of forging their key collectivities—patriclans, chiefdoms, and social status

within chiefdoms—on the basis of genealogical descent and acts of submission, these speakers, including those who belonged to the earliest Zulu
and Xhosa polities and clans, largely disregarded language as a marker of
belonging. This conclusion is important because it shows that modern-day
Zulu and Xhosa language-based identities are not embedded in the deeper
history of the region but emerged gradually over the course of history.

The next step in the process began when European mariners, officials,
and naturalist explorers arrived in South Africa between 1500 and 1800
CE. Equipped with deeply rooted (but periodically reworked) ideas about
the relationship between race, skin color, and language, they gradually
categorized the region's indigenous peoples into distinct "races." By the
early 1800s, most European observers claimed that the so-called Caffres
extended over much of southern Africa and were unified by a common
skin color and language that separated them racially not only from the
"Hottentots" to the west but also from "true Negroes" to the north. As I
demonstrate, this claim marked an important moment in South African
history because it not only created the "Caffre-Hottentot" divide, but it also
introduced the idea of a distinct "Caffre" race and language that influenced
missionary linguists, ethnographers, anthropologists, and apartheid ideologues for the next two hundred years.

A third step began with the arrival of European and American missionaries in South Africa after 1800—the former establishing themselves primarily in the eastern Cape region and the latter in the Natal-Zululand area.
Shortly after their arrival, they embarked on translating didactic and liturgical materials, including versions of the New and Old Testaments, into the
region's vernacular speaking practices. I argue that, influenced by the preexisting idea of the "Caffre" language, both missionary communities initially
assumed that the target language for these translations extended over much
of southern Africa, notably from South Africa's eastern Cape region to Delagoa Bay in southern Mozambique. They gained additional confidence in this
"Caffre" language continuum when they learned that it was possible to use
skills in the speaking practices of the people from one end of the continuum
to communicate successfully with the people on the opposite end.

Confidence in this "Caffre" language paradigm increased further among
European missionaries when they traveled throughout the coastal belt in
the company of African interpreters who confirmed that the region's various speaking practices were mutually intelligible and thus part of a single
language. I show that these interpreters came to this conclusion because

they were not culturally conditioned to attribute significance to the relatively small linguistic differences they encountered on their travels with the missionaries. They lacked this conditioning because they belonged to the Gonaqua, Gqunukhwebe, and Ntinde polities, who had historically ignored language as a marker of belonging in order to forge viable polities in the linguistically complex environment of the eastern Cape borderlands.

By the 1840s the combination of deeply ingrained African ideas about language and belonging, the practical experience of language in the region, and the long-standing trope of the "Caffre" language continuum motivated European and American missionaries to attempt to harmonize the coastal region's various speaking practices into a single literary language. Indeed, in 1853, the Wesleyan-Methodist missionary William Shaw sought to bring this harmonizing project to conclusion by proposing that European and American missionaries work together on the creation of a single "Caffre" translation of the Bible.

Yet the American missionaries rejected this proposal in 1854 based on the novel assertion that the speaking practices of Natal and Zululand formed a separate "Zulu" language that was not only different from the "Caffre" language but also superior to it. I show that this change of heart can be explained largely by the American missionaries' growing reliance on the language expertise of local African intermediaries whose understanding of language had been shaped by their upbringing in the Zulu kingdom, which had begun to differentiate between "superior" and "inferior" speaking practices in the late 1810s.

The American missionaries' rejection of Shaw's proposal was of long-term significance because it bifurcated what used to be considered a single "Caffre" language into distinct Zulu and "Caffre" (soon to be renamed Xhosa) languages. To develop these languages, missionaries, African intellectuals, and other stakeholders pursued language standardization and language education programs. I demonstrate that language standardization involved missionaries and Africans jointly identifying which mode of speaking in each region represented *the* standard one—a process that centered on "purification" in the case of Zulu and "harmonization" in the case of Xhosa. Language education involved Africans and non-Africans, in their capacity as lawmakers, superintendents of education, and teachers, promoting standardized Zulu and Xhosa as part of "mother-tongue" education in various school settings between the middle of the nineteenth and the last decade of the twentieth centuries. These processes helped set up the standards as prestige languages in education and, more significantly, encouraged a growing number of people to conceptualize their forms of everyday speech as part of these standardized languages and ultimately as markers of their Zuluness and Xhosaness.

This long history holds the key to understanding the development of Zulu and Xhosa as powerful language-based identities in South Africa. It explains why these identities had enormous explanatory power in the 1990s on the Rand and wider South Africa. They did not hold power because they reflected the primordial essence of the region's indigenous populations. Nor did they possess this power because colonial and apartheid rule had unidirectionally imposed invented "tribal" identities on passive, helpless Africans. Instead, the language-based Zulu-Xhosa divide had explanatory power in the 1990s because it was the product of a long historical process that involved indigenous and foreign-born actors weaving together strands of African and European ideologies of language and belonging and popularizing their syntheses through language standardization and education. Understanding this long history, detailed in the chapters that follow, is instrumental for making better sense not only of the transition violence of the 1990s but also of the new South Africa writ large.

"What Does Stick to People—More Than Their Language—Is Their *Isibongo*"

Language and Belonging in South Africa's Deeper Past

A s explained in the introduction, modern-day Zulu and Xhosa identities are first and foremost language-based identities, which means that people believe they are Zulus or Xhosas because they speak languages known as Zulu and Xhosa. Did language also determine collective belonging in South Africa's deeper past? As Paul Landau has noted, "Understanding that tribes or ethnic groups had no recognizable ancient corollaries does not mean there are not *other*, real, ancient continuities, stemming from a common heritage and history."[1] What does this common heritage and history look like for the communities in South Africa's coastal belt?

The current chapter addresses these questions by using evidence from historical linguistics, archeology, and history to discuss two different perspectives of language for the region during the period before 1800. The *outsider perspective* shows that the long expansionary movement of Bantu speakers through subequatorial Africa and their subsequent encounter with South Africa's Khoesan-speaking firstcomers unleashed dynamics of language divergence that produced the forms of speech modern linguists like to classify as Zulu and Xhosa.

The second part of the chapter adopts the *insider perspective* to show that the Bantu speakers involved in these encounters did not themselves shape this divergence through deliberate language policies, because, in the period before 1800, they established their most important collectivities, such as patriclans, chiefdoms, and social statuses within chiefdoms, on the basis of genealogical descent and acts of submission rather than language. This does not mean that they did not recognize the differences between various forms of speech, but rather that they chose not to mobilize these differences as part of their discourses of collective belonging. My conclusions about the insider perspective are significant because they suggest that modern-day Zulu and Xhosa language-based identities are not embedded in the deeper history of the region but emerged gradually only after 1800.

The Outsider Perspective

While modern linguists record and compare linguistic features in order to classify extant speech forms into language families and branches, and from there into languages and language variants (dialects), historical linguists explain why these features are present to reconstruct the history of the speakers. For instance, when two extant neighboring speech communities have many linguistic features in common, it is possible that they inherited these features from a common ancestral (proto) speech community from which they diverged spatially by way of migration. Some linguistic differences, meanwhile, may have come about because migrant communities developed new words or attached new meanings to old words as they developed new technologies, ideas, or cultural practices. Alternatively, the linguistic differences may have emerged because migrants had intense contact with other speech communities and borrowed from them not only new technologies or ideas but also the words for these novelties.

To find out which historical process best explains the presence of specific linguistic features in extant and ancestral languages, historical linguists use sophisticated methods—the comparative method, lexicostatistics, glottochronology, and contact modelling—and combine their data with archeological, genetic, climatic, and historical evidence.[2] Their findings suggest that many of the important similarities across the Bantu language family are best explained by a history of slow expansion away from a single ancestral (proto) speech community and that many of the important differences between the languages within this family can be best explained by a history of borrowing from other language families.[3]

The consensus is that the ancestral, proto-Bantu speech community was located in the borderland region between modern-day Nigeria and Cameroon in about 5000 BCE. From there, members of this community began to migrate into the lowland region around the Sangha and Nyong Rivers by 3500 BCE, initiating an expansion that would bring some of their descendants to South Africa sometime between 300 BCE and 200 CE. One factor that explains this expansionary achievement is the skill of farming, which proto-Bantu speakers developed by domesticating yams, oil palm, peanuts, kola nuts, and black-eyed peas. Not surprisingly some of the oldest words in proto-Bantu are *-kùá ("yam") and *-kúndè ("black-eyed peas").[4]

Farming improved proto-Bantu speakers' ability to feed their expanding populations. But it was not enough to sustain them indefinitely because, in the tropical zone where they lived, abundant rainfall steadily "leached the soil," rendering it less and less productive over time.[5] In search for new farmland, the farmers expanded from modern-day Cameroon into the interior of what is now the Democratic Republic of the Congo between circa 3500 and 2000 BCE. As they penetrated the unfamiliar rainforest of the Congo River basin, they encountered populations who still relied predominantly on hunting and gathering. The newcomers called the hunter-gatherers *-túá (which survives in some modern Bantu languages as Batwa and abaThwa), and they shared knowledge, traded, intermarried, and fought with them.[6]

From the Congo River basin, subsequent generations pushed on eastward across the forest and woodland savannas located immediately south of the equatorial rainforest zones. These proto-Savanna-Bantu speakers formed two migratory wings. The proto–Western Savanna Bantu moved in a southwest direction. The proto–Eastern Savanna Bantu moved in an eastward direction, fragmenting along the way into proto–Luban, Lega, Sabi, Botatwe, and Mashariki speech communities. In about 1000 BCE, the proto-Mashariki speech community encountered Nilo-Saharan (Central Sudanic and Eastern Sahelian) speakers in the Great Lakes region, from whom they adopted grain (sorghum and pearl millet) farming, iron smelting and forging, and probably cattle herding. As they adopted these new skills, the migrants also borrowed words of Nilo-Saharan origins, such as *-bèlé (grain) and *-òndò (hammer), and developed new ones, such as *-gòmbè or *-ka (cow), which survive in modern-day Zulu and Xhosa in the form of amabele (sorghum), isando (hammer), and inkomo (cow).[7]

Following this knowledge transfer, proto-Mashariki can be divided into two daughter communities. The northern, proto-Kaskazi community moved east along the southern edge of Lake Victoria, while the southern, proto-Kusi community expanded south along Lake Tanganyika, gradually diverging into proto-Nyasa, proto-Makua, proto-Shona, and proto–Southeast Bantu. In the possession of grain, iron, and some cattle, this latter speech community moved into South Africa's coastal belt in the first centuries of the Common Era.

In South Africa, this proto–Southeast Bantu speech community continued to change incrementally over the course of the succeeding centuries.
The exact nature of these changes and the contexts in which they unfolded
is not completely known yet and thus must be imperfectly pieced together
from a variety of sources.[8] In fact, even though the simplified account below
will identify population movements (migration) as the crucial engine of
historical and linguistic change, it is possible that these changes resulted
from the movement of ideas (diffusion) rather than people.[9]

Around 100 CE, groups of proto–Southeast Bantu speakers—whose
predominant subsistence activity was grain agriculture but who also practiced iron smelting and forging, small-scale cattle herding, and hunting and
gathering—moved in a southward direction through one of the many passes
that dissect the *uKhahlamba* (the Drakensberg Mountains). The destination
of these "Bantu-speaking farmers" was the fertile coastal grassland belt of
South Africa, which is physically separated from the higher-lying region
(highveld) by the Great Escarpment, a mountain range that reaches up
to ten thousand feet in height and runs parallel to the Indian and Atlantic
Ocean coastline roughly one hundred miles inland (see map 1). Extending
some thousand miles (1,600 km) from southern Mozambique to modern-
day Cape Town, the coastal belt is rich in rainfall and features a multitude of
rivers—the Phongolo, Mfolozi, Thukela, Mkomazi, Mzimkhulu, Mtamvuna,
Great Kei, Keiskamma, Sundays, and Gamtoos Rivers (to name a few)—
running from the higher to the lower-lying areas before entering the sea. As
one moves through this coastal region from northeast to southwest, the climate is generally warm and subtropical in the region between the Phongolo
and the Sundays Rivers. But it cools steadily thereafter, evolving into the
mild Mediterranean-type weather typical of the broader region surrounding
Table Bay. Annual rainfall also gradually decreases in this westerly direction,
from a high of forty to twenty inches at about the Sundays River.

This twenty-inch annual rainfall line was important for Bantu-speaking
farmers because to the west of this line, rainfall was not enough to sustain
their main crops (sorghum, millet, beans, and, later, maize) although livestock (sheep, goats, and cattle) herding was possible all the way to Table Bay.
At the latter place rainfall was again sufficient to support non-Bantu crops
such as wheat and grapes for wine. Even though rainfall varied greatly from
season to season and droughts were frequent (often persisting for as long
as a decade), the costal belt was generally fertile and free of the diseases
such as yellow fever and sleeping sickness that ravaged Bantu populations

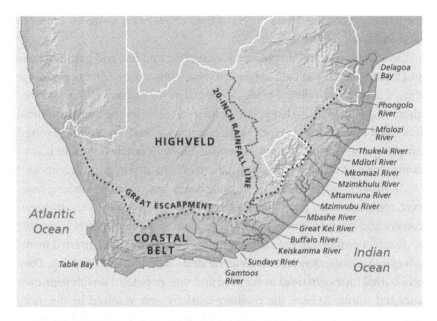

MAP 1. South Africa's coastal belt.

in tropical Africa. Even malaria occurred only in the northeasternmost corner of the coastal belt.

Compared to the tropics and the highveld, the farmers were thus entering a veritable paradise. But they did not enter empty land; they encountered there firstcomers, notably hunter-gatherers whose ancestors had
arrived in the coastal belt some six thousand years earlier.[10] These hunters
lived in bands of twenty to eighty people, valued egalitarianism, and called
themselves Ju/'hoansi, G/wikhoe, Hai//om, and !Kung in a language with
many distinct but related speech patterns that linguists classify as part of
the "Khoesan" language family. A unique characteristic of Khoesan is that
it is rich in click sounds, some of which are transcribed by graphemes such
as /, //, and !.

The Bantu-speaking farmers identified these hunters by the already-
mentioned term, *-túá, which in modern Zulu and Xhosa becomes abaThwa,
and whose original meanings probably include "chief," "neighboring people," and "despised group."[11] The varied meanings can be explained by the
changing relationship between the two communities over time. Recogniz-
ing their own position as newcomers, the farmers acknowledged the hunters as firstcomers with a prior claim to the land and critical knowledge of
the ancestral spirits that control the land and its fertility. Initially, therefore,

the farmers recognized the hunters as their chiefs in exchange for access to land and spiritual guidance.[12]

Once in place, they laid out farms, mined for iron ore, and pastured their small cattle herds, gradually forming a prospering village community. Over time, a lively cross-cultural trade developed as the farmers exchanged sorghum and millet, decorated pottery, and iron wares for the hunters' animal hides and rainmaking services.[13] Intermarriage, moreover, produced mixed offspring who reinforced these economic ties with family bonds and, in so doing, ensured that the farmers and hunters coexisted as good neighbors.[14]

As villages prospered and the farming community expanded in size, however, competition for land increased, and the relationship between the newcomers and the firstcomers soured. The Bantu-speaking farmers were able to disassociate themselves from the hunters because they had inserted themselves into the latter's ancestral ties to the land via their mixed offspring. They also buried their own dead in the land and thus populated it with their own ancestral spirits. At best, the resulting tensions were resolved by the more numerous and therefore more powerful farmers incorporating hunters as wives, clients, or tributaries; at worst, the farmers treated the hunters as a despised group, violently pushing them into remoter areas.[15] Once the farmers had established their hegemony, they used their malleable oral histories to legitimize their power in a variety of ways. Perhaps the most common strategy was to erase from memory their extreme dependence on and intense interactions with the hunters during the early stages of their history. A good example of this erasure is the practice of tracing descent patrilineally, which led Bantu-speaking farmers to "forget" the family ties they had established when their men had married the daughters of Khoesan-speaking hunters.

How did these events affect language change in the region? One effect was that hunters became bilingual over time, adding Bantu to their Khoesan speech pattern. Christopher Ehret, for instance, argues that hunters traveled to the farming villages to obtain the goods that were manufactured there; to navigate the village space successfully, they had to learn "the Bantu tongue of the village" which thereby became "the language of interethnic contact."[16] But this was never a unidirectional language exchange. First, Bantu-speaking farmers assimilated from the Khoesan-speaking hunters the names for unknown animals, rivers, and places. Moreover, Bantu men's Khoesan-speaking wives transmitted their Khoesan speech to their sons and daughters and, as long as this language skill remained useful in day-to-day interactions with other Khoesan speakers, the offspring of these unions remained bilingual. Both reasons help explain how some Khoesan click sounds first entered Bantu speech patterns of the coastal belt of South Africa.[17] The influence of Khoesan on Bantu speech, however, remained limited because of the Bantu society's rapid economic and political ascendency and practice of historical erasure.

Bantu-speaking farmers dominated the region between the Phongolo and Mzimkhulu Rivers until about 1000 CE, when another group of newcomers arrived. The products of the Late Iron Age, the newcomers were true mixed farmers who paid at least as much attention to their cattle keeping as to their farming activities. They also brought with them new ceramic styles, more elaborate organizational structures characterized by more powerful rulers, and new Bantu speech patterns linguists classify as "proto-Nguni."[18]

The dynamics of the encounter between these proto-Nguni-speaking "mixed farmers" and the Bantu-speaking "farmers" probably unfolded in a similar way as the farmer-hunter encounters had. This suggests that a period of initial subordination of the newcomers to the established population was followed by a phase of lively trade, intermarriage, and good neighborliness. This in turn gave way to a period of increased competition for land, which eventually led to conflict. The period of conflict ended when proto-Nguni speakers incorporated the earlier Bantu-speaking farmers, a process that, as archeologists note, was accompanied by earlier *Ntshekane* ceramic styles giving way to *Blackburn* styles.[19]

What linguistic consequences did this process of encounter and incorporation have? Ehret suggests that the political dominance of the newcomers led to their speech forms exercising a dominant influence over the speech forms of incorporated peoples.[20] In the most extreme case, dominant influence could have meant that incorporated people replaced their older Bantu speech forms with the proto-Nguni forms of their new political masters. But political dominance did not necessarily have to produce this outcome. Consider the Soutpansberg region, where Kalanga-speaking newcomers conquered Venda-speaking firstcomers during the seventeenth century. Following the conquest, however, the newcomers "adopted the Venda speech of their new subjects" rather than the other way around.[21] In South Africa's coastal belt the process may have been similarly complex. Carolan Ownby, for instance, suggests that when the proto-Nguni-speaking newcomers incorporated large communities of earlier Bantu speakers, proto-Nguni speech forms borrowed words from the older Bantu speech layer and, in so doing, produced new variants (dialects) such as "Lala."[22]

Richard Bailey offers a similar argument. He suggests that when the newcomers incorporated the established population, the latter shifted their older Bantu speech forms to proto-Nguni forms by way of relexification—that is, they adopted the newcomers' proto-Nguni vocabulary but maintained some aspects of their own phonology.[23] Indeed, both Ownby's and Bailey's arguments suggest that the population movements and encounters that occurred north of the Mzimkhulu River at this time helped produce so-called northern Nguni speech variants—notably the Zulu (*zunda, khuluma*), Qwabe (*thefula*), and Cele (*tekeza, lala*) speech forms—that modern-day linguists classify as part of the Zulu language.[24]

Around four centuries later, sections of these northern Nguni-speaking mixed farmers began to move from the Mzimkhulu River in a southwestward direction toward the twenty-inch rainfall line, a region attractive to them because its "temperate grassland" supported both agriculture and cattle herding.[25] Most likely these migrant groups featured minor sons of chiefly families seeking to establish their own chiefdoms by "inch[ing] their way down the coast."[26] As part of this movement, Nguni speakers entered a land inhabited by a pastoralist (herding) people whose ancestors had settled in the region between the Mzimkhulu and Table Bay as early as the first century CE.[27]

Although the exact relationship between South Africa's herders and hunters is subject to debate, there were some noteworthy differences between them.[28] For starters, the herders distinguished themselves from the hunters by owning fat-tailed sheep and cattle.[29] And while the hunters traced descent bilinearly because they had little property to pass on to their offspring, the herders' property in livestock encouraged them not only to distinguish between rich and poor but also to trace descent as clearly as possible through the paternal line.[30] Finally, whereas the hunters organized themselves into bands of twenty-five to fifty people, property ownership and dependency on pasturage and water for grazing their livestock incentivized the herders to unite for the purpose of common defense into chiefdoms, which consisted of a chief and one hundred or more followers. Although the herders may occasionally have used a collective name—*Khoekhoen (Khoekhoe, Khoikhoi)*—they preferred to identify themselves by the names of the specific chiefdoms to which they belonged.[31] Thus they were the Cochoqua, Chainouqua, Hessequa, Gouriqua, Attaqua, and Inqua (the latter becoming the dominant power of the upper reaches of the Sundays River by the second half of the seventeenth century).[32] But, remarkably, the herders, like the hunters, used speech patterns that belong to the click-filled Khoesan language.[33]

As they proceeded toward the twenty-inch rainfall line, the northern Nguni-speaking migrant groups thus encountered speech patterns not entirely unknown to them but that were in many ways radically different from their own. Nevertheless, they began to interact with the Khoekhoe herders (whom they possibly began to call amaQèya) as their ancestors had previously interacted with Khoesan-speaking hunters and Bantu-speaking farmers further north.[34] Likely, ad hoc cross-cultural trade quickly developed, as part of which the newly arrived farmers offered the herders farming products—sorghum, millet, pumpkin—and highly desirable metal products, since the region south of the Mzimkhulu was poor in raw iron and copper. Initially, they might have traded these goods for access to some of the land in use by the herders, but once this access was secured, they became more interested in the herders' livestock.

Unlike the transhumant herders, the northern Nguni-speaking mixed farmers established permanent settlements; consequently, their villages gradually evolved into "the focal point of interethnic relations" and for this reason, their form of speech began to function as the lingua franca of inter-ethnic contact.[35] As this happened, the herders' Khoesan speech assimilated aspects of the mixed farmers' Nguni speech, a tendency that was reinforced when fathers of the mixed-farming community married off their daughters to Khoekhoe men in exchange for cattle.[36] In their roles as mothers, these women passed on their speech patterns to their children before the latter learned Khoesan from the wider society. The linguistic complexity was reinforced when mixed farmers joined some of the herder chiefdoms such as the Inqua and, later, the Gonaqua.[37]

But language influence also took place in the other direction.[38] In fact, as newcomers, the northern Nguni-speaking mixed farmers assimilated the herders' names for the region's rivers, flora, and fauna. This explains how Nguni speakers adopted click-filled words (c, q, and x indicate click sounds) such as kuQoboqobo (the area of Keiskammahoek) and eXesi (the area of Middledrift), iNxuba (the Great Fish River) and iNciba (the Great Kei River), and ingca (grass) and igusha (the latter derives from the Khoesan root *-gu and means "fat-tailed sheep"). Perhaps, as newcomers, the mixed farmers also recognized the herders' stronger ancestral ties to the spirits of the land and, therefore, keenly assimilated their religious knowledge and religious leaders.[39] This would explain why the Nguni speakers in this region began to use the click-filled word *igqwirha* for "healer" and *uThixo* for creator deity (the latter tracing back to the herders' "founding ancestor" *Tsui-//goab*).[40]

Khoesan sounds and words also entered the Nguni speech community because the women of migrant groups were required to *hlonipha*—"to show respect" toward men in their families—by avoiding the use of words and syllables in everyday speech that sound similar to the names of male family members. This practice encouraged women to use Khoesan sounds and even Khoesan words as substitutes. As they shared this unique form of Khoesan-rich *hlonipha* speech with their children, the Nguni speech community as a whole gradually became populated with these sounds and words.[41]

Khoesan words and sounds also entered the Nguni speech community as its men married herder women, who then raised their children bilingually, learning Khoesan from the mother and Nguni from the wider community. The first recorded example of this type of intermarriage occurred when the Nguni-speaking Chief Togu took the daughter of the ruler of a herder chiefdom as one of his minor wives, possibly in the late seventeenth century.[42] Khoesan influence on Nguni speech probably peaked in the eighteenth century when the mixed farmers violently incorporated more and more herders into their chiefdoms and some of them began to identify themselves by the Khoesan term *//kosa* ("angry men").[43] Pronounced "Xhosa" by the Nguni-speaking mixed farmers, the word is a testament to the ways in which the human encounters south of the Mzimkhulu River generated dynamics of language change that gave life to new "southern Nguni" variants—notably the Ngqika, Mpondomise, and Mpondo forms of speech—that modern-day linguists tend to classify as part of *the* Xhosa language.[44]

As this brief recapitulation has shown, centuries of human expansion and interaction below South Africa's Great Escarpment produced a wide range of localized Nguni speech forms that modern linguistics likes to classify as distinct Zulu and Xhosa languages. However, while these classifications—and the differences on which they rest—are meaningful for linguistics, they were not necessarily meaningful to the speakers themselves. Indeed, it is crucial to adopt an insider perspective on language and ask what the Nguni speakers made of the lexical, phonological, morphological, and syntactical features that characterized their speech communities in the period before circa 1800 CE.

The Insider Perspective

Unlike the linguists who create the outsider perspective, the Nguni-speaking populations of the coastal region did not regard language as a recordable, classifiable, abstract object of knowledge. As scholars have noted of the Tswana speakers of the South African highveld, the inhabitants of the region thought of language as a person actively using his or her tongue and, therefore, described it with the word *loleme* (tongue).[45] Since the Nguni speakers of the coastal belt used similar words—*ulimi* and *ulwimi* (tongue)—it can be assumed that they, too, thought of language as action rather than object.[46] However, even though Nguni speakers did not objectify and classify their speech communities into abstract languages before 1800 CE, there is evidence that they paid at least some attention to the differences between speech communities.

Evidence pointing in this direction comes from the colonial official James Stuart. In about 1900, Stuart conducted personal interviews with Africans who had been born during the early days of the Zulu kingdom (see table 1). These informants recalled that, before the rise of this kingdom in 1817 (they used terms such as "olden days," "old days," "formerly" and "ancient Zulu people"), the residents of the coastal region of modern-day KwaZulu-Natal used the term *amantungwa* for people from the upland areas who visited them to sell the medicinal plant *ikatazo*. Stuart's interlocutors claimed that *amantungwa* included "Zulus," "Khumalos," and "Hlubis," which shows that the term was not used as the marker of one specific clan or polity at this time but as a catchall term for people vaguely associated with the upland areas where the *itakazo* plant could be found. Importantly, all the interlocutors asserted that the *amantungwa* were identified not only by peddling *itakazo* but also by their uttering the expression *Ofe mkozi* or *Hofe mkozi* (whose specific meaning is unclear). Based on this evidence, it can be tentatively argued that before the rise of the Zulu kingdom, the region's Nguni speakers not only recognized specific speech forms such as *Ofe mkozi*, but also used them as "soft" markers of "vague" regional identities such as *amantungwa*.

It should be noted that assigning vague regional identities to others was a fairly common practice in precolonial southern Africa. People in precolonial Zimbabwe, for example, occasionally identified people as *Korekore* ("northerner") and *Zezuru* ("highlander"); thus these terms did not reflect political or ethnic identities but rather vague regional ones.[47] Whether people

TABLE 1. Evidence of *Ofe mkozi*–speaking *amantungwa*

Mbovu kaMtshumayeli	"People of the olden days carried *ikatazo* and said, '*Ofe mkozi!*' They went about selling it. . . . I do not know the meaning of the phrase."
Mruyi kaTimuni	"In the old days we made use of this expression, '*Ofe Mkozi*,' i.e. *amaNtungwa* used it. The name *amaNtungwa* means 'those from the north.' . . . Special medicines used by our tribe are . . . *ikatazo*. We came from the north with a knowledge of these."
Jantshi kaNongila	"'*Ofe mkozi*' is an expression used at the beginning of a conversation by the ancient Zulu people."
Ngidi kaMcikaziswa	"Mbovu says the Zulus formerly used to go about the country selling *ikatazo* (medicine), and saying to people they met, '*Hofe mkozi!*' . . . The Zulus were peddlers, but not of tobacco but *ikatazo*, which they dug up-country (*enhla*), where they lived."
Mmemi kaNguluzane	"The *amaNtungwa* are from the north. . . . The Zulus used to arrive in the Qwabe tribe with *indungulu* and *ikatazo* medicines, and say on arrival, '*Ofe mkozi*,' speaking of themselves as *amaNtungwa*."
Madhlebe kaNjinjana	"We Kumalo spoke the '*Hofe*' language."
Maziyana kaMahlabeni	"The *amaHlubi* people are *amaNtungwas*. They are those who used to say, '*Ofe, Mkozi!*'. . . . I heard from them that formerly in their tribe they said, '*Ofe, mkozi!*' My belief is that the *amaHlubi* bartered the *ikatazo* plant."

Source: Colin de B. Webb and John B. Wright, eds., *The James Stuart Archive of Recorded Oral Evidence Relating to the History of the Zulu and Neighbouring Peoples*, 6 vols. (Pietermaritzburg: University of Natal Press, 1976–2014), Mbovu kaMtshumayeli, 1903, 3:25; ibid., Mruyi kaTimuni, 1903, 4:37; ibid., Jantshi kaNongila, 1903, 1:176; ibid., Ngidi kaMcikaziswa, 1904, 5:31; ibid., Mmemi kaNguluzane, 1904, 3:263; ibid., Madhlebe kaNjinjana, 1905, 2:45–46; ibid., Maziyana kaMahlabeni, 1905, 2:277, 281.

assigned these two identities on the basis of unique speech patterns or purely on the basis of their alleged regional origins is unclear. Another precolonial example provides more evidence. According to Elizabeth MacGonagle, it appears that in the eighteenth century, people in southern Mozambique used the name *Ndau* for people who came from north of the Save River and greeted people by saying, *Ndau-we, Ndau-we* (We salute you! We salute you!).[48] If this is correct, then the people in southern Mozambique used speech as a "soft" marker of a "vague" regional identity called *Ndau*.

It is possible that the Nguni speakers of South Africa's coastal belt ascribed similarly vague regional meanings to terms such as *abenguni*, *abambo*, and *amalala* before 1800.[49] Daniel Hedges, for example, argues that *abenguni* did not refer to a specific political entity in the sixteenth century but to the "early residents of lower areas of Zululand."[50] The vagueness persisted into the early nineteenth century, when the inhabitants of the coastal belt appear to have associated the term with Nguni-speaking chiefdoms who lived "to the southwest."[51] Hedges notes the same phenomenon for *abambo*, which in the form of *Vambe* may have referred "to the people of Natal rather than to a specific political unit" in the sixteenth century.[52] It retained this vagueness into the late seventeenth century, when people used versions of the word—*emboas* or *semboes*—for "the people of southern Natal."[53] The term's geographic vagueness also carried over into the nineteenth century, when the Nguni speakers from the eastern Cape region used *eMbo* as well as *abambo* to refer to people who lived in or came from the east.[54] A good example of this usage comes from William Wellington Gqoba, who explained in 1887: "Someone will ask, 'Where do you come from?' and he will reply, 'I come from *Mbo* [*Hayi ndivela e Mbo*].' Where is that? 'Over there to the east [*Ngapá e Mpumalanga*].' Is it not a personal name? 'No, it isn't. It's the name of the direction from which we came.'"[55] Based on this evidence, it is possible to conclude that whereas an early meaning of *abenguni* was "people to the west (of us)," an early meaning of *abambo* was "people to the east (of us)."[56] There is no clear indication, however, whether Nguni speakers associated these terms with specific speech forms or geographic regions only.

We have better circumstantial evidence for the term *amalala*, whose meanings have been explored most thoroughly by John Wright. He explains that one of the word's older meanings included "people who, from some unspecified time in the past, lived mainly south of the Thukela River, particularly in the coastal region and its hinterland as far south as about the Mkhomazi River."[57] Wright adds that the term was also associated with "people who spoke one or other variants of the *tekeza* dialect."[58] Together, the two statements suggest that *amalala* originally functioned (similar to *abenguni* and *abambo*) as a vague regional identity, circumscribed loosely (in ways similar to *Ndau* and *amantunga*) on the basis of people's speech patterns. It can thus be tentatively concluded that in the "olden days," the Nguni speakers below the Great Escarpment not only recognized differences between regional speech forms but also used them as *soft* markers of *vague* regional identities. It remains unclear, however, whether they also used these differences as *hard* markers of *specific* collective identities, such as patrilineages and patriclans, and chiefdoms and social status within chiefdoms in the period before 1800 CE.

Nguni and other Bantu speakers have historically placed significant value on belonging to collectivities, because this "helped to ensure one's security in an uncertain world."[59] The value they placed on collective belonging reverberates powerfully in well-known proverbs such as *Um[u]ntu ngum[u] ntu ngabantu* (A person is a person through other people). Popular knowledge assumes that they should have mobilized language as markers of these collectivities and collective identities. As shown in the introduction, this assumption has its roots in the ideas of eighteenth-century German philosophers, including Johann Herder, who argued that language and belonging are naturally related phenomena. Scholars, however, have long doubted an overly deterministic relationship between language and collective identity. Herder's counterpart, Max Weber, for instance, noted as early as the nineteenth century that "there are no universal cultural traits (notably language) characterizing ethnic groups" because any group decides for itself which traits it wishes to deploy as markers of difference.[60] Following Weber, most modern scholars agree that *descent* rather than language is the marker most universally mobilized in collective identity discourses. Harald Haarmann puts it best: "On a world-wide scale it is paternity, not patrimony associated with language, that is the 'central experiential concept.'"[61]

The importance of descent-based notions of collective belonging for Bantu (and later Nguni) speakers cannot be overstated. The belief in ancestral spirits and the tendency to accumulate property, which created a need to clarify inheritance patterns, motivated them early on to trace genealogical descent unilineally, either through the mother (matrilineally) or the father (patrilineally). By tracing genealogical descent, they created collectivities—notably lineages—that included all those people ("living, deceased, and those yet unborn") who allegedly shared a common ancestor.[62] Linguistic evidence suggests that Bantu speakers initially traced descent matrilineally, using the word *-cuka*—whose original meanings included "female fertility"—to describe a matrilineage.[63] As Bantu societies moved into eastern and southern Africa after circa 1000 BCE, however, some of them began to trace descent patrilineally and use the word *-lòngò*—which originally meant "a line of objects"—to denote a patrilineage.[64]

Perhaps as early as 1000 CE, South Africa's Nguni-speaking populations used the word *uhlanga* to refer in very abstract terms to the idea of "genealogical origins" and to the patrilineages to which they belonged.[65] The basic unit that connected people to a patrilineage was probably "the House" (household) which some early Bantu speakers described as *-júbò*, a term that probably evolved into *umuzi* and *umzi* in modern Zulu and Xhosa, respectively.[66] If more recent anthropological evidence can be projected into the deeper past, then, in a genealogical sense, a household among Nguni speakers included ideally a polygyny-practicing father and his sons ranked according to the rank of each son's mother (great wife, right-hand wife, left-hand wife).[67] Because the senior son of the great wife outranked his brothers, it was he who inherited the father's household upon the latter's death, compelling his brothers to establish new households of their own, which normally continued to recognize their genealogical ties and inferior rankings to the original (senior) household. Over time, this process of ranking, succession, and segmentation led to the emergence of a series of related and ranked patrilineages.[68]

When the members of patrilineages recognized (or asserted) their descent from a common ancestor, they formed an even bigger descent-based collectivity called a patriclan (*isizwe* in Zulu and Xhosa).[69] In recognition of their clan ties, moreover, the members of these patrilineages used the mythical ancestor's name as their clan name (*isibongo* and *isiduko* in Zulu and Xhosa, respectively). In the specific context of the Natal-Zululand region, one Ndukwana kaMbengwana explained this phenomenon in the early twentieth century in these terms: "The *isibongo* identifies all people. . . . It is the name which indicates the origin (*ukudabuka*) of people. . . . The word is connected with *bonga*, meaning to praise, because when one is praised, one is praised by means of it. It indicates one's clan . . . of origin."[70] For instance, several patrilineages among the Xhosa believed that they shared the mythical Tshawe as a distant common ancestor and thus, constituted together the Tshawe clan. Several patrilineages among the Zulu, meanwhile, traced their descent to the common mythical ancestor Zulu and, therefore, constituted the Zulu clan. Nguni speakers in general and the Zulu and Xhosa in particular, therefore, formed important collectivities such as patrilineages and patriclans by emphasizing genealogical descent relations rather than by paying attention to the differences between people's speech forms.

Although genealogy-based collectivities were important to Bantu speakers, the more immediate reality was that they lived in political communities that included related and unrelated people. Dating back to the beginning of their expansion, the already-mentioned "House" (household) functioned not only as Bantu speakers' most fundamental social unit but also as their most fundamental political unit. Because of this political character, a household "was always competing for membership with other establishments" and, consequently, was not "a closed-door kin-group" but was open to all kin and nonkin who willingly accepted the authority of the leader of the household.[71] Some of the early Bantu-speaking people began to call this leader *-kósì, a term whose meaning approximated something akin to "a strong or mature person, particularly (though not necessarily only?) male, having authority over a small group."[72]

By the time proto-Nguni speakers arrived below the Great Escarpment in about 1000 CE, *-kósì had evolved into something akin to inkosi ("chief"). The chief's power had also evolved: it now derived to a significant extent from his ability to accumulate cattle by settling disputes, performing religious rituals, controlling trade, making war, and redistributing cattle to loyal followers.[73] A chief who used this power effectively attracted more followers and thus formed a larger political unit called a chiefdom (isizwe in modern Zulu and Xhosa).[74]

Even though Nguni speakers often named their chiefdoms after the chiefs' clan, chiefdoms usually included people of different clan backgrounds.[75] As the aforementioned Ndukwana explained: "The people belonging to any particular tribe [i.e., chiefdom] are not necessarily all of one isibongo [i.e., clan name]. . . . All chiefs, without exception, have, as members of their tribe, persons of different izibongo [i.e., clan names]."[76] The willingness to incorporate people of different genealogical backgrounds stemmed in part from the long-term practice of Bantu-speaking newcomers to integrate firstcomers so as to acquire knowledge of the land and its spirits. A second impulse came from the practical reality that, below the Great Escarpment, numbers mattered for the Nguni speakers' own survival and security. As the anthropologist Monica Wilson notes, "In Southern Africa men were scarcer than land, and because the power of a group depended upon its fighting strength, strangers were welcome; they added to the dignity and power of a chief."[77]

This open attitude toward strangers can be illustrated by focusing on the Nguni-speaking chiefdoms who called themselves "Xhosa" and who were ruled by chiefs belonging to the Tshawe ruling clan. As Jeff Peires explains, these chiefs incorporated a variety of Nguni- and Khoesan-speaking strangers between 1600 and 1800.[78] For instance, they incorporated members of the Maya, Ntshilibe, Ngwevu, and Zangwa clans who originally belonged to Thembu, Sotho, Mpondomise, and Mpondo chiefdoms. Although Xhosa chiefs were at times in conflict with Khoesan-speaking hunter-gatherers, they accepted some of them as marriage partners and subjects. Khoesan-speaking herders also became part of Xhosa chiefdoms. Perhaps as early as

1700, Xhosa polities incorporated members of the Inqua chiefdom as the Sukwini, Gqwashu, and Nkarwane clans. After 1750, they also incorporated the remnants of Chieftainess Hoho's Khoekhoe polity as the isiThathu clan and of Chief Ruiter's Hoengiqua chiefdom as the Giqwa clan. Moreover, as Monica Wilson has shown, Xhosa chiefdoms and other Nguni-speaking polities also regularly incorporated European- and Asian-born shipwreck survivors.[79] This evidence suggests that Nguni speakers formed political communities that united people not only from different clans but also from very different cultural and linguistic backgrounds.

Nguni-speaking chiefs did not necessarily treat these newcomers as inferior members of their polities. Chiefs north of the Mzimkhulu River, for instance, were known to treat newcomers "in exactly the same way as other members of [their] tribe[s]."[80] South of the Mzimkhulu River, Nguni-speaking chiefs operated in a similar manner. Consider the family history of the Xhosa *imbongi* (traditional poet) Samuel Edward Krune Mqhayi. He recalled that one of his distant ancestors had left the Thembu polity for the Dange section of the Xhosa polities in the late eighteenth century. His great-great-grandfather also switched allegiance, this time from the Dange to the Ngqika section of the Xhosa. Rather than discriminating against the stranger, however, the ruler of the Ngqika-Xhosa made him one of his trusted councillors.[81]

There is no evidence that newcomers had to culturally or linguistically assimilate to be accepted as members of Nguni-speaking chiefdoms. In fact, evidence suggests that Nguni-speaking chiefs allowed newcomers to retain "their ancient customs" so as to better secure their loyalty.[82] However, the newcomers had to submit to the chief, an act as part of which the latter increased the number of his followers and the former gained access to resources under the chief's control, such as loan cattle, pasturage, and farmland. Among proto-Nguni and Nguni speakers, submission meant to *-konza* the chief, a practice modern Zulu expresses as *ukukhonza* ("to pay homage," "to subject oneself," "to serve").[83] It involved making a formal declaration of allegiance, which in modern Zulu would be similar to *Ngizokhonza, Nkosi; ngifake ikhanda lapha kuwe* ("I have come to serve, O Chief; that I may put my head in your control").[84]

The practice of *ukukhonza* means that political identities among Nguni speakers did not revolve around culture or language but formal declaration of allegiance. This is expressed nicely by Jeff Peires, who notes that all newcomers who submitted to the ruling Tshawe clan automatically "became Xhosa with the full rights of any other Xhosa."[85] Consequently, while lineages and clans represented genealogical descent-based collectivities, Nguni-speaking chiefdoms were first and foremost allegiance-based collectivities.

Although speaking the chief's language was clearly not a prerequisite for becoming a member in a chiefdom, it is likely that new members began to adapt their speaking practices to the chiefdom's dominant speech form over time.[86] They most likely did so to better navigate the social world to which they now belonged. They may have also associated the dominant form of speech with superior status in the chiefdom. However, this latter factor should not be overstated, because social rank depended on a person's genealogy rather than his or her language.[87]

This was certainly the case at the upper echelons of early Nguni-speaking societies. Among the Xhosa, for instance, chiefs used their genealogies to claim for themselves positions of superior status, a practice that stemmed from the long-standing Bantu idea that (ancestral) spirits conferred special powers on their most immediate living descendants.[88] Based on this ideology, the *inkosi enkhulu*—the paramount chief or king—among the Xhosa was the male descendant who could claim to be "most closely related to Tshawe himself."[89] It was this genealogical rank that gave him the authority to mobilize all Xhosa chiefdoms for war, serve as the supreme judge in all disputes, command "the allegiance of the Great Councillors . . . and their armies," and commence "the first-fruits ceremony," an annual event at which "the junior chiefs reaffirmed their loyalty" to him.[90] Immediately below the paramount ruler were all the other Xhosa chiefs, who also legitimized their authority by asserting membership in the royal Tshawe clan and thus patrilineal descent from Tshawe himself.[91] They acknowledged, however, that their more distant genealogical ties to Tshawe translated into inferior social ranks, which they expressed by referring to themselves as *umninawa* (younger brother) in relation to their genealogical superior, whom they called *umkhuluwa* (older brother).[92]

Genealogical descent conferred social status more broadly in Nguni polities for several reasons. First, other influential roles besides chieftainship were also frequently assigned on the basis of genealogical descent. For instance, in the case of the Xhosa, a chief's son and the sons of the chief's principal councillors were usually circumcised together with the result that "the political unit of chief and councillors was reproduced every generation, and councillorship, like chiefship, became hereditary" over time.[93] Furthermore, these polities included related and unrelated people from the very beginning of their existence. Consequently, as they expanded in size by adding new members, those who possessed genealogical links to a polity's founding generation had an incentive to recall and assert such links so as to claim a higher status for themselves.[94] Finally and perhaps most importantly, Nguni speakers demarcated social status on the basis of genealogical descent because they believed that cultural practices and language could not play this role effectively because the latter were too transient. It was reported, for example, that, when the Ngqosini and Zangwa clans, who were of Khoekhoe and Mpondo ancestry, submitted to Xhosa chiefs, they assimilated the local custom of body painting with red ochre and circumcising their children, thereby rendering themselves indistinguishable from the chiefdom's long-standing members.[95]

Language was believed to be similarly transient. "Those who, of one *isibongo,* have *konza'd* those of another," the aforementioned Ndukwana explained, "will gradually forget their language, dialect and, to some extent, their customs, modifying them by those of the people they live among."[96] According to William Wellington Gqoba, this happened to the Khoesan-speaking members of the Ngqosini, Ngqosoro, Gqwashe, and Gwangqa clans when they became part of the Xhosa chiefdom. "These clans became quite mixed up with the Amaxosa so that no one would detect any difference. Their language has altogether been absorbed by the Xosa."[97] In contrast, Nguni speakers believed that their genealogies, as expressed by lineage and clan memberships, were more permanent aspects of their identities. Socwatsha kaPhaphu articulated this idea in 1905, stating: "What does stick to people—more than their language—is their *isibongo* [clan name]."[98] These assumptions go a long way to explain why Nguni speakers focused on genealogy to determine social status in their chiefdoms.

Precisely because they saw them as the key marker of social status, however, Nguni speakers were prone to manipulate genealogical descent relations. They were not exceptional in this. Max Weber recognized the general malleability of genealogies across time and space when he explained that, as a general rule, collective identities are "based on the perception of common descent," which is to say "what counts is the existence of this perception rather than its historical accuracy."[99] Based on the scholarship of Ian Cunnison, Mahmood Mamdani described the practice of crafting rather than merely recording genealogical ties among the Humr of Sudan in these terms: "The . . . genealogy of the Humr is ten or eleven generations deep and easily divides into two periods: five or six for the immediately remembered ancestors and the next five or six linking the Humr to a prestigious ancestor. Often, the result is to link strangers as close kin. . . . Claims of kinship, in this instance, rest less on evidence of filial affiliation in the distant past than on political affiliation in the present."[100] Paul Landau came to the same conclusion for the Tswana speakers of the South African highveld, where totemic icons, such as crocodiles, hippos, and lions made it easier for people to invent genealogical ties in order to "cover the tracks of amalgamations."[101] Among Nguni speakers, it was not totems that played this role but the distant, mythical ancestors, notably the putative clan founders Zulu and Tshawe. In other words, they, too, manipulated clan genealogies and lineage rankings in order to build larger polities and organize status relations among the members of their polities.[102]

Such manipulations probably occurred often in the period before 1800, when Nguni-speaking chiefs had to worry about the loyalty of their subjects.[103] A good example is the Xhosa Chief Ngqika who is said to have lost twenty-five hundred and ten thousand subjects to rival chiefs in 1803 and 1809, respectively.[104] Preoccupied with the loyalty of their subjects, Nguni chiefs developed methods to bind them more closely to their rule, for instance, by turning unrelated followers into "pseudo-kinsmen" through the invention of fictive kinship ties.[105] Among the Xhosa in particular, the process was simplified by clans assuming that lineages with the same name belong to the same clan. "Since relationship need not be demonstrated," Peires explained, "it was easy for clans to expand through the incorporation of individuals or groups of alien origin."[106]

Perhaps the best example of the invention of kinship ties involved the Tipha, Ngwevu, Qocwa, Ngqosini, Cete, and Nkabane polities. It appears that the members of these polities joined the Xhosa chiefdoms as conquered subjects sometime in the sixteenth or seventeenth century.[107] To bind them more closely to their rule, Xhosa chiefs moved them from the status of unrelated subjects to (pseudo-) kinsmen by creating "a false genealogical affiliation" which portrayed them as the descendants of the mythical Cira and Jwara, who had been defeated and subordinated by their brother—the equally mythical Tshawe.[108] By asserting kinship ties, the Xhosa chiefs turned the newcomers into more reliable subjects while the newly incorporated individuals gained higher social status in the Xhosa polities.

Collectively, this historical evidence suggests that, before 1800 CE, Nguni speakers circumscribed their most important collective identities—clans, chiefdoms, and social status within chiefdoms—on the basis of genealogy and acts of submission rather than by mobilizing language differences. This may strike us as surprising because these differences were often quite substantial, notably when and where Nguni speakers encountered and incorporated Khoesan-speaking hunters and herders. It may also strike us as surprising because the outsider perspective of language attributes a lot of importance to these language differences. Modern linguists, for instance, use them to attach classificatory labels such as Zulu and Xhosa to the various Nguni speech variants below the Great Escarpment. And historical linguists study them to draw conclusions about the deeper history of the region and its peoples.

The insider perspective reveals a very different attitude toward these language differences, however. It shows that before the nineteenth century, Nguni speakers recognized these differences and occasionally deployed some of them as *soft* markers of *vague* regional identities such as *amantungwa* and *amalala*. But they did not emphasize them as part of their more meaningful identity discourses. They could afford to ignore these language differences because they established their most important collectivities by other means, notably by tracing genealogical descent and performing acts of submission. This attitude toward language and identity contrasts radically from modern-day notions of Zuluness and Xhosaness, which are first and foremost language-based identities. The subsequent chapters will explain how these modern notions emerged by fusing African and European ideologies of language and belonging in new ways.

• 2 •

"Surrounded on All Sides by People That Differ from Them in Every Point, in Color . . . and in Language"

The Birth of the "Caffre" Language Paradigm

Anyone researching the history of nineteenth- and twentieth-century South Africa will inevitably encounter the word "Caffre" and its manifold variants (Cafre, Kafir, Kaffir, etc.).[1] For a considerable portion of these two centuries, people of European descent (or "whites") used this term to classify the region's Black population as an inferior race of Africans.[2] South African author Mark Mathabane, in his autobiography, offers a powerful description of the term's derogatory meaning in the twentieth century: "In South Africa it is used disparagingly by most whites to refer to blacks. It is the equivalent of the term *nigger*. I was called a 'Kaffir' many times."[3] While this more recent historical context explains why the word "Caffre" is rightfully considered hate speech in post-apartheid South Africa, the term's history dates back to the beginning of Europe's engagement with the region, when it had rather different connotations.[4]

The existing scholarly literature does not adequately explore the full range of meanings that Europeans attached to the term before the nineteenth century. Of course scholars have not completely ignored the word's deeper history. The available literature argues, for instance, that the term derives from the Arabic word for "unbeliever" and that Muslims first applied it to people of the East African interior whom they characterized as infidels or heathens.[5] As the story goes, over the course of the sixteenth century, the Portuguese then assimilated the term and used it to refer to people of southern African descent; then, in the seventeenth and eighteenth centuries, the Dutch and British employed the term as a synonym for the "black African inhabitant(s) of the region now covered by KwaZulu-Natal and the northeastern parts of the Eastern Cape."[6] Finally, scholars have argued that the term "Caffre" applied to Xhosa chiefdoms and their populations only.[7]

The word's deeper history has been treated in a cursory fashion only, however, with scholars usually analyzing all of these themes in less than one or two pages. This is why it has become marred by oversimplifications. For instance, the existing historical accounts fail to realize that the Portuguese, not Muslims, first linked the term explicitly to Black skin color in the sixteenth century. Similarly, it oversimplifies the transition from the Portuguese to the Cape Colony's usage of the term and, in so doing, overlooks that the latter usage emphasized differences in skin color and language to establish a "Hottentot-Caffre" race dichotomy, a divide with long-term significance for southern African history. Perhaps most importantly, the existing narrative fails to acknowledge that, by the turn of the nineteenth century, the Cape Colony's European settler population used the term "Caffre" primarily as a synonym for the Xhosa chiefdoms only, while European naturalists claimed that the "Caffres" were unified by a common skin color and *language* that separated them racially not only from "Hottentots" but also from "true Negroes." The naturalists, moreover, argued that the "Caffres" occupied much of southern Africa, notably the coastal region from the Keiskamma River to Delagoa Bay.

As I lay out in this chapter, the term evolved over the centuries to come to signify two different things to two different groups of Europeans. However, it was the European naturalist understanding of the "Caffres" that influenced missionary linguists when they first arrived in the region in the early nineteenth century. For this is reason, it is of great significance for the historical development of languages and language-based identities below South Africa's Great Escarpment.

"Caffres"

Europeans first made contact with southern Africa and its indigenous peoples as part of their sea voyages to Asia in the late fifteenth and early sixteenth centuries. One of the principal driving forces behind Europe's growing interest in the riches of that region was the commercialization of European civilization, which, in turn, motivated Portugal, Spain, England, France, and the Netherlands to seek out the wealth of the wider world.

For Portugal, plotting a seaborn path to Asia began with exploring the west coast of the African continent. They reached the Senegambia region in 1444, the Gold Coast in 1471, and the mouth of the Congo River in 1482. Six years later, Bartolomeu Dias reached the tip of South Africa; another nine years later, Vasco da Gama entered the Indian Ocean world.[8] Over the course of the next decades, the Portuguese tried to extract resources from this world by controlling commerce rather than large territories or populations. As part of this strategy they used a combination of violence and diplomacy to establish fortified bases at commercial choke points. In order to corner the gold, ivory, and slave export trade from southeastern Africa, Portuguese forces under Francisco de Almeida and Pero de Anhaia occupied Kilwa and Sofala in 1505, respectively. With similar aims in mind, Vasco Gomes set up a trading post at Mozambique Island in 1507, and Lourenço Marques established a settlement at Delagoa Bay in 1545.[9]

The initial Portuguese approach to southern Africa and its peoples was shaped by the views of (sub-Saharan) Africa and Africans that had dominated the Mediterranean world at least since the Middle Ages and that were indebted to the Judeo-Christian tradition.[10] Among other things, this tradition divided the peoples of the (known) world into three related groups—Africans, Europeans, and Asians—based on the biblical story about the peopling of Africa, Europe, and Asia by Noah's sons Ham, Japheth, and Shem in the aftermath of the great flood. More importantly, medieval reinterpretations of the book of Genesis identified darker skin color as the crucial characteristic of Africans by suggesting that it represented the visible mark of the curse Noah had cast on the descendants of Ham.[11] Equipped with this theory, the Portuguese sailed along the coast of West Africa and began to classify the Muslim and animist Wolofs, Mandinka, Tukulors, Serers, and Bakongo they encountered as "blacks" on the basis of their darker skin color and to define the region south of the Senegal River as the "land of the blacks (*terra dos negros*)."[12]

This perspective still dominated the Portuguese knowledge system when Vasco da Gama's fleet rounded the Cape of Good Hope between 1497 and 1498. Consequently, the crew identified the people they encountered near St. Helena Bay, Mossel Bay, Inhambane, and the Quelimane River as "blacks (*negros*)" because of their darker skin color.[13] A change, however, occurred in the ways in which the Portuguese classified the inhabitants of southern Africa between 1498 and 1505. As the list of fleets for 1505 makes clear, the Portuguese no longer described the inhabitants of Inhambane as "blacks" but as "Caffres." According to the list, "João de Queirós, as he sought anchorage 60 leagues to this side of Cabo das Correntes, was killed by the Kaffirs [os cafres] together with the master pilot and nearly all the others who were with him in the longboat."[14] One year later, the term featured in several orders issued by Pero de Anhaia, the Portuguese captain-major of Sofala.[15] Usage increased steadily during the next few decades, such that the Portuguese chronicler, João de Barros, remarked in 1552, "The name Kaffirs [Cafres] is already in general use among us, because of the number of slaves of this people that we have."[16]

It is most likely that the Portuguese adopted the term "Caffre" after 1500 because they came into sustained contact with preexisting Arab-Muslim and Persian-Muslim ideas about the inhabitants of East Africa. These Muslims identified the people of East Africa as Zanj (also Zinj; plural Zunūj) based on the belief that the continent of Africa had been peopled by the descendants of Noah's son Ham, whose son Kush had fathered Habasha who, while moving southeastward into Africa, had given rise to the Habasha, Nuba, Buja, and eastern Barbara peoples, as well as the Zanj.[17] According to their assessment, the Zanj lived in a region—the "land of the Zanj" (Bilād al-Zanj in Arabic, Zanguebar in Persian)—that extended along the East African coastline from circa 11.8° north to 26° south latitude.[18] Furthermore, Muslim observers associated the term Zanj with dark skin color. The Maghrebian traveler and scholar Ibn Battuta, for instance, explained in 1332 that at Kilwa "most of its people are Zunūj, extremely black [al-zunūj al-mustahkamū al-sawād]. . . . They are a people devoted to the Holy War because they are on one continuous mainland with unbelieving Zunūj [kuffār al-zunūj]."[19] Finally, as the quote makes clear, Muslim observers recognized that, while many Zanj were believers ("devoted to the Holy War"), they also included many unbelievers whom they described as kuffār (plural) and kāfir (singular).

The Portuguese were aware of this ethnography. Thus, the aforementioned João de Barros, explained in 1552: "The Arabians and the Persians who have learning, and who live in its vicinity, call it [East Africa] in their writings Zanguebar, and the inhabitants they call Zanguy [Zanj] and also by the common name of Kaffirs, which means people without a creed, a name they give to all who are idolaters."[20] As Barros's quote shows, the Portuguese were not only well informed about the ways in which Arab and

Persian Muslims thought about the inhabitants of East Africa, but they also clearly understood that the Arabic word *kāfir* referred to religious difference rather than differences in skin color. Nevertheless, as the Portuguese assimilated the term *kāfir* into their own ethnography of the region, they began to explicitly associate it with Black skin color (perhaps because of their own habit of thinking about sub-Saharan Africans in terms of Black skin color). Already Barros observed in 1552 that the key characteristic of the "Caffres" was that they were "black."[21] By the end of the century, the term "Caffre" had become quasi-synonymous with Black skin color among the Portuguese. As Jan Huygen van Linschoten, who had earlier served with the Portuguese at Goa, remarked in 1596, "These black people [*Swerten*] or Caffres of the land of Mozambique, and all the coast of Ethiopia, and within the land to the Cape of Good Hope . . . are in general as black as pitch."[22]

As was characteristic for the pre-Enlightenment period, the Portuguese did not systematize their knowledge about the "Caffres" beyond the focus on skin color.[23] This allowed them to use the term with considerable flexibility, notably by identifying all the inhabitants of the region as "Caffres" even if the latter's subsistence activities varied significantly.[24] Similarly, even though they recognized differences in local speaking practices, the Portuguese insisted that all the indigenous inhabitants of the region were "Caffres." In 1609, for instance, the Dominican friar João dos Santos argued that the "Mocarangas" (Karanga) and "Botongas" (Tonga) of modern-day Zimbabwe and Mozambique were all "Caffres," even though they allegedly spoke different languages.[25] Admittedly the differences appeared to be small, for one shipwreck survivor who had traveled through the Transkei to Sofala in the 1590s remarked, "The language is almost the same in the whole of Kaffraria, the difference between them resembling that between the languages of Italy, or between the ordinary ones of Spain."[26]

The only factor counteracting this flexibility was the rapidly expanding trade in gold, ivory, ambergris, and slaves from the region.[27] To circumscribe this valuable trade more clearly, the Portuguese added geographic specificity to the term as the sixteenth century progressed. While they initially associated it with the region that Muslim geographers had identified as the *Bilād al-Zanj* (*Zanguebar*) situated anywhere between the Horn of Africa (11.8° north latitude) and Delagoa Bay (circa 26° south latitude) on the east coast of Africa, by 1552 the Portuguese argued that "Caffraria" extended only as far as Melinde (circa 3° south latitude) in the northeast

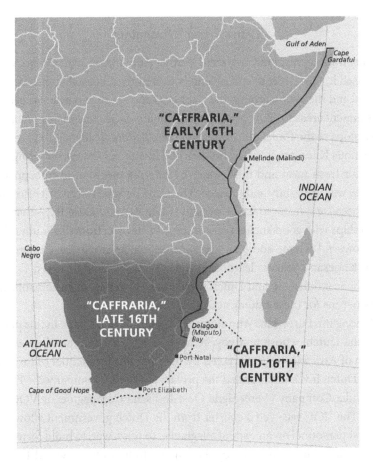

MAP 2. "Caffraria," ca. 1500 to 1600.

but as far as the Cape of Good Hope (34.2° south latitude and 18.3° east longitude) in the southwest.[28] The Portuguese changed the terminology again over the course of the next century, when the trade began to center increasingly on the region south of the Zambezi River Valley. They detached "Caffraria" entirely from the *Bilād al-Zanj* at this time, situating the northeastern boundary line at Mozambique Island (circa 15° south latitude).[29] At the same time, they extended the northwestern boundary from the Cape of Good Hope to Cabo Negro (15.7° south latitude).[30] As a result of these adjustments, "Caffraria" emerged as a region that included all of modern-day Namibia, Botswana, and South Africa and much of modern-day Zimbabwe and Mozambique (see map 2).

"Caffres" and "Hottentots"

As the trading relations between Europe and the Indian Ocean world increased in the sixteenth and seventeenth centuries, coastal South Africa in general and the region around the Cape of Good Hope in particular became refreshment areas for European ships on their voyages to and from Asia. On these stops at the Cape, Europeans interacted sporadically with the region's indigenous Khoesan-speaking hunters and livestock herders, bartering with them for fresh meat and fresh water by offering pieces of iron, copper, or brass as well as brandy and tobacco. The Cape became the favorite stopover place because it featured bays—notably Table Bay and False Bay—that provided ships with good anchorage and some protection from the South Atlantic's powerful winter and summer winds. Regular stopovers ensured that some Khoesan speakers learned European languages and served English, French, Scandinavian, and Dutch mariners as messengers, informants, and go-betweens for these trading activities.[31]

Among the Europeans who stopped frequently at the Cape in this period were the Dutch, whose first voyage to the East Indies rounded the southern tip of Africa in 1595. Attracted by the high profit potential of the spice trade, Dutch investors founded the private joint stock company the United East India Company (Vereenigde Oost-Indische Compagnie, or VOC), in 1602. The VOC received a charter from the Dutch government allowing it to enlist personnel on an oath of allegiance, to wage war, to build fortresses, and to establish trading monopolies in the Indian Ocean world through military conquest. Over the course of the seventeenth century, the VOC's executive Council of Seventeen—the Heeren XVII—deployed its six thousand ships and forty-eight thousand men to gain control over the spice-producing regions of modern-day Indonesia (Batavia).[32]

Given the Cape region's relatively temperate climate and disease-free environment, the VOC established a permanent refreshment station there in 1652 in the form of a fortress and vegetable garden. Some five years later, the company released nine of its employees from their contracts and allowed them to become settlers under the status of "free burghers." These settlers established fenced livestock, vegetable, and wheat farms in the area of modern-day Rondebosch and were required to sell their produce to the company at fixed prices.[33] Faced with European settlers on their traditional grazing lands, Khoesan-speaking herders mounted armed opposition. But military defeats due to the combination of inferior arms, internal divisions, and vulnerability to diseases such as smallpox caused indigenous resistance to collapse and their polities to disintegrate in the eighteenth century.[34] Claiming land by "right of conquest," meanwhile, the company made land grants to the growing number of incoming French- and German-speaking settlers. In 1707, the settler community consisted of some two thousand free burghers, some of whom owned large wheat- and wine-growing estates in the fertile valleys of the wider Cape region (notably at places like Stellenbosch) and satisfied their labor needs by indenturing the defeated Khoesan-speaking herders and hunters and by importing slaves.[35]

The first shipments of enslaved West Africans and Angolans were landed in 1658. As the demand for labor increased due to successful wine and wheat farming, the VOC began to import slaves from Mozambique, Madagascar, Indonesia, India, and Ceylon. By 1793, the Cape population numbered 13,830 free burghers and 14,747 slaves, who were subject to a governor and a council of policy who, in turn, were subject to the instructions of the VOC's Council of Seventeen and the governor-general of Batavia.[36]

When the VOC staff established themselves at the Cape of Good Hope in 1652, they inherited the Portuguese term "Caffre" and other European terms—"savages," "negroes," "Saldaniers," "Strandlopers," and "Watermen"— for the indigenous peoples of southern Africa.[37] Over time, they also adopted the names some of the indigenous communities used for themselves or applied to one another, including "Goringhaiconas," "Cochoquas," and "Soanquas."[38] Perhaps more importantly, soon after the establishment of the Cape settlement, VOC personnel referred to the Cape region's inhabitants collectively as "Hottentots" because the latter frequently used a similar-sounding word in their dance songs.[39]

Company personnel did not draw a clear distinction between Khoesan-speaking herders and hunters before the eighteenth century.[40] Indeed, although the Dutch associated the term "Hottentot" with a herder lifestyle, they included communities among them who did not possess cattle or sheep.[41] The "Strandlopers" or "Watermen" who eked out a living by collecting mussels, fish, and dead seals were subsumed within the classification as were peoples referred to as "Soaquas," "Ubiquas" and "Bosjesmans" (also "hill people," "mountaineers," "banditti" and "struijkrovers") who allegedly lived in the woods and mountains to the north and east of the Cape, where they survived by hunting, shore fishing, and allegedly stealing.[42]

Similarly, VOC personnel did not initially draw a clear distinction between "Hottentots" and "Caffres." This explains why they occasionally used these terms interchangeably, as in 1668 when the Dutch compiler Olfert Dapper titled his book on southern Africa *Kaffraria, or Land of the Kafirs, Otherwise Named the Hottentots*.[43] This flexible attitude began to change in the last quarter of the seventeenth century, however, when VOC officials learned from indigenous informants that "far off" to the east lived a different people known as the "Choboquas," who were as Black as the slaves from Guinea and Angola.[44] The differences between the "Hottentots" and the "Choboquas" appeared so substantial that VOC officials began to classify the latter as "another race of people."[45] Moreover, they began to actively inquire if these "Choboquas" were "real (*opregte*) Kaffers" and "where the Hottentots end and where the Caffres begin."[46]

Because reliable intelligence was not immediately forthcoming, Cape residents assumed on the basis of rumors that north of the Cape Colony's boundary, the land of the "Caffres" began somewhere beyond the Cedarberg, Roggeveld, and Nuweveld mountain chains, but readily admitted that "the actual land of the Caffres [*Kaffern*] . . . has never really been discovered or visited" in that direction.[47] The situation was better to the east of the Cape where, in 1688, the Dutch vessel *Centaurus* picked up several Europeans near the Buffalo River; most had survived a shipwreck near the Mzimkhulu River two years earlier. These survivors claimed they had encountered various communities on their overland journey to the Buffalo River, including a people called "Magossche" (most likely the Nguni-speaking Xhosa chiefdoms mentioned in chapter 1). Although they were confused about the exact identities of these groups, all of them agreed that the "Magossche" were "Caffres."[48]

The VOC personnel's desire to obtain more accurate information about the dividing line between the "Hottentots" and "Caffres" suggests a period of transition from pre-Enlightenment to Enlightenment-era thinking. During the age of Enlightenment, notably in the eighteenth century, Europeans came to believe that there was an order in the natural world that could be discovered through scientific observations and made visible through scientific systems of classification (taxonomies). Enlightenment-era naturalists applied these ideas to the study of mankind, which was thought to occupy the apex of a hierarchically ordered natural world.[49] Despite some notable differences, the most influential naturalists of the time—Carl Linnaeus, Georges-Louis Leclerc, the Comte de Buffon, and Johann Friedrich Blumenbach—believed that skin color could be used to divide mankind into distinct races.[50]

Because these color-coded taxonomies suggested that different shades of Blackness were indicative of racial subgroupings, European naturalists began to fine-tune their assessment of indigenous peoples' skin color in southern Africa.[51] Although Europeans had claimed previously that all the inhabitants of the region were "blacks," by the turn of the eighteenth century an increasing number of them agreed with the German-born Peter Kolb, who explained that the "Hottentots are olive-coloured" whereas "the Caffres are totally black [absolument noirs]."[52] The corollary of this fine-tuned color-coded classification system was that "Hottentots" and "Caffres" represented two distinct racial varieties.

Additional expeditions helped territorialize these two "races" during the second half of the eighteenth century. The Dutchman Robert Jacob Gordon traveled along and across the Orange River in 1779, for instance; in remarks about the local "Briqua" he encountered on this journey, Gordon stated that they were "Caffres" because they possessed Black skin color.[53] Based on this information, Cape Colony officials eventually concluded that the Orange River represented the approximate boundary line between the "Hottentot" and "Caffre" races in the northern Cape region. Europeans also elaborated the "Hottentot-Caffre" dichotomy in the context of the eastern Cape region. An important step in that direction occurred in 1737–38 when the survivors of a colonial hunting party reported that "there were not . . . any Kaffres residing west of the Kysee [Keiskamma River]."[54] In 1752 company officials confirmed the river's function as a boundary line between the two so-called "races" when they sent out an expedition under Ensign August Frederick Beutler. Following the apparently well-established trading route to the "Caffres" they found the region west of the Keiskamma River occupied by "Hottentots" and the region east of it belonging to the "Caffres," whose skin color they described as "blacker" than that of the "Hottentots."[55] In accordance with these observations, the expedition concluded that the Keiskamma River represented the dividing line between "Hottentots" and Caffres" in the eastern Cape region.[56]

Observations of indigenous speaking practices reinforced the dichotomy. The focus on language made sense in the context of eighteenth-century comparative philology, which suggested that languages and nations (races) overlapped neatly, so that identification of the former resulted in the identification of the latter and vice versa.[57] Taking a cue from natural science, linguists argued further that distinct languages could be discovered by collecting lexicological and phonological "facts" and organizing them into comparative lists. Significant differences between the speaking practices of the "Hottentots" and "Caffres" first became apparent when Europeans

TABLE 2. Samples of "Caffre" and "Hottentot" word lists

	GREVENBROECK		BARROW	
ENGLISH	CAFFRE	HOTTENTOT	CAFFRE	HOTTENTOT
One	Mounje	Chiu	Eenyé	Qŭœ
Two	Mabile	Kham	Zimbeenie	Kăm
Three	Matato	Nhona	Zintaté	Gŏna

Source: Johannes G. Grevenbroeck, "An Elegant and Accurate Account of the African Race living round the Cape of Good Hope Commonly called Hottentots (1695)," in Schapera and Farrington, eds. and trans., The Early Cape Hottentots, 281–83; John Barrow, An Account of Travels into the Interior of Southern Africa, in the Years 1797 and 1798, 2 vols. (London: Cadell and Davies, 1801, 1804), 1:220.

compared "Caffre" words with "Hottentot" terms of the same meaning and recognized that a lexicological boundary separated these two modes of communication (see table 2).

The same observers also identified a phonological boundary between these speaking practices. Early on in their studies, they had become convinced that click sounds represented a unique feature of the "Hottentot" language.[58] Although they learned that different "Hottentot" groups used somewhat different speaking practices, they claimed that all modes of communication that included these sounds formed part of a single "Hottentot" language. One of them, Carl Peter Thunberg, remarked in the 1780s that "the language of the Hottentots . . . includes dialects that are noticeably different from one another. However, in almost all of them one can hear a certain rattling, clapping, or clicking."[59] Having identified click sounds as the most important phonological marker of the "Hottentot" language, European naturalists tried to assess whether the "Caffres" used similar sounds.

At first, they denied this possibility categorically. Referring to the "Caffre" communities of "Terra de Natal," Peter Kolb, for one, claimed that "[they] do not smack their tongue against the roof of the mouth when they speak."[60] Similar information reached the Cape Colony from the Orange River, where Europeans learned in 1762 and 1779, respectively, that the "Birina [a group classified as "Caffres"] . . . spoke a language that was very different from that of the Namacquas [a group classified as "Hottentots"]" because "in this language no clicks of the tongue are heard."[61]

Encounters in the eastern Cape region suggested less radical differences, however. The Beutler expedition of 1752, for instance, explained that the difference was not that the "Caffres" did not use click sounds at all but that they did not click in the same manner ("se klocke ook niet gelijk") as the

"Hottentots."[62] Writing more than a decade later, Thunberg specified that the crucial issue was the frequency with which the two groups used these sounds. "The language of the Caffres is much easier," he remarked; it "employs clicks only in a couple of words."[63] European commentators eventually concluded that the two groups or races were indeed separated by a linguistic boundary. Among them were Beutler's men, who concluded in 1752 that the "Caffre" language "differs completely [*verschilt ten eenmal*] from that of the Hottentots."[64]

By the end of the eighteenth century, European naturalists' desire to establish clear boundaries on the basis of skin color and language had led to the identification of "Hottentots" and "Caffre" as two distinct racial varieties. Now the term "Caffre" was no longer associated with all the inhabitants of southern Africa but only with those inhabitants who possessed Black skin color, spoke the still poorly defined "Caffre" language, and resided somewhere north of the Orange River and east of the Keiskamma River.

"Caffres" and "True Negroes"

European naturalists were not satisfied with the elaboration of the "Caffre-Hottentot" dichotomy. Driven by what Michel Foucault has called the "taxonomic impulse," they used a series of expeditions to identify the extension of the "Caffres" into the interior of the African continent. The findings from these expeditions led them to believe that the "Caffres" were hemmed in by another race—the "true Negroes."

In the northern Cape region, Dutch explorer Robert Jacob Gordon had already identified the "Bitjoana" (Tswana) as "Caffres" in 1779.[65] Drawing on information collected by the British colonial official Pieter Jan Truter, Englishman John Barrow seconded Gordon's opinion at the turn of the century, declaring, "That the *Booshuanas* [Tswana] are of the same race of people as the Kaffers on the sea-coast is a position that will scarcely admit of a doubt."[66] Based on these other findings, the German-born naturalist Heinrich Lichtenstein concluded that, in this direction, the "Caffres" inhabited a region that extended "from the river Kuruhman, as its southern boundary, thirty or forty days' journey northwards."[67]

A similar classificatory development took place in the eastern Cape region, where the survivors of the *Grosvenor* shipwreck had previously identified the Mpondo and Bomvana polities as "Caffres" in 1782.[68] Six years later, Dutch East India Company official Franz Winckelmann argued that "the Tambucki [Thembu], a nation that resides further east, represent different tribes of Caffres."[69] In the early 1800s, Lichtenstein and the Dutch colonial administrator Ludwig Alberti advanced more ambitious theories regarding the eastward expansion of the "Caffres." While Lichtenstein argued that "the more distant tribes of Caffres" included the "Mambuckis" (Mpondo) and the "Maduanas" (Qwathi), Alberti claimed that the people living "in the vicinity of Rio de la Goa" were also "proper Kaffirs (wirkliche Kaffern)."[70]

Following the prevailing theories of racial classification and comparative philology, European naturalists focused once again on skin color and language to determine whether or not these groups belonged to the "Caffre" race. Most commentators agreed that skin color served as an important marker of the "Caffre" race, though descriptions of their skin color ranged from "jet black," "nearly black," "deep bronze," and "pale black" to "blackish brown."[71]

More importantly, they agreed that the "Caffres" were unified by a common language. Gordon explained in 1779 that the "Caffres" north and east of the Cape Colony spoke "the same" language "but a different dialect and without any click of the tongue."[72] Contemporary observers advanced similar views about the various communities between the Cape Colony and Delagoa Bay. Lichtenstein, for instance, reported that the Thembu spoke "exactly the same" language as the "Koossas" (Xhosa).[73] Regarding the "Maduanas" (Qwathi), who lived beyond the Mzimvubu River, he reported that he had been informed by travelers that "there was scarcely any difference between their language and that of the Koossas [Xhosa]."[74] Colonel Richard Collins reinforced these claims when he explained in 1809 that the language underwent only "some changes" as one traveled beyond the Thembu to the "Mambookees" (Mpondo) and the "Manduanas" (Qwathi).[75] The most far-reaching opinion came again from the Dutch administrator Alberti. Having met several emissaries from "the vicinity of Rio de la Goa" at the residence of Chief Ngqika of the Rharhabe-Xhosa, he became convinced that the "Caffre" language extended as far as the Portuguese settlements at Delagoa Bay. "My interpreter, a Gonaqua," Alberti explained, "told me that the language of these visitors was the same as that spoken by the Kaffirs, in whose company I found myself."[76]

Inspired by comparative philology, these European observers established the unity of the "Caffre" language on the basis of lexicological and phonological comparisons. Lichtenstein explained that "there is a certain lisp in all the Caffre dialects . . . [that] is produced by thrusting the point of the tongue

TABLE 3. Samples of Lichtenstein's Beetjuan and Koossa word lists

ENGLISH	CAFFRE DIALECTS	
	BEETJUAN	KOOSSA
A man	Muhntŏ	Uhmtŏ
People	Baatŏ	Gabaantŏ
A child	Unjana	Uhmtoána
A mouth	Mulumŏ	Mloomu
Flesh	Nama	Jamma

Source: Heinrich Lichtenstein, *Travels in Southern Africa, In the Years 1803, 1804, 1805, and 1806*, 2 vols., trans. A. Plumptre (London: H. Colburn, 1812–15), appendix 2, "Vocabulary of Words of the Beetjuan Language"; ibid., vol. 1, appendix "Vocabulary of Words from the Language of the Koossas."

against the gums."[77] He explained further that "all the Caffre dialects" were "smooth" because they consisted primarily of words that included "simple sounds," "two syllables," "open vowels," and "clear intonation of the last syllable."[78] Lexicology was also important. In 1779, Gordon suggested that, while the "Caffres" of the northern and eastern Cape regions used different words for some things, such as *water*, they employed the same or similar words for other things.[79] Lichtenstein's "Beetjuan" and "Koossa" word lists, which represented the "Caffre" speech forms of the northern and eastern Cape regions, seemingly confirmed that "the principal radical words" showed "a striking conformity" between these speaking practices (see table 3).[80]

The question remained whether these speaking practices were mutually intelligible. Lichtenstein provided an affirmative answer in the first decade of the nineteenth century. "A Koossa [Xhosa] and a Beetjuan [Tswana], meeting by chance," he explained, "must understand each other ultimately, though perhaps slowly."[81] Alberti likewise noted that his Gonaqua interpreter, who spoke fluently the language of the Xhosa of the eastern Cape region, had required less than two days of practice to be able to converse with the emissaries from "the vicinity of Rio de la Goa."[82] On the basis of such evidence, European naturalists concluded that, in one way or another, all so-called Caffre dialects were mutually intelligible and thus formed part of a single language.[83]

These conclusions, in turn, gave rise to estimates of the geographical dimension of "Caffraria" that deviated from the earlier Portuguese ones. In the first decade of the nineteenth century, Barrow insisted that "the belt of country. . . . inhabited by the Caffres" stretched "across the southern part of Africa," extending in the west from 20° to 25° south latitude (roughly modern-day Namibia) and in the east from 24° to 32° south latitude (approximately the southern tip of modern-day Mozambique to KwaZulu-Natal).[84] Lichtenstein was more generous in his estimates. As he explained: "I consider all the tribes . . . southward from Quiloa [i.e., Kilwa at about 10° south latitude], and eastward from the colony of the Cape, very decidedly as a great nation . . . [and] would include them all under the general name of Caffres."[85] Both Barrow and Lichtenstein thus agreed that the "Caffres" extended across much of southern Africa.

Their geographic estimates also implied that the "Caffres" were not only distinct from the race of the "Hottentots," whose historical home was believed to be the region close to the Cape of Good Hope, but also from the "true Negroes," who allegedly inhabited the regions to the immediate north of "Caffraria." Focusing on alleged differences in skin color, the French naturalist Georges-Louis Leclerc, the Comte de Buffon, argued as early as the middle of the eighteenth century that "it appears . . . that the Negroes proper are different from the Caffres, who are blacks of a different species. . . . The true Negroes, that is to say, the blackest among the Blacks, are found in the Western region of Africa, whereas the Caffres, that is to say, those least black among the Blacks, are found in the Eastern regions."[86] European naturalists operating in southern Africa agreed with Buffon's conclusion. Lichtenstein, for example, claimed that the "Caffres" were "equally distinct from the Negroes and Mohammedans on one side, and from the Hottentots on the other."[87] Similarly, Barrow noted at about the same time that "the Caffres [are] . . . surrounded on all sides by people that differ from them in every point, in color . . . and in language."[88]

Importantly, their assessment of these differences was not value-neutral. While they deemed the "Caffres" inferior to Europeans, both naturalists intimated that, in terms of their appearance and language, the "Caffres" were superior to the "Hottentots" and the "true Negroes." Lichtenstein, for instance, argued that the "Caffres" represented "a great nation" whose "external form and figure" differed "exceedingly from the other nations of Africa" because "they are much taller, stronger, and their limbs much better proportioned."[89] Barrow's musings entailed a similar coded message. "There is perhaps no nation on earth," he explained, "that can produce so fine a race of men as the Caffres: they are tall, stout, muscular, well made, elegant figures. . . . They have not one line of the African negro in the composition of their persons."[90] Studies of language pointed in the same direction. In Lichtenstein's view, the "Caffre" language was "pleasing to the ear" because, unlike the "Hottentot" language, it was "full-toned, soft, and harmonious, and spoken without clattering."[91] Barrow was more explicit when he asserted that the "Caffre" language "appears to be the remains of something far beyond that of any savage nation."[92]

How could these differences and the perceived superiority of the "Caffre" race be explained? Barrow and Lichtenstein did so by tentatively placing the historical origins of the "Caffres" outside of the African continent. The former, for instance, surmised that the history of the "Caffre" race began with the arrival in Africa of "the tribes of those wandering Arabs known by the name of Bed[o]uins."[93] Agreeing in principal but differing in detail, Lichtenstein posited, "They appear to me of much more ancient descent . . . and nothing is adverse to the supposition that the people of the northern coasts of Africa, who were of Asiatic origin, may have been the immediate ancestors of the Caffres."[94]

It is noteworthy that by explaining the "superiority" of the "Caffres" with non-African origins, Barrow and Lichtenstein in effect articulated an early version of the Hamitic hypothesis. This late nineteenth-century hypothesis claimed that Hamites represented a branch of the Caucasian (white, European) race who had invaded Africa in the deeper past, bringing early civilizational development to the continent.[95] As one of the proponents of the Hamitic hypothesis, Charles Gabriel Seligman argued in 1930: "The civilizations of Africa are the civilizations of the Hamites, its history the record of these peoples and of their interaction with the two other African stocks, the Negro and the Bushman. . . . . The incoming Hamites were pastoral 'Europeans'—arriving wave after wave—better armed as well as quicker witted than the dark agricultural Negroes."[96] Writing more than a century earlier, Barrow and Lichtenstein offered their own version of this racialized thinking. However, whereas Seligman differentiated between superior Hamitic invaders and inferior "Negro" and "Bushman" races, Barrow and Lichtenstein identified the "Caffres" of southern Africa as a superior race of invaders, distinguishable from "Hottentots" and "true Negroes" on the basis of their skin color and language.

"Caffres" and "Xhosas"

It is an irony of history that, at the same time as the Hamitic hypothesis gained ascendancy among European naturalists in the nineteenth century, the same naturalists began to question the racial distinctiveness of the "Caffres." In the 1830s, for instance, the naturalist James C. Prichard rejected Barrow's and Lichtenstein's "Caffre-Negro" race dichotomy by claiming that the "Caffres" and "Negroes" represented two "branches of one race."[97] In 1850, his counterpart Robert Knox similarly classified the "Caffres" as "closely allied to the Negro race."[98] Both Prichard and Knox may have been encouraged to question the eighteenth-century "Caffre-Negro" race dichotomy because they came into contact with a settler-colonialist discourse about the "Caffres" that associated the term more narrowly with those indigenous chiefdoms who self-identified primarily as Xhosa and blocked the settlers' eastward expansion.

This expansion was the product of the VOC's late seventeenth-century decision to allow direct immigration to the Cape. As the settler population increased, the most fertile land within the colony's existing boundaries was quickly occupied. After 1700, therefore, new arriving settlers habitually crossed these boundaries to claim new land.[99] For instance, while Beutler's expedition of 1752 still identified "Hagelcraal" near Mossel Bay as the easternmost place inhabited by European stock farmers, VOC records indicate that twenty years later, some of them resided east of the Camdeboo Mountains and the mouth of the Gamtoos River.[100] Wary of the settlers' uncontrolled eastward migrations, the company decreed in 1770 and again in 1774 that settlement beyond these places was illegal.[101] However, these directives went against the interests of the land-hungry settlers who, in 1775, successfully petitioned the VOC for the extension of these limits to the Great Fish River and the Bushmans River.[102]

Precisely in this broader region, however, the settler expansion started to be challenged by "Caffre" communities who self-identified as the Xhosa chiefdoms. In the late 1770s, for instance, Gordon encountered the homesteads of several "Caffer [here meaning Xhosa] chiefs" along the Great Fish and Bushmans Rivers.[103] In fact, by 1778, farmers and Xhosa lived in such close proximity to each other that company governor Joachim van Plettenberg felt compelled to meet with several Xhosa chiefs to negotiate a boundary agreement, which, if the Dutch records can be trusted, established the Great Fish River as the official line of demarcation between the two groups.[104]

As a result of the intense contact along this boundary, European settlers and some VOC officials began to associate the term "Caffre" more narrowly with these Xhosa chiefdoms only, a trend that intensified after 1779, when the two groups began to compete with each other for land, cattle, and other resources, commencing a century of warlike conflicts (three of which took place between 1779 and 1799).[105] This explains why the Dutch official Ludwig Alberti, who as shown above maintained that the "Caffre" race extended to Delagoa Bay, also claimed that the "country occupied by the Kaffirs [here meaning Xhosa] . . . is bounded in the East by the River Key [Kei], in the West by the Great Fish River, in the South by the sea, and in the North by a range of mountains."[106] The same context of competition and violence also explains why some settlers began to attach decidedly negative meanings to the term. Both the Frenchman François Le Vaillant and the Englishman John Barrow observed this tendency among the colony's settler population in the 1780s and 1790s, respectively. As Le Vaillant remarked about the Xhosa: "The report of this Nation being barbarous and bloody . . . was industriously circulated by the Colonists."[107] Barrow agreed, noting that "it is a common idea, industriously kept up in the colony, that the Kaffers [here meaning the Xhosa] are a savage, treacherous, and cruel people."[108]

This trend intensified in the first half of the nineteenth century when European settlers and colonial officials regularly accused the Xhosa chiefdoms of "thievishness" and "indolence" and characterised them as "treacherous savages" and "merciless barbarians" in order to justify the dispossession of their land.[109] In 1836, for instance, one prominent settler by the name of Robert Godlonton characterized the Xhosa polities as "uncivilized and barbarous" and incapable of attaining "a high point in the scale of humanity."[110] Only one year prior, the British military official Colonel Harry Smith, had identified them as "a perfidious set, actuated by the feelings of the moment . . . slaves of momentary feeling, possessing nothing but a love of mischief, rapine, and injustice."[111] Most likely, these negative characterizations and descriptions helped to gradually transform the meaning of the term "Caffre," contributed to its reclassification by Prichard and Knox in 1836–37 and 1850 respectively, and ensured that it eventually became a term of denigration and hate speech in South Africa.

In 1800, this development had only just begun, however, allowing two very different sets of ideas about the "Caffres" to coexist. The settler-colonialist discourse used the term as a shorthand for the Xhosa polities only, while the naturalist discourse identified the "Caffres" as a racial category that was distinct from and superior to the "Hottentots" and the "true Negroes" in terms of their skin color and language. Knowledge of this latter conception of a distinct "Caffre" race and language, which European naturalists believed extended over much of southern Africa, is useful because it opens up insights into the history of the Zulu-Xhosa language divide. Most scholars tell this history through distinct Zulu and Xhosa case studies, a binary approach which is encouraged by the bifurcated character of the wider historiography and the erroneous assumption that when eighteenth-century naturalists (and nineteenth-century missionaries) wrote about the "Caffre" language, they used the term in the settler sense, referring to the speaking practices of the "Xhosa" only.

The evidence above, however, suggests that when eighteenth-century naturalists wrote about the "Caffres" and the "Caffre" language, they referred to a single language community that unified much of southern Africa and included all the Nguni variants that modern linguistics likes to classify as distinct Zulu and Xhosa languages. This means that history of the Zulu-Xhosa language divide must ask who divided a *single* "Caffre" language into two *distinct* Zulu and Xhosa languages and why. The following chapters will provide answers to these questions, showing that missionaries and Africans contributed to this outcome in complex ways.

3

"All Speak the Caffre Language"

Missionaries, Migrants, and Defining the
Target Language for Bible Translation

D r. Johannes Vanderkemp and John Edmond of the London Missionary Society (LMS) were the first European missionaries to visit the so-called Caffres (in this case, the Xhosa) of South Africa's coastal belt. Their visit to this region in 1799 and 1800, however, did not result in a permanent mission station.[1] The first permanent mission station among the "Caffres" was not established until Joseph Williams, in his capacity as British government missionary agent, settled on the banks of the Kat River in 1816, serving the region's Xhosa, Gonaqua, and Khoekhoe communities until his death in 1818. Following Williams's passing, the colonial government sent missionary John Brownlee to establish Chumie (Tyhume) Station among the Xhosa in June 1820. Several European missionary societies, along with one American missionary organization, joined these government-sponsored proselytizing efforts over the next three decades, steadily widening Christianity's influence in the coastal belt.

As part of their engagement with the coastal belt and its peoples, the missionaries translated a wide range of didactic, liturgical, and missiological materials into vernacular speaking practices, which, until the early 1850s, they believed to belong to a single "Caffre" language that extended from South Africa's eastern Cape region to Delagoa Bay in southern Mozambique. While the eighteenth-century European naturalist idea of the "Caffre" race and language had conditioned them to assume that the target language for these translations extended across this vast space, the missionaries gained additional confidence in this paradigm when they interacted with people of European and African descent who migrated throughout this region and who used their skills in the speaking practices of the people from one end of the coastal belt to communicate successfully with the people from the other end.

British Rule in the Coastal Belt

The Cape Colony was in the hands of Great Britain by the time the missionary project got fully underway in the early decades of the nineteenth century. A British military expedition had gained permanent control of the formerly Dutch colony in 1806, during the Napoleonic Wars. However, aside from preventing the French from gaining a foothold in this strategically important location for their seaborne trade with the Indian Ocean world, British imperial officials had no clear vision for the Cape Colony.[2]

Although Britain's interests in the Cape Colony were limited, its officials pursued a liberal reformist agenda by ending indentured servitude and abolishing slavery between 1828 and 1838.[3] They also attempted to stabilize the colony's conflict-ridden eastern boundary with the so-called Caffres, which, in this case, referred primarily to the Xhosa chiefdoms who still resided on both sides of the Great Fish River at this time (in a region extending approximately from the Bushman's to the Mbashe Rivers). These attempts provoked additional wars, however. In the Fourth Frontier War (1811–12), the British violently removed all Xhosa residents from the region west of the Great Fish River, which the Dutch had established as the eastern boundary of the colony in 1778.[4] When Xhosa warriors tried to regain their land west of the river in the Fifth Frontier War (1818–19), the British forces waged a brutal campaign against them and, one year later, resettled some four thousand lower-middle-class men, women, and children from the British Isles along the boundary.[5] Although these "1820 Settlers" remained "culturally distinct" from the earlier European stock farmers who began to refer to themselves as Afrikaners, they did come to share the latter's thirst for indigenous land and labor power and, thus, for colonial expansion.[6]

The colony's eastern boundary remained a contested area. In 1834, Xhosa chiefs triggered the Sixth Frontier War (1834–35) when they conducted a surprise attack against British and Afrikaner settlements along the boundary. Colonial Governor Benjamin D'Urban retaliated with a ten-month campaign that achieved a negotiated settlement and required the defeated Xhosa chiefs to give up their Mfengu clients, accept nominal British rule, and acknowledge the Keiskamma River as the new boundary line. However, the liberal-humanitarian lobby both in the colony and the metropole vociferously protested against these policies and convinced the British government to rescind the last two of these measures in 1836. Already disenchanted with British rule, a significant faction of the Afrikaners responded by moving beyond the boundaries of the Cape Colony, where they gradually established additional European possessions.[7] In the coastal belt specifically, they wrested control of the region between the Thukela and Mzimkhulu Rivers (including the small European outpost at Port Natal) from the Zulu kingdom, transforming it into the Republic of Natalia in 1839, which the British officially annexed as the Cape Colony's District of Natal in 1844 and organized as a separate Natal Colony in 1856.

Back in the eastern Cape region, British soldiers and settlers and Xhosa chiefs and warriors fought two additional wars against each other. Victory in the Seventh Frontier War (1846–47) allowed Britain to extend the Cape Colony's eastern boundary from the Great Fish River to the Keiskamma River by adding the District of Victoria and to organize the region between the Keiskamma and the Great Kei Rivers as British Kaffraria, a Crown-governed dependency for the defeated and displaced Xhosa.[8] These policies set the stage for the Eighth Frontier War (1850–53), during which the British and Xhosa suffered about fourteen hundred and sixteen thousand deaths, respectively.[9] This loss of life and the outbreak of a bovine lung sickness epidemic in 1854 prepared the ground for the millenarian-inspired Cattle-Killing Movement among the Xhosa polities two years later, in which an additional forty thousand of their men, women, and children perished from starvation.[10] British officials fully exploited this heightened distress among the Xhosa to add economic exploitation to political subordination: they forced the Xhosa to accept exploitative wage labor regimes circumscribed by colonial laws such as the "Kaffir Pass Act" and "Kaffir Employment Act" of 1857.[11]

Thus, without following a clear plan, the British had expanded their control over significant portions of South Africa's coastal belt by the middle of the nineteenth century. In the eastern Cape region, they had gained control of the Xhosa chiefdoms west of the Kei River, including some of their affiliated Gonaqua, Gqunukhwebe and Ntinde polities. By annexing the District of Natal in 1844, the British had also extended their control over African communities in the Natal-Zululand region between the Thukela and Mzimkhulu Rivers. However, the coastal belt was still largely in the hands of independent African polities, notably the Xhosa, Thembu, Mpondomise, Mpondo, and Bhaca chiefdoms who resided between the Kei and

Mzimkhulu Rivers, and the powerful Zulu kingdom, which still ruled the area north of the Thukela River.

Missionaries in the Coastal Belt

While British colonial expansion in the coastal belt occurred without a clear plan, European and American missionaries established numerous mission stations in the region with a strong sense of purpose (see map 3). They intended to save souls by converting the region's indigenous populations to Christianity. This desire resulted from a global development between the seventeenth and nineteenth centuries. Successively, the Protestant and Catholic Reformations, the Atlantic Revolutions, the Napoleonic Wars, and the onset of industrialization and capitalism all gave rise to an atmosphere of millennial expectations. This atmosphere, in turn, produced large-scale religious revivals and Protestant movements throughout Europe and North America whose followers felt a strong desire to bring spiritual renewal, repentance, and conversion to the world, including to the coastal belt of South Africa.[12]

After 1820 several missionary societies joined the earlier government-sponsored missionizing efforts of Joseph Williams and John Brownlee. Founded in 1796, the Glasgow Missionary Society, one of several Scottish Presbyterian mission societies (hereafter collectively abbreviated as SPMS), sent John Bennie and John Ross to Brownlee's Chumie Station in 1821.[13] Over the course of the next two decades, they and other SPMS missionaries established their own stations, notably Incehra Station (the future Lovedale) in 1824. Not wanting to fall behind, the LMS recruited John Brownlee, who founded the Buffalo River Station (the site of present-day King William's Town) among the Ntinde in 1826. Several LMS missionaries soon followed Brownlee, including the German-born Frederick Gottlob Kayser, who opened the Knapp's Hope Station among the Rharhabe-Xhosa in 1833, and the English-born Richard Birt, who helped found Umxelo Station among the Dange-Xhosa in 1839 and Peelton Station among the Mfengu in 1848.

Two German missionary societies became active in the eastern Cape region during the same period. The Moravian Missionary Society (MMS) established Shiloh Station among the Thembu polities in 1828.[14] The Berlin Mission Society (BMS) sent out missionary Jakob Ludwig Döhne, who founded Bethel Station (present-day Stutterheim) among the Rharhabe-Xhosa in 1837.[15] In the aftermath of the Seventh Frontier War, Döhne and his colleague Karl Wilhelm Posselt moved to Natal, leaving the rebuilding

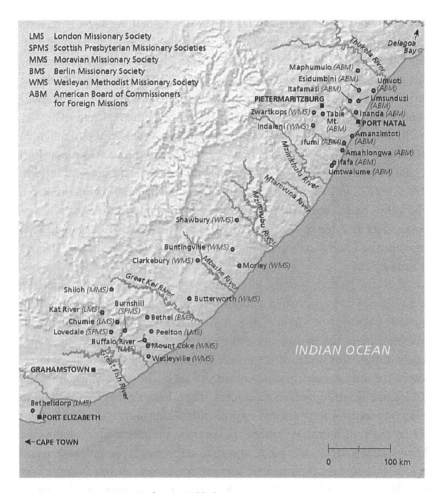

MAP 3. Mission stations in the coastal belt, ca. 1850.

efforts to Johann Heinrich Albert Kropf (usually referred to as Albert Kropf only), who reestablished the BMS's Bethel Station in 1848.[16]

All these efforts paled in comparison to those of the Wesleyan (Methodist) Missionary Society (WMS). Founded in England in 1813, the WMS's entry into the eastern Cape region began with Reverend William Shaw, who arrived in South Africa as a Wesleyan chaplain attached to the "1820 Settlers" and almost immediately developed an ambitious plan to extend the work of the WMS beyond the colonial frontier.[17] Supported by a steady stream of new missionaries, notably William Shrewsbury, William Boyce, and John Appleyard, he turned his plan into a reality over the next two decades. In 1823, for instance, the WMS established Wesleyville mission station among the Gqunukhwebe.[18] Several other stations followed, including Mount Coke among the Ndlambe-Xhosa in 1825, Butterworth among the Gcaleka-Xhosa and their Mfengu clients in 1827, (Old) Morley among the Bomvana in 1829, Clarkebury among the Thembu in 1830, Buntingville among the Mpondo in 1830, and Shawbury among the Bhaca in 1839.

By the early 1840s, the Wesleyan missionaries crossed the Mzimkhulu River into Natal-Zululand, where they established stations at Durban (Port Natal), Pietermaritzburg, Zwartkops (Kwangubeni), and Indaleni in 1841, 1845, 1846, and 1847, respectively. In the Natal-Zululand region, however, the WMS had to compete with members of the American Board of Commissioners for Foreign Missions, who had first arrived in the region in 1835 and operated twelve mission stations between the Mzimkhulu and Thukela Rivers by 1850.

Thus, by the middle of the nineteenth century, European and American missionaries had established stations throughout much of the coastal belt, notably between the Great Fish and Thukela Rivers. They operated with the blessing of the British colonial government in this vast region, especially in the areas under direct British control. But the missionaries' interests were not necessarily identical with those of the colonial government. Colonial officials supported missionary efforts because they expected these efforts to transform the region's African inhabitants into loyal subjects, docile laborers, or harmless "others." In contrast, the missionaries supported the colonial government's political agenda in the region primarily when and where that agenda promised to advance the project of religious conversion. In other words, even though there was at times considerable overlap between the two agendas, the missionaries were first and foremost interested in promoting Christianity or, as one of them put it, "communicating the light of the Gospel to the heathen tribes who inhabit the coast country from the Keiskamma to Delagoa Bay."[19]

Missionary Translations: Defining the Target Language

To properly communicate "the light of the Gospel to the heathen tribes," the missionaries studied local speaking practices, produced word lists, vocabularies, phrase books, dictionaries, grammars, philological surveys, spelling books, and reading primers of local vernaculars and, finally, translated the Bible, hymns, and other liturgical materials into what they called the "Caffre" language.

Although this process began as early as 1800 when Johannes Vanderkemp of the LMS had published a rudimentary grammar and vocabulary
titled *Specimen of the Caffra Language* and *Vocabulary of the Caffra Language*,[20] it was the Scottish missionaries who initiated a more comprehensive approach in the 1820s. One of their first actions consisted of, as they
put it, "reducing to form and rule, this language, which hitherto floated in
the wind."[21] The system of writing that resulted from this effort was then
used by missionary John Bennie and others as the basis for the first language primer of its kind, *Incwadi yokuqala ekuteteni gokwamaxosa* (First
elementary book of the Xhosa), published in 1824.[22] For the next fifteen
years, Bennie was in charge of the SPMS's language development efforts.
He published didactic materials and linguistic materials, notably *A Systematic Vocabulary of the Kaffrarian Language* in 1826, which included his
Introduction to the Kaffrarian Grammar.[23]

The Wesleyans also worked on the language, with William Shaw preparing a makeshift vocabulary between 1823 and 1826.[24] The crucial breakthrough for the Wesleyans, however, came when William Boyce published
A Grammar of the Kafir Language in 1834, which for the first time explained
the rules governing the prefix changes and sound patterns that rendered the
language melodious sounding .[25] As early as March 1832, Boyce referred to
these rules in these terms:

> One principal word in a sentence governs the initial letters or syllables
> of the other words: this is independent of any grammatical concord,
> or variety of inflexion. Thus, in speaking the language, the following
> points must be ascertained in order to insure correctness: first, the
> principal or governing word in a sentence; second, the principal letter
> in that word, to the sound of which the initial letters or syllables of the
> other words must be assimilated; third, the changes which must be
> made in the initial letters or syllables of the word which is governed
> by this euphonic concord.[26]

In the aftermath of this breakthrough, the WMS published a number of
didactic materials that facilitated reading instruction in the language. These
works included, among others, *Incwadi yezifundo ibalelwe izikolo zaba-Wesli.
Emaxoseni* (Lesson book written for Wesleyan Schools among the Xhosa),
which was published in 1838.[27] They also produced linguistic materials that
rendered the "Caffre" language more accessible as an object of knowledge.
Included among these publications were John Ayliff's *A Vocabulary of the*

Kafir Language (1846) and John Appleyard's *The Kafir Language: Comprising a Sketch of its History* (1850).[28]

The publication of the first vernacular reading materials, including tracts and periodicals, complemented these efforts. Among the former, some of the most significant were the LMS's *Igqihra* (The Sorcerer), the SPMS's *Iziqwenge zembali yamaxosa* (Extracts of a history of the Xhosa), and the WMS's *Ukukuleka, gu-Jesusi Kirisitusi* (The Salvation, through Jesus Christ), published in 1836, 1838, and 1840, respectively.[29] As for periodicals, the SPMS published *Ikwezi* (The Morning Star) between 1844 and 1845, while the WMS produced *Umshumayeli wendaba* (The News Teller) between 1837 and 1841, *Isibuto samavo* (A Collection of Tales) between 1843 and 1844, and *Isitunywa sennyanga* (The Monthly Messenger) in 1850.[30]

The missionaries' primary focus, however, was on translating liturgical materials. Yet rather than a European missionary, it was Ntsikana, a Rharhabe-Xhosa of the Cira clan, who composed the first vernacular hymn with a Christian theme, *Ulo Thixo omkhulu ngosezulwine* (He, the Great God in Heaven) in about 1817.[31] The success of Ntsikana's hymn encouraged the missionaries to translate their own hymns into the vernacular. At least on paper, Bennie was the main SPMS composer and translator, submitting thirty-two hymns (revisions of ten old hymns and twenty-two new ones), of which thirty were published as part of the first Caffre-language hymnal in 1832.[32] But the Scottish mission church's African members—Vimbe (baptized John Muir), Dukwana (Ntsikana's son), and Festiri Soga—also played an important role. Three hymns by Vimbe and five by Festiri were also included in the 1841 hymnal *Inncwadana inamaculo gokwamaxosa* (Little book of hymns of among the Xhosa).[33] About a decade later, the Scottish missionaries proudly reported that they had printed "500 copies of the new Hymn Book," which included eighty-seven hymns.[34]

The Wesleyans rivaled these efforts. By 1824, William Shaw had already tried his hand at composing a small hymn containing the lines "Sifun ukutanda wena, Uyasitanda tina; Sifuna wen ukukunga, Uyakusina tina [We seek to love thee, (for) thou wilt love us; We seek to pray to thee; (for) thou wilt hear us]."[35] As singing became a key aspect of their proselytizing efforts, the Wesleyans devoted more resources to composing and translating hymns. In 1835, these efforts resulted in the publication of the first Wesleyan hymn book, *Le yincwadi yamaculo okuvunywa gamaxosa eziskolweni zaba-Wesley* (This book of hymns which are to be sung by the Xhosa in the Wesleyan schools), which included forty-eight hymns composed or translated by WMS missionaries John Ayliff, William Boyce, Henry Dugmore, and Richard Haddy, as well as government interpreters George Cyrus and Theophilus Shepstone.[36]

The Wesleyan and Scottish missionaries also took a leading role in translating prayers, commandments, catechisms, and other missiological materials. In 1824, the Scottish missionary John Ross translated the catechism, publishing it as a volume called *Incwadana yokubuza encinane*, which also included translations of the Ten Commandments (*Imiteto yeshumi lika-Tixo*), the Lord's Prayer (*Isikungo senKosi*), and the Creed (*Inkolo*).[37] Wary of the Scottish missionaries' Calvinist leanings, the Wesleyans prepared their own rudimentary translations of the Ten Commandments, the Creed, and the Lord's Prayer as early as 1826.[38] They translated the Lord's Prayer as *Ubawo wetu osezulwini* (Our Father in Heaven), and several of their short prayers, notably *O Inkosienkulu! Senika ufefe lwako pezu 'kwetu; lika inkhliziyo zetu, ukuba secine lomtetu* (Lord have mercy upon us, and incline our hearts to keep this law) and *siantandaza wena, Balainnkhlizweni zetu, yonke Iimiteto yako* (And write all these thy Laws in our hearts, we beseech thee).[39] It was not until 1832, however, that the first Wesleyan translation of the Catechism appeared under the title *Incwadi yokubuza yezi zi-skola, zama-Khristi Ekutiwa gama-Wesli, ema-Xosene* (Book of questioning for Wesleyan Christian schools among the Xhosa).[40]

Although these materials were of great importance to the missionary enterprise, the missionaries' key desire was to translate the Bible. The SPMS approached this work cooperatively. As early as 1825, all Scottish missionaries "examined separately and successively" each completed translation before it went to press.[41] In this manner, they hoped that "errors, which otherwise might have escaped the eye of the most scrupulous, are . . . corrected."[42] But progress was slow: by 1830 they possessed little more than Ross's translation of the first epistle of John.[43] The LMS experienced similarly slow progress, completing only preliminary translations of the gospels of Mark and Matthew, the epistle to the Ephesians, and a "free translation" of a compilation of the Lord's miracles.[44] The same was true for the Wesleyans, who accomplished little other than William Shaw's early attempts at translating the book of Genesis and William Shrewsbury's preliminary translations of parts of the gospel of Mark (1829) and the book of Hebrews (1830).[45]

In January 1830, representatives of the WMS, LMS, and SPMS met at the Buffalo River in order to agree on a common orthography for writing the "Caffre" language. As part of the meeting, they also decided to coordinate their translation and revision efforts so as to speed up the process.[46] As part of this cooperative effort, different societies began to translate different books of the Bible. The Scottish missionaries, for example, worked on Colossians (1832) and the book of Revelation (1833).[47] The LMS missionaries Brownlee and Kayser worked on the gospel of John, the epistle to the Romans, Philippians, Thessalonians, and Galatians, as well as the Psalms, Acts, and First Timothy.[48] The Wesleyans took charge of the remaining parts, and between 1831 and 1833, Shrewsbury translated the book of Joel, the epistle of James, the gospel of Luke, the book of Isaiah, the gospel of Matthew, and the epistles to the Romans.[49]

The Sixth Frontier War (1834–35) derailed these cooperative efforts, forcing each society to pursue Bible translations on their own. On the side of SPMS, Bennie found refuge at Somerset East, where he translated several books of the New Testament in 1836.[50] The Wesleyans produced their own (revised) translations of some of these works during the same time period.[51] The end of the war did not lead to renewed cooperation. In 1840, the SPMS planned the next phase of its translation activities without taking into consideration the simultaneously occurring efforts of the Wesleyans.[52] The Wesleyans had done the same several years earlier when they appointed Henry Dugmore as the "final reviser" of their translations and settled among themselves "the orthography of the Kaffer language."[53] Although they did occasionally cooperate with BMS missionaries Döhne and Posselt, typically the Wesleyans worked on their own, completing (revised) versions of the gospel of Matthew and the epistles to the Romans by 1842, and the gospels of Luke and John and the Catholic Epistles by 1846.[54]

These individualistic approaches ran into complications in 1844 when the Scottish and Wesleyan missionaries simultaneously appealed to the British and Foreign Bible Society (BFBS) to fund the publication of their respective translations of the New Testament. Established four decades earlier, the BFBS financially supported the worldwide publication and distribution of Bible translations. The society had started its activities in South Africa in 1806, supplying Bibles to British soldiers serving at the Cape. Four years later, they had supplied the London missionaries at Bethelsdorp with Dutch Bibles and testaments.[55] In 1820, the BFBS established its first South African Auxiliary organization with government support.[56] Smaller BFBS auxiliaries emerged in the eastern Cape region about a decade later, notably at Salem and Grahamstown in 1833 and 1834.[57]

In the latter year, the Wesleyan missionaries successfully secured funding from the BFBS for the publication of some of their existing Bible translations.[58] Encouraged by this experience, the Wesleyans requested additional funding in 1844, notably for the publication of the first complete translation of the New Testament.[59] However, the Scottish and London missionaries also contacted the BFBS with a similar funding request around that time. Unsure about which of the two translation projects to support, the BFBS proposed that these initiatives be combined into one collaborative effort.[60]

In April 1845, representatives of the WMS, LMS, SPMS, and BMS met at Umxelo Station in the eastern Cape, where they agreed to pursue "a united effort to print an authorized Version of the New Testament."[61] They also organized a "committee of revision" consisting of missionaries Henry Dugmore and William Davis (both of the WMS), James Laing and William Chalmers (both of the SPMS), Henry Calderwood (LMS), and Jakob Döhne (BMS). In a letter to the BFBS, William Shaw summarized the meeting: "All were . . . anxious that the Version should be made as accurate as possible, and that it should go forth with all the authority that the joined approval of the several societies can give it, so that there may be but one Version in general use, on the various Mission Stations, and among the Native Christians of the country."[62] Working from existing translations, the eastern Cape missionaries were able to publish the first authorized version of the New Testament in 1846, using two slightly different titles, one of which read I-Testamante entsha yenkosi yetu ka-Yesu Kristu, gokwamaxosa.[63]

The Seventh and the Eighth Frontier Wars (1846–47, 1850–53) once again disrupted the missionaries' efforts, this time to complete the translation of the Old Testament. Although they produced several extracts from the Old Testament between 1849 and 1854, they did not publish a complete version until 1859, when John Appleyard concluded his Itestamente endala: okukuti, inncwadi zonke zocebano oludala, engekafiki uKristu: ikunyushelwe kokwamaXosa.[64] It took another five years before the first complete and revised edition of the entire Bible appeared. Known as "Appleyard's Version," it bore the title Inncwadi yezibalo ezingcwele, e zetestamente endala ne zetestamente entsha, ziguqulwe kwezonteto zanikwa kuqala ngazo.[65]

It had taken the European missionary societies almost three decades to translate the New Testament and another decade to complete the translation of the entire Bible into the "Caffre" language. Repeated interruptions caused by the frontier wars and the lack of cooperation among the missionary societies explain in part why it took such a long time to produce a vernacular translation of the scriptures. However, translating from well-known written languages, such as Greek, Latin, English, and Dutch, into poorly understood and circumscribed oral vernaculars raised a number of additional obstacles for the missionaries that delayed their progress.

One such obstacle was the absence of a widely accepted (i.e., standardized) orthography for the target "Caffre" language. In order to solve this predicament, the missionaries followed the rule of assigning to each audible sound (phoneme) in the language a distinct sign (grapheme).[66] William Shaw explained the process of representing speech in writing in these terms: "We all concurred in the adoption of the Roman character, as being on the whole the most convenient and suitable form in which we could write and print it. The power or sound given to the vowels was in accordance with the practice of most of the languages of Southern Europe. The consonants represented the same powers as in English, with the exception that *g* was always to be pronounced hard, as in 'give.'"[67] Because some sounds in the target language—notably click sounds, guttural sounds, and some compound sounds—did not fit neatly into familiar sound-sign systems, the missionaries had to develop new signs. Eventually, they agreed to represent the dominant click sounds by way of the letters *c, q,* and *x,* while using the letter *r* for the guttural sound.[68] They also agreed that compound sounds should be "reduced as nearly as the ear can distinguish into their elementary parts, and represented, accordingly, by a combination [of signs.]"[69]

The problem was that different missionaries heard these sounds differently and, consequently, transcribed them differently. As Shaw explained: "When we began to collect words, however, we discovered the existence of . . . variations in the consonantal powers, which, as we did not wish to introduce new characters, required in some cases a combination of consonants; and these from time to time occasioned differences of opinion: *ex. gr.,* the word for 'elephant' was spelt three different ways by the Missionaries, *in-ghlovu, in-thlovu, in-dhlovu.*"[70] To solve this and other orthographic problems, the missionaries organized joint meetings, notably at Umxelo in April 1845. As John Appleyard later explained, at Umxelo the eastern Cape missionaries decided to abandon the "disjointing system," according to which the prefixes and roots were written separately, and adopted the "uniting one" which demanded that prefixes and roots be always written together.[71] They favored this system because, in their view, prefixes and roots were not distinct ideas or words but codependent parts of a single idea or word.[72] They also preferred the "uniting system" because it seemingly facilitated the reading process for indigenous readers. As one of the missionaries explained in 1853, "The phrase 'amambatise ingubo,' spoken as two words, with proper accent, the Kaffir, I believe, will understand without the least difficulty. But when he turns to his Testament and meets with 'a m ambatise,' he is bewildered just from the absurd way in which the word is divided."[73] It was through these meetings and decision-making processes that the eastern Cape missionaries gradually developed a "uniform orthography."[74]

Aside from orthography, the target language also posed difficulties because it did not always possess easily identifiable equivalents for crucial Christian concepts. As SPMS missionary John Ross remarked after returning from a meeting of the "Translation Committee" in June 1832, "The difficulties we experienced were the choosing and seeking out of proper terms. Some had been used formerly but were not fixed; some were formed after much inquiry; and others, such as ordinary, common, free, &c., have not been found."[75] WMS missionary Shrewsbury encountered the same problem when he tried to explain to his African listeners "the great doctrine of Justification by Faith" that forms part of Romans 8:4–5 and Luke 7:36–50. "[He] found it exceedingly difficult to do so," Shrewsbury explained in 1831, "the Caffre Language having no word that answers to those important terms in the Text—'Ungodly,' 'Justify,' or 'Righteousness'"[76] Moreover, even if a missionary believed he had identified a word whose meaning approximated the Christian concept, the other missionaries did not always agree. For instance, in the New Testament translation of 1846 they used the word "UKUGWEBELA . . . for justification, or judgment for, or in favor of."[77] Not everyone was pleased with this decision. "The term . . . is very objectionable," one missionary complained in 1853.[78]

Defining the geographical reach of the target "Caffre" language posed another and for the development of South Africa's Zulu-Xhosa divide a particularly significant problem. LMS missionary Richard Birt followed the settler-colonialist idea, which defined the "Caffres" narrowly as consisting of the Xhosa communities only; he therefore criticized the use of non-Xhosa words in "Caffre" translations of the Bible.[79] The majority of European missionaries, however, defined the target "Caffre" language much more broadly. The initial inspiration for this broad conceptualization of the target language came from the missionaries' reading the works of naturalists such as Alberti, Barrow, and Lichtenstein as described in the previous chapter.[80]

Regarding the northward extension of the "Caffre" language, missionary John Brownlee claimed in 1823 (only three years after his arrival in the Cape Colony's frontier region) that "[the] change of dialect is such, that . . . the tribes to the northwest of Lattakoo [i.e., the Tswana] can be understood by the Caffres [i.e., the Xhosa],"[81] an assertion that mirrored Lichtenstein's earlier declaration that "a Koossa [Xhosa] and a Beetjuan [Tswana], meeting by chance, must understand each other ultimately, though perhaps slowly."[82] And regarding the eastward extension of the "Caffre" language, missionary William Shaw argued in the same year (and also barely three years after his arrival in southern Africa) that the Xhosa and the people of southern Mozambique were "evidently of the same origin, . . . speaking a language, which, notwithstanding very considerable differences in dialect, is doubtless substantially the same,"[83] a claim that matched Alberti's earlier statement that "the language of these visitors [from Delagoa Bay] was the same as that spoken by the Kaffirs [i.e. Xhosa]."[84]

The tendency to include residents from the northern highveld in the "Caffre" language community continued into the early 1830s, as testified by WMS missionary Richard Haddy's claim from 1832 that the language of "the Abasutu nation [Sotho] . . . is fundamentally the same as the Caffre; but there is a difference in dialect, which prevents easy communication at first."[85] Over the course of the 1830s, however, some missionaries began to doubt the logic of including the speaking practices of highveld residents.[86] One of the first doubters was the Scottish missionary James Laing, who remarked in 1832 that "the Bechuanas . . . differ in language from the Kaffers [Xhosa], whereas those along the coast to a considerable distance speak a dialect much the same as that of the Kaffers [Xhosa]."[87] WMS missionary William Boyce seconded this impression five years later, stating "that the relationship subsisting between Kafir and Sechuana is that of descent from a common parent is evident. . . . Yet each dialect has peculiarities of its own, sufficient to oblige the learner to consider it, for all practical purposes of speech and composition, as a distinct language."[88]

However, the majority of missionaries upheld the idea that the "Caffre" language community extended below the Great Escarpment as far east as Delagoa Bay. Boyce was particularly outspoken about this idea. Around 1832, for instance, he informed the mission board that "the Caffer language, with slight dialectical varieties, is spoken by the Caffers, Tambookies, Amapondas, Zulus under Dingaan, . . . and by many tribes inland, northwest of Delagoa Bay."[89] Five years later, he reiterated this view, explaining,

"The Kafir [language] is confined to the Amaxosa, Abatembu, Amapondo, and Amazulu tribes, extending from the Great Fish River as far as the River St. Lucie, about halfway between Port Natal and Delagoa Bay."[90] He doubled down on this assessment in 1844 when, in a letter to the BFBS, he explained that "the population of Kafferland (including the Zulu Country) . . . all these speak the Kaffer language with trifling dialectic differences, affecting however the pronunciation of a few words only. . . . As far north as Mozambique (about 5° South) the Kaffer is understood."[91] Boyce was not alone in his assessment. "The natives [in Natal] are all Kaffirs, of the Zoola and other nations," William Shaw explained in 1848, "and all speak the Kaffir language, with slight variation in their dialects from the language spoken by the Kaffirs on the border of the Cape Colony."[92] Nor were the Wesleyan missionaries the only ones who thought this way. SPMS missionary William Govan agreed with their assessment, claiming in the same year that "the country occupied by tribes speaking the Caffre language extends . . . along the shores of the Indian Ocean, from the eastern boundary of the Cape Colony, several hundred miles at least beyond the district of Natal."[93]

Defining the geographic reach of the "Caffre" language was part and parcel of the missionaries' translation and proselytizing efforts in South Africa. Following the guidance of eighteenth-century naturalists such as Barrow and Lichtenstein, they initially assumed that this language extended across much of southern Africa and included the indigenous speech communities of the South African highveld and coastal belt. By the 1830s most missionaries began to exclude the speech forms of the highveld from the "Caffre" language paradigm based on the idea that these speech forms were not mutually intelligible with those of the coastal belt. However, they continued to believe that the "Caffre" language extended from the eastern Cape region to Delagoa Bay precisely because in that direction the various speech communities, including those that we now know as Zulu and Xhosa, appeared to be mutually intelligible.

Migrancy and Communication in the Coastal Belt

This idea of mutual intelligibility arose from the missionaries' sustained interactions with people who were fluent in the speech forms of the eastern Cape and used this skill to communicate successfully with people from Natal-Zululand (and vice versa). These migrants and their experiences of language demonstrate the risks associated with dividing the history of

South Africa's coastal belt into convenient binaries such as the Cape and Natal colonies, Eastern Cape and KwaZulu-Natal provinces, or Xhosa and Zulu languages. Prior to the mid-nineteenth century, neither Europeans nor Africans thought or acted according to these binaries. As mentioned in chapter 2, in the eighteenth century, European hunters and naturalists traveled beyond the borders of the Cape Colony to the environs of Port Natal without organizing into binaries the regions they traversed, the people they met, or the speaking practices they heard. In the first decade of the nineteenth century as well, Africans from Delagoa Bay visited Chief Ngqika of the Rharhabe-Xhosa without either of the two parties thinking of the other as speakers of wholly different languages. Indeed, well into the 1850s, people of European and African descent circulated freely in this region, defying the geographic, ethnographic, and linguistic boundaries that were slowly beginning to emerge. The experiences, impressions, and testimonies of these individuals suggested to the missionaries that the speaking practices of the people residing between the eastern Cape and Delagoa Bay were mutually intelligible and formed part of a single "Caffre," language for which a single Bible translation could be produced.

Jakob Msimbiti

Perhaps the first migrant who shared such impressions with the missionaries was Jacob Msimbiti.[94] Having grown up in Chief Ndlambe's Xhosa polity, Msimbiti entered the service of a Dutch-speaking farmer on the frontier, which was not an uncommon practice in the early decades of the nineteenth century.[95] Around 1820, however, Msimbiti came into conflict with British colonial law, which had become more draconian toward the Xhosa in the aftermath of the Fifth Frontier War (1818–19). Arrested for allegedly "trespassing" the newly established border, he found himself imprisoned at Robben Island by the middle of 1822, just about the time when Captain William Owen of the Royal Navy was preparing a sea voyage designed to chart the southeastern African coastline.[96] Because Owen anticipated making contact with the indigenous inhabitants of this coastal region, he went to the Robben Island prison to recruit six Africans, including Msimbiti, to serve as his interpreters on the voyage. [97]

When the expedition arrived at Delagoa Bay, Owen and his men made contact with the local Tembe and Mabhudu people, as well as the "warlike Kaffers, called Zoolos, . . . [whom] the people of Delagoa call . . .

Hollontontes."[98] Owen was somewhat disappointed with his interpreters' ability to translate from the local vernacular into English or Dutch, for when they had an "interview with the Hollontontes" conducted "through the medium of the interpreters," the latter's performance had been "very bad."[99] Although Msimbiti and the other interpreters were not adept at translating into English or Dutch, Owen came to believe that they were able to communicate with the local populations in their own speaking practices, having witnessed Msimbiti "persuad[ing] a native . . . to try his assegaye at a small tree, which he did."[100] When two of the other African interpreters later "deserted" to join the local people of Delagoa Bay, Owen became convinced that the mutual intelligibility of their and the local language had encouraged them to do so. As he explained, "Shortly after their departure, two Kaffers, whom we had embarked at the Cape of Good Hope, deserted. . . . We afterwards learnt that the language of these men was nearly the same as that of the Zoolos, while that of Mapoota, was a sort of mixed dialect between the language of the Kaffers and that spoken about the English River; in short, they [the languages] all appeared to have the same origin, and were easily acquired by the natives."[101]

Owen communicated precisely this assessment to the European missionaries when he returned from Delagoa Bay to the Cape Colony in April 1823. After his conversation with Owen at Cape Town, WMS missionary Barnabas Shaw explained that "the language of the Delagoas is the same as that of the Caffrees. . . . There is, no doubt, a difference of dialect, but they can converse so as to be understood."[102] Moreover, Owen's conviction that these languages were mutually intelligible encouraged him, while at Port Elizabeth in June 1823, to supply F. G. Farewell's first commercial expedition to Delagoa Bay with "two Kaffers as linguists," one of whom was Msimbiti.[103]

On this journey to Delagoa Bay, Farewell stopped at Port Natal; several indigenous people later remembered that Farewell was accompanied by an African interpreter whom they called "Nhlamba" (short for Hlambamanzi), a nickname Msimbiti received later in his life.[104] The subsequent journey, however, did not proceed smoothly; the other interpreter was accidently killed, and Msimbiti, after having been assaulted by one of the English crew, deserted Farewell's expedition while anchored at St. Lucia. From there, the adventurous Msimbiti made his way to Shaka kaSenzangakhona's Zulu kingdom, where Farewell and others encountered him again in 1824.[105] By that time, he had firmly established himself in the Zulu polity, for "when Mr. Farewell formed his settlement at Port Natal, he found that Jackot [Msimbiti] was with Chaka, with whom he had become a great favorite, serving as interpreter, with the rank of 'Chief.'"[106]

The eastern Cape missionaries were surely aware of Msimbiti's experiences at King Shaka's court, given Owen's and other commentators' references to them in their writings.[107] There is reason to believe, moreover, that they had opportunities to directly converse with Msimbiti about his life in the Zulu kingdom, for both Shaka and his successor King Dingane sent him, along with other Zulu ambassadors and the Natal trader John Cane, to the Cape Colony in 1828 and 1831, respectively.[108] If Msimbiti did indeed accompany the first journey all the way to the Cape Colony, he must have met WMS missionary William Shrewsbury at Butterworth Station, where the latter encountered the Zulu embassy in 1828.[109] It is a matter of record that Msimbiti was with the second embassy when it reached Grahamstown in 1831.[110] Even if the missionaries did not directly ask Msimbiti about his views on the "Caffre" language continuum on these occasions, they surely concluded that his favor with the Zulu monarchs arose at least in part from his ability to communicate effectively with them, a conclusion that likely strengthened their confidence in the idea that the "Caffre" language extended all the way to Delagoa Bay.

George Cyrus and Richard Hulley

If the missionaries remained doubtful, however, they only had to consider the experience of other migrants, such as George Cyrus.[111] Born in England in 1811, the nine-year-old Cyrus had arrived in the Cape Colony's eastern borderland region in 1820 and initially attended the Wesleyan school at Salem (located in the Albany District roughly sixteen miles (26 km) south of Grahamstown); he subsequently moved to William Shaw's Wesleyville Station among the Gqunukhwebe-Xhosa, where he and Aaron James Aldum were trained "as Government Interpreters."[112]

Cyrus's skills in the local speaking practices evolved steadily. On 7 April 1830, he served as interpreter in a legal case involving two indigenous men in the Somerset Circuit Court.[113] At about this time, moreover, he composed or translated one of the hymns included in the hymn book the WMS published in 1835.[114] Most importantly, Allen F. Gardiner, formerly a captain in the Royal Navy, hired him to serve as his interpreter during an overland journey from the Cape Colony to Port Natal and the Zulu kingdom in 1835.[115] For the next twelve months or so, Cyrus interpreted Gardiner's conversations with members of the indigenous communities in this region, including Ntinde chief Tshatshu, Mpondo chief Faku, Thembu chief Vadana, a Natal African chief called "Mambayendi," and Zulu king Dingane.[116]

Given Gardiner's reliance on Cyrus in almost all of his communications with the communities residing between the Cape Colony and Delagoa Bay, it is very likely that Cyrus's perspective shaped Gardiner's ideas about regional speaking practices, including the theory that, although there existed significant lexicological and phonological differences between them, "the Kafir [Xhosa] and the Zoolu [Zulu] languages are very similar."[117] Following his return from Gardiner's expedition, Cyrus served as government interpreter and as Wesleyan schoolmaster and Bible translator in the eastern Cape region, which makes it probable that he communicated the same assessment to the Wesleyan missionaries and, in so doing, increased their confidence in the idea that the "Caffre" language community extended all the way to the Zulu kingdom and perhaps as far away as Delagoa Bay.[118]

Cyrus's assessment was, in turn, reinforced by the experience of another individual who traveled from the Cape Colony to the Zulu kingdom at about the same time. Born in Ireland, Richard Brangan Hulley was ten years old when he arrived in South Africa in the company of his parents, siblings, and other settlers in 1820. For the next decade or so, he attended a rural school for children of European settlers near the Kowie and George Rivers in the Albany District.[119] While it is possible that he had direct contact with some of the Xhosa people who lived and worked in the Albany area, it appears that he acquired some proficiency in the local speaking practices while conducting trading journeys beyond the Kei River. Additional opportunities to improve his skills arose when he and his family moved to Butterworth Station, a WMS missionary outpost among the Gcaleka-Xhosa and Mfengu people, sometime in the 1830s. By 1837, his language skills were proficient enough to recommend him to Church Missionary Society missionary Francis Owen, who hired Hulley to serve as his interpreter on his journey to King Dingane's Zulu people.[120]

During the subsequent journey, Hulley used his language skills to communicate with Owen's indigenous interlocutors, including members of the Bhaca and Zulu people, among whom they resided between August 1837 and February 1838.[121] In the Zulu kingdom, Hulley's language skills were in particularly high demand as Owen had frequent conversations with King Dingane.[122]

As Hulley explained, "For several days the king would send for us early in the morning and until nine o'clock of each day would keep us to answer any questions that he might put."[123] His conversations with the Zulu king intensified when Dingane asked Hulley to teach him how to read. Speaking to Owen, the king allegedly said, "I won't trouble you [Owen] as we cannot understand each other. . . . I appoint your interpreter as my teacher."[124]

Following a sojourn of several months at King Dingane's court, the relationship between Hulley and the Zulu monarch came to an abrupt end when the latter had a party of emigrant Afrikaners led by Piet Retief killed in February of 1838. In the aftermath of this event, Hulley and Owen left Zululand and, after a brief sojourn at Port Natal, returned to the Cape Colony, where Hulley's language skills continued to recommend him for work with the indigenous populations.[125] Hulley served as "local preacher" and "master of a school held in the chapel of the Wesleyans" at the "Caffers' Drift Post" (among the Ngqika-Xhosa) in 1839 and in similar positions at the WMS stations of Clarkebury (among the Thembu and Mfengu people) in the 1840s, Shawbury (among the Bhaca and Mfengu people) around 1849, and, finally, Osborn (among the Bhaca and Mfengu people) in the 1860s.[126] While serving at these stations, Hulley had frequent opportunities to share with the missionaries his impressions of the "Caffre" language community. Given his long conversations with King Dingane, it stands to reason that he suggested to them that there existed a "Caffre" language continuum that extended from the Cape Colony to the Zulu kingdom, if not beyond.

Orson Magerman, Joseph Kirkman, and Charles Brownlee

In addition to Jacob Msimbiti, George Cyrus, and Richard Hulley, three young interpreters—Oerson Magerman, Joseph Kirkman and Charles Brownlee—likely also shared similar impressions with the missionaries. These three young men accompanied American Board missionaries Newton Adams, Aldin Grout, and George Champion on their initial journeys to the Natal-Zululand region between December 1835 and May 1836.

Oerson Magerman was of Khoekhoe descent and had acquired quasi fluency in the speaking practices of the Xhosa communities while growing up at Chumie mission station.[127] Joseph Kirkman was the son of an 1820 settler and had assimilated similar language skills while growing up at LMS missionary John Brownlee's Buffalo (River) Station among the Ntinde population, where his parents worked as traders.[128] A testament to his linguistic abilities was the fact that John Brownlee personally recommended Kirk-man to the American Board missionaries.[129] The most well-known member of the group, however, was Charles Brownlee, missionary John Brownlee's son. Born in 1822, Charles acquired fluency in the speaking practices of the Xhosa while growing up among the indigenous residents of his father's mission stations at Chumie (circa 1820–26) and the Buffalo River (1826–31).[130] When Charles agreed to accompany the American Board missionaries, he was a thirteen-year-old pupil at Salem School and already possessed a reputation as a "good interpreter."[131]

Upon their arrival in Natal-Zululand, Magerman, Kirkman, and Brownlee noticed some differences between their own speaking practices and those of the local population.[132] They must have quickly adapted, however, because they continued to serve the American Board missionaries as interpreters for the next two years. Magerman assisted them in their communications with the indigenous populations of the region until 1838.[133] Similarly, Kirkman worked with Champion in Natal (south of the Thukela River) before moving with the same missionary to Nginani Station in Zululand (about 10 miles or 16 km north of the river) in September 1836.[134] He was also at Nginani in February 1838, helping Champion communicate with a messenger sent by King Dingane in the aftermath of the massacre of Retief's party.[135] Brownlee resided at the same station; he was still there in February 1838 when King Dingane specifically sent for him to serve as his personal interpreter in his dealings with Retief's party.[136] He arrived too late to do anything to save them, however, and, together with the other interpreters and the American Board missionaries, Brownlee withdrew to Port Natal and from there to the eastern Cape region in 1838.

Upon their return, Magerman, Kirkman, and Brownlee had good opportunities to share their impressions of the speaking practices of Natal-Zululand with the Cape Colony's European missionaries. Kirkman stayed in the eastern Cape region only for a short time, though, accompanying American Board missionaries to Natal-Zululand again in 1839 and staying there at least until 1843.[137] In contrast, Magerman remained in the eastern Cape, serving at the LMS mission station of Philipton "in the capacity of interpreter" for the station's Mfengu, Gonaqua, Xhosa, and Thembu residents.[138] Although he may have joined the anticolonial Xhosa-Khoekhoe alliance in the Eighth Frontier War, one missionary described him as late as 1853 as "one of the most respectable men" of the eastern Cape's Blinkwater area.[139] Like Magerman, Brownlee remained in the eastern Cape, working for instance as the clerk and interpreter for a government agent at Block Drift in 1839, and government commissioner to the Ngqika-Xhosa between 1847 and 1850, and between 1853 and 1867.[140] During this period, Brownlee stayed in close contact with the missionary community, providing language education, and translation assistance to them, notably to his father John Brownlee, LMS missionary Richard Birt, and WMS missionary John Appleyard.[141]

Although it is impossible to reconstruct what precisely Magerman, Kirkman, and Brownlee told the missionaries about the speaking practices of the coastal region, it is possible to gauge their collective impression from a letter Brownlee wrote to the BFBS in 1855. In it, he acknowledged that the speaking practices of eastern Cape and Natal-Zululand regions included many words that were different; nevertheless, he insisted that the languages were "essentially the same" and thus formed part of a single "Caffre" language community.[142]

Theophilus Shepstone

Theophilus Shepstone's experience provided the strongest support for the idea that the "Caffre" language community extended to Delagoa Bay.[143] Born in England in 1817, Shepstone arrived in South Africa in 1820 with his father William Shepstone, a builder, lay preacher, and later regular missionary in the Wesleyan Missionary Society.[144] Accompanying his father, Shepstone lived among indigenous populations during some of the most formative years of his linguistic life, including Wesleyville mission station among the Gqunukhwebe (1823–27), Butterworth Station among the Gcaleka-Xhosa and Mfengu (1827–29), and Morley Station among the Bomvana and Mpondo people (1829–31). He became fluent in the indigenous speaking practices of the region, a skill which brought him to the attention of WMS missionary William Boyce in 1831. Commenting on this skill, Boyce noted in 1832: "Theophilus Shepstone is fully competent to translate into Caffer, since that language has been familiar to him since he was five years old. His command of the language, and his judgment, displayed in the selection of suitable expressions, have been much admired by intelligent natives."[145] For the next three years, Shepstone lived at Boyce's Buntingville Station among the Mpondo people, where he and a Xhosa-born interpreter known by the baptismal name "John Burton" helped Boyce translate various portions of the Bible and several hymns into the

"Caffre" language and, more significantly, prepare the groundbreaking *Grammar of the Kafir Language* in 1834.[146]

Shepstone's language skills subsequently recommended him for several positions in the government of the Cape Colony. He served as "Caffer Interpreter" on the staffs of three governors between 1835 and 1838, participating in the removal of some sixteen thousand Mfengu from Gcaleka-Xhosa chiefdom to the Cape Colony, in the peace negotiations with Gcaleka-Xhosa Chief Hintsa on 29 April and 10 May 1835, and the announcement of "a treaty of reciprocal trust" (known as the *Ucebo lwobukolwana o lwenziweyo Gama-Ngisi nama-Kwane*) with three chiefs of the Gqunukhwebe polity on 19 June 1838.[147] Shepstone occupied a similar position in a military expedition to Port Natal between late 1838 and early 1839, during which he assisted with communications with the Mpondo Chief Faku and the indigenous population of Natal.[148] After his return to the eastern Cape region, he worked as a diplomatic agent among the Gqunukhwebe, Ndlambe-Xhosa, and Mfengu in the Fort Peddie area between 1840 and 1846; during this time, he also continued to assist various WMS missionaries with their Bible translation work.[149]

In 1846, Shepstone's language skills recommended him for the position of diplomatic agent to the native tribes of Natal Colony, a post he held under a different title (secretary of native affairs) until 1878. "For such an office," WMS missionary William Holden later recalled, "he was well fitted by his long residence at Fort Peddie, as diplomatic agent, and his intimate acquaintance with the Kafir language and character."[150] Although the indigenous people of Natal-Zululand noticed that Shepstone's pronunciation of the language resembled that of "the Pondos (or the amaXoza)," he was apparently able to communicate effectively with them.[151] The bishop of Natal likewise noted after a journey through the Natal Colony in Shepstone's company that "it was most touching to observe how his [Shepstone's] perfect knowledge of their language and modes of thought . . . brought these poor savages to his feet at every kraal we visited."[152]

This background explains why missionaries, settlers, and colonial administrators alike valued Shepstone's opinion on the linguistic landscape of the coastal region of South Africa. In 1852, for instance, when a Natal government commission wanted to know if the Natal Africans spoke a different language than "the surrounding . . . tribes" or merely a different dialectical variation of a common language, they did not hesitate to consult Shepstone on the matter. "The Language spoken by all the Kafir tribes between the Cape colony and Delagoa Bay," Shepstone informed the commissioners at the time, "is one with dialectic or local differences [only]."[153] Two years later, in response to a similar question from the BFBS, Shepstone answered: "I believe that the degree of affinity between the Zulu and Kafir [Xhosa] is such as to render it quite possible to persons intimately acquainted with both to frame such a translation of the Scriptures as would be perfectly understood by both, without even the dialectical modification contemplated by your question."[154]

As the case studies above suggest, several people with significant linguistic skills traveled from the eastern Cape region to Natal-Zululand in the first half of the nineteenth century and came to the conclusion that the two region's indigenous speech communities formed part of a single "Caffre" language continuum. If there remained any doubts among the European missionaries about this continuum, they were further alleviated by the reverse experience: people who traveled from Natal-Zululand to the eastern Cape region and transferred their skills from the old speech environment to the new one with similar success.

The Mfengu (Fingoes)

Perhaps the first recorded example of this type of transfer occurred in the first decade of the nineteenth century, when the Dutch administrator Ludwig Alberti met several emissaries at the residence of Chief Ngqika of the Xhosa people, whom the latter identified as strangers "from that land, from which all the Kaffirs were descended" (that is, the region between Natal and Delagoa Bay).[155] At first the strangers experienced some difficulties in communicating with the locals; when the emissaries tried to speak with Alberti's Gonaqua interpreter, they "did not understand each other without a great deal of trouble."[156] The indigenous parties, however, adapted to the other side's peculiarities within two days and, henceforth, communicated with each other with ease, leading Alberti to conclude that the speaking practices of the eastern Cape region and Delagoa Bay formed part of a single "Caffre" language community.[157]

Subsequent observations pointed in the same direction. For instance, when Captain Owen returned from Delagoa Bay to the Cape Colony in first half of 1823, he was accompanied by several people from that region. LMS missionary John Philip interviewed these new arrivals and collected information about their speaking practices. "I introduced them to one of Gaika's

Caffers [i.e., Ngqika-Xhosa] from the Keiskamma," Philip noted, "and we found that they could converse together, on common subjects, so as to be understood by each other."[158] This experiment convinced Philip that "the different tribes, inhabiting the extensive regions beyond the colony of the Cape of Good Hope . . . are known to speak different dialects merely of the same language."[159]

A third recorded case involved Henry Francis Fynn. In 1824, the English-born Fynn traveled from the eastern Cape to Port Natal in the company of his interpreter, Frederick.[160] Over the next decade, Fynn became reasonably proficient in the local speaking practices, because he not only traded with local people but also married several of their women and recruited many of their members into his own makeshift *iziNkumbi* chiefdom. Importantly, when Fynn returned to the eastern Cape region in 1834, he used the speaking practices he had acquired in Natal-Zululand to carry out various government appointments that required him to apply these language skills, including that of "Caffre interpreter" during the Sixth Frontier War (1834–35), diplomatic agent to the Mpondo chief Faku (circa 1835–36), diplomatic agent to the Thembu (1837–48), and resident agent to the Mpondo (1848–52).[161]

Even if the missionaries were unaware or simply ignored Alberti's testimony, Philips's observations, and Fynn's experience, they could not do the same with the Mfengu. The exact origin of the Mfengu remains a subject of considerable debate. Historians initially agreed that they were the remnants of a number of chiefdoms—Hlubi, Bhele, Zizi, Ngwane, and others—from the Natal-Zululand region, who, after being scattered by a series of wars in that region, ascribed to the Zulu king Shaka in the early decades of the nineteenth century, migrated to the eastern Cape, where they became clients of the Xhosa and Thembu chiefs.[162] Several scholars subsequently criticized this narrative, arguing instead that many Mfengu were in fact Xhosa people who were brought into the Cape Colony as war captives by British soldiers and settlers in the aftermath of the Battle of Mpholompo (1828) and the Sixth Frontier War (1834–35).[163] To cover up these enslavement activities, colonial officials, settlers, and European missionaries imposed on these war captives a new Mfengu identity, including the two claims that this identity entailed, notably their alleged displacement from the Natal-Zululand region by Shaka's wars and their alleged enslavement by the Xhosa. A growing number of Xhosa opportunists willingly adopted this identity, modifying their oral traditions and clan names accordingly, to gain access to government- and missionary-controlled resources after 1847.[164]

This revisionist approach to the Mfengu is correct in suggesting that many contemporary reports erroneously ascribed to Shaka all the wars that scattered the Hlubi, Bhele, Zizi, and other chiefdoms in the period between 1820 and 1830. The frequent contemporary references to Shaka, however, should not necessarily be seen as evidence of a massive colonial cover-up of their enslavement actions but rather as a trope describing real conflicts in the Natal-Zululand region and marking the beginning of a complex and complicated history of African and European usages of the image of Shaka.[165]

Similarly, while contemporary statements about Xhosa keeping Mfengu as slaves are incorrect, they did originate from real problems Mfengu clients experienced among their Xhosa patrons over time.[166] And while it is true that Europeans (and Africans) used captive laborers in nineteenth-century South Africa, it appears odd that not a single European or African criticized the alleged enslavement of Xhosa men, women, and children during a period when abolitionist thought was particularly strong in the Cape Colony and throughout the British Empire.

Although it is very likely that, over time, some Xhosa opportunists embraced the Mfengu identity to gain access to government- and missionary-controlled resources, it is less likely that this occurred on a large scale before 1850, when Xhosa society had not yet experienced the widespread destruction that came in the wake of the Eighth Frontier War (1850–53) and the cattle killing episode (1856–57). More importantly, none of the revisionist historians rejects the idea that some Mfengu were originally from the Natal-Zululand region; this would indeed be difficult to argue given that a large number of them self-identified as Hlubi, Zizi, and Bhele refugees before 1835 and maintained strong memories of their blood relatives from the Natal-Zululand region beyond that time. BMS missionary Posselt, for instance, explained in 1852 that when his group migrated from the eastern Cape to the Natal-Zululand in 1847, "we had some people with us from the Amamfengu in Kafraria, who accidently met with their relatives here [in Natal] and knew each other."[167] European and African contemporaries, moreover, noticed differences between Xhosa and Mfengu cultural practices and modes of speaking, which suggest that they were not originally from the same region.[168]

The Mfengu identity, then, likely had no precedent in late independent Africa and therefore represents an ethnic identity that colonial officials, missionaries, and Africans together constructed over the course of the nineteenth century. Yet the idea that they were mostly captive Xhosa rather than displaced people from the Natal-Zululand region is unconvincing for the period between 1820 and 1853 in general and for the period between 1820 and 1835 in particular.

European missionaries first encountered the people who came to be known as Mfengu when they established several mission stations—Chumie, Lovedale, Burnshill, Buffalo River, Wesleyville, and Butterworth—among the Rharhabe- and Gcaleka-Xhosa as well as the Ntinde and Gqunukhwebe polities in the early 1820s.[169] After 1828, missionary contact intensified when groups of Mfengu, amid Xhosa accusations of witchcraft, removal of property, and various forms of violence, moved into the colony or onto mission stations.[170] This contact, in turn, reached a climax during the Sixth Frontier War when the colonial government removed some sixteen thousand Mfengu from among the Xhosa, an act that colonial officials and missionaries (erroneously) characterized as the "deliverance of the Fingoes from the state of slavery."[171] When the Mfengu migrants reached Peddie, they gathered "near an *umqwashu* (milkwood tree)" to mark the event by swearing a mighty oath "to be faithful to God, to be loyal to the British Government, and to do all in their power to support the missionaries and educate their children."[172] In the aftermaths of the Seventh and Eighth Frontier Wars, the colonial government resettled additional Mfengu parties near colonial towns such as Grahamstown, Port Elizabeth, and Fort Beaufort; on mission stations such as Clarkson, Lovedale, and Burnshill; and in a series of "Fingo settlements" near Fort Peddie between the Great Fish and Keiskamma rivers.[173] In these areas, they provided a source of labor for European farmers, a protective buffer against Xhosa attacks for colonial farms and towns, and a captive audience for missionaries.

Although the exact origin and identity of the Mfengu remains a subject of historical debate, the missionaries were convinced that they represented the fragments of various chiefdoms from the Natal-Zululand region that had been destroyed by a series of wars (frequently, if erroneously) ascribed to King Shaka. This included Wesleyan missionaries William Shaw and William Shrewsbury, who explained in 1826 that "Far north of Kaffer Land, and between it and Delagoa Bay, in about the Latitude of Port Natal . . . resides a powerful African Prince, named Tshaka. . . . He is the terror of the Northern Tribes, having subdued and slain multitudes. Many have fled at his approach, and many fragments of Tribes, called Fingoes, have been scattered and migrated in the most wretched and distressed state into Kaffer Land."[174] Interestingly, this narrative frequently originated with Xhosa and Mfengu individuals rather than the missionaries. Tente, a minor son of Chief Ngqika of the Xhosa, for instance, remarked in 1840 that "the Amam-Fengu ... were dispersed by enemies in their own country before they came among the Kaffres [Xhosa]. Whilst my father was yet living he gave his word that they should reside at the Lenye."[175] Members of the Mfengu told similar stories, as William Shaw recounted: "I held many conversations with Sigliki about his country and the surrounding tribes. He used to tell me that it would take a man 'three or four moons' to travel from his country to Wesleyville. He had been wandering with various dispersed hordes for several years. It became evident that his tribe had originally occupied some country westward from Delagoa Bay, and not very remote from that place."[176] Mfengu communities near Healdtown and Fort Beaufort told similar stories about their origins. In a letter to Queen Victoria in 1857, they explained: "We are only fragments that are left of great nations; ... we came from far, from the rivers Tugela, Zinyate, and Umvolose, beyond Port-Natal; ... we were broken up and scattered in the wars of Chaka, King of the Zulus; ... we travelled through a country without inhabitants, many months, ... till at length we came into Kaffraria, a great host of strangers, and were called by the Kaffirs FINGOES."[177]

The word "Mfengu," which contemporary Europeans anglicized into "Fingo" and "Fingoes," derived from the verb *ukumfenguza* ("to wander destitute") and from actual sentences such as *siyamfenguza* ("we are wandering about being hungry and seeking shelter"), with which the migrants addressed Xhosa chiefs when they entered their domains and asked for their protection.[178] In doing so, the refugees submitted to the authority of Xhosa chiefs, and the latter welcomed them as new subjects and clients. Indeed, accounts of oral history claim that the Xhosa paramount chief Hintsa sought to bind the newcomers closely to his rule by instructing his leading men to take the newcomers' daughters in marriage "so that you may be united and be one; so that these people may not leave and their fingoism may disappear."[179]

Differences between the speaking practices of the Mfengu and the Xhosa also suggested different geographical origins for both groups and a history of migration that brought them together. While visiting the Gcaleka-Xhosa in 1827, William Shaw, for instance, noticed that the "Amafengoo" spoke the "Caffre language, with various degrees of difference as to the pronunciation."[180] Later he added that "the difference in their pronunciation was chiefly occasioned by interchanging the consonants, more especially the dentals and labials."[181]

These phonological differences appear to have been strongest for those Mfengu who identified themselves as Zizi. Contrasting Xhosa speech patterns with those of a self-identifying Zizi man, Scottish missionary William Thomson explained in 1824 that "the Caffers say *emanzie* for *water*, he says *ematenzi;* they say *sonka* for *bread*, he says *sinka;* they say *hamba* for *get you gone*, he says *kamba*."[182] Missionary John Brownlee remarked that "[the language of the Zizi was] more nearly related to Sechoana than that of the Kaffirs [Xhosa]."[183] The different phonologies rendered it difficult for some Zizi clients to communicate with their Xhosa patrons; one Mfengu man of Hlubi origins claimed in 1855 that "there are some Fingoes (the Amazizi) that did not well understand the Kafir [Xhosa]."[184] However, Thomson stated about one of his Zizi informants that "excepting some words, the Caffers [Xhosa] understood him well."[185]

The contradictions between these statements can be explained with the peculiar history of the Zizi people. Originally from the coastal belt of Natal-Zululand, some Zizi broke off and moved into the Caledon River valley in the seventeenth century and, through assimilation with that region's Sotho-speaking peoples, created the Baputhi chiefdom, developing a Sotho-ized speech pattern in the process. Around 1825, Matiwane's Ngwane attacked this Baputhi chiefdom and pushed some of that polity's Sotho-ized Zizi into the eastern Cape region. At the same time, some of the "original" Zizi from Natal-Zululand were also displaced and moved into the eastern Cape region. This region thus became a place of refuge for Zizi people with very different histories and language profiles: because of their more complex Sotho-ized speech patterns, the former group of Zizi had, as the testimonies above show, more difficulties communicating with the Xhosa; in contrast, the latter group of Zizi refugees, having a simpler speech pattern, experienced less problems in their communication with the local Xhosa populations.[186]

Irrespective of this rather unique case, the majority of the Mfengu appear to have communicated rather well with the Xhosa and vice versa. As the Wesleyan missionary William Shrewsbury remarked in 1826, "We have often ourselves, when traveling, observed that they [Mfengu and Xhosa] conversed together with as much ease as a Lancashire man would talk with a man of Kent."[187] Missionaries who worked particularly closely with Mfengu communities held similar opinions. One of them was Wesleyan missionary John Ayliff. In October 1830, Ayliff took charge of Butterworth mission station among the Gcaleka-Xhosa, who had a large number of Mfengu clients residing among them.[188] At the time of Ayliff's arrival, the station itself already included several Mfengu converts.[189] Ayliff then attracted additional Mfengu to the station over the next four years.[190] During the Sixth Frontier War, he also facilitated the Mfengu exodus out of Gcalekaland, and, following the completion of that war, he served as missionary to various Mfengu communities in the Cape Colony and the region between the Fish and Keiskamma Rivers.[191] At this time, Ayliff became an avid student of Mfengu history and, through conversations with them, recorded their Hlubi, Bhele, Zizi (etc.) origins.[192]

All this contact gave Ayliff considerable insight into the relationship between the speaking practices of the Mfengu and Xhosa. Already in 1836, for instance, he implied that the two speech communities overlapped when he stated: "As the Kaffer [Xhosa] language is used by the brethren in the Colony . . . the spiritual concerns of the Fingoes are attended to."[193] He was more explicit in 1853 when he explained in a letter that "the language spoken by the Fingoes is the same as that spoken by the Kaffirs with some slight unimportant variations."[194]

Ayliff's conclusions were supported by the Scottish missionary James Laing, whose engagement with the Mfengu began in 1831 when they first found their way to Burnshill mission station looking for paid work.[195] A couple of years later, several of them began to attend his church services, while a Mfengu woman named "Mahlamene" became a servant in his household.[196] Laing also began to visit the Mfengu communities attached to the Rharhabe-Xhosa at this time.[197] His contact with them intensified in the aftermath of the Sixth and Seventh Frontier Wars, when the Mfengu settlements of Ely, Sheshegu, Gaga, Macfarlane, and Ncwazi emerged in the neighborhood of Lovedale and Burnshill Stations. From then on, Mfengu children became a common sight at the Burnshill outstation schools.[198] Following Laing's move to Lovedale in 1843, he encountered an increasing number of Mfengu as regular church members.[199] Laing also hired a Mfengu man named Ntibane Mzimba as a teacher for the school at Sheshegu, which included many Mfengu children, including Ntibane's son, Pambani Mzimba, who became one of the Scottish mission church's first ordained African ministers in 1877.[200]

Due to his extensive contact with Mfengu people, Laing was in a good position to assess the relationship between the speaking practices of the two groups. While Laing recognized that they "use a few words which are not in common use by the [Xhosa] people here," he nevertheless believed that these differences did not prevent them from communicating effectively with each other. "It is scarcely necessary to say," he explained in 1848, "that the Fingoes and Kaffirs [Xhosa] speak one and the same language."[201]

Together with the testimonies of Jacob Msimbiti, George Cyrus, Richard Hulley, Oerson Magerman, Joseph Kirkman, Charles Brownlee, and Theophilus Shepstone, the case of the Mfengu suggested powerfully that the various forms of speech in the coastal belt were mutually intelligible and thus formed part of a single "Caffre" language that extended from the eastern Cape to Natal-Zululand and Delagoa Bay. Consequently, the missionaries agreed that this "Caffre" language represented the target language for the translation activities that would enable them to communicate the "word of God" to the indigenous people of South Africa's coastal belt.

Translating the "word of God" into the local language had been a chief concern for the missionaries since their arrival in the region in the early decades of the nineteenth century. This arrival occurred with the support of the British colonial government, who hoped that the missionary influence would transform the coastal belt's indigenous populations into loyal subjects or peaceful neighbors. Although the agendas of missionaries and colonial officials did often overlap, the missionaries were more interested in the indigenous peoples' spiritual transformation rather than their political domination and control. To bring about this religious change, the missionaries wanted to bring the source of Christian revelation—the Bible—directly to them, a task that necessitated translation.

Eighteenth-century naturalist ideas about the "Caffre" race and language encouraged the missionaries to adopt a broad view of the target language for these translation activities. While they narrowed the "Caffre" language's geographical reach by excluding the highveld speaking practices in the 1830s, they held on to the notion that the "Caffre" language continuum extended through the coastal belt from the Great Fish River to Delagoa Bay. They held on to this notion because they interacted with people who circulated throughout this coastal belt and who used their fluency in the speaking practices of one area to communicate successfully with the people of other areas. The impressions these individuals shared with the missionaries suggested strongly that the speaking practices of the coastal belt's diverse communities and polities were mutually intelligible and thus formed part of a single "Caffre" language. This assumption, as the next chapter will show, became a firm belief when the missionaries traveled themselves throughout this region in the company of African interpreters who consistently downplayed the differences between the region's various speaking practices.

4

"Their Language Had an Affinity with That of Both of These Nations"

African Interpreters, Métissage, and the Dynamics of Linguistic Knowledge Production

Preexisting African ideas about language played one of the biggest roles in shaping European missionaries' understanding of the "Caffre" language community. These ideas entered the missionary knowledge system as a result of their close interactions with African interpreters.[1] Such interactions were common because, rather than being linguistic geniuses, as older hagiographies claimed, missionaries depended on the language expertise of African interpreters across the continent.[2] As a result of this dependence, some interpretive power shifted to the interpreters, especially in the context of Bible translation and the development of written languages throughout Africa.[3] These broader patterns held true for South Africa during the first half of the nineteenth century as well.[4]

Most studies of missionary–interpreter interactions in the context of Bible translation are primarily concerned with the ways in which such interactions helped identify or create equivalent terms in the vernacular for crucial concepts of Christianity (such as God, sin, salvation) and whether the use of such terms resulted in the Christianization of African consciousness or the Africanization of Christianity.[5] Generally, the outcome depended on who controlled meaning during these interactions, which changed in accordance with shifting power relations between missionaries and their African interlocutors.[6]

The same dynamic applied to the mapping of languages in Africa. In contexts where missionaries depended on the expertise of African interpreters, the latter and their preexisting ideas exercised some control over the missionaries' understanding of African languages and their geographical reach.

In these situations of dependence, then, the interpreters helped Africanize the missionary knowledge system of African languages.

This was the case in South Africa's coastal belt. As I will show below, the missionaries who arrived in this region during the first half of the nineteenth century became adult learners of a radically different new language. Therefore, they were never able to acquire native-speaker proficiency in the local speaking practices. As a result of this limitation, they remained dependent on the linguistic expertise of their African interpreters for the duration of their activities in the South African mission field. At crucial moments of linguistic knowledge production, this dependence on African interpreters was particularly intense, which created opportunities for African ideas about language to shape and Africanize the missionaries' understanding of the "Caffre" language community, notably its purported extension from the eastern Cape to Delagoa Bay.

European Missionaries: Skills and Dependence

All European missionaries working in nineteenth-century South Africa encountered an often overlooked but important obstacle in the path to acquiring native-speaker proficiency—age. They arrived in the region as adults, which limited the level of proficiency they were able to acquire in the local speaking practices over the course of their lifetimes.[7] As studies in support of the Critical Period Hypothesis in linguistics argue, the human brain stores language information "most efficiently and effectively" before the age of twelve. After this critical period, the brain seems to employ different ways and areas to store the information, with the result that "learning a new language later in life is difficult and rarely completely mastered."[8] Regardless of how hard and diligently they worked at improving their language skills, the missionaries' advanced age actively prevented them from acquiring native-speaker proficiency in what they called the "Caffre" language. The missionaries were cognizant of this harsh reality, including James Laing of the SPMS, who explained: "People who learn a language like the Kaffir, when they are grown up, are apt to speak and write in the order and idiom of their own vernacular. This is what may be seen daily in the manner in which the missionaries, who acquired the language when they were advanced to manhood, speak it to the people. The remark applies to writing as well as to speaking."[9]

For this reason, the SPMS expected its missionaries to raise their children in country *and* bilingually. The society's plan of education in 1839 stipulated that the children of missionaries receive their "elementary education" at the schools of their parents' mission stations so that they "have the foundation of their acquirements laid in the language of the country and be made familiar with the native mind."[10] The importance the SPMS ascribed to this issue is further exemplified by its attempts to actively prevent missionaries from removing their children from the mission stations before the latter had acquired native-speaker proficiency. Responding to the request of a missionary spouse to remove her children to Scotland for the purpose of education, the Mission Board replied: "The Committee will consent to her removal . . . but only on condition suggested by the final object, viz: that definite and systematic means be used to prevent the children from losing their familiar acquaintance with their native tongue."[11] The SPMS thus sought to address the language problem by raising the next generation of missionaries in South Africa and in ways that ensured their early acquisition of the coastal belt's indigenous speech forms.

The Wesleyan missionaries also believed that native-speaker proficiency was acquired in the early years of childhood or not at all. As one of their own, William Boyce explained in 1832, "Children brought up in the country, and who learn the language as their mother tongue, will of course become perfectly acquainted with it, *and they alone.*"[12] This assessment was correct. Those who learned the coastal belt's vernaculars in childhood— Charles Brownlee and Theophilus Shepstone and others—were considered fluent (*aba bafo bonke babesazi kakuhle isi Xosa ukusiteta*) by the African populations among whom they lived, earning for themselves sobriquets such as "white Xhosa" (*ama Xos'amhlope*).[13] Those who did not acquire the vernaculars in their childhood, however, struggled with them for the duration of their activities in the mission field.

LMS missionary Frederick G. Kayser is a good example. Born in 1800 near Leipzig, Germany, Kayser began his labors in South Africa when he was twenty-seven years old. Given his relatively advanced age, it is not surprising to find him, two years after his arrival in the region, admitting that speaking the language "fluently in long sentences is very difficult."[14] Kayser's struggles with the language continued thereafter; during an encounter with an indigenous woman three years later, he was still communicating in "*broken* Kaffers."[15] Wesleyan missionary William J. Davis faced similar challenges. Born in England circa 1810, Davis arrived in South Africa in 1832 when he was twenty-two years old.[16] Despite his diligent work, Davis's progress was so slow that, after a year in the field, he prayed for divine intervention. "I find it a hard language," he noted in his journal in 1833. "May He who enabled the Apostles to speak with other tongues assist me."[17]

Given his desperation in 1833, it is rather surprising to find Davis credit himself with having begun "the translation of the books of Chronicles into Kafir" less than a year later.[18] Another six months later, he even claimed to be able to "speak and preach with some degree of fluency" in "the Kafir language."[19] There is good reason to be wary of such assertions of linguistic grandeur. The German missionary Posselt, for instance, disparaged missionaries who claimed to be able to preach in the language after only "six or nine months"; he argued that this type of preaching should be considered no more than "childish babbling [*kindisches Lallen*]."[20] In fact, missionaries who reported of preaching in the local language usually referred to reading from previously prepared texts. Kayser is again a good example. In 1830, he admitted that while the Xhosa could understand him well when he read the language from a previously translated text, they "could not follow me so well when I spoke to them otherwise."[21] Kayser and Davis were not unique cases. Even the most respected linguists among the missionaries faced the same dilemma: in spite of achieving notable improvements in their command of local speaking practices over time, they struggled with the language and therefore remained dependent on the linguistic expertise of African interpreters.

John Brownlee was one of these missionaries. Born in Scotland in 1791, Brownlee established the government mission station at Chumie among the Rharhabe-Xhosa in 1820 and the LMS station at the Buffalo River among the Ntinde in 1826. If his own assertions can be trusted, Brownlee's language skills improved steadily during these years. In 1833, for instance, he took sole credit for having translated various sections of the Bible.[22] His fellow missionaries lauded him for having prayed "in the native tongue," preached "in the native language," and conducted "worship . . . in the Kaffer language" on various occasions between 1825 and 1834.[23] During the same time, however, Brownlee depended heavily on the language expertise of his African interpreter, Diyani (Jan) Tzatzoe.[24] "I have . . . Tzatzoe with me," Brownlee wrote in 1820; "I could not have done well without him; he interprets for me, and assists me in the language."[25] This dependence continued during the next decade. "I have got nearly the whole of Mark's gospel translated into Caffre," Brownlee explained in August 1827; "Brother Jan Tzatzoe is valuable in this respect as an assistant in the work of translating."[26] He still depended on Tzatzoe three years later: "Brother John [Jan] Tzatzoo . . . continues to render assistance . . . particularly . . . in translating and in the study of the language."[27]

When Brownlee was catechizing in the language during this time, he did so from materials previously translated with Tzatzoe's assistance. "After school I generally catechise from Watt's Catechism," he explained in 1827, "which we [i.e., Brownlee and Tzatzoe] have translated into the Caffre language."[28] In fact, Brownlee was not secure enough in the vernacular to speak freely with the Xhosa, which explains why, in 1828, he and Kayser declared themselves unable to visit them if Tzatzoe did not join them. As they wrote to the LMS directors that year, "These visits have not been so frequent. . . . The chief reason is that it not only is necessary to have a good interpreter but also one qualified to meet all their objections[;] Jan is the only person on the Institution qualified so to act."[29] Five years later, Brownlee and Kayser asked Tzatzoe again to interpret for them during their negotiations with Chief Maqoma regarding the establishment of a new mission station among the Rharhabe-Xhosa.[30] As this evidence suggests, although Brownlee undoubtedly improved his command of the local speaking practices over time, he remained dependent on Tzatzoe's language expertise when and where intimate linguistic knowledge was required.

John Bennie, the acknowledged language expert of the SPMS, experienced similar levels of dependence. Born in Scotland in 1796, Bennie arrived in the eastern Cape region in 1821 and served at Chumie, Lovedale, and Burnshill Stations over the next two and half decades. His language skills improved steadily over the course of this period.[31] In 1831, for instance, Bennie conducted an entire church service without the help of an interpreter, which was a great achievement because, as fellow missionary Laing explained, "This has rarely been done by any of us. We speak by interpreters."[32] Bennie's skills, however, were not advanced enough to repeat this feat on a regular basis. As Laing remarked later that year, "Mr Bennie in general prays in Kaffer but he does not in general preach in it."[33] Bennie's language skills continued to improve, but even seventeen years after he had first arrived in the region, he was able to conduct impromptu conversations with indigenous interlocutors only if these conversations were concerned with "common or doctrinal subject" rather than "something . . . unknown" or communicated to him "in highly figurative language."[34]

Bennie addressed his weaknesses by relying on the African interpreter Noyi Gciniswa, who also went by the baptismal name of Robert Balfour. In 1831, for instance, the SPMS missionaries reported, "Assisted by Robert Balfour, he [Bennie] is much engaged in translating the Scriptures into the language of Caffraria."[35] In this context, "assisting" meant that Noyi provided Bennie with the linguistic expertise that only a native speaker possessed, notably with "appropriate and idiomatic Kaffre expressions."[36] In fact, during Bennie's most productive phase of translation work, conducted during a brief sojourn at Somerset East in 1836, Noyi "corrected" all of his written translations.[37] Thus, even after some fifteen years in the region, native-speaker proficiency eluded Bennie, ensuring his continued dependence on Noyi's language skills.

Wesleyan missionary William Shrewsbury depended on the language expertise of African interpreters in a similar manner. Born in 1795, Shrewsbury arrived in the eastern Cape in October 1826.[38] He spent eight months at Wesleyville Station among the Gqunukhwebe to study "Caffre words" before moving to Butterworth Station among the Gcaleka-Xhosa and Mfengu, where he resided between 1827 and 1830.[39] In the latter year, Shrewsbury penned a paragraph into his journal that reveals both the state of his language skills as well as his dependence on African interpreters:

> The difficulty . . . of translating the Scriptures . . . can hardly be exhibited in too strong a light. . . . A Missionary sits down with his interpreter, who cannot read a single line of a word of God in any language; and perhaps his knowledge of divine things is very imperfect, and some of his notions erroneous. He opens the sacred volume, and has to translate that, in the first instance, into barbarous Dutch, that his interpreter may comprehend its meaning; and then his interpreter tells him how that barbarous Dutch ought to be worded in the Caffre language. And thus every verse being a double translation.[40]

As the quote shows, Shrewsbury was not only unable to communicate effectively in the local language (he spoke to his African interpreter in Dutch), but he also completely depended on his African interpreter to shoulder the crucial aspect of the translation work: that of expressing meaning in the target language.

Although Shrewsbury, similar to other missionaries, did not speak or write much about his African interpreters, it is possible to identify two of them by their baptismal names—Peter (surname unknown) and John

Burton.[41] In his diary entry for 10 April 1829, Shrewsbury reveals that Peter was helping him with translating the fifth chapter of the book of Matthew.[42] John, meanwhile, was at Shrewsbury's side during other moments when a good command of the local language was required. While visiting four captive Xhosa men at Fort Wilshire in March 1829, for example, Shrewsbury "requested John to pray with them, as I could not pray myself in Caffre."[43]

As expected, Shrewsbury became more comfortable with the vernacular over time, and some five years after he had first arrived in the region, he began "to speak" and "conduct the services . . . without an Interpreter."[44] He was, however, by no means fluent; in 1832 he admitted that his interlocutors did not always understand his "imperfect Caffre."[45] Moreover, when Shrewsbury moved to Grahamstown in 1834 to oversee the translation department of the Wesleyan mission, he continued to make use of people who possessed native-speaker fluency even if not all of them were of African descent. "We have great facilities for pursuing a faithful & correct translation of the Word of God," Shrewsbury explained in July 1834, "as we are favored with the help of two European youths, who acquired the Kafir Language in their childhood, by residing among the natives."[46] There is little doubt that he also drew on the expertise of the department's unnamed African-born interpreter, of whom it was said that "he could speak English, Dutch, and Kafir languages with fluency. Hence he became very useful as an interpreter, and took great delight in assisting in the translation of the Scriptures."[47] Although Shrewsbury became more proficient in the local modes of communication over time, like Brownlee and Bennie, he, too, was unable to achieve a level of linguistic proficiency that would have enabled him to dispense with his African interpreters. All three depended on African interpreters such as Jan Tzatzoe, Noyi Gciniswa (Robert Balfour), John Burton, and Peter.

This type of dependence persisted well into the 1860s. When WMS missionary John Appleyard's first complete version of the Bible in the "Caffre" language appeared in 1864, European missionaries discussed the quality of this translation by consistently referencing the impressions of people with native-speaker proficiency. Wesleyan missionary Robert Lamplough, for instance, asked Charles Pamla, who was of Mfengu descent, to verify if the translation "represented a faithful rendering of the English."[48] Similarly, the Moravian missionary Heinrich Meyer, who had first arrived in South Africa in 1855, asked Africans for assistance. "Not trusting my own opinion," he explained, "I have asked intelligent natives" to review the translation.[49] Even Albert Kropf, who had arrived in the region in 1848 and had soon developed a reputation as a formidable linguist, acknowledged that the quality of Appleyard's Bible translation could only be properly assessed by people with native-speaker proficiency—a skill that eluded him. Writing in 1866, he declared, "It would be presumptuous of me, to give a decided opinion on the necessity of a new translation, which can only be decided by those, who have acquired the idiom of the Kaffir language from their childhood."[50]

The discussion of the Appleyard's translation brings several claims made so far into focus: first, that European missionaries who came to South Africa as adults never acquired native-speaker proficiency and remained keenly aware of this deficiency; second, that the missionaries were willing to address this problem by surrounding themselves with African interpreters (and others) who possessed that proficiency and expertise. The resulting dependence on African interpreters suggests that African ideas about language had ample opportunity to influence the ways in which the missionaries thought about the "Caffre" language community in general and its geographical reach in particular.

Interpreters and the Geographical Reach of the "Caffre" Language

James Laing, who had arrived in the eastern Cape region in 1830 at the age of twenty-seven, is one of the best examples of a missionary who drew significant conclusions about the "Caffre" language community from his interactions with African interpreters. Laing resided for twenty-five years at the Scottish mission's Lovedale (1830–31 and 1843–55) and Burnshill Stations (1831–43). Like other missionaries, he struggled with the language and was frustrated about his dependence on an African interpreter by the name of Thomas Fortuin.[51] In 1832, he began to take paid language instruction from Klaas Love, the African interpreter at Burnshill Station.[52] The lessons resulted in some improvements, enabling Laing to read prayers and religious lessons from prepared scripts. Yet Laing relied heavily on the language skills of Love and, whenever possible, communicated through him to the indigenous people he met on the mission station or during visits to neighboring communities.[53] When Klaas was unavailable, Laing also asked one of the station's leading African members, Charles Henry Matshaya, to accompany him.[54] Importantly, Laing described the geographical reach of the "Caffre" language community in his journal in 1832: "According to information on which I can depend . . . the Tambookies speak the same language as the Kaffers. . . . Beyond the Tambookies are the Mambookies and beyond the Mambookies are the Amapinda people. . . . Parallel with these last tribes, are the Bechuanas who differ in language from the Kaffers [Xhosa] whereas those along the coast to a considerable distance speak a dialect much the same as that of the Kaffers."[55] Who had provided him with this information? Given Laing's ongoing problems with the language, this information came most likely from the men on whose language skills he depended on a daily basis: Klaas Love and Charles Henry Matshaya.

Laing continued his language studies for the next two decades. Native-speaker proficiency, however, eluded him, and he continued to rely on his African interpreters in situations that demanded advanced language skills, notably during "public worship."[56] The interpreter who usually helped him on these occasions was an African man named Moset.[57] Two African teachers, John Muir Vimbe and Tente kaNgqika, also helped Laing, notably with his translation work.[58] When Tente died in 1842, Laing recruited another young African man, Tshetshe Kleinveldt, to assist him.[59]

While his dependence on indigenous language experts persisted, Laing interacted with the Mfengu settlements of Ely, Sheshegu, Gaga, Macfarlane, and Ncwazi, whose children attended the outstations schools under his supervision. It was in this context that Laing announced in a letter in 1848 that "it is scarcely necessary to say that the Fingoes and Kaffirs [Xhosa] speak one and the same language."[60] Six years later, he reiterated this point in a letter to the BFBS: "The Fingoes here, who in former times lived on the Tugela, the present boundary of Natal to the N.E., . . . understand the Kafir translations quite well, the language being, except in a few words, the very same."[61] Whose perspective is reflected in this assessment of the coastal belt's linguistic landscape? Given Laing's continued deficiencies in the region's vernaculars and his continued dependence on African interpreters, it is likely that this assessment was once again shaped by the latter, notably Moset, Vimbe, Tente, and Tshetshe.

The influence of African interpreters is also perceptible in Wesleyan missionary William Shaw's statements about the "Caffre" language community. Born in Scotland in 1798, Shaw arrived in the eastern Cape region in 1820. Over the course of the next two years, he worked near Grahamstown among the region's European settlers and Khoekhoe soldiers, which explains why he initially focused on acquiring the Dutch language rather than the vernacular of the neighboring African communities.[62] Not surprisingly, when Shaw ventured beyond the Cape Colony's boundary for the first time in August 1822, he was accompanied by the African interpreter Diyani (Jan)Tzatzoe.[63] Shaw depended on Tzatzoe's language skills again one year later when he traveled beyond the colonial boundary to the Gqunukhwebe to negotiate the establishment of a mission station there.[64] When Shaw founded Wesleyville Station among this community several months later, he was accompanied by another African interpreter named Jantje Nooka, on whose language skills he henceforth depended in all his interactions with the Gqunukhwebe and their Mfengu clients.[65]

While interacting with the Gqunukhwebe and Mfengu by way of his African interpreters, Shaw also came to some important conclusions about the "Caffre" language, notably that beyond the border of the Cape Colony resided "countless multitudes of untutored Pagans; all of whom are evidently of the same origin . . . and speaking a language, which, notwithstanding very considerable differences in dialect, is doubtless substantially the same."[66] Given Shaw's dependence on his African interpreters at this time, it appears that this statement was based at least in part on Tzatzoe and Nooka's assessment of the region's speech patterns.

Shaw continued to depend on his African interpreters, who later also included the Wesleyville residents Yosef Wesley, Daniel Kotongo, and David Boozak. In 1826, for instance, Shaw preached in Dutch, "which his interpreter rendered into Caffre."[67] Moreover, in December 1826 and again in May 1827, Shaw, in the company of these interpreters, traveled to the Gcaleka-Xhosa and their Mfengu clients to negotiate the establishment of another mission station (Butterworth).[68] Shortly after his return from this journey, he wrote down the following conclusions:

> In the immediate vicinity of the spot selected [Butterworth Station], are a number of villages, formed by Africans of several distinct nations, who, in consequence of wars and commotions in the interior, have been scattered and driven from their native countries, and have sought refuge in the country of Hintsa, who has treated them kindly, and allowed them to settle among his people. They are known among the Caffres [Xhosa] under the general name of Amafengoo [Mfengu]; they are, however, of many different nations, (some of them from the neighbourhood of the Portuguese settlements on the east coast,) but all speak the Caffre language, with various degrees of difference as to the pronunciation.[69]

Given Shaw's dependence on his African interpreters at the time of this journey, his conclusion regarding the geographical extension of the "Caffre" language community must have originated at least in part with the African interpreters who surrounded him at this time—notably Nooka, Wesley, Kotongo, and Boozak.

Shaw's language skills improved over the course of the next two years, but he continued to depend on African interpreters in the context of translation work and impromptu conversation with indigenous inhabitants.[70] Thus, when Shaw traveled as far as the Mpondo chiefdom in 1829, he was accompanied by John Burton, the African interpreter attached to William Shrewsbury's Butterworth Station.[71] Shaw used his conversation with the Mpondo chief and councillors to gain a better understanding of the "Caffre" language community and noted in his journal that "their language is the same as that of the Caffres [Xhosa], with only such a slight difference in the pronunciation of some words, that we found no difficulty of understanding them, or of making ourselves understood."[72] Whose assessment of the differences between the speaking practices of the Xhosa and Mpondo did this statement reflect? Given Shaw's limited language skills at this time, it most likely reflected the views of the African interpreter Burton.

Shaw relocated to England in 1833 but returned to the eastern Cape region four years later to serve as the general superintendent of the Wesleyan missions in southeastern Africa.[73] For the next decade, Shaw's time and energy were focused on expanding the mission field to Natal-Zululand.[74] In 1848, he traveled to this region to visit the Wesleyan mission stations at Pietermaritzburg and Zwartkops, which had been established in 1845 and 1846.[75] Similar to his previous journeys, Shaw used the opportunity to engage in linguistic knowledge production and shortly after his return from the Natal in 1848 expressed the view that "the natives are all Kaffirs, of the Zoola and other nations, and all speak the Kaffir language, with slight variations in their dialects from the language spoken by the Kaffirs on the border of the Cape Colony."[76] Shaw's quotation illustrates that he returned from Natal convinced that the Zulus also spoke the "Caffre" language and that, consequently, this language extended from the eastern Cape to Delagoa Bay.

But whose assessment of the "Caffre" language continuum does Shaw's statement represent? It is noteworthy that at the time of his visit to Pietermaritzburg and Zwartkops, these stations included several African interpreters from the eastern Cape, including Thomas Fortuin and John Muir

Vimbe, who had previously worked as interpreters for the Scottish missionary James Laing. After being cut off from the Cape Colony by the outbreak of the Seventh Frontier War in March 1846, both Fortuin and Vimbe trekked overland to Natal, where they began to work as teachers and interpreters in the WMS's Pietermaritzburg and Zwartkops Stations.[77] Thus, by 1848, the two WMS stations in Natal that Shaw visited included African interpreters who were fluent in the speaking practices of the eastern Cape and now used their language skills to work among the indigenous communities of Natal. There is no documentary evidence that confirms that Shaw spoke with Fortuin or Vimbe during his visit to these stations. It is very likely, however, that he did meet them because these mission stations were relatively small, tight-knit communities. Moreover, Shaw had a deep interest in the language situation, a long track record of relying on the language expertise of African interpreters, and now the unique opportunity to obtain the perspective from two African interpreters who knew the language situation in both areas intimately. It is therefore likely that Shaw spoke with them and that his subsequent conclusion about the language situation—notably that the Zulus spoke the same "Caffre" language as the Xhosas in the eastern Cape—reflected at least in part the perspective of Fortuin and Vimbe.

William Shaw was not the only missionary who traveled to Natal in 1848. At about the same time, Shaw's colleague, John Appleyard, traveled to Pietermaritzburg to stay several weeks with his father-in-law, James Archbell.[78] Born in England in 1814, Appleyard had arrived in the eastern Cape in 1840. His approach to studying the local language was noticeably mechanical. As he noted in November 1840, "To-night I began the Kafir Grammar a second time. I shall reduce all that I possibly can into tabular form, adopting the plan of the declensions of nouns, and singular and plural euphonic letters."[79] Progress was slow, and it was not until April 1843 that Appleyard began to interact with the local communities without the assistance of an African interpreter.[80]

Three years later, Appleyard took charge of the Wesleyan printing press and began to work on the language in cooperation with his colleague Henry Dugmore, who had been entrusted with overseeing "the revision and printing of the Kaffir version of the Scriptures."[81] He was now deeply involved in the translation of the Bible and the publication of several philological studies of the language, including an article titled "The Kaffir Dialects" in 1847 and the aforementioned monograph on *The Kafir Language* in 1850.[82] But he was not doing this work alone; instead he worked in close cooperation with individuals who possessed native-speaker proficiency, including an African interpreter named "Old Joseph" and the aforementioned Charles Brownlee.[83] Several years later, Appleyard readily admitted that he had depended on these language experts while working on his publications. "In order to ensure as much correctness in this as possible," he explained in 1859, "all my translations have been usually read over, sheet by sheet, previous to their going to the press, with an intelligent native Teacher, and in most instances I have gained something by so doing, though at the cost of much time consumed in questioning and the like."[84]

With this background information in mind, it is possible to better understand why a major shift in Appleyard's thinking about the "Caffre" language community occurred during his stay in Natal in 1848. Before Appleyard embarked for Natal, he expressed the opinion that the differences between the "Caffre" speech forms of the Xhosa, Thembu, and Mpondo and the "Caffre" forms used by the Zulus were so substantial that these speech forms represented two distinct branches of the "Caffre" language family.[85] Following his return from Natal in 1848, however, Appleyard introduced an important correction to this opinion. He now believed that the differences between these speech forms were less significant than previously assumed, and that they formed part of a single branch of the "Caffre" language family. As he explained, "Further inquiries respecting the dialects of the Kafir family, made during a few weeks' sojourn in the Natal colony, have led the writer to doubt the propriety of the division adopted [previously]."[86] Why did Appleyard change his mind about the "Caffre" language family during his sojourn in Natal? Given his habit of consulting African interpreters for their language expertise, it appears likely that he also spoke to the African interpreters, notably Fortuin and Vimbe, who worked on the WMS stations in the Pietermaritzburg area and possessed intimate knowledge of both regions' speaking practices. Indeed, there is good evidence that African interpreters influenced Shaw's *and* Appleyard's view of the "Caffre" language family and its geographical reach from the eastern Cape to Delagoa Bay.

African Interpreters: Culture, Identities, Knowledge

The likelihood that European missionaries' understanding of the "Caffre" language community reflected at least in part the views held by their African interpreters raises questions about the context that produced these views. Why did these interpreters consistently downplay the significance of the very real if relatively small differences that existed between the various indigenous speech communities between the eastern Cape and Delagoa Bay?

One potential answer has to do with the social context in which these African interpreters operated. As John and Jean Comaroff remind us, in the northern Cape region, African interpreters "held unusual power—they were the best paid of the work force that undergirded the mission."[87] There are no data available for the pay rates Africans in the eastern Cape received for their language services from the missionaries. However, many of them performed these language services as part of their "teaching" activities, for which clearer data are available. For instance, the aforementioned Noyi Gciniswa (Robert Balfour) received a salary of £8 per annum for his duties as the Glasgow Missionary Society's "native" teacher in 1826.[88] About a decade later, Noyi, John Muir Vimbe, and Tente kaNgqika earned each an annual salary of £12 for their work as schoolmasters.[89] These wages were substantial, considering that, in 1834, the African residents of Philipton and the Kat River settlements were paid 6d to 9d per day of labor (which translated to £9.1 to £13.7 per year provided the laborer was willing to work 365 days per year) but sometimes had to be content with being "given alcohol in lieu of wages."[90] By the 1850s, the Scottish missions paid "native" teacher salaries of £20 per annum, which compared very favorably with the £12 per annum salaries the Cape Colony offered to Gqunukhwebe chief Kama's principal headmen in 1856.[91]

African teacher-interpreters thus occupied positions that were relatively well remunerated and, given their close association with European missionaries, tended to command significant prestige at least within mission station communities. Both pay and prestige, however, depended on Africans performing their duties satisfactorily, which, in the case of interpreting, meant being able to accompany the missionaries on their travels and communicate on their behalf with the various African communities the missionaries encountered on these journeys. In this context, it may well have been advantageous for these interpreters to downplay the differences between their own speaking practices and those of the Thembu, Mpondo, Natal Africans, and Zulu in order to remain valuable to the missionaries.

There is, however, a second explanation for why the interpreters consistently downplayed these differences, and it has to do with their cultural backgrounds. Reconstructing those is not an easy task, given the complex ethnic backgrounds and political allegiances of mission station residents.[92]

That said, the microbiographies of some of the African interpreters I've been able to reconstruct below do suggest that they had broader cultural roots among the Khoekhoe and Xhosa and narrower roots among the métis (mixed) chiefdoms of the eastern Cape borderlands, notably the Gonaqua, Gqunukhwebe, and Ntinde.

Diyani Tzatzoe

One of the most important African interpreters in the eastern Cape region was the aforementioned Diyani (Jan) Tzatzoe. Born around 1791, Diyani was the senior son of Kote Tzatzoe (the son of Mbange, son of Ntinde), who was the ruler of the Ntinde chiefdom. This chiefdom included people of Khoekhoe descent, which explains why Diyani himself had a Khoekhoe mother and was probably bilingual, speaking a form of so-called Hottentot (which I will call "Khoesan" here) as well as the so-called Caffre speech of the eastern Cape region (which I call "Nguni" here).[93] At the age of fifteen, Diyani became a member of the LMS mission station of Bethelsdorp, where Dutch functioned as the "official" station language.[94] Diyani quickly added competency in Dutch to his language repertoire. "He writes the Dutch language extremely well," one visitor to Bethelsdorp noted in 1809, "and translates from it into his own tongue [Nguni]."[95] All these language skills recommended Diyani for the position of African interpreter in 1816. For the next three years, he served in this role under missionary Joseph Williams at the Kat River Station.[96] In the aftermath of Williams's death, Diyani began to work as interpreter for a number of missionary societies, notably the LMS, SPMS, and WMS. Referring specifically to Diyani's Nguni and Dutch language skills, Wesleyan missionary Shrewsbury noted in 1829: "He first read his Text, Matt. 19:1–6 with fluency from the Dutch Bible, and afterwards, with great care and exactness, gave a verbal translation thereof, sentence by sentence, before he proceeded to expound the passage. . . . Without doubt he ranks first in point of qualifications for translating the Scriptures into the Kafir [Nguni] Language."[97]

Noyi Gciniswa

Initially the most influential of the Scottish mission's African interpreters was Noyi Gciniswa (Robert Balfour). Born in 1783, Noyi traced his lineage to the royal Tshawe clan of the Xhosa through his father, Gciniswa (the son of Phazima, son of Gandowentshaba, son of Ngconde, . . . , son of Tshawe).[98] He also had ties to the Gonaqua polity because his great-grandfather, Gandowentshaba, had given his sister to Chief Hinsati of the Inqua, a chiefdom of Khoesan-speaking herders, a union that produced a young man named Cwama, the subsequent ruler of the Gonaqua chiefdom.[99] The genealogical connection to the Xhosa and the Gonaqua gave Noyi the credentials to reside near the Kat River, where people from both groups lived in the early decades of the nineteenth century.[100]

As a member of this community, Noyi came into contact with missionary Joseph Williams, Diyani Tzatzoe, and Ntsikana (a spiritual leader of Rharhabe-Xhosa descent) between 1816 and 1819. When Williams and Ntsikana died in 1818 and 1819, Noyi led a portion of this Kat River community (notably his Ntinde wife Nobuyiswa, Ntsikana's children, and several other members) to Chumie Station, where they were hailed as the Scottish mission's "first fruits of the Caffre nation" in 1823.[101] The people who joined Chumie Station from the Kat River spoke both Nguni and Dutch and possibly still some Khoesan.[102] In Noyi's case, this multilingualism came to the attention of John Bennie, who made him his interpreter, a position that usually required translating between Dutch and Nguni.[103] As shown above, Noyi soon became indispensable to Bennie, correcting all his translations in the 1830s.[104]

Thomas and Anna Fortuin

Thomas and Anna Fortuin began to reside and work as interpreters at the Glasgow Missionary Society's Lovedale Station sometime in the mid-1820s.[105] The family's social standing in the Lovedale community increased over time, reaching a high point around 1840, when one of their daughters, Mamata, married Noyi's son, Jan Beck Balfour.[106] Their standing however, took a dive in April 1843 when Thomas was wrongfully accused of having illegally sold a gun to a Xhosa.[107] Some six months later, moreover, the marriage between Mamata and Jan Beck Balfour ended amid mutual accusations of adultery.[108] The family relocated to Pirie Station, where they found little peace because a local African prophet demanded that the Fortuins and the other African church leaders "desist from hearing the word of God."[109] It was six months after these events that the Scottish missionaries asked Thomas to establish a new station among the Gcaleka-Xhosa on the Cefane River.[110] As mentioned before, the outbreak of the Seventh Frontier

War forced the Fortuins to move to Natal, where they attached themselves to the Wesleyans.

The Fortuins' ethnic and linguistic background was complex. Thomas was possibly of Gonaqua background because he was described as "a Hottentot by birth but brought up in Kafferland."[111] Of Anna it was said that she had a European (Irish) father and a Khoekhoe mother but had grown up among Chief Hintsa's Gcaleka-Xhosa.[112] Their background explains why the Fortuins possessed the Nguni and Dutch language skills that made them ideal interpreters in the eastern Cape region. About Anna, Laing explained that she "understands both the Dutch and Kaffre [Nguni]," which made her a useful person "particularly when acting as our interpreter in cases of conscience."[113] "Thomas the interpreter," Laing added, "turns the sermon into Kaffer as it is spoken in Dutch by the Missionary."[114]

Klaas Love, John Muir Vimbe, and Tshetshe Kleinveldt

A second generation of African interpreters became active in the 1830s. One of them was Klaas Love, whose parents had moved with Noyi from the Kat River to Chumie Station, where they received the baptismal names of John and Elizabeth Love in 1823.[115] Although the missionaries identified the Loves as "Caffres," the fact that they had resided at the Kat River and named their children "Klaas" and "Lentje" suggests that they had genealogical ties to Xhosa and Khoekhoe communities and may in fact have belonged more narrowly to the Gonaqua.[116] Capable of speaking both Nguni and Dutch, Klaas likely began his work as interpreter in 1831, when he moved from Chumie Station to Burnshill.[117]

When Klaas left Burnshill in 1834 or 1835 to become a government interpreter, his place was filled by a man named Vimbe.[118] Born around 1810, Vimbe grew up on a small tributary of the Kat River.[119] In 1820, he and his parents relocated to Chumie Station, attaching themselves to the aforementioned Charles Henry Matshaya.[120] Vimbe spent the next decade working as a cattle herder at different mission stations, notably at Incerha (later Lovedale) and Burnshill. At the latter station, he learned the fundamentals of reading, writing, and the Christian faith under the tutelage of missionary Laing.[121] Baptized John Muir on 24 August 1834, Vimbe, who by then had a wife and a child, continued his studies at Burnshill in the company of Matshaya and Matwa (a minor son of the former Chief Ngqika of the Rharhabe-Xhosa).[122] At this time, he also composed or translated two hymns, which were printed at Lovedale in 1836.[123] Two years later, Vimbe, after having been "examined in reading in Caffre and Dutch," became "schoolmasters" of one of Burnshill's outstations, which provided opportunities to assist Laing with his translation work.[124] Vimbe had a Khoekhoe father and Xhosa mother (Nomantu) who had lived near the Kat River when he was born; he had been circumcised "according to the custom of the Kaffers," and he married a woman from the Kat River who "can read three languages."[125] This information suggests that he probably had Gonaqua ancestry. This would also explain his own bilingualism and his ability to serve as Laing's interpreter until he went to Natal in the wake of the Seventh Frontier War and entered the service of the Wesleyan's Zwart-kops Station in 1847.

Following Vimbe's departure, Laing began to rely on the linguistic exper-tise of Tshetshe Kleinveldt.[126] Born near Lovedale around 1828, Tshetshe lived at Pirie Station until 1841,[127] when he formed part of the first incoming class at Lovedale Institution.[128] There, Tshetshe learned how to "read and understand English" and soon was able to "read from the English Bible" and translate passages "into Kaffre."[129] In the aftermath of the Seventh Frontier War, these skills enabled Tshetshe to serve as a teacher at the Lovedale mis-sion school and to assist Laing, who had moved from Burnshill to Lovedale in 1843, with his translation activities.[130] His Nguni-sounding first name and his Dutch-sounding last name and his ability to speak Nguni fluently suggests that he was of mixed ancestry, most likely of Gonaqua, Ntinde, or Gqunukhwebe background.[131]

John Burton

Like their Scottish counterparts, the Wesleyan missionaries usually sur-rounded themselves with several African interpreters. William Shrewsbury, for instance, depended on the assistance of a "young man" who received the baptismal name "John Burton" on 4 January 1829.[132] Shortly after his bap-tism, Burton accompanied Shrewsbury on a visit to Grahamstown, serv-ing as his guide and interpreter.[133] He served in the same capacity during Shaw's journey to the Mpondo chiefdom later in the same year.[134] This area appealed to Burton, for one year later he moved to that region to serve as William Boyce's interpreter between 1830 and 1833.[135] Both Shrewsbury and Boyce identified Burton as a "Caffre" and acknowledged his skills in that language on several occasions.[136] Burton, however, also spoke Dutch, which he appears to have acquired while living in close proximity to Dutch farmers during his youth.[137] These pieces of evidence suggest that he may have been of Gonaqua descent or that, at the very least, he was a member of the Gqunukhwebe or Ntinde, who occupied the border region with the colony and its Dutch-speaking farming community.

Daniel Kotongo, Yosef Wesley, David Boozak, and Jantje Nooka

William Shaw also used several African interpreters during his tenure in the eastern Cape region. Baptized "Daniel" in October 1829, Kotongo served as Shaw's interpreter between 1825 and 1830.[138] In the 1820s Shaw described Kotongo as his "faithful Caffre servant," who worked as "our Interpreter from Wesleyville," and credited him with possessing "complete knowledge of the native feelings and customs."[139] Because Wesleyville had been founded in the domain of the Gqunukhwebe chiefdom and because Kotongo apparently spoke fluent Nguni and Dutch, it is most likely that he was of Gqunukhwebe descent, or, alternatively, of Ntinde or Gonaqua background.

Shaw's second interpreter at Wesleyville was a man whose baptismal name was "Yosef Wesley."[140] Before moving to Wesleyville in 1825, Yosef had spent some time in the frontier region, possibly at the Kat River or Theopolis.[141] He spoke Nguni and Dutch, which allowed him to work as an interpreter at Wesleyville, a role he executed diligently for the next two decades.[142] Although the missionaries never specified Yosef Wesley's identity and original name, his former residence in the border region and his bilingualism suggest that he, too, may have been of Gonaqua, Gqunukhwebe, or Ntinde background.[143]

David Boozak was Shaw's third interpreter at Wesleyville.[144] Boozak already lived among or near the Gqunukhwebe chiefdom by the time Shaw first visited the polity in 1823, for it was said that Boozak had "left his Garden and all its contents as soon as he heard that a Missionary had come to Wesleyville."[145] Although not much else is known of him, his last name and his Nguni and Dutch bilingualism suggest that he was most likely of Gonaqua heritage.

Shaw's fourth and final interpreter at Wesleyville was Jantje Nooka.[146] Jantje was descended from a family of Gonaqua who had inhabited the eastern Cape region since the last quarter of the eighteenth century. This emerges from the journal of the Dutch naturalist traveler Robert Jacob Gordon, who, while traveling in the vicinity of modern Port Elizabeth in

1778, "found . . . a kraal of the Gounaqua chief, Nouka, who had ten straw huts belonging to the people with him."[147] Three decades later, some of the descendants of this chief lived at the Kat River, where missionary Joseph Williams remarked in 1816 that "Hendriek Nucker with ten families joined us. This man is appointed by Gika [Ngqika] as the Chief of the people residing here."[148] A man named Hendrik Nooka appears several times in the colonial records for the same year, each time identified as a "Gonaqua Hottentot . . . [and] the interpreter of the Caffre Chief Ngqika."[149] In 1823, William Shaw hired the Nguni- and Dutch-speaking Jantje Nooka—who was probably the son of Hendrik and who, by then, was married to a woman identified as "Hottentot"—to accompany him as his interpreter to the Gqunukhwebe.[150] Jantje served in this role at Wesleyville until the Sixth Frontier War (1834–35), when he returned to the neighborhood of the Kat River, where it was said that "the Nooka family of Gona Caffers" represented an influential family and where Jantje henceforth worked for the LMS.[151]

Although spotty, these microbiographies suggest that the African interpreters who worked for the European missionaries had their broader cultural roots among the Khoekhoe and Xhosa chiefdoms of the eastern Cape region. This suggests that, at least on the Xhosa side, they grew up in a context in which people established their key collectivities, such as patriclan, chiefdom, and social status within chiefdoms, on the basis of genealogical descent and acts of submission rather than by overtly mobilizing language differences. Language differences existed and were noted, of course. And, as detailed in chapter 1, at times they were deployed as "soft" markers of "vague" regional identities. But well into the nineteenth century, Xhosa communities did not use these language differences to demarcate the collectivities—clans, chiefdoms, status—that mattered.

This context helps explain why people from these communities did not attribute significant meaning to the differences between speaking practices, especially when these differences were relatively small. This is supported by a remark made by Stokwe, son of Chief Nqeno kaLanga of the Mbalu-Xhosa, to Scottish missionary John Cumming in 1845. After listening to Stokwe's complaint that one of Nqeno's subjects had joined the Thembu in the capacity of an evangelist without having asked the chief's permission first, Cumming asked if the subject's guilt was not reduced by his continuing to reside "amongst a people who spoke the same language." Although

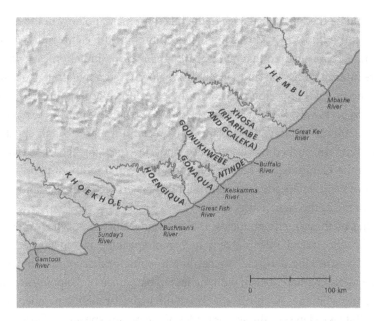

MAP 4. Eastern Cape borderlands and métis polities, ca. 1750.

Stokwe remained adamant about the subject's guilt, he readily admitted that it was true that the subject remained "amongst a people who spoke the same language."[152] The African interpreters' wider cultural background thus encouraged them to downplay the significance to the real (if small) differences they encountered between the region's speaking practices. This tendency was even more pronounced among those interpreters whose narrower cultural roots traced to the Gonaqua, Gqunukhwebe, and Ntinde polities—the métis (mixed) chiefdoms of the eastern Cape borderlands, a region that extended approximately from the Buffalo River to the Bushman's River by the middle of the eighteen century (see map 4).[153]

Borderlands and Métissage

As discussed in chapter 1, the eastern Cape region had functioned as a meeting place between Khoesan-speaking herders and Nguni-speaking mixed farmers since the first millennium CE. Mutual trading, intermarriage, and political incorporation ensured that both groups gradually assimilated some of the other's cultural and linguistic characteristics. It is generally accepted, for instance, that these activities allowed Khoesan click sounds to populate the Nguni language of the mixed farmers, notably of those who came to be known as Xhosa. By the beginning of the eighteenth century, several factors ensured that cultural and linguistic assimilation gave way to more intense métissage (mixing) in this region. First, population expansion and the process of fission incentivized the region's Xhosa polities to move more aggressively westward across the Kei River. Second, the expanding Cape Colony, notably the advance of the land-hungry Dutch-speaking stock farmers, pushed more and more Khoesan-speaking herders eastward across the Gamtoos and Sundays Rivers. This rapid influx of people gave rise to several métis (mixed) polities in the eastern Cape borderlands over the course of the eighteenth century.[154]

One of these métis polities was the Ntinde chiefdom, which included people who traced their descent to Nguni-speaking mixed farmers and Khoesan-speaking herders.[155] According to some oral accounts, the chiefdom's métis character began with the mixed parentage of the polity's founding figure—Ntinde—who was the son of the highest-ranking member of the royal Tshawe clan (i.e., the senior leader of the Nguni-speaking Xhosa chiefdoms) and his Khoekhoe wife (possibly the daughter of Chief Ngqosini, who ruled a polity made up of Khoesan-speaking herders).[156] Tellingly, the same oral accounts explain that it was the Ntinde chiefdom that initiated "the mixing of the blood, skin tone, and language" between the Xhosa and Khoekhoe, and that this mixing explained why "the Ntinde . . . have a lighter skin tone."[157]

Documentary evidence points in a similar direction. In the 1750s, the Ntinde chiefdom, then ruled by Ntinde's son Mbange, controlled the region immediately east of the lower Keiskamma River and thus in the eastern Cape borderlands.[158] Not surprisingly, when the VOC's Beutler expedition reached Mbange's domain in 1752, they noticed that the chiefdom also included people identified as "Gonaqua Hottentots."[159] The chiefdom maintained its métis character into the nineteenth century. When Colonel Richard Collins visited the region in 1809, he was informed that the appearance of the Ntinde chief, now Kote Tzatzoe (the son of Mbange), "is said to be more that of a Hottentot than a Kaffer, and he has Hottentot wives."[160] By the time European missionaries became fully active in the eastern Cape borderlands, the Ntinde chiefdom's heir apparent, the already-mentioned Diyani (Jan) Tzatzoe (the son of Kote Tzatzoe), had also married a woman of Khoekhoe background in order to continue the métis character of the chiefdom's ruling house.[161]

Another métis polity in the region was the Gqunukhwebe chiefdom. The Gqunukhwebe explain the métis character of their chiefdom with a peculiar origin story.[162] They report that their history began with a man named Khwane, who was a councillor of Tshiwo, the highest-ranking member of the royal Tshawe clan at the time and thus the principal chief of the Nguni-speaking Xhosa polities. Instead of executing Xhosa subjects convicted of witchcraft, Khwane hid them "in a forest where they . . . intermarried with the local Khoi [i.e., Khoekhoe]."[163] When Tshiwo faced a military defeat a while later, Khwane forged out of this métis community a "secret army" that rescued Tshiwo.[164] Having been saved by this army, Tshiwo rewarded Khwane by "appointing him a chief equal in rank to the amaTshawe," thereby giving him the authority to forge out of his Xhosa-Khoekhoe métis community the Gqunukhwebe chiefdom.[165]

Documentary evidence, meanwhile, suggests that the chiefdom was "located in the area between the Kei and the Keiskamma rivers" by the 1750s.[166] Some four decades later, during the rule of Chief Tshaka, the Gqunukhwebe polity had relocated to the area between the Sundays and Fish Rivers.[167] Because this latter region was also claimed by European stock farmers, the Gqunukhwebe allied with and incorporated some of the local Khoesan-speaking herders, notably following the death of Chief Tshaka at the hands of European settlers.[168] In spite of the tensions with the settlers, the new chief, Chungwa, moved the chiefdom's center of gravity to the Gamtoos River in the first decade of the nineteenth century, a movement as part of which the chiefdom added additional Khoesan-speaking herders to their numbers.[169] As an indigenous informant told Colonel Collins at the time, "Some Hottentots are also said to be intermixed with them [the Gqunukhwebe]."[170] Chungwa's successor, Chief Phato, made peace with the Cape Colony in 1819, allowing, as we have seen, Wesleyan missionaries, notably William Shaw, to establish Wesleyville Station in their midst and hiring some of the members of this métis polity as interpreters.[171]

The third and final métis community in the region were the Gonaqua. There is reason to believe that the word "Gonaqua" originally functioned as a generic term for "strangers" because, according to linguists, it was related to the Korana word "<≠gona," which simply meant "foreigner."[172] It is possible that people identified as "strangers" (Gonaqua) by others eventually adopted the name for themselves, with the result that the word also became associated with a specific community of a particular locality, notably the eastern Cape borderlands. This would explain why a VOC expedition in 1689 was told by Khoesan-speaking members of the Inqua chiefdom, which was located near the upper reaches of the Sundays River at the time, that further east along the coast lived several groups of people, notably the "Gonaqua" and the "Kabuquas" (the latter term referred to the Xhosas).[173]

Who exactly were these Gonaqua? Xhosa oral accounts tell us that the history of this Gonaqua polity began when the Xhosa chiefdoms experienced a succession dispute between Gandowentshaba and his brother and heir apparent, Tshiwo. When the dispute evolved into open conflict, Gandowentshaba and his followers fled westward across the Great Fish River and eventually found refuge among the Inqua chiefdom, which was then ruled by Hinsati. Gandowentshaba gave his sister in marriage to Hinsati, a mixed union that produced a young man named Cwama. The accounts also explain that, after some time, Gandowentshaba and Tshiwo resolved their differences and then formed an alliance that attacked the Inqua chiefdom, killing Hinsati in the process.[174] It is appears that Cwama, who had already proven himself as a capable military leader,[175] broke away from the Inqua polity at this time and established his own chiefdom—the Gonaqua, who occupied lands east of the Inqua and close to the Xhosa.[176]

Perhaps because of his métis background, Cwama attracted to his rule not only Khoesan-speaking herders but also Nguni-speaking mixed farmers. The latter may have included some of Gandowentshaba's erstwhile followers who, as oral accounts explain, stayed in the region in the aftermath of the Inqua-Xhosa war "as they loved the area because it was open, well stocked with game, and unoccupied."[177] Although it is difficult to know with certainty how this chiefdom organized itself culturally at this stage, it is likely that the Gonaqua polity developed "a peculiar blend of Khoekhoe and Xhosa culture."[178]

It is unclear how long the Gonaqua chiefdom sustained itself as an independent métis polity in the eastern Cape borderlands. Both the Inqua and Gonaqua chiefdoms prospered until at least 1702, when both polities (in the Dutch records referred to as "Hequons" and "Genocquaas," respectively) were attacked and robbed of many of their cattle and sheep by a group of European adventurers from the Cape Colony.[179] Documentary evidence also tells us that the Gonaqua still represented an independent chiefdom located "east of the [Great] Fish [River], being ruled over by a chief named 'Babbelaan'" in 1736.[180] However, when the Beutler expedition reached the borderlands in 1752, they noticed some loss of political sovereignty. "The

Gonaquas Hottentots live among them [i.e., Xhosa chiefdoms] and mix with them," the expedition journal noted. "The Caffres [i.e., Xhosa] use them as servants and in time of war also as soldiers."[181]

By the second half of the eighteenth century, some Gonaqua groups also fell under the increasing control of the Cape Colony's advancing European stock farmers. In 1778, for instance, the VOC envoy Robert Jacob Gordon met the "Gounaqua chief Nouka" (probably the ancestor of Jantje Nooka, William Shaw's interpreter at Wesleyville), who told him that he had until recently lived peacefully along the Van Staden's River "fetching [the colony's] runaway slaves from the Caffers [Xhosa]."[182] At about the same time, a VOC officer reported that the Xhosa polities complained that the European stock farmers were harboring Gonaqua cattle thieves: "Because the Gonna Hottentots [Gonaqua], who had formerly lain among them, and now resided among the Christians, constantly carried off their cattle, and brought them to this side of the Bushmans river, wherefore they, the Kafirs [Xhosa], presumed that the Christians acted with the said Gonna Hottentots; they desired, therefore, that the Christians would dislodge the said Gonna Hottentots, and drive them back to them, in order that they might again obtain possession of their cattle."[183]

Occupying a position between Europeans and Xhosas proved to be unsustainable in the long run. During the Third Cape Frontier War (1799–1803) the Gonaqua waged war against European farmers, who were in the process of depriving them of their "land, stock, and independence."[184] As the war turned against them, a number of Gonaqua found refuge among the Xhosa polities.[185] Other Gonaqua joined some of their relations who had earlier been absorbed into the Gqunukhwebe chiefdom.[186] A second section of Gonaqua rebels chose a different path. They made peace with the (by then) British-ruled Cape Colony, accepting the governor's offer to settle under the tutelage of the LMS at Algoa Bay. This group became part of the founding stock of the LMS mission stations of Bethelsdorp and Theopolis and, in the 1830s, of the Kat River settlement.[187] It was from these fragments of the Gonaqua chiefdom that European missionaries recruited many of their interpreters.

As these brief historical accounts of the Ntinde, Gqunukhwebe, and Gonaqua illustrate, the eastern Cape borderlands was a region where métissage flourished throughout the eighteenth and early nineteenth centuries. These métis communities represented a classificatory challenge in terms of language. Bilingualism, for instance, was a common occurrence. Thus, when Beutler's men reached the Keiskamma River in June 1752, they met "three Hottentots" who spoke their own Khoesan language but also "understood the Caffer [Nguni] language."[188] Similarly, near the Great Fish River twenty-seven years later, the Scottish naturalist William Paterson hired as his interpreter a "Hottentot" man who spoke Khoesan but was also "perfectly acquainted with the language of the Caffres [i.e., Nguni]."[189] Finally, while traveling along the Bushmans River in January 1778, Gordon visited the Gqunukhwebe chief Tshaka, who in addition to "Caffre [Nguni]" also "spoke Hottentot [Khoesan]."[190]

What complicated the situation even further was that these métis communities were not only bilingual but also appear to have mixed their languages in ways modern linguist would most likely describe as code mixing. For instance, when the Swedish naturalist Anders Sparrman met a group of Gonaqua near the Van Stadens River in 1775, he noticed that "their language had an affinity with that of both of these nations," which suggests that they mixed Khoesan and Nguni speech forms in ways that made it difficult to discern whether they spoke one or the other language.[191] The Frenchman François Le Vaillant met some Gonaqua near the Great Fish River in the 1780s and relayed that "though their language is very similar, my people [Khoesan speakers] could not always understand them."[192] He suggested that the difficulties of communication arose from the fact that these "Gonaquais . . . clucked with their tongues like the other Hottentots" but employed some words "used among the Caffres, but not among those properly called Hottentots."[193] Thus at least some members of the borderlands' métis communities came to speak a mixed language that is best described as Khoesan-Nguni or Nguni-Khoesan, depending on which of the two languages was dominant.[194]

When European stock farmers with their slaves and servants arrived in the eastern Cape borderlands, these métis communities also added Dutch to their preexisting language skills. The German naturalist Heinrich Lichtenstein made contact with three "bastards of the Gonaaquas and Caffres," two of whom "spoke broken Dutch."[195] They assimilated more elements of the Dutch language over time, in line with the growing political and economic importance of Dutch-speaking European missionaries and stock farmers and their servants and slaves, who tended to be conversant in pidgin Dutch or spoke a mixture of Khoesan and Dutch.[196] At the LMS mission station of Bethelsdorp, for instance, the missionaries' Dutch language and the Gonaqua members' mixed language coexisted into the 1810s.[197]

The fact that these métis communities practiced bilingualism and language mixing indicates that they did not demand that their members speak one specific language only and purely. This conclusion is suggested by modern language studies that demonstrate that people who live in social settings where two languages coexist tend to become bilingual as long as there exist no strong social pressures that compel them to speak just one language.[198] Moreover, these studies show that in contact situations between speakers of different languages, "language mixing may occur" as long as "the speakers of the languages involved do not have an emotional investment in keeping their home language free of influence from other languages."[199] Consequently, the apparent laissez-faire attitude toward bilingualism and language mixing of the eastern Cape borderland's métis communities suggests that they did not mobilize language as part of their discourses of belonging. Most likely, they had a long-standing distrust of language as a useful marker of belonging, because they had to forge meaningful polities out of people who tended to speak two radically different languages—Khoesan and Nguni.

Precisely because they did not use language as a marker of belonging, the members of these métis communities were not culturally conditioned to perceive as significant the relatively small differences between the coastal belt's various (Nguni) speech forms even if they recognized them otherwise.[200] Recall when Dutch administrator Ludwig Alberti and his Gonaqua interpreter met several emissaries from "the vicinity of Rio de la Goa" at the residence of Chief Ngqika of the Rharhabe-Xhosa (see chapter 2).[201] These emissaries were of Tsonga, Swati, or Zulu background, which meant that the differences between their speaking practices and those of their Xhosa hosts were surely noticeable. And yet, according to Alberti, his Gonaqua interpreter categorically rejected the notion that the visitor spoke a different language when he explained that "the language of these visitors was the same as that spoken by the Kaffirs [Xhosa] . . . , only that . . . the former did not speak it well."[202] As the statement "the former did not speak it well" suggests, the interpreter recognized the differences between the two forms of speech. However, being a Gonaqua and therefore not culturally conditioned to perceive these differences as significant, he identified both forms of speech as belonging to the same language.

The Gonaqua, Gqunukhwebe, and Ntinde interpreters who worked for European missionaries in the first half of the nineteenth century had the same attitude toward language. When they accompanied their missionary

FIGURE 1. Detail, "Cafrerie," ca. 1850. Victor-Adolphe Malte-Brun, *Carte itinéraire des explorations faites de 1849 à 1856, 7 ans l'Afrique australe, par le Rd David Livingstone* (Paris: Imp. de Bineteau, 1857). (gallica.bnf.fr/Bibliothèque nationale de France)

patrons—James Laing, William Shaw, John Appleyard, and others—on their journeys through the coastal region and encountered the speaking practices of the Xhosa, Thembu, Mpondo, Mfengu, Natal African, and Zulu polities and communities, they recognized the differences between these speaking practices but did not perceive them as delineating distinct languages. And when and where they communicated this assessment to their missionary patrons, they helped strengthen the latter's conviction that a single "Caffre" language extended from the Cape Colony to Delagoa Bay and that it was possible to create for this single "Caffre" language a single translation of the Bible that would form the basis of a single written language (see figure 1).

Wesleyan Linguistic Harmonizing Efforts

In fact, the Wesleyan missionaries began to work on such a project as early as 1850, designed to transcend the differences between the speaking practices of the Xhosa, Thembu, Mpondo, Mfengu, Natal Africans, and Zulu. They were keenly aware of the historical precedents for this type of linguistic harmonization, notably in the case of England, where the translation of the Bible had created a written language that unified a wide range of spoken dialects. "[The] plain people in the rural districts of the north and west of England," the Wesleyan missionary William Shaw explained in defense of the project, "although speaking dialects that differ from the written English very materially, yet read with an understanding the English version of the Scriptures."[203] Moreover, philological studies in general and those of Wesleyan missionary John Appleyard in particular testified to the historical changeability of the "Caffre" language. On the broadest level, he saw this changeability evinced by the language's alleged evolution from a Semitic tongue to its present condition, a process that, in his opinion, had been accompanied by the addition of its most distinctive feature—the euphonic concord.[204] On a narrower level, Appleyard saw proof of its changeability in the language's prefix contracting from *umu* to *um* as the people had migrated westward.[205] From the perspective of the Wesleyan missionaries, this evidence strongly suggested that the "Caffre" language could be made to bend to their will and that any different speaking practices could be harmonized into a single unifying written language.

They gained additional confidence for this harmonization project from the experience of the Mfengu, a people who, the missionaries believed, had come to the eastern Cape as refugees. While the missionaries had always insisted that, as shown above, the differences between the speaking practices of the Xhosa and Mfengu were insubstantial, by the late 1840s, they saw evidence that even these minor differences were beginning to disappear as the latter assimilated the speaking practices of the former. As Appleyard explained in 1849, the Mfengu "lost many of their peculiarities in consequence of that people's close and familiar intercourse with the Kafirs [Xhosa]."[206] The missionaries themselves contributed to this process by drawing no distinction between these two groups in the context of their proselytizing work. On the Wesleyan mission at Farmerfield in 1840, for instance, Xhosa and Mfengu were grouped together into one area, while Europeans, freed slaves, and Tswana- and Sotho-speaking people each inhabited distinct areas of their own.[207] More importantly, in the mission schools, both Xhosa and Mfengu pupils learned to read the same "Caffre" language with the help of the same didactic materials.[208] In 1840, Tente, the Ngqika-Xhosa schoolmaster of the SPMS's outstation school at the Lenye River, had his Xhosa and Mfengu pupils read from the same "Caffre" translation of the gospel of Mark.[209] Indeed, one of the best "Caffre" readers at Tente's school was a Mfengu boy.[210] The other mission societies operated in the same manner. "The Amafengu," the Wesleyan missionary Appleyard explained in 1849, "use . . . Kafir publications, thus rendering it probable that any peculiarities which their dialects still retain, will soon disappear."[211]

The result of this process was most advanced among the younger generation. The Scottish missionary Bryce Ross, who possessed native-speaker proficiency in the language and interacted with Mfengu communities in and around Lovedale Institution, observed this trend. "Nearly all the young Fingoes on the frontier speak the Amaxosa dialect," he explained in 1856. "The Fingo dialect will, in all probability, die out of this part of the country, together with the generation that brought it hither."[212] His colleague Laing agreed. "It is but fair to state that these Fingoes have been many years among the Kafirs," he noted in 1854, "and have become accustomed to their mode of speaking."[213]

Although Mfengu speech forms persisted well beyond the mid-nineteenth century, the Mfengu example, especially when viewed in conjunction with missionary conclusions about the language history of Europe and the historical changeability of the "Caffre" language, suggested that it was possible to harmonize the speaking practices of the various populations in the coastal belt into a single unifying written language.[214] It was the hope of the Wesleyan missionaries that this could be achieved with the help of publications that avoided terms and idiomatic expressions that were unique to individual speech communities and substituted them with terms and expressions common to and understood by all of them. The Wesleyan missionary Horatio Pearse explained this modus operandi in 1853: "We have no portion of the Sacred Scriptures printed solely in the Zulu dialect of the Kaffir language. We have hitherto used the translations issuing from the mission press in British Kaffraria. . . . It is proper to observe, that in those translations we have kept in view the dialectical differences of the different tribes from the frontier of the old colony to this [Natal] district, *so as to render them intelligible to all*, instead of confining their use to the Amaxosa tribes."[215] Indeed, as Pearse added, the Wesleyan mission had already established a committee whose purpose was to identify universally intelligible words, "with a view to assimilate, as far as practicable, the two [Xhosa and Zulu] dialects for the contemplated revised translation of the entire Word of God."[216] Appleyard, in his capacity as translator, editor, and superintendent of the Wesleyan mission press at Mount Coke, produced some of these new translations and supplied them "to [all] stations, including those beyond the Kei River and at Natal."[217]

The titles of these updated translations indicate that they were no longer intended only for the Xhosa, Thembu, and Mfengu but also for the people of "Emboland"—a term the missionaries used to refer to the region inhabited by Mpondo, Natal African, and Zulu communities. Thus, in 1851, the Wesleyan mission replaced the 1835 translation *Le yincwadi yamaculo okuvunywa gamaxosa eziskolweni zaba-Wesley* (This book of hymns which are to be sung by the Xhosa in the Wesleyan schools) with the *Inncwadi yamaculo okuvunywa ezikolweni zaba Kristu ezisemaxoseni nezisembo* (Book of hymns, which are to be sung in the Christian schools among the Xhosa and in Emboland).[218] In 1854, they also replaced the 1838 translation *Incwadi yezifundo ibalelwe izikolo zaba-Wesli. Emaxoseni* (Book of lessons for Wesleyan schools. Among the Xhosa) with the new version, titled *Inncwadi yezifundo: ibalelwe izikolo ezisema-Xoseni neziseMbo* (Book of lessons for schools among the Xhosa and in Emboland).[219] In the same year, the Wesleyans likewise substituted the 1832 translation *Incwadi yokubuza yezi ziskola, zama-Khristi Ekutiwa gama-Wesli, ema-Xosene* (Book of questioning for Wesleyan Christian schools among the Xhosa) with a new Catechism entitled *Eyokuqala inncwadi yemibuzo, ebuzwayo ezikolweni esisemaxoseni nezisembo* (First book of questions for schools among the Xhosa and in Emboland).[220]

The revised translations and titles were inspired by the missionaries' belief that the "Caffre" language extended from the eastern Cape to Delagoa Bay. This belief was the product of a complex convergence of ideas. The writings of eighteenth-century naturalists such as Barrow and Lichtenstein about the "Caffre" race and language encouraged the missionaries early on to adopt not only the term "Caffre" for the target language of their translation activities but also a broad conception of the geographical reach of this language. The missionaries' subsequent interactions with people who moved throughout the coastal belt reinforced this broad conception of the "Caffre" language because these migrants seemingly used their skills in the speaking practices from one end of the coastal belt to communicate with the inhabitants of the other end. This belief in a "Caffre" language continuum became a firm conviction when the missionaries explored the coastal belt in the company of African (Gonaqua, Gqunukhwebe, and Ntinde) interpreters on whose language skills they depended and who downplayed the differences between the region's speech forms because of their own habit of disregarding language as a marker of belonging. Consequently, preexisting African ideas about language played a crucial role in shaping the missionaries' understanding of the "Caffre" language and, by the early 1850s, the belief that this language included the speaking practices of the Zulu kingdom *and* Xhosa chiefdoms.

5

"The Natives. In What Respects, If Any, Do They Differ from the Southern Caffres?"

American Missionaries and the Zulu Question

I n 1853, the British Foreign Bible Society (BFBS) sent out a "circular" designed to take stock of "the progress which had already been made in translating, printing, and circulating the Word of God in the different Native Languages or Dialects of South Africa."[1] In his response, the Wesleyan missionary William Shaw proposed that the European and American missionary societies in the coastal belt join forces to advance the publication of a complete translation of the Bible. As Shaw explained, "I have formed the opinion that it is not needful to have two versions of the Kafir Scriptures, one for this part of the country [the eastern Cape region], and the other for Natal; although there is much difference in *dialect*, there is no essential difference in the *language*. A careful examination of the *verbiage*, which should be accommodated to suit both districts, would in my view meet all the wants of the case."[2] Shaw's proposal was squarely in line with the Wesleyan missionaries' harmonizing translation activities in the early 1850s, notably those carried out by John Appleyard at Mount Coke. These translations were not intended to impose one dialect on the speakers of another dialect. Instead, they were designed to bring the speakers of different dialects together. This was achieved by avoiding words and idiomatic expressions that were unique to one or the other dialect and replacing them with verbiage understood by speakers of both dialects.

More importantly, Shaw's statement that "there is no essential difference in the language" reflected the long-held view about the geographical reach of the "Caffre" language in the coastal belt. For this reason, his proposal received support from other European missionaries and persons close to them. The Scottish missionary James Laing, for instance, explained to the

BFBS in August 1854: "As to the Zulu and Kafir languages . . . I am of the opinion that one Bible would suffice for Natal and Kaffraria."[3] Charles Brownlee, the son of LMS missionary John Brownlee, also commented favorably on Shaw's proposal. When asked by the BFBS if a single Bible translation would suffice for all the coastal belt's indigenous communities, he answered in the affirmative: "The publication of an edition of the Bible, suited to Zulus as well as Kafirs—may, I think, be accomplished, though many words in the two languages are different. The languages are, however, essentially the same."[4] Finally, there was Theophilus Shepstone, who was the son of a Wesleyan missionary and who by the 1850s worked for the Natal government and sat on its Commission for the Compilation of the Zulu Grammar & Dictionary. In his response to the BFBS, he also commented favorably on Shaw's plan: "I believe that the degree of affinity between the Zulu and Kafir is such as to render it quite possible to persons *intimately acquainted with both* to frame such a translation of the Scriptures as would be perfectly understood by both, without even the dialectical modification."[5]

Rather surprisingly, the WMS's John Appleyard became one of the first detractors of Shaw's proposal. Writing to the BFBS from Mount Coke in 1854, he argued: "I do not think that one version of the Scriptures would be sufficient to meet the case of all the Kafir and Zulu speaking tribes. . . . The opinion which I at present hold on the subject of this query, is, that there should be two separate versions prepared and printed in the first instance."[6] Appleyard's reply to the BFBS's query is surprising because he was actively involved in producing the WMS's harmonized translations, and his own philological scholarship acknowledged the historical changeability of the "Caffre" language in general and the recent linguistic assimilation of the Xhosa and Mfengu in particular (see chapter 4). The wording "in the first instance" is particularly noteworthy because it suggests that he did not reject Shaw's plan categorically. The best explanation for Appleyard's attitude is that, in 1854, he was already working on his "Caffre" translation of the first complete edition of the Old Testament, a project that would surely have been derailed by the adoption of Shaw's plan and the arduous committee work that this plan would have inevitably entailed.[7]

In any event, Appleyard's example highlights that missionary linguists could be very flexible in their engagement with African languages and quick to sacrifice alleged philological "truths" to more pragmatic considerations, changing their discourses accordingly. The members of the American

Board of Commissioners for Foreign Missions in Natal-Zululand (ABM) experienced a similar volte-face between 1835 and 1854.

The ABM missionaries discussed Shaw's proposal in June 1854. Following short deliberations, they rejected it, citing a series of linguistic arguments as the basis for their decision.[8] These arguments must be treated with caution, however, because nonlinguistic factors played a crucial role in this rejection. After all, between 1835 and 1850, members of the ABM had promoted their own plans for producing a single literary language for the indigenous populations in the region between the eastern Cape and Delagoa Bay. As I argue in this chapter, the American Board missionaries self-identified as a "Mission to the Zulus"; they therefore searched for ways to differentiate "Zuluness" from "Caffreness" from the beginning of their activities in the South African mission field. Initially, they particularized "Zuluness" on the basis of cultural markers (such as "honesty" and "chastity") rather than language; as long as this sentiment prevailed, they willingly supported plans of harmonizing the coastal belt's speaking practices into a single literary language.

Several factors changed this attitude toward language drastically over time. First, when the American Board missionaries began to work exclusively among "Zulu" refugees in Natal during the 1840s, they became less and less convinced that the "Zulus" were culturally distinct from the "Caffres." While searching for new ways to particularize "Zuluness," the members of the ABM expanded their "Zulu" translations and publications in response to an influx of monetary support from the American Bible Society and the Natal government. There is no evidence to suggest that the Natal government's financial contribution to the ABM's language work was part of a grand strategy to prevent a unified "Caffre" language. After all, as noted above, Theophilus Shepstone, a powerful figure in the Natal administration, responded quite positively to Shaw's plan as late as May 1854. Indirectly, however, the money did play a role because the funds together with those of the American Bible Society allowed the American Board missionaries to increase their material investment in and emotional attachment to the "Zulu" language.

Exactly this investment and attachment came under threat by the late 1840s from Wesleyan missionaries who arrived in Natal not only in large numbers but also accompanied by so-called Caffre-speaking intermediaries, equipped with Appleyard's harmonized "Caffre" language materials. I argue that rejecting Shaw's plan in 1854 based on the argument that the "Zulu" language was distinct from "Caffre" promised to address all three issues: it curbed the Wesleyan threat to the ABM's operations in Natal-Zululand; it protected the ABM's investment in "Zulu" translations and publications; and perhaps most importantly, it redefined "Zuluness" on the basis of language, and, in so doing, reaffirmed the ABM's identity as a "Mission to the Zulus."

The ABM in South Africa: A Mission to the Zulus

As part of North America's Second Great Awakening, Christian preachers and theologians organized revival meetings across the United States of America between the 1790s and 1830s. At these meetings, they exhorted listeners to secure their salvation by converting the heathens of the world.[9] Accordingly, in 1810, American Presbyterians and Congregationalists established the ABM, which organized multiple missionary operations over the next two decades, including in India (1813), the Hawaiian Islands (1819), and China (1829).[10] By the early 1830s, the ABM was ready to carry its missionary zeal to the African continent.[11] They sent a mission to West Africa in 1834 and a mission to South Africa in 1835.[12]

As the product of two decades of revivalism, the ABM and its missionaries faced the future with an "unabashed millennial optimism."[13] This optimism, paired with an emerging sense of American nationalism, led them to believe that Americans were "providentially favored to carry the gospel overseas."[14] This self-confident attitude, in turn, encouraged American Board missionaries to take literally the Bible text of Matthew 28:19—"Go you therefore, and teach all nations, baptizing them in the name of the Father, and of the Son, and of the Holy Ghost"—and focus on the conversion of nations in toto rather than individuals. As the ABM declared as early as 1810, "The Lord is shaking the nations; his friends in different parts of Christendom are roused from their slumbers; and unprecedented exertions are making for the spread of divine knowledge, and the conversion of the nations."[15] Early successes with the nation-based approach to missionizing, notably "in Hawaii in 1822 where the conversion of the aristocracy had led to the baptisms by the thousands," seemingly confirmed the idea that whole nations could be converted en masse.[16] Archibald Alexander, a professor in the Theological Seminary at Princeton, reinforced this idea in 1829 when he asked American Board missionaries to "contemplate the strange spectacle of whole nations casting away their idols, and princes and people, the aged and the young, sitting down at the feet of the missionaries, to be instructed in the things which relate to their salvation."[17] But which specific "nation" should the American Board missionaries target for conversion in South Africa? A letter from Dr. John Philip of the London Missionary Society in South Africa held the answer; he recommended that the American Board missionaries be sent to "the people called Zoolahs [Zulus]."[18]

Accepting their divine commission, the ABM began to identify its mission project in South Africa closely and exclusively with the Zulus. "I confess I have a strong impression that the Lord will smile upon your career," the secretary of the ABM declared to the missionaries who had recently departed for the South African mission field. "The Zoolahs [Zulus] are given to Christ, & we are commanded to preach His gospel to them."[19] Thus, whereas the European missionaries who worked in the eastern Cape region in the first half of the nineteenth century tied their mission project to the broadly defined "Caffres," the American Board missionaries who came to South Africa in 1835 tied their identity to the "Zulus" only.

The first members of the ABM mission to South Africa arrived in Cape Town in the early months of 1835. Under the impression that the Zulus were divided "in two separate independent communities," the missionaries split up their operations accordingly.[20] The first group consisted of southern Presbyterians and included Reverends Daniel Lindley, Henry I. Venable, and Alexander E. Wilson, MD, three graduates of the Union Theological Seminary in Virginia. They were destined for work among the "Interior Zulus" of King Mzilikazi who, in the early 1820s, had led his followers from Natal-Zululand onto the highveld, where they established their own conquest state by defeating and incorporating local populations. Traveling via the LMS station at Griquatown, the missionaries reached their destination in February 1836 and soon afterward received permission to establish a mission station in Mzilikazi's highveld domain.[21]

The second group of missionaries intended to work among the "Maritime Zulus" of King Dingane, who had participated in the assassination of Shaka kaSenzangakhona and succeeded him as the new ruler of the Zulu kingdom in 1828. This group of missionaries consisted of Congregationalists and included Reverends Aldin Grout and George Champion, two graduates of Andover Theological Seminary, and Newton Adams, MD, a trained medical professional. To gather more information on Dingane's people and hire interpreters, Adams and Aldin Grout moved on to Grahamstown in May and September 1835.[22] With the overland route to Port Natal blocked by the Sixth Cape Frontier War, however, Grout, Adams, and Champion proceeded to Port Natal by sea, arriving there in December 1835. At Port Natal, the three missionaries encountered a community of some thirty English traders, who informed them that Allen Gardiner, formerly a captain in the Royal Navy, had already received permission to establish a mission station in Dingane's Zulu kingdom for the Church Missionary Society.[23]

Gardiner's departure for England in early 1836, however, provided the American Board missionaries with an opportunity to approach Dingane separately and secure his tentative support for their own evangelistic work in the region.[24] With the king's approval, the missionaries established one mission station, Umlazi, near Port Natal and a second one, Nginani, about ten miles north of the Thukela River, in the same year.[25] Thus, by 1836 the two groups of American Board missionaries had successfully established stations among the "Zulus," successes that helped reinforce their self-conception as a mission to the "Zulus," even if they had to organize into separate "Interior" and "Maritime" parties.[26]

Yet the ABM's position in South Africa began to deteriorate shortly after this promising start, most notably on account of the arrival of Afrikaners, who, displeased with British policies, had begun to migrate out of the Cape Colony at the beginning of 1836. By August of that year, one Afrikaner group reached the vicinity of Mzilikazi, the inhabitants of which attacked them successfully on two separate occasions. The survivors of these attacks retreated to Thaba Nchu, where they organized a punitive commando that successfully dispersed King Mzilikazi's followers on 16 January 1837. In so doing, the Afrikaners deprived the American Board missionaries of their mission field in the highveld. Disillusioned, Lindley, Venable, and Wilson descended the Great Escarpment to join their fellow missionaries in Natal-Zululand.[27]

The withdrawal from the highveld did not rid the now reunited American Board missionaries of the problem posed by the Afrikaners, for another party of them reached Port Natal on 19 October 1837. Under the command of Piet Retief, this group tried to negotiate access to land with King Dingane. The Zulu king's regiments, however, attacked and killed Retief and many of his followers on 6 and 17 February 1838. Here, too, Afrikaner survivors responded by organizing a punitive commando, which attacked the Zulu kingdom in April 1838 but suffered a decisive defeat at the hands of Dingane's regiments. Fearful of a major Zulu offensive against Port Natal itself, the American Board missionaries withdrew temporarily from the mission field, with Grout, Venable, Wilson, and Champion returning to the United States and Lindley and Adams finding refuge in the Cape Colony.[28]

However, these reverses did not diminish the American Board mission-aries' self-conception as a mission to the Zulus because these setbacks con-vinced them that there was no alternative target population for them in South Africa.[29] The ABM director expressed this idea clearly in 1838 when he reminded his "Brethren of the S. African Mission" that their "business" was primarily with "the Zulus."[30] Moreover, the ABM's position in Natal-Zululand began to improve soon afterward. First, Dingane suffered a defeat at the hands of another Afrikaner commando in the Battle of Blood River (Ncome) in December 1838. This allowed the Afrikaners to establish the "Republic of Natalia" between the Thukela and Mzimkhulu Rivers and opened the way for the American Board missionaries' return to the region. Second, the outbreak of a Zulu civil war (1839), in which Dingane was displaced by his brother Mpande, made it possible for missionary Aldin Grout to establish Nkanyezi Station in the Zulu kingdom (1841).[31] For all intents and purposes, the ABM's focus on the mission to the Zulus had paid off by 1841.

The political situation in the region remained extremely volatile, how-ever. King Mpande, for instance, withdrew his support for Nkanyezi Sta-tion in 1842, forcing Aldin Grout to remove himself with his followers to Natal.[32] The silver lining was that Mpande's rule also pushed many of his own subjects across the Thukela River into Natal. As a result of this forced migration of so-called Zulus, the American Board missionaries began to believe "that the facilities for prosecuting missionary operations [among the Zulus] will be greater here [in Natal] than there [in the Zulu kingdom]."[33] Not surprisingly, when writing to his family in the United States in 1844, Aldin Grout emphasized that they were now working among "the Zulus of Natal."[34] Thus, although King Mpande had compelled the American Board missionaries to abandon the Zulu kingdom, they remained confident in their identity as missionaries to the Zulus.

This self-identification received another boost in 1846 when the British government, which had formally annexed Natal two years earlier, asked the ABM to help with the implementation of a Location system.[35] To better man-age the relations between Natal's growing European and African populations, British officials moved Africans in Natal, except those who were "aboriginals" of the region, onto specially demarcated and administered areas called "Loca-tions."[36] Furthermore, they asked missionaries to establish mission stations in these racially segregated living areas to help manage, Christianize, and "civilize" Natal's African population. Natal's diplomatic agent to the native tribes, Theophilus Shepstone, established the first Location—Zwartskop—in the vicinity of Pietermaritzburg in November 1846. He created six additional ones—Umlazi, Umvoti, Inanda, Umzinyati, Impafana, and Tugela—shortly afterward.[37] Although these Locations consisted of the poorest farmland, became overcrowded and impoverished over time, and were always subject to criticism from land- and labor-hungry European settlers and their allies in the colonial administration, they did give the American Board missionaries better access to the region's Zulu population.

A second generation of American Board missionaries traveled to South Africa to take advantage of this situation. Reverends Lewis Grout, James C. Bryant, William Ireland, Hyman Wilder, Seth Stone, and others arrived in Natal between 1847 and 1851. Jakob L. Döhne joined their ranks in 1850, following a decade of service in the eastern Cape region for the Berlin Missionary Society and nearly three years of work in Natal on behalf of the Dutch Reformed Church. With the help of these reinforcements, the ABM maintained some twelve mission stations in Natal by 1854, notably Umvoti (Aldin Grout), Amanzimtoti (Adams), Inanda (Lindley), Umsunduzi (Lewis Grout), Ifumi (Bryant), Table Mountain (Döhne), and Umtwalume (Wilder).[38]

All these developments ensured that the American Board missionaries identified themselves evermore confidently as a "Mission to the Zulus" even though they did not maintain a single mission station in the Zulu kingdom.[39] In 1851, the general meeting of the members of the ABM in South Africa agreed to formally adopt "Mission to the Zulus" as their official name.[40] Although the name morphed into "Zulu Mission" and "American Zulu Mission" between 1851 and 1855, it demonstrates the extent to which the American Board missionaries tied their sense of purpose in South Africa to the Zulus at this time.[41] As I will argue below, this self-conception also contributed in important ways to the ABM's rejection of Shaw's plan in 1854.

The Rejection of Shaw's Proposal

The American Board missionaries discussed Shaw's proposal at their general meeting at Amanzimtoti (Umlazi) Station in June 1854. The minutes of this meeting show that the missionaries rejected the proposal as "impracticable" and tasked Lewis Grout, Jakob Döhne, and Seth Stone to communicate this decision to the South African Bible Society.[42] In subsequent letters sent to the BFBS, the three missionaries emphasized linguistic reasons as the basis for this rejection. They claimed, for example, that the Africans among whom they worked in Natal-Zululand were unfamiliar with words and idioms, such as *iqinqa* for "counsel" and *umkumkani* for "king," used by Africans in the eastern Cape region.[43] They alleged that these lexical and idiomatic differences rendered reading materials in the "Caffre" language of the eastern Cape useless in Natal-Zululand. "The difference between the Zulu and the Kafir," one letter explained, "shows itself to us in the fact that neither our people, nor we, as Missionaries, have ever been able to use books, prepared in the Kafir language, to any advantage, though the attempt was not unfrequently made before our Mission had a tolerable supply of books in the Zulu."[44]

Differences in orthography were cited as another problem.[45] At the time, the American Board missionaries preferred the "disjointing system," whereas the missionaries in the eastern Cape region used the "uniting system."[46] In the disjointing system, the simple expression "We love" had to be written as *si ya thanda*, whereas the uniting system expressed it as *siyathanda*. Proponents of the former system claimed that *si* represented, as in English, the independent personal pronoun "we" and *thanda* the verb "love" and, thus, separate ideas that needed to be expressed with distinct words.[47]

European missionaries disagreed based on the argument that "there is not the slightest affinity in the *formal* construction" between the European languages and the "Caffre" language.[48] John Appleyard, for instance, explained that, rather than understanding *si* and *thanda* as separate ideas, the former represented the verbal prefix of the verb-root *thanda*. In his view, this understanding of the language was more correct because *si* could never be used on its own but had to be attached to a verb root.[49] Yet the American Board missionaries were unwilling to compromise on this issue. As Lewis Grout stated,

> For myself—so fully persuaded am I of the great practical utility and philosophic propriety of writing the pronouns and auxiliaries separate from the principal verbs in Zulu—or as some would say, "Separating verbal prefixes from their roots,"—that I should be very sorry to see our Mission adopt any system very essentially different, on that point, from that which we now follow. And if *all* the Missionaries in Kaffirland [the eastern Cape region], and elsewhere, be *unanimous* in the opinion that the pronouns and auxiliaries must be *joined* to the principal verb, I should not expect a conference on this subject would result in uniformity on *that* point.[50]

The members of the ABM in South Africa rejected Shaw's proposal on the basis of these linguistic arguments in 1854. This rejection, in turn, meant that European missionary societies and the American Board missionaries would pursue separate Bible translation projects and develop separate standardized literary languages—Zulu and "Caffre" (later referred to as Xhosa)—for the coastal belt of South Africa.

However, it is important to underscore here that these two languages did not grow naturally out of the linguistic differences between the eastern Cape and Natal-Zululand regions. Indeed, the American Board missionaries' arguments about these differences were questionable. It is obvious, for instance, that their focus on orthographic differences, notably those created by the use of the disjointing system in Natal-Zululand and uniting system in the eastern Cape, represented a man-made obstacle that had little to do with people's actual speaking practices and their mutual intelligibility. The claim that idiomatic differences prevented effective communication between the speakers of the two regions must also be questioned. Only a couple of years earlier, the American Board missionaries had assessed these idiomatic peculiarities very differently. "So similar are the dialects," American Board missionary James Bryant explained in 1849, "that the Zulus find but little difficulty in understanding the Kafirs."[51]

At this time, moreover, they still acknowledged that the language situation in the coastal belt region defied easy categorization. In 1851, American missionary Hyman Wilder admitted that in southern Natal, Wesleyan publications were generally "better understood than those printed by us."[52] The reason for this was that speech patterns throughout the coastal belt varied incrementally rather than absolutely. The American Board missionary Seth Stone drew attention to this when he explained that near the Mzimkhulu River (which represented Natal's southern border with the eastern Cape region at this time), "people all speak a dialect or dialects something near the Zulu, or between the Zulu and the Amaxosa dialects."[53] Moreover, people were moving from one region to another region, which rendered the linguistic situation in any one place highly complex. "There are those at Ifafa," Stone added, "who have lived in the Zulu country, and others who have lived with or near the Amaxosa, and Amaponda, and other places remote."[54] In response to this complexity, the American Board missionaries initially promoted their own plans for harmonizing the coastal belt's various speaking practices into a single literary language. At the time, Bryant argued that this was possible because "these different dialects comprise in the aggregate a much more perfect language than that now in use by any one tribe."[55]

Yet, as we have seen, when William Shaw proposed the creation of one standard version of the scriptures and a single literary language, the American Board missionaries denied this complexity and their own previous efforts to deal with it. They tersely replied: "Our people [in Natal] do not well understand services, conducted in the Kafir dialect."[56] The contradictions in these assertions are striking, and they suggest that the rejection of Shaw's proposal was tied only superficially to linguistic arguments. This is all the more likely because not all of the American Board missionaries agreed with the decision to reject Shaw's proposal. The aforementioned Wilder, for instance, explained in 1856 that publishing one edition of the Bible in the "Caffre" language "as will make it accessible to all the Kafir tribes" was "a very desirable object and I think it can to a great extent be accomplished if all the missionaries, throwing away all ambition and personal views will cordially cooperate with the plans of the Society."[57] The last sentence in his letter strongly indicates that some of Wilder's colleagues rejected Shaw's proposal for personal rather than linguistic reasons. One of these personal reasons had to do with the American Board missionaries' assumed identity as a "Mission to the Zulus."

The Zulu Question

The self-conception as a "Mission to the Zulus" encouraged the American Board missionaries to particularize "Zuluness" from the very beginning of their activities in South Africa. Thus, whereas European missionaries in the eastern Cape region looked for traits that the various "Caffre" communities—including the "Zulus"—had in common, the American Board missionaries searched for traits which set "Zuluness" apart from "Caffreness." This attitude was perceptible as early as 1835 when the ABM's George Champion asked a trader at Port Natal: "The natives. In what respects, if any, do they *differ* from the Southern Caffres?"[58]

The American Board missionaries soon learned that it was rather difficult to particularize "Zuluness" in any meaningful way. The instructions they had received shortly before their embarkation for South Africa did not help because they suggested that the Zulus were both territorially and politically fragmented: "The Zoolahs. . . . Not many years since they became divided into two separate independent communities . . . Dingaan, the ruler of the maritime nation, resides *somewhat* more than a hundred miles from Port Natal; and Masalikatsi, the head of the interior nation, *may possibly* be not far distant from Latakoo."[59] The withdrawal from the highveld and Mzilikazi's people in 1837 opened the path for a tighter territorial and political demarcation of "Zuluness." For instance, the American Board missionaries began to see the Thukela River as a crucial boundary of "Zuluness" in this period.[60] This marker, however, became useless once refugees escaped into Natal from the civil wars that began to ravage the Zulu kingdom after 1839.[61] Indeed, soon after the outbreak of the first of these civil conflicts, Mpande led his followers into Natal, an act that became known as the "breaking of the rope" (*ukugqabuk' igoda*) precisely because it split the Zulu kingdom, which was said to be figuratively united from generation to generation by an imaginary grass rope (*igoda*), into two opposing camps.[62] The polity remained fragmented after Mpande's victory in 1840, because a large section of his followers stayed in Natal where they lived independent of his rule.[63] Moreover, additional numbers of Zulu subjects relocated to Natal, fleeing from Mpande's rule throughout the 1840s, prompting the American Board missionaries to envision the complete disintegration of the Zulu state.[64]

While they struggled to define "Zuluness" in territorial and political terms, the American Board missionaries believed, at least initially, that a cultural boundary circumscribed this identity. The focus on culture had a long tradition in the region, as the rulers of the Zulu state had themselves used cultural practices to demarcate belonging to their realm.[65] One such practice was that the kingdom's male and female age-set regiments (*amabutho*) were not allowed to marry until they received the king's permission to do so (a permission that was usually granted to men in their thirties and women in their twenties).[66] At the same time, certain sections of society were prohibited from engaging in courtship (*ukuqomisa* or *ukuqoma*) and premarital sex in the form of external intercourse (*ukuhlobonga* or *ukusoma*).[67] Although they were not the only regional power that organized semipermanent regiments (*amabutho*) and expansionary military campaigns, the fact that the kingdom's armies had defeated most of their regional rivals encouraged many of its members to think of their (warrior) culture not only as different but also as superior to those of other peoples.[68] King Shaka, for example, had explained to several European traders in 1826 that for his followers, "it would be no difficult matter" for his regiments "to conquer" European troops armed with guns.[69] Some nine years later, while watching a performance by some of his female *amabutho*,

Shaka's successor, King Dingane, asked Captain Allen Gardiner rhetorically: "What black nations can vie with us?"[70] Both statements indicate a sense of cultural difference and superiority that some members of the Zulu state felt vis-à-vis their neighbors.

Some European commentators reworked these preexisting ideas of cultural difference and superiority as part of their attempts at particularizing "Zuluness." Given their own fascination with war and conquest, they commented frequently on the allegedly superior military skills of the Zulus.[71] After having observed a Zulu army in action, the Natal trader Henry Francis Fynn, who resided in the region between 1824 and 1834, noted, "The frontier Kaffir tribes . . . could be in no way compared to the *superior* standing of the Zulu nation."[72] Two French missionaries agreed, adding: "These Zulus are a fine race of blacks, *superior* in stature, in elegance of shape, and in muscular strength, to the Bechuanas."[73] Europeans were even more fascinated with those aspects of "Zulu" culture that seemingly matched their own Protestant-bourgeois value system. Accordingly, in 1836, one of the European traders at Port Natal singled out the Zulus by emphasizing "the freedom from theft" that allegedly existed among them, which, given the widespread rhetoric about the thievishness of the "Caffres" of the eastern Cape region, made them appear extraordinary indeed.[74] They also singled out the Zulus for their allegedly harsher laws regarding marriage and sexuality. While residing at Dingane's capital, "Umgungundhlovu," in 1837, missionary Owen observed with a mixture of trepidation and admiration that "two persons were put to death . . . for the crime of Adultery."[75]

Shortly after their arrival in South Africa, the American Board missionaries made similar arguments about the cultural difference and superiority of the Zulus. Regarding military culture, they remarked in 1842 that this culture, in combination with Shaka's superior generalship, had "made the Zulu nation the largest and most powerful in all South Africa."[76] They were even more outspoken about issues of crime and sexuality. Writing from Port Natal in 1836, Aldin Grout explained that, while the "Caffres" of the eastern Cape region were "often detected . . . in *stealing and deceiving*, . . . the Zoolahs have two most remarkable traits of character for a heathen community, *honesty and chastity*."[77] Five years later, they continued to single out the Zulus for their allegedly superior sexual restraint. "What a mother of harlots and all uncleanness is licentiousness, in every heathen nation upon the globe," missionary Aldin Grout remarked in 1841, "*except* the Zulus. . . . The Zulus have not their equal in this respect."[78]

As long as they focused on culture, the American Board missionaries did not see in language an important marker of "Zuluness." This can be partly inferred from situations in which they identified communities as "Zulus" while attributing to them "non-Zulu" speaking practices. For example, they continued to classify King Mzilikazi's followers as "Zulus" even after they had learned that this polity consisted of diverse people using speaking practices identified as "Sitibela" or "Sichuana" or both.[79]

Similarly, the American Board missionaries referred to King Dingane's people as "Zulus" even though the latter were believed to speak the "Caffre" language or a dialect almost identical to it. This explains why the American Board missionaries studied the "Caffre" language at Bethelsdorp in the eastern Cape region before continuing their journey to Natal-Zululand.[80] Moreover, as long as they believed that the two modes of speaking were just about identical, it made sense for them to hire as their "Zulu" interpreters people who spoke fluently the "Caffre" language of the eastern Cape region, notably Oerson Magerman, Joseph Kirkman, and Charles Brownlee.[81]

After their arrival in Natal-Zululand, these interpreters noticed some differences between the local speaking practices and those of the eastern Cape region.[82] As American Board missionary George Champion wrote in 1836, "As far as we learn [from our interpreters], the ground-work of the language, (by which I mean the principles on which it is constructed,) is the same as that of the Kaffer language, but a great many things have different names, and the same words have different significations from what they possess in the Kaffer tongue."[83] At first sight, this issue appears to explain why, when Aldin Grout and Newton Adams traveled to King Dingane's place in the same year, they did so in the company of Thomas Halsted, an English settler who had first arrived in Port Natal in 1824 and allegedly "spoke Zulu as well as English."[84] But a closer look at the sources shows that they hired Halsted not because of his language skills but because he was "well known to the king" and "professed to understand Zulu court etiquette."[85] Moreover, the American Board missionaries noticed that their own interpreters (Magerman, Brownlee, and Kirkman) successfully adapted to the peculiarities of the local speaking practices "by repetitions, and change of phrases," to the extent that King Dingane specifically called for Brownlee to act as his interpreter during his conflict with Retief's Afrikaner party.[86] Perhaps more tellingly, Kirkman still worked as Aldin Grout's interpreter when they traveled together to the Zulu kingdom to establish and run Nkanyezi Station between May 1841 and July 1842—more than five years after they had first arrived in the region.[87]

The American Board missionaries also took notice of other newcomers from the eastern Cape region who seemingly adapted without too much difficulty to the speaking practices of Natal-Zululand. They certainly knew of Theophilus Shepstone, who used his skills in the speaking practices of the eastern Cape to work as the diplomatic agent of Natal, a position he first occupied in 1846. The American Board missionaries were particularly familiar with the BMS missionaries Wilhelm Posselt and Jakob Döhne, who traveled from the eastern Cape region to Natal-Zululand in 1847 and whose skills in the "Kafir language" impressed them so much that they invited both to help with the translation of the Bible into the "Zulu" language.[88]

All of this evidence suggested to the American Board missionaries and many other observers that the speaking practices of Natal-Zululand and the eastern Cape represented mere dialectical variations of a single "Caffre" language. And as long as they defined "Zuluness" on the basis of cultural markers rather than language, the American Board missionaries had no reason to question this single "Caffre" language paradigm. Thus they not only adopted a relaxed attitude toward plans to harmonize these speaking practices into a common literary language, but they actively promoted such plans themselves. They sought, for instance, to promote the creation of such a common language by exchanging words between the different "dialects." As Bryant explained in 1849, "These different dialects comprise in the aggregate a much more perfect language than that now in use by any one tribe. The Kafirs, for instance, have a word to express 'king,' in distinction from 'chief,' which the Zulus have not; and another tribe has a word for 'concubine,' which is found neither among the Zulus nor Kafirs. Such words, having the native form and prefix, could be easily transferred from one tribe to another."[89] One year later, they also sought the elimination of orthographic differences by promoting the creation of a uniform system orthography in the region.[90] They claimed that in this manner "a much more copious, flexible, and in every respect complete language might be obtained for all the tribes of Southern Africa."[91] Therefore, at least until 1850, the American Board missionaries themselves promoted the harmonization of the different speaking practices into a single literary language. To make the point once more, they adopted this attitude toward language because they particularized "Zuluness" on the basis of culture ("honesty" and "chastity") rather than language.

Questioning Cultural Difference

However, these ideas came gradually under pressure in the period between 1845 and 1855. Some of the American Board missionaries had their first doubts about the cultural superiority of the Zulu people when King Mpande expelled them from the Zulu state in 1842. Whereas Aldin Grout had earlier described Mpande as "a plain, honest man," he now referred to the Zulu king as characterized by "littleness, meanness, and thirst for blood."[92] His disillusionment with Zulu politics grew steadily thereafter, and by 1845 he began to pray for the collapse of the "Zulu nation."[93]

The Zulu kingdom was indeed in trouble by the middle of the 1840s. Large numbers of people fled from Mpande's rule to Natal, where they entered the colonial government's Location system.[94] As explained earlier, this development strengthened the American Board missionaries' self-perception as a "Mission to the Zulus" because they gained more immediate access to so-called Zulus. However, it began to adversely affect their views of Zulu culture. As they lived and worked in close proximity with these Zulu refugees, they developed more critical views of their cultural attributes. In contradiction to earlier statements about the superior honesty and chastity of the Zulus, Dr. Adams, for instance, claimed in May 1845: "The mass of people among whom we have to live and labor, are in a state of deep degradation, strongly attached to their evil customs, and almost beyond description vile and corrupt in their habits and practices. Chastity is scarcely, if at all, known among them. All of them will cheat and lie, some will kill and steal."[95] Six months later, he added: "This people are very licentious. . . . Perhaps it will give you a tolerable idea of their character in this respect, to state that the usages and opinions of Zulu society require chastity only in married women. Lying and deception are very prominent vices of the Zulu. From their infancy they are trained to these habits, which, consequently, grow with their growth and strengthen with their strength."[96] As these testimonies demonstrate, the missionaries' characterizations of the Zulus as a people who excelled in honesty and chastity started to give way to descriptions that accused them of excelling in lying and licentiousness instead.

The rhetoric changed for two reasons. First, many of the younger refugees who arrived in Natal left the Zulu kingdom precisely because they wanted to escape the restrictive laws that governed marriage and sexual behavior north of the Thukela River.[97] Once in Natal, these individuals engaged in activities that challenged not only these laws but also the Protestant-bourgeois sensibilities of the American Board missionaries.[98] Moreover, the majority of these refugees resisted the missionaries' attempts to impose Christianity and their bourgeois morality on them. In the face of these attitudes, the American Board missionaries did not merely become disillusioned with "Zulu" culture but gradually came to regard it as the key obstacle to conversion. These sentiments were expressed by Bryant. "Our intercourse with this people," he explained in 1847, "shows us more and more clearly, that they [Zulus] are . . . the voluntary slaves of appetite and lust, they have no relish for those truths, which lay a stern prohibition on their darling sins."[99] By the late 1840s and early 1850s, the American Board missionaries' rhetoric approached that of the European settlers who had for some time characterized the coastal belt's African population as savages and barbarians.[100]

These negative representations raised serious doubts about the distinctiveness and superiority of the Zulus vis-à-vis the coastal belt's other "Caffres" and, by extension, about the ABM's identity as a "Mission to the Zulu." It is ironic that Africans who left the Zulu kingdom in this period exacerbated this problem, because many of them identified themselves not as Zulus but people returning to their original homeland. "Remnants of tribes conquered by Chaka and Dingane are leaving Umpandi and the Zulu country," one American missionary commented in 1848, "[they are] returning here to their old homes, so that these people are not properly Zulus, but Caffirs who dwelt here before their captivity and now the government assigns them land tracts."[101] This remark suggests that the American Board missionaries supported the notion that the refugees were Caffres rather than Zulus, even if this argument made it more difficult to claim, as Aldin Grout had done in 1844, that the ABM was working among "the Zulus of Natal."[102]

In part, they felt compelled to support the refugees' "Caffre" identity because the Location system, which helped safeguard Africans' access to land in Natal and thus the ABM's access to Africans, came under pressure from European settlers and their allies in the colonial administration. It was the British high commissioner to South Africa, Sir Harry Smith, who launched the first assault against the Locations. On a visit to Natal in 1848, he took the side of the land-hungry settlers and promised to revisit the land question by creating a Land Commission. Made up of European military men and civil servants, this commission concluded that the majority of Africans in Natal "had no rights to the land" because they were "Zulus" and thus "foreigners" and that the Locations should be broken up and the "foreigners" resettled among European farmers or beyond the Mzimkhulu River.[103] Although this plan, and similar initiatives that followed it, were never implement, they did encourage the American Board missionaries to protect the Locations by claiming that the refugees possessed genuine ancestral claims to land in Natal.[104] As Lewis Grout explained in 1852,

> These tribes were living more or less separated from each other & independent . . . until the . . . powerful invasions of Tyaka [i.e., King Shaka], when they were, for a time, entirely broken up & destroyed or scattered or subdued & incorporated with his own people. . . . [Some] made the best of their situation by uniting with & following the enemy. Many, probably most, of these also watched the signs of the times & secured the earliest opportunity for escaping from bondage & return-ing to their father land. . . . And hence the only sense in which they can be called [Zulu] "refugees" is that they fled from a land of strangers and returned from an involuntary exile to the land of their birth and the home of their fathers.[105]

While this argument helped protect Natal's Location system, it implied that "Zuluness" consisted of nothing but a thin cultural veneer that Africans could adopt or shed without much effort. In doing so, the argument raised new questions about the true nature of "Zuluness" and, moreover, put into question the American Board missionaries' identity as a "Mission to the Zulus." For how could they claim to be working among the "Zulus" if most of their charges were "Natal Caffres"? To restore their own identity, there-fore, they had to find a new way of particularizing "Zuluness," preferably one that disconnected "Zuluness" from culture and from residence in the Zulu kingdom. Several developments gradually pushed them toward seeing language as the solution to this problem.

The Turn to Language

One factor that pushed ABM members to base "Zuluness" on language was the sudden increase in their "Zulu" translation and publication activities. Although Bible translation was an important aspect of missionary work, all missionary societies had difficulties funding these activities and, in particu-lar, the printing and publication of translated texts. Although the American

Tract Society provided some financial support for these purposes around 1840, it never provided enough for the American Board missionaries to make significant advances in publishing vernacular texts.[106] They experienced significant frustration over this slow progress. As Lewis Grout noted in a letter to the board in June 1849, "A small book of sixteen printed hymns, a little spelling book of about thirty pages, and two tracts of selections of Scripture, of about sixty pages each, make up the substance of our catalogue of available books in the Zulu language. Our press has done nothing for two years and our mission is already suffering the sad consequence."[107] This situation changed drastically in 1850, however, when the American Bible Society granted the ABM $500 (about $15,000 today) to cover the printing costs associated with "the Scriptures for the Zulas."[108] In 1853, the society provided another $400 (about $12,000 today) for the same purpose.[109] These grants improved the ABM's situation to the extent that Aldin Grout proclaimed confidently to the BFBS that year that "the American Bible Society stands ready to furnish us with the means to print the Scriptures as fast as we can translate them."[110]

Buoyed by this financial support, the American Board missionaries increased their efforts to translate and print so-called Zulu language texts. In 1850, they printed the book of Psalms (*Incwadi yezihlabelelo*).[111] Three years later, they added *The African Servant* (*Inceku yase yafika indaba e qinisileyo*) and a second edition of their spelling book (*Incwadi yezifundi*).[112] In 1853, they were in the process of printing the epistle to the Romans (*Incwadi ka Paule e balelwe Amaromani*) and translating the gospel of John (*Ivangeli Ngokuloba ku ka Johane*), Acts of the Apostles (*Izenzo zabaPostile*), Proverbs (*Izaga*), Bunyan's *Pilgrim's Progress* (*Incwadi ka'bunyane okutiwa ukuhamba kwesihambi*), and a book on geography (*Incwadi yezwe*).[113] Writing that same year, the missionaries reported proudly that they had printed a total of 1,241,886 pages since the inception of their mission in South Africa.[114] They also decided that henceforth copies of all their "Zulu publications" were to be sent to the American Oriental Society to showcase their linguistic achievements.[115]

These activities established the American Board missionaries' reputation as experts in the Zulu vernacular by the time Natal government officials recognized that, for colonial rule to function properly, "all functionaries of the Government, engaged among the natives, shall pass an examination in the Zulu language."[116] To help facilitate the language learning process in preparation for such an examination, the government became an active supporter of the preparation and publication of language learning aids. In 1853, it appointed a six-person commission charged with the "publication of a dictionary and a concise grammar of that dialect of the Kafir language spoken in Natal and commonly called Zulu."[117] Chaired by Theophilus Shepstone, the commission included three American Board missionaries— Jakob Döhne, Lewis Grout, and Hyman Wilder—in addition to the Berlin missionary Karl Wilhelm Posselt and Wesleyan missionary William J. Davis.[118] The American Board missionaries were particularly proud of their appointment to this commission and informed not only the head office in Boston but also the American Oriental Society of the news.[119] Moreover, because the American Board missionaries had already worked on similar projects since 1849 and 1852, they were able to convince the commission to entrust two of their own—Döhne and Grout—with preparing the Zulu language dictionary and grammar, respectively.[120]

These developments ensured that the American Board missionaries experienced not only an increase in their intellectual and monetary investment in so-called Zulu language translations and publications between 1850 and 1853 but also an increase in their emotional attachment to the very idea of a Zulu language separate from "Caffre." The notion that this Zulu language was distinct from the "Caffre" language became ever more appealing in these years because of the influx of more and more Wesleyan Methodist missionaries. The Wesleyans were not alone, of course; Lutherans of the Norwegian and Berlin Missionary Societies, as well as Anglicans and Catholic missionaries, also came to Natal in this period. But the Wesleyans were particularly worrisome to the ABM, because they came to Natal in the company of African interpreters armed with Appleyard's integrated "Caffre" translations and publications.

The Wesleyan Threat

The first Wesleyan missionary who settled in the Natal-Zululand area was James Archbell; he moved to Port Natal in 1841. Because Archbell worked only among the European (mostly English-speaking) settlers and military personnel of Port Natal, the American Board missionaries did not see him as a rival.[121] This impression was confirmed in 1845 when Archbell moved to Pietermaritzburg, where he paid more attention to his interests as a landowner and newspaper editor than to his mission work, a development that led to his dismissal from the WMS in 1848.[122]

The American Board missionaries' assessment of the Wesleyans changed, however, when they learned that Archbell was only the spearhead of the WMS's entry into Natal. Aldin Grout, for instance, wrote alarmingly to the ABM in Boston in September 1845, "I learn the Wesleyans design to prosecute their work here as fast as their men and means will allow and I fear that our own society will move so slow, that others will step in before them to reap the harvest of souls."[123] Almost panic-stricken, he sent off another letter in December, explaining: "A little more delay, and we may see the Wesleyans occupying the most eligible places."[124] His fears were confirmed when Wesleyan missionaries William J. Davis, John Richards, and William C. Holden, coming from the eastern Cape region, and James Allison, entering from the area occupied by the Swazi kingdom, arrived in Natal in 1846–47.[125] The American Board missionaries noticed that one crucial difference between Archbell and the newcomers was that the latter targeted not only Natal's European settlers but also its African population.[126]

Importantly, the American Board missionaries did not consider the Wesleyans a theological threat. Both groups of missionaries "preached a muscular, agrarian faith, where work and education were emphasized alongside worship."[127] Moreover, Aldin Grout's claim above, that the Wesleyans' forceful entry into Natal might allow them to "reap the harvest of souls" before the ABM, suggests that he did not accuse the Wesleyans of promoting a false theology. Instead, the American Board missionaries perceived the Wesleyans as a threat against their overall territorial influence in the region, notably among the Zulus. This perception increased further when they learned that the Wesleyan missionaries were accompanied by African intermediaries. While two of these intermediaries arrived with Davis and Richard, two more (most likely Vimbe and Fortuin, mentioned in chapter 4) joined them after being pushed into Natal by the outbreak of the Seventh Frontier War.[128] Allison, moreover, brought an entire group of African intermediaries with him from the Swazi kingdom.[129]

These African intermediaries, acting as interpreters, teachers, and evangelists, increased the effectiveness and reach of the WMS in Natal. As Lewis Grout noted in 1847, with the help of these African intermediaries, the Wesleyans were moving into territory that the members of the ABM claimed for themselves:

I was told by good authority that Mr Allison's (a Wes Miss) assistants (of which he has many, colored men) are to visit and hold service on the Sabbath on the part of this (Inanda) location. . . . Again, some weeks since I spent a night few hours this side of the Umgeni . . . and the family when I stopped spoke of a Wesleyan assistant from D'Urban holding forth to the natives in that quarter. . . . Again two of these itinerants (Wes assistants and colored men) spent a Sabbath and preached to the larger tribe of people not far inland from Dr Adam's station.[130]

Adding insult to injury, the head of the Wesleyan mission in Natal, Davis, approached his American counterparts as early as 1846 to request a distinct sphere of influence for the WMS in the region. Davis's letter is worth quoting at length because it highlights the confidence and ambition with which the Wesleyans entered the Natal-Zululand mission field:

I wish to inform my American Brethren that from the appointment of the first Wesleyan Missionary here in 1841, it has always been the intention of the Wesleyan Missionary Society to prosecute its labours . . . among the native population. . . . It will thus be seen that probably ere long the number of Wesleyan Missionaries will be much larger in Natalia than at the present time. . . . I think it desirable and therefore with deference would propose to my American Brethren that . . . each society should . . . have a distinct line of country assigned to its missionaries. . . . It will prevent all painful collision in the prosecution of our missionary labours. . . . I wish also to observe that the Wesleyans have at present missions in the territory of the chief Faku, near the Western boundary of the colony, and it certainly would be most desirable to the Wesleyan Society, to extend its missions within the Natal territory, so as to connect them with those in Kaffraria near the Western boundary of the colony.[131]

The American Board missionaries did not reject the proposal out of hand, because agreeing to it promised to protect a substantial portion of Natal from Wesleyan interference. "If we must have Wesleyan missionaries near us," Bryant explained in 1847, "we thought the proposal of Mr D a good one and accordingly decided to occupy the coast ourselves, and let the Wesleyans occupy the interior."[132] Even before a formal agreement could be reached, however, the Wesleyans requested that the mouth of the Mgeni River (near Port Natal) be excluded from these stipulations, a request that the American Board missionaries forcefully rejected: "The first American missionaries came to this country when it was wholly unoccupied; and considering the amount of labor and money which has been expended, they hope they will not be regarded as arrogant in their assumptions, if they say that they regard themselves as fairly entitled to and disposed to occupy all the territory which they have reserved. . . . In view of these other considerations that might be named, we feel bound to decline the request of our Wesleyan brethren."[133] This exchange settled the issue and led to a formal agreement whereby the Americans claimed all Locations situated on the coast between the Mvoti and the Mzimkhulu Rivers, while the Wesleyans claimed the Locations situated inland between Pieter-maritzburg and the Mzimkhulu River.[134]

The agreement, however, did not end the American Board missionar-ies' anxieties about the Wesleyans. Aldin Grout, for instance, feared that as soon as the Wesleyans "have filled up the ground we have now left them . . . they find some pretext for showing some of their men into ground they have now promised to leave us."[135] Lewis Grout shared these con-cerns, claiming that the Wesleyans were already sending out their men to see whether there were unoccupied areas in Locations that the ABM had claimed per the agreement. "We are in danger of serious interruptions," he noted in late 1847, "unless we have more men."[136] Their fear of what they called "the aggressive habits of our Wesleyan brethren" persisted into the 1850s because, as one American Board missionary noted in 1850, "[they] are flocking in by ship loads."[137] The number of Wesleyan missionaries and African intermediaries did indeed grow in this period to the extent that in 1855, the WMS made Natal a separate administrative district of their South African operations.

What rendered the Wesleyans all the more threatening to the American Board missionaries was that they arrived in Natal not only with African intermediaries (who were apparently able to communicate effectively with the African population of Natal) but armed with an impressive archive of vernacular texts, which they had been accumulating since the 1820s. Moreover, as detailed in chapter 4, in the early 1850s the Wesleyan mis-sionaries, notably Appleyard, began to adapt these texts to the dialectical peculiarities of the Mpondo and the communities north of the Mzim-khulu River (including the members of the Zulu kingdom), adding to the titles of their publications the word "*eMbo*" or "Emboland" to reflect this characteristic.[138]

Thus, by the early 1850s, the perceived Wesleyan threat to the ABM's position in Natal-Zululand had a linguistic dimension, which Shaw's 1853 proposal dramatically amplified. To defend their investment, reputation and overall position in the region, the American Board missionaries argued in their rejection of Shaw's proposal that the Wesleyans' hybrid translations were poorly understood in Natal and that the differences between "Zulu" and "Caffre" were too substantial for these speaking practices to be fruitfully assimilated into a single Bible translation and literary language.[139]

What made this argument that "Zulu" and "Caffre" were distinct languages particularly enticing to the American Board missionaries in 1854 was that it not only helped defend their interests against the Wesleyan threat, but it also provided them with the opportunity to redefine "Zuluness" on the basis of language, a definition that could be applied to all Africans in the Natal-Zululand region regardless of their cultural mores and political affiliation. Indeed, in the same year, 1854, that the American Board missionaries discussed and rejected Shaw's proposal, they apparently used their influence on the Natal Commission to establish "Zulu" as the standard language for all Africans north of the Mzimkhulu River and began to identify them as "Zulus" on the basis of that language. As the newly arrived John Colenso, the bishop of Natal, explained at this time, "The Kafir population of Natal. . . . To all these the name Zulu is now given; and the language, as it will be settled by this Commission . . . and finally adopted as the standard for the whole district, will be the *Zulu-Kafir language*."[140]

Perhaps most significantly, defining "Zuluness" in linguistic terms allowed the American Board missionaries to reaffirm their own identity as a "Mission to the Zulus," which had always been important to their sense of purpose in South Africa. Not surprisingly, this identity also featured prominently in the rejection letter the American Board missionary Seth Stone sent to the BFBS in 1854: "The [American Board] Missionaries . . . saw a smoothness and a beauty in the (King's) Zulu which they had not discovered in the other [dialect], and subsequent observations on other dialects have confirmed them in the belief that the Zulu is superior to all the kindred dialects in the vicinity. This and the fact that this is, and was from the first considered as *a Mission to the Zulus*, gave them the impulse in acquiring, and has confirmed them in the use of the Zulu rather than any other dialect."[141] In addition to drawing attention to their identity as a "Mission to the Zulus," the last sentence in Stone's quote illustrates clearly that the American Board missionaries in 1854 sustained this identity by asserting a close correlation between "Zuluness" and the "Zulu language," a language they considered—due to its "smoothness" and "beauty"—distinct from and superior to the coastal belt's other dialects.

When the American Board missionaries first arrived in the region, they sustained their identity as a "Mission to the Zulus" by reworking preexisting ideas about cultural difference. However, the discourse about the superiority of Zulu culture came under pressure in the 1840s, when large numbers of Africans abandoned their Zulu identities, entered Natal as returnees to "the land of their birth and the home of their fathers," and, more importantly, resisted the American Board missionaries' value system. The resulting disillusionment with Zulu culture caused the American Board missionaries to gradually shift their attention to language. Although they had previously resisted the idea that language and Zuluness were intimately related, their mounting investment in the idea of the Zulu language, combined with the Wesleyan threat to their material interests in Natal, pushed the American Board missionaries to define Zulu as a distinct language from "Caffre" after 1850. Once this was achieved, they used this Zulu language as a marker of Zuluness and, in so doing, successfully reaffirmed their own identity as a "Mission to the Zulus" even though all their mission stations were located outside the Zulu kingdom. The combination of all these factors goes far to explain why the American Board missionaries rejected Shaw's plan for the creation of a single Bible translation and literary language in 1854. The significance of this moment for the history of language development in South Africa cannot be overstated; by rejecting Shaw's proposal based on the argument that the Zulu language was distinct to "Caffre," the American Board missionaries helped set the stage for the emergence of two distinct Zulu and "Caffre" (soon to be called Xhosa) literary languages and language communities. What remains to be explained in the American Board missionaries' line of argument is that they considered the Zulu language not only different from "Caffre" but, as the Seth Stone quote illustrates, also superior to it. The next chapter will trace the genealogy of this idea to the ABM's African intermediaries and from them to the Zulu kingdom itself.

• 6 •

"To Speak Properly and Correctly, viz. *Uku-Kuluma-Nje*"

Americans, Africans, and Zulu as a Superior Language

When the American Board missionaries rebuffed William Shaw's proposal to develop a single literary language for the coastal region in 1854, they tasked Seth B. Stone with writing one of the rejection letters. As quoted in the previous chapter, his rejection letter included the remark that "Zulu is superior to all the kindred dialects in the vicinity," revealing the American Board missionaries' belief that the Zulu language was not only different from "Caffre" but also superior to it. They supported this claim both with philological arguments—including the idea that Zulu was superior to "Caffre" because it did not contract words (for instance, *umuntu* rather than *umntu* for "person")—and with rhetorical statements, such as Stone's comment in the same letter that there was "a smoothness and a beauty in the (King's) Zulu which they had not discovered in the other [dialect]."[1]

As I will detail below, the intellectual origins of these rhetorical statements can be traced back to the early Zulu kingdom (1817–28) and its habit of differentiating high-status subjects from low-status tributaries on the basis of "superior" and "inferior" speaking practices known as *ukukhuluma* and *ukutekeza*. These ideas began to influence the American Board missionaries' views of local speaking practices only at the turn of the 1850s, because it was at this time that they began to rely on the language expertise of African intermediaries such as Davida, Nanise, Nembula, Hangu, Ntaba, and others, whose own understanding of language had been shaped by their exposure to the Zulu state's ideology of rule. Just like their European counterparts in the eastern Cape, then, the American Board missionaries in Natal-Zululand derived important linguistic ideas from African intermediaries and African ideologies of language. Indeed, in the end these intermediaries and ideologies—rather than intrinsic linguistic differences—contributed decisively to the American Board missionaries' rejection of Shaw's proposal in 1854. Consequently, the Zulu-Xhosa language divide is the product of a historical and culturally contingent process, which can be traced to a precise moment in time, the interaction of African and foreign-born actors, and the convergence of their respective ideologies of language and belonging.

Zulu Is Superior to Caffre

The American Board missionaries were not the first people who made the argument that Zulu was superior to the coastal belt's other "Caffre" vernaculars. Shortly after his arrival in Cape Town in 1835, for instance, Dr. John Philip of the LMS informed Aldin Grout that "the Zoolah language is but the more perfect Caffer."[2] The idea that the so-called Zulu language was superior did not stick with the American Board missionaries at this time, however, because, as the use of the word "but" implies, Philip viewed the differences between the two speech patterns as insignificant. He reinforced this perception when he suggested that, before moving to Natal-Zululand, the American Board missionaries ought to "go to Cafferland [i.e., the eastern Cape region] and stop at one of the mission stations there a year or two to learn the Caffer language," a suggestion that implied that the two modes of speaking were mutually intelligible.[3]

The first recorded ABM claim for the superiority of Zulu over "Caffre" appeared in 1849 when Lewis Grout explained that "The Kafir. . . . seeks to abbreviate and contract its words, while the [Zulu] . . . delights in full forms."[4] His deliberate use of "delights" suggests that he attached a superior status to the Zulu vernacular because it did not use abbreviations and contractions. This argument did not achieve lasting traction, either, however. In the same year, James Bryant, who was considered the most linguistically gifted of the American Board missionaries, reiterated that all the vernaculars in the coastal belt were nearly identical and should be assimilated into a single "more perfect language."[5]

American statements favoring Zulu became more forceful in the early 1850s. In 1854, for instance, Jakob Döhne, now a member of the ABM, employed a mother-child metaphor to establish the superiority of Zulu over "Caffre." "Being the mother," he explained, Zulu used words with "pure roots," employed expressions "in their full forms," and preserved its *great simplicity*" by "joining . . . verb to verb, without interference of conjunctions, or . . . independent particles." In contrast, "the Kafir being the child" employed "derived words" and was "fond of new expressions" and "contractions."[6] Lewis Grout agreed. In his *Zulu Grammar* (1859), he declared Zulu to be the purest of all the African languages, including "Caffre," because it had been shielded for a longer period of time from the adulterating influences that usually accompanied "connection and collision with other nations and languages." He concluded that "there is no part of South Africa, where foreign influence has come later, or been felt less, than in case of the language and tribes of which we speak, particularly the Zulu."[7]

As these statements suggest, Döhne and Lewis Grout expressed their claims for the superiority of the Zulu with the help of philological terminology (roots, forms, contractions, nouns, verbs, conjunctions, particles) and substantiated them with philological theories of language change (connections and collisions with the speakers of other languages). However, the American Board missionaries did not support these claims with philological arguments alone. They also supported them with rhetorical claims whose existence predated their own arrival in the region. Importantly, these preexisting rhetorical arguments were much more narrowly concerned with differentiating speech patterns to the north and south of the Thukela River.

The American Board missionaries Newton Adams, Aldin Grout, and George Champion first encountered these preexisting arguments when they settled at Port Natal in early 1836. In August of that year, they explained in a letter to the mission board in Boston that "some progress has been made in the language, and for this purpose is Mr. Champion stationed *in the Zoolah country*, that the language generally in use may be *correctly* acquired, and the Bible translated, it being our wish that he is devoted mainly to this business."[8] The letter clarified that Champion was about to establish Nginani Station in the Zulu kingdom's heartland at "a spot in the district assigned us by the [Zulu] king" that was located "about eight miles distant from the *Um Togelam [Thukela] River*, the *western boundary* of the Zoolah country [i.e., the Zulu kingdom]."[9] The careful placement of Champion to acquire the "correct" language suggests that the American Board missionaries were under the impression that the speech forms north of the Thukela River in the Zulu kingdom were superior to the allegedly less correct and therefore inferior speech forms south of the river in Natal. Given that their arrival in the region had only just occurred, it is likely that they were led to this impression by their interactions with Port Natal's local community of English merchants and their African clients and that it reflected a commonly held idea in the region.[10]

There is no indication that the American Board missionaries assimilated this specific rhetorical argument into their own discourse about the region's linguistic landscape before 1850. In 1851, however, Jakob Döhne refused to be appointed to a station in southern Natal because "the dialect spoken by the people in that direction was not pure Zulu"; he asked to be located in "a suitable field north of Durban" (i.e., closer to the Thukela River) instead.[11] Döhne's claim that people in southern Natal did not speak "pure Zulu," whereas people close to or beyond the Thukela River apparently did, is noteworthy because it shares obvious similarities with the earlier claim that the language was spoken correctly to the north of the Thukela River in the Zulu kingdom.

Stronger evidence emerges for the year 1854, when, again, Stone explained that there existed an unparalleled "beauty in the (King's) Zulu."[12] Because the expression "King's Zulu" referred directly to speech patterns used north of the Thukela River in the Zulu kingdom, it mirrors the early rhetorical claim that the language was spoken more correctly there. The earlier rhetoric also reverberates in Lewis Grout's *Zulu Grammar,* where the author argued that the rulers of the Zulu polity spoke a language of a "higher standard" than their regional neighbors.[13] By the 1850s, then, the American Board missionaries had apparently assimilated a preexisting rhetoric that claimed that the speech forms north of the Thukela River were superior to those south of the river.

Missionary Language Skills and African Interpreters

It is possible to probe for the origins of this older ideology of language by asking why its rhetorical content gained traction with the American Board missionaries only after 1850. What had changed in their approach to the region's speaking practices that could explain their sudden inclusion of rhetorical arguments grounded in an older ideology of language? Put simply, it was only in the 1850s that they began to increase their translation and publications efforts and, in so doing, became more dependent on African intermediaries whose own understanding of language had been shaped by this older ideology of language.

Although the American Board missionaries relied on European and Khoekhoe interpreters when they first arrived in the region (see chapter 3), they did, like their counterparts in the eastern Cape region, work diligently at improving their language skills as quickly as possible. Aldin Grout is a good example. Soon after his arrival in the region, he "did what [he] could to acquire the language of the people."[14] Although he was forced to relocate to the United States during the troubles between 1838 and 1839, when he returned to Natal in 1840, he committed himself again to learning the language.[15] He initially lived with Adams at Umlazi Station, where the two of them studied the language together in the hope that they would soon make enough progress "to be able to dispense with an interpreter altogether."[16] This hope was disappointed, however, and in 1841 when Aldin Grout traveled to the Zulu kingdom to establish Nkanyezi Station, he was once again accompanied by his tried and trusted interpreter from the eastern Cape region, Joseph Kirkman.[17] Undeterred, he continued his studies, using Kirkman as his teacher and Champion's translation of the gospel of Matthew as his textbook.[18] There is no reason to believe that these efforts remained fruitless, but there is evidence that suggests he continued to struggle with the local speaking practices.[19] In 1846, he was still busy "translating phrases which we need to use every day in our intercourse with the people," an activity that implies that even some of the more mundane interactions in the language remained fraught with difficulties.[20]

Aldin Grout was not the exception. Even James Bryant, considered the most gifted of the American missionary linguists until his untimely death in 1850, struggled with the local speaking practices. Few of them, Bryant included, were willing to admit this publicly, however. In 1849, for example, Bryant explained enthusiastically to the ABM in Boston that "our knowledge of the language is becoming more and more accurate, our senior members being well qualified to engage in the work of translating and composing books in the native tongue."[21] Based on this optimistic information, the ABM in Boston circulated stories about the ease with which their missionaries acquired proficiency in the local speaking practices and advanced their translation activities. In Bryant's specific case, the ABM circulated the claim that he had begun "preaching in Zulu in ten weeks after arriving in Natal." It was only after Bryant's death that Lewis Grout set the record straight, notably explaining in 1852:

The very short time in which Br Bryant acquired the Zulu language, you no doubt have authority from somebody for the statements which have appeared from time to time on that point, but to me they seem extravagant and I think they are calculated to mislead the reader. Br Bryant studied the language on his passage to Natal, and then he may have written down some Zulu words taken one by one from an imperfect vocabulary to the amount of a sermon and [he may] have read them to an assembly of natives, yet it is doubtful if they got many ideas from it and if it should be called preaching. Br Bryant who saw the notice of his first essay at preaching was surprised as well as his wife. . . . If along with that habit of "preaching in Zulu in ten weeks after arriving at Natal," it should be said that one of our missionaries who has been here the longest (16 years and more) speaks the Zulu very imperfectly, making mistakes . . . in almost every sentence . . . , the impression given . . . should be much more correct concerning the acquisition of the language.[22]

The mistakes alluded to by Lewis Grout were often humorous. One American Board missionary, for example, confused *lalelani* (give attention) with *lalani* (go to sleep), while a missionary wife confused *amadoda* (men) with *amadada* (ducks).[23] Such testimonies show us that the American Board missionaries, Bryant included, shared the experience of their counterparts in the eastern Cape region: both groups of missionaries continued to struggle with the local speaking practices even though their language skills improved over time. This problem was caused in part by the fact that, when the American Board missionaries first arrived in the region in 1835, they did not possess any language learning aids such as vocabularies, dictionaries, or grammars. Painfully aware of this problem, Seth Stone explained in 1857: "It is one thing to learn Arabic or one of the Languages of India, with their Sapies and very intelligent living teachers, and Grammars and Dictionaries. . . . It is quite another thing to learn so totally uncivilized a language as the Zulu."[24] The next generation of American Board missionaries who arrived in South Africa in the second half of the 1840s benefited from the language expertise acquired by their predecessors. The new arrivals usually stayed for several months at Aldin Grout's mission station of Umvoti and Newton Adams's station of Umlazi, where they devoted most of their time to studying the local speaking practices. Writing from Umlazi in August 1847, one newly arrived missionary, Silas McKinney, explained that he was actively studying the grammar of the language.[25] About one month later, he found himself at Umvoti Station, where he "devoted [himself] wholly to the study of the language."[26] He was very pleased with his progress and very optimistic about his prospects for becoming fluent. One year later, however, now located at Ifumi Station, the reality of second-language acquisition compelled him to be less sanguine:

> My circumstances . . . were in many regards peculiar and unfavorable
> for acquiring a thorough knowledge of the language. After a residence
> of three months in the country—at two different places forty miles
> apart, with only an acquaintance with the most common principles
> of the language and an ear and tongue almost totally untrained to the
> peculiar sounds, . . . I was placed at the distance of twelve miles from
> the nearest mission brother, . . . and with nothing but . . . a Grammar,
> and an imperfect vocabulary.[27]

McKinney's admission that he was unable to acquire "a thorough knowledge of the language" is noteworthy because it appears to be in tension with Hyman Wilder crediting him with "conduct[ing] evening worship in Zulu for the benefit of the natives" only six month later.[28] The tension can be resolved, however, by probing more closely as to what "conducting worship in Zulu" actually meant. The evidence suggests that, as in the eastern Cape region, conducting worship in the vernacular usually involved the missionary reading passages from various texts (sermons, catechism, the Lord's Prayer, Sabbath Liturgy, and various Bible passages, etc.) that had been translated well before the service. It rarely involved preaching in an impromptu manner. As American Board missionary William Ireland explained, "I have written one sermon together with two shorter exercises in Zulu one of which I delivered last Sab[bath]. . . . I have hardly dared to extemporize in my Sabbath exercises yet, as I find that it is very easy to say exactly the opposite of what you intend to." [29]

It is reasonable to assume that, over time, most of the American Board missionaries acquired a level of fluency in the local speaking practices that allowed them to converse with the indigenous population in a more ad hoc manner. When reaching this stage, however, most of them also realized (even better than before) that a significant difference remained between their level of fluency and the proficiency of native speakers. Having studied the coastal belt's speaking practices for some two decades, American Board missionary Döhne explained the difference between these two skill levels in 1857:

> It is . . . not so difficult for an educated man to pick up part of the
> language and make himself understood to natives who are daily with
> him and can observe his mode of expressing himself. But that is not
> yet the language which the native speaks. In its best quality taken, it is
> but an English rendered by Zulu-Kafir words, and therefore far from
> the Zulu idiom. The same is the character of translation. A translation
> which is easily understood by Missionary members . . . may . . . be . . .
> utterly defective . . . because the mode of thinking in Zulu and speak-
> ing in Zulu must be studied in its proper way, and is difficult for the
> mind of foreigners.[30]

As Döhne's statement shows, the members of the ABM recognized that
their skills in "Zulu" remained quite distinct from what linguists would call
"native-speaker proficiency." The crucial reason for this problem was that,
as mentioned in chapter 4, the American Board missionaries, like their
counterparts in the eastern Cape, arrived in the mission field as adults
and thus at a stage in their life when their ability to acquire native-speaker
proficiency in a language radically different from their mother tongue had
vanished. Döhne's statement also suggests that the American Board missionaries recognized not only that native-speaker proficiency eluded them
but that the absence of this proficiency also undermined the quality of their
written work in the language, most importantly, their Bible translations. It
stands to reason that they became most aware of this problem when they
expanded their translation and publication activities after 1850 due to the
influx of new monetary resources (also discussed in chapter 4). In order to
address this weakness, the members of the ABM began to rely more heavily
on the language expertise of their African followers, whose number, as luck
would have it, began to increase at the same time.

The American Board missionaries' reliance on African language intermediaries is not always easily established. Döhne, for example, never
indicated that he benefited from the language expertise of Africans while
preparing the Zulu language dictionary he published in 1857. Yet circumstantial evidence suggests strongly that he took advantage of such expertise. For instance, the quotation above suggests that he was acutely aware
that his knowledge of the language remained defective because he lacked
native-speaker proficiency. It is also clear that Döhne had worked closely
with African interpreters, notably a man named Joshua Hermanus (the son
of a councillor of the minor chief Tola of the Dange-Xhosa), during his

decade-long tenure in the eastern Cape region.[31] There is good reason to believe that he followed the same modus operandi when the ABM's General Meeting, held at D'Urban on 12 December 1849, asked him (as well as Aldin Grout and Adams) to "prepare a Zulu+English vocabulary for the press" and to help with "the work of translating the Psalms into Zulu."[32] For soon after taking on these tasks, Döhne asked to be moved to a station "north of Durban" because the people there "spoke a purer dialect."[33] This request implies that Döhne wanted to involve Africans directly in his language work once again, and it is highly likely that he subsequently relied once more on the language expertise of African intermediaries even though he never mentioned them by name.

Similar evidence is available for Lewis Grout, who arrived in South Africa in 1847 and spent the first months in the region at Umvoti Station, where he devoted his time "to the study of the language."[34] His language skills advanced quickly, prompting Aldin Grout to credit him with preaching in the language only a couple of months after his arrival—although "preaching" meant "read[ing] to the congregation what I had written during the past week in Zulu."[35] His language skills continued to improve to the extent that, in the early 1850s, his colleagues entrusted him with preparing translations of various Bible segments as well as a grammar of the Zulu language. Despite these developments, however, Lewis Grout, like Döhne, recognized that his knowledge of the language remained inferior to native-speaker proficiency. In a letter to the ABM in Boston in September 1851, he acknowledged this deficiency in himself and his colleagues:

> The . . . work of translating the Scriptures into the Zulu Language and of preparing other books is yet in its infancy, and moreover most if not all of us feel that we are yet in mere infancy of preparing for it. In a language so new and peculiar, without a thorough analysis of its principles and a vocabulary of its words, . . . and moreover without a suitable school or any appropriate measures in operation for raising up competent Native assistants . . . , the mission has before it an almost untouched Herculean task.[36]

The quote shows that Lewis Grout was aware that his skills in this "new and peculiar" language remained deficient and that this deficiency undermined the quality of his translation work. His lamenting the absence of "competent Native assistants" furthermore suggests that he was already involving Africans in his translation work, but that he found them poor assistants because they were proficient in the Zulu language but did not possess adequate skills in the English language and biblical theology.

Davida, Nanise, and Nembula

Seth Stone was uncharacteristically outspoken about his dependence on the language expertise of Africans. He also more clearly identified the individuals who helped him with his language work. Writing in December 1852, Stone explained that he used two methodologies for language acquisition, both of which involved Africans: "Besides trying the analytical method of learning the language (i.e.) by translating from the Zulu to English out of our books; and cross-questioning natives to find their way of employment of certain terms; . . . I have also tried the synthetical [method], by translation from English to Zulu and getting native criticism upon the same."[37] Stone depended on Africans not only for learning the language but also for his translation activities. He certainly did so in 1866 when he was working on the Book of Daniel and the epistle to the Romans with the help of "our best native critic to help make them more idiomatic Zulu."[38] In a letter that same year, Stone explained in detail the method he and other American Board missionaries used for producing their translations: "When we find what we wish to say in Zulu . . . there is no difficulty; but if not which is constantly happening, we call the first native and try our ingenuity to make him produce the thoughts in his own idiom; and frequently we try many persons on the same. We have to get our facts . . . by many witnesses; lastly for the major difficulties we have some natives who know English pretty well. . . . They are our critical apparatus on the Zulu side."[39] Stone also identified by name at least one of the Africans who provided him this sort of help. "Udavida [Davida] has been of much help to me," he explained in December 1852. "I have had an inquiry exercise with him, and others once a week ever since I commenced preaching, to elicit information respecting the language; reserving my difficulties for these occasions."[40] Stone was more tight-lipped about Davida's background, except for mentioning that he knew "several of the idioms . . . of this region" and that he had been a church member of James Allison's mission station of Edendale near Pietermaritzburg before joining Stone's Ifafa Station in southern Natal sometime in the early 1850s.[41]

Davida was not the only person clearly identified as an African language intermediary. During his visit to the ABM's Inanda Station in 1854, John

Colenso, the Anglican bishop of Natal, learned that the station missionary, Daniel Lindley, preached "through an interpreter" who was a "young half-caste woman" called Nancy.[42] Nancy also helped Lindley and most likely some of the other American Board missionaries with their Bible translation activities. This becomes apparent from records of the ABM's general meeting at Durban in January 1855, at which the missionaries voted to "approve the employment of Nancy of Inanda to assist in correcting the translations of books into Zulu prepared for the press [and] that Mr Lindley & any [other missionary] who may require her assistance be a committee to engage her services."[43]

"Nancy of Inanda" was in fact Nanise, the daughter of John Cane, one of the first English residents at Port Natal, and his Khoekhoe or mixed-race wife, Rachel.[44] At Port Natal, Nanise appears to have grown up in a multilingual environment, made up of her (most likely) Cape Dutch–speaking mother and her English-speaking father, as well as Chief Dabeka kaDube's vernacular-speaking Qadi people who had attached themselves to the European community at Port Natal sometime after 1837.[45] When her father, John Cane, was killed in an unsuccessful military expedition against King Dingane's Zulu regiments in 1838, Nanise joined the Lindley household, where her language skills quickly earned her a reputation as an excellent mission school teacher and interpreter.[46] It was said, for example, that Theophilus Shepstone, upon hearing Nanise translate one of Lindley's sermons, was so thoroughly impressed by her abilities that he considered them superior to his own.[47]

In addition to Nanise and Davida, a man named Nembula kaDuze (Makhanya) also worked as the interpreter for Aldin Grout and possibly for Newton Adams.[48] Nembula first came into the sphere of influence of the Adams household at the age of eight when his mother joined Umlazi Station. While his mother quickly established herself as an influential (native) evangelist, Nembula became a pupil in the Adams's family mission school, where he soon added English to his preexisting vernacular language skills.[49] By the mid-1840s, Nembula had acquired enough education to work as one of the ABM's paid African intermediaries (the official titles for these positions ranged from "native assistant" and "native helper" to "native teacher") and included a wide range of responsibilities, notably teaching the day school of Adams's Station.[50] Following his baptism in 1847, Nembula became "Ira Adams Nembula" and added preaching to his duties, often filling in for American Board missionary James Bryant, whose health began to fail at this time.[51] "[Nembula] took the English testament in his hand," one of Bryant's colleagues observed in 1848, "and fluently translated it to the people and then preached them of the judgment and warned them to flee from the wrath to come."[52] His ability to move effortlessly between the two languages nicely explains why Nembula became one of the American Board missionaries' language intermediaries at this time.[53]

Hangu and Ntaba

The cases of Davida, Nanise, and Nembula suggest that the American Board missionaries usually recruited language intermediaries from the people who first attached themselves to their families and participated in their evening (family) schools in the late 1830s and early 1840s.[54] It was by living with missionary families and going to these schools that Africans added English to their preexisting vernacular language skills and, in so doing, acquired the bilingualism that made them potential language intermediaries a decade later.

One of these potential intermediaries was Hangu (uHangu). He first entered the household and family school of Aldin Grout in 1841, when the latter resided at Nkanyezi Station in the Zulu kingdom.[55] When King Mpande expelled the American missionary in 1842, the then thirteen-year-old Hangu accompanied Grout back to Natal and, shortly thereafter, began to teach at the day school of Umvoti Station.[56] In 1844, Aldin Grout described Hangu in these terms: "I have employed one of the boys that has lived with us for several years to teach. . . . Uhangu the teacher can read tolerably well in his own language and some in English. . . . He is perhaps sixteen years old. . . . Being a native and knowing all the feelings [and] habits of his people, I see that he has some important advantage over a white man from our country who knows nothing of natives."[57] As the quote shows, Aldin Grout recognized Hangu's intercultural abilities and therefore hired him as a teacher. His reference to Hangu's skills in the vernacular and English suggests, furthermore, that he probably employed him as his language intermediary when the need arose for a bilingual interpreter.

A second individual who may have worked as Aldin Grout's cultural and language intermediary in the late 1840s and early 1850s was Ntaba (uNtaba) Luthuli. Like Hangu, the thirteen-year-old Ntaba had joined Aldin Grout in 1841, when the latter lived at Nkanyezi Station.[58] When the American missionary had to relocate to Natal one year later, Ntaba, like Hangu, went with him and helped him establish Umvoti Station. During this time, Ntaba worked as a "laborer" but "possessed such a desire to learn" that Grout taught him to speak English and to read his own vernacular language.[59] By 1846, these skills recommended Ntaba for a teaching position in the station's day school, whose wages of £1 per month he invested into a European-style house, a small cotton farm, and Western-type goods such as a wagon, a plow, and a spade.[60] Ntaba's developing bilingualism meant that he was, like Hangu, in a good position to help the American missionary with his language work. As Aldin Grout explained in 1850, "[Ntaba teaches] from two to three hours per day" and devoted the rest of the time "to his own scholar affairs and sometimes to those of the station."[61] Given his bilingualism, it is likely that these affairs included serving as Aldin Grout's language intermediary.

By the turn of the 1850s, all ABM stations in Natal-Zululand had begun to employ Africans as teachers and preachers. Indeed, in the annual report for 1851, the "Zulu Mission, South Africa" identified several additional individuals—Mqiko, Makanya, Patayi, Bili, Famana, Msingaphansi, and Matanda—working as teachers and preachers at various ABM stations in the region.[62] Similar to Ntaba and Hangu, and Nembula and Nanise, they had been trained in the schools of the American Board missionaries and thus had added English language skills to their preexisting knowledge of the vernacular speaking practices. In 1853, moreover, some of these individuals began to receive more advanced training in the English language when they joined the first incoming class of the ABM "Seminary for lads" at Aman-zimtoti Station.[63] Thus, in the early years of the 1850s, most if not all of the American Board missionaries had within easy reach an African teacher or preacher whose developing bilingualism they could use to their advantage in the context of their own language and translation work.

Convert Populations

Even if an African teacher or preacher for each and every station cannot be identified, in the early years of the 1850s all ABM stations included African converts whose vernacular language expertise the American Board missionaries could access. In addition to Hangu and Ntaba, for instance, Aldin Grout's Umvoti Station included a young man named Mlawu, a woman by the name of Mfisikazi, two mothers identified as Mamuni and Ngangati, and their respective sons, Nyokana and Sotyangane, as well as Sotyangane's wife, Sana, and Ntaba's wife, Tititsi.[64]

Missionary Lindley's Inanda Station had at least nine converts. In addition to Nanise, the station included Mayembe "Dalida" Dube and her son, Kakonina "James" Dube, "Joel Hawes" and "John" Mavuma, "Jonas" Mfeka and Taulisa, Patayi "George Champion" Mhlongo, and "Klaas" Goba (quotation marks indicate baptismal names).[65] Döhne and Lewis Grout had also been able to surround themselves with converts. Döhne's Table Mountain Station, for instance, included only one convert in 1851, but eleven individuals two years later.[66] Lewis Grout's Umsunduzi Station had "ten adult converts" in 1854, including an older man named Mehlwana and another man by the name of Tambusa, who had joined Grout's household and family school in 1847 when he was still a boy.[67]

By the turn of the 1850s, therefore, the American Board missionaries found themselves in the company of convert populations who not only possessed native-speaker proficiency but were often bilingual to varying degrees because they had frequented the missionaries' schools. And they found themselves in the company of people with these language skills precisely at the time when they recognized that their deficiencies in the vernacular language undermined the quality of their language work, notably their Bible translations. In this context, it was quite natural for the American Board missionaries to increase their reliance on the language expertise of Africans in whose midst they resided.

By relying on the language expertise of these African intermediaries, however, the American Board missionaries acquired not only the former's native-speaker proficiency in the vernacular speaking practices but also the rhetorical claims embedded in their preexisting ideology of language. This included the belief that speech patterns to the north of Thukela River in the Zulu kingdom were smoother, purer, more beautiful, and more correct than those used by the people to the south of the Thukela River.

Ukukhuluma Nje

The African intermediaries hold the key to understanding the exact nature of this preexisting ideology of language. While it is impossible to reconstruct the cultural background of each and every one of the ABM's intermediaries, many of them had experienced significant exposure to the rule and culture of the Zulu kingdom before moving to Natal. One piece of evidence pointing in this direction is that the ongoing civil war within the Zulu state forced many of its subjects to flee across Thukela River into Natal in the early 1840s. "Several thousands have left the Zulu country and settled in this region [Natal] during the past two years," the American Board missionaries reported in 1843. "If the emigration continues, this community will soon equal the Zulu country population, and I believe that the facilities for prosecuting missionary operations will be greater here than there."[68] Because the ABM established mission stations among these "refugees" from the Zulu kingdom, its missionaries tended to attract their first converts from people who had a had significant exposure to the Zulu kingdom's culture and ideology of rule.

A good example of this is Lewis Grout's convert, Mehlwana, of whom it was said that he had served in King Shaka's regiments (*amabutho*) in his younger years, long before moving across the Thukela River to Natal.[69] Even better examples are the first converts of Lindley's Inanda Station— Mayembe Dalida Dube, Klaas Goba, Joel Hawes, and John Mavuma. They all belonged to the remnants of the Qadi chiefdom, which had been incorporated into the expanding Zulu kingdom by King Shaka in the late 1810s, and of whom it was said that they "had been instrumental in the final defeat of his oldest and most formidable rival, Zwide of the Ndwandwe, in 1826."[70] Specifically, Mavuma had served as a member of King Shaka's personal bodyguard detachment, while Maymbe had been the wife of Dube, who had served as the reigning chief of the Qadi and as a powerful officer (*induna*) of the Zulu state.[71] Perhaps because they had been Shaka's loyal subjects, King Dingane, who took the throne after his half-brother's death in 1828, did not trust them and had many of them, including Chief Dube, executed in 1837. The survivors, including Mavuma, Mayembe, Hawes, and Goba, fled across the Thukela River into Natal, where they became members of Lindley's Inanda Station about a decade later.[72]

In this context it should also be recalled that Hangu and Ntaba joined Aldin Grout in their teenage years, when the latter resided at Nkanyezi Station in the Zulu state and that they left for Natal only when King Dingane expelled Grout in 1842.[73] Finally, there is the example of Nembula kaDuze (Makhanya), who worked closely with Aldin Grout and possibly Newton Adams. Nembula's father was Duze kaMnengwa, the chief of the Makhanya, a polity which in spite of long-standing ties to the Qwabe chiefdom, had *konza'd* King Shaka's Zulu kingdom. However, sometime after this act of submission, Shaka exploited a succession dispute among the Cele confederation to reorder the political landscape south of the Thukela River in his favor; he had the stronger of the two Cele contenders, Mande, and his key supporter, Duze kaMnengwa, executed to help the weaker contender, Magaye, become the Zulu state's supreme tributary ruler in the Natal region. In the aftermath of this event, the one-year-old Nembula was taken by his mother, Mbulazi Makhanya, to the Mlazi River, where Newton Adams established Umlazi Station in 1836.[74]

Because all these individuals (or their parents) had been raised within the Zulu state's sphere of influence or among people who had been exposed to this influence, it is possible that they had assimilated the claim, based on an ideology of language difference that originated with the Zulu state, that the speech patterns of the Zulu kingdom were more correct, purer, and smoother than those used south of the Thukela River. Given that the Zulu state's ideology of language distinguished between superior and inferior speech patterns for the purpose of separating the kingdom's insider subjects (*amantungwa*) from its outsider tributaries (*amalala*) and that the approximate dividing line between these two population groups was the Thukela River, this supposition is almost a certainty.

The Zulu State and Language

As chapter 1 showed, prior to the late eighteenth century, the inhabitants of South Africa's coastal belt recognized patriclans, chiefdoms, and social status within chiefdoms as the three most important collective identities. While membership in a chiefdom was established by a person submitting to the authority of a particular ruler, both clan and social status identities were established by asserting (real or fictive) genealogies. This meant that the process of incorporating strangers into an existing chiefdom usually ended with the act of submission, unless rulers and subjects considered it advantageous to deepen their mutual bonds by establishing kinship ties either through intermarriage or the invention of fictive genealogical ties. The massive expansion that accompanied the rise of the Zulu state in the early decades of the nineteenth century appears to have outpaced the ability of this system to consolidate power rapidly by transforming strangers into loyal subjects efficiently. This problem, combined with transformations in the security and economic needs as well as the military and coercive capabilities of the Zulu state, gave rise to a language-based discourse of collective identity that had no precedent in the coastal belt of South Africa.

Scholars agree that the region between the Phongolo and Mzimkhulu Rivers witnessed significant transformations between the late eighteenth and early nineteenth centuries, as smaller chiefdoms gave way to larger conquest states, such as the Mthethwa, Ndwandwe, and eventually the Zulu.[75] In 1817, the defeat of Dingiswayo's Mthethwa state at the hands of Zwide kaLanga's Ndwandwe state opened up the opportunity for Shaka kaSenzangakhona and his then relatively small Zulu chiefdom to expand their power in the region. While this expansion took place, Shaka established his own ruling house—the royal house—and legitimized its right to rule over an expanding number of subjects by monopolizing usage of the term *amaZulu*, which can be translated as "people of the sky or heavens."[76] He also appropriated the old term *abenguni* (see chapter 1) in order to link his person and the royal clan with "ancient residence in the land" and, thus, seniority and primacy.

The actual expansion of Shaka's Zulu polity took place in two phases. In the first phase, when their polity was still small, Shaka, and the members of the ruling house focused on subjugating their immediate neighbor chiefdoms between the Black Mfolozi and Thukela Rivers.[77] The key motivation behind this first phase of expansion was most likely the Zulu rulers' desire to quickly increase their subject base and military resources to face the Ndwandwe state, which, in the aftermath of their victory against the Mthethwa, had become the most powerful polity in the region. The desire to protect themselves against the Ndwandwe would also explain why the Zulu rulers tried to tie newly conquered populations as effectively as possible to their rule. Thus they enrolled the (young) men and women of these chiefdoms into the Zulu state's male warrior and female labor regiments (*amabutho*) and, in so doing, encouraged them to see the Zulu royal house rather than their own hereditary chiefs as their true benefactors and superiors.[78] At the same time, the Zulu rulers forbade conquered people to express independent forms of authority and culture so as to accelerate their assimilation as subjects of the Zulu state. One informant described this process in these terms:

> Tshaka did not scatter the nations; he unified (*qoqa'd*) them. . . . [The leading men of formerly powerful and independent chiefly lines, such as] Somapunga ka Zwide (Ndwandwe), Myandeya (Mtetwa), Msicwa ka Pungatshe and Mtshubane ka Pungatshe (Buthelezi)—none of these sang their *ingoma* [i.e., chants that accompany coming of age ceremonial dances], nor did they hold their *umkosi* [first fruit ceremonies] according to previous custom, for it would be said they wished to make kings of themselves. They were not allowed to *buta* people

[enroll people in their own regiments]; . . . only the Zulus retained their old laws and customs. *Other tribes were made to relinquish many old customs by the Zulus* . . . for after their defeat all people became the king's subjects.[79]

Finally, the rulers of the Zulu state encouraged their new subjects, as well as members of the royal house and related clans, to adopt the preexisting label *amantungwa* (see chapter 1 for details) as a key aspect of their identity as bona fide members of the Zulu state. This label implied a common place of origin, notably in distant upland regions from where in the distant past they had allegedly all "come or rolled down [to the coastal region of Natal-Zululand] using a grain basket [as a floating or rolling device]" (*ukwehla ngesilulu*).[80]

The Zulu rulers experienced some difficulties in convincing the core members of the Qwabe state (i.e., those who traced their descent back to the mythical ancestor "Qwabe") to adopt this *amantungwa* identity, as they had "a clearly marked out and named cultural identification as lowlanders (*abasenzansi*)."[81] This predicament explains why Shaka employed a personal touch to convince some members of the Qwabe to embrace the *amantungwa* identity. A particular powerful description of this process of assimilation comes from the 1905 testimony of an informant named Mkehlengana. Born into the Ncwana section of the Qwabe, Mkehlengana argued in 1905, "Like the Zulu tribe we are *amaNtungwa*."[82] However, from the rest of his account it is clear that this identity resulted from his father's submission (*ukukhonza*) to Shaka and the latter's acceptance of the former as a fellow member of the *amantungwa*. As he noted, "Tshaka said to Komfiya [Mkehlengana's father, also known as Zulu kaNogandaya] when he came to *konza*. . . . 'Komfiya, approach.' In fear my father approached him. Shaka tapped him on the head and said, 'Do not show fear here among us. . . . You will be a close friend, for you are of our people; we originated together with you. We are *amaNtungwa* together with you.'"[83] The same predicament also explains why the Zulu rulers tried to accommodate the "lowland" aspect of the Qwabe identity by inventing a story of common origin, which held that the original ancestors of the Qwabe and Zulu peoples were two brothers, Qwabe and Zulu, the sons of a man from the north by the name of Malandela.[84] The origin story allowed the Qwabe to think of themselves as *amantungwa*, because it suggested that their ancient origins were in the upland region in spite of their more recent self-identification as lowlanders.

The most powerful and novel aspect of the *amantungwa* identity was the claim that the *amantungwa* were unified by linguistic ties as well. This idea seems to have first emerged when the Zulu rulers established their own mode of speaking as the "official" language of the Zulu state in general and the *amantungwa* in particular. Although some people would later refer to this speaking practice as the "King's Zulu," "Ntungwa Nguni," or even "Zunda," the Zulu rulers themselves referred to it simply by way of the verb *ukukhuluma*.[85] Evidence for the use of this term comes from missionary linguist Döhne, who explained in 1857 that "the Zulu language . . . was . . . called the *Ukukuluma*."[86] He added that *ukukhuluma* distinguished itself from other speaking practices in the region in "that it is comparatively free from many harsh and flat sounds, and always compounds the nasal or liquid sounds before d, g, b, p, &c., as *tanda, tenga, hamba, mpompa*, &c."[87]

The Zulu rulers expended considerable energy on encouraging their new subjects to assimilate this way of speaking and to embrace it as a marker of their *amantungwa*-ness. For instance, they implemented a custom known as *ukukhuluma nje*, which compelled all *amantungwa* to use *ukukhuluma* in specific settings, notably in the royal court and councils, and military villages and regiments.[88] As Wilhelm Bleek explained in an unpublished manuscript in 1856, "The Zulu custom . . . requires every man, if speaking in public, either in their courts of law, or at court, to speak properly and correctly, viz. *uku-Kuluma-nje*."[89] One year later, Döhne expressed a similar idea when he noted: "[Shaka's] ambition seemed not so much to destroy the neighbouring tribes, as to subdue and incorporate them with his own. . . . Those of them who spoke another dialect than the Zulu were prohibited from doing so in his presence, and addressed him by means of an interpreter. This was continued until they were able to express themselves properly in the Zulu language, . . . *Ukukuluma*."[90] Given this context, it appears that the best translation of the word *ukukhuluma* is not "to speak" (the meaning it has in the modern Zulu language) but rather "to speak the official court language" or "to speak properly." This way of translating the word *ukukhuluma* also appeared in some of the early published Zulu-language dictionaries. In 1899, for instance, missionary linguist Albert Kropf translated *uku-Kùluma* as "to speak the high court dialect," and *isi-Kùlumo* and *u-Kùlumo* as the "Court language with the Zulus."[91]

The success of the custom of *ukukhuluma nje* can be gauged by looking at communities that experienced language shifts following their submission to Zulu rule. It appears that the "Khumalo people" were one of these communities. As an informant named Magidigidi explained in 1905, "They had a separate dialect of their own, these Kumalo people. [But] it was altered by Tshaka."[92] There is also the case of the Ntuli section of the Bhele people.[93] Although the Ntuli had first submitted to Shaka's father Senzangakhona, they became recognized as *amantungwa* during the subsequent reign of Shaka. As part of their assimilation into the Zulu state's *amantungwa*, they adopted the story of migration from the north by way of the grain basket required by this identity.[94] More importantly, they stopped using their own mode of speaking (*ukutekeza*) and began to use *ukukhuluma*. This would explain why an informant recalled having witnessed the Ntuli chief Ndlela kaSompisi speaking "in the ordinary Zulu way" during King Dingane's reign.[95]

Not all subjugated people embraced this custom with the same enthusiasm and success as the Ntuli and Khumalo. This is suggested by Bleek, who, while traveling through Natal and the Zulu kingdom in 1855 and 1856, wrote in his diary: "I interrogated several aMatonga. I discovered that their language . . . is the language which the Zulus call uKutugeza. . . . It was spoken far more frequently, until under the rule of the Zulus the *nKukulumanje*, meaning the slaughter of a language, was effected."[96] Although it is likely that Bleek both misspelled and mistranslated the term in his diary, his association of the term *ukukhuluma nje* with the "slaughter of a language" may have nevertheless made sense from the perspective of his interlocutors. As speakers of *ukutekeza*, a mode of communication viewed as particularly offensive by the Zulu rulers, these "aMatonga" probably experienced the many adjustments they had to make in order to abide by the custom of *ukukhuluma nje* as akin to *ukukhukhula manje*, the "slaughtering" or rather "sweeping away" of their own language.[97]

It is noteworthy that the Zulu rulers took the sting out of this process of language assimilation for the people who were particularly important to the success of their conquest state, the numerous and powerful Qwabe. They did so by identifying the speaking practices of the Qwabe and other coastal communities between the Thukela and Phongolo Rivers (for example, the Mthethwa) as *ukuthefula* and classifying it as a legitimate, if inferior, mode of communication among the *amantungwa*.

Evidence for the contemporary use of the term *ukuthefula* comes from a variety of sources. Bleek explained in the 1850s that "there are chiefly the aMagwabi [i.e., Qwabe] to be mentioned as a *Tefula*-tribe."[98] African informants around 1900 provided similar evidence: "A characteristic of the Qwabe people is that they *tefula*."[99] Providing more detail, Bishop Colenso explained in 1859 that "the *ukutefula*, in fact, is rather a sort of lisping Zulu [i.e., *ukukhuluma*]."[100]

Probably for this reason, the Zulu rulers classified *ukuthefula* as a legitimate but inferior mode of speech among the *amantungwa*. Apparently the very top of Zulu society practiced this inclusive approach. "[King] Dingana *tefula'd* in his speech to some extent," one African informant recalled in 1909.[101] Another informant noted in 1909 that King Mpande "sometimes *tefula'd*."[102] Despite this inclusive approach, the Zulu rulers did classify *ukuthefula* as an inferior mode of speaking. This can be gathered from the very meaning of the term, which can be translated as "to be oily, slippery."[103] It is also apparent from the Zulu rulers' insistence that this mode of speaking be avoided on official, public occasions. As Bleek explained in 1856, "The *uku-Tefula* is indeed so very general that one nearly may say that half the Zulu nation is speaking it ... although most who speak so in common will, on public occasions, have recourse to the proper Zulu enunciation; for the *uku-Tefula* is considered as incorrect, and its popularity of pronunciation pointed out and sneered at."[104]

Even though the tolerant attitude toward *ukuthefula* may be explained by Shaka having lived for many years among the *ukuthefula*-speaking Mthethwa, it should probably be seen as the Zulu rulers' attempt to accommodate the linguistic peculiarities of the numerous and powerful Qwabe and, in so doing, encourage them to adopt the *amantungwa* identity. Indeed, in the same way as the Zulu rulers' discourse of *amantungwa*-ness accommodated the Qwabe's self-identification as lowlanders through a carefully crafted story of origin about Malandela and his sons, it accommodated the Qwabe's linguistic differences by classifying *ukuthefula* as a legitimate, albeit inferior, speaking practice among the Zulu state's subject base. In doing so, the Zulu rulers created a collective identity (*amantungwa*) whose principal markers were the myth of their common "upcountry" descent and their common language, notably *ukukhuluma*. With the help of this collective identity, they transformed the communities subjugated during the first phase of expansion into subjects who identified more closely with the Zulu state and were willing to defend it against the Ndwandwe threat.

UkuTekeza

This threat began to wane following two Zulu victories against the Ndwandwe in 1821 and 1826.[105] What remained, however, was the Zulu rulers' need to continuously acquire and redistribute resources to support their subject base of *amantungwa*. It was this need that encouraged the Zulu rulers to embark on a second phase of expansion, notably across the Thukela River into Natal, where they subjugated the Thuli and Cele polities.[106] With the Ndwandwe threat contained but the need for resources increased, the Zulu rulers lost the desire to incorporate these newly conquered polities as subjects (*amantungwa*). On the contrary, to legitimize and maximize the exploitation of these groups, the Zulu rulers desired to "trap" them permanently in an inferior tributary status. They achieved this in part by excluding the leaders of these polities from the Zulu state's key offices of power. Furthermore, the Zulu rulers did not enroll the young men and women of these polities into the Zulu state's *amabutho* but organized them as irregular support units responsible for collecting, guarding, and transporting the resources destined to benefit the Zulu state and its subject base of *amantungwa*.[107]

Most importantly, the Zulu rulers deployed a discourse of exclusion to entrench the separate and inferior status of these tributaries. The use of (potentially preexisting) derogatory names was an important component of this exclusionary discourse.[108] For instance, the Zulu state identified those tributaries residing to the south of the Thukela River by a variety of derogatory names, notably *amazo(t)sha* (face-slitters), *izindiki* (stump-fingered ones), *inyakeni* (dirty people), and *amalala* (menial know-nothings).[109] The last term was an old term (see chapter 1 for details) that the Zulu state now appropriated, invested with contempt, and applied specifically to its tributaries from the region south of the Thukela River. As one African individual by the name of Mqayikana kaYenge explained in 1916, "We . . . are amaLala, having been so called by the Zulus who defeated us. By so speaking they insulted us . . . for people that defeat others insult them."[110]

Particularly significant here is the fact that the Zulu rulers also mobilized language differences (however small) as means of entrenching the inferior status of the polities referred to as *amalala*. This mobilization of language differences for the purpose of exclusion and exploitation may have been triggered by their preexisting use of language as a marker of *amantungwa*-ness. In other words, having used language as a means to construct a well-bounded *amantungwa* identity during the first phase of expansion, the Zulu rulers were compelled to also use language differences as a means of circumscribing its "inferior" counterpart—*amalala*-ness—during the second phase of expansion. And whereas the Zulu rulers tied *amantungwa*-ness to the use of *ukukhuluma*, they tied *amalala*-ness to the use of *ukutekeza*.

According to Döhne (1857), *ukutekeza* (also called *ukutekela* or *isilala*) omitted "the nasal sounds, and transmutes some consonants" and, in some of its variations, used only "low, broad, and flat sounds."[111] Colenso added that people who "*tekeza* in their speech" pronounced *inkomo*, "bullock," as *iyomo; umlomo*, "mouth," as *unomo;* and *abafazi*, "women," as *abafati*.[112] The Zulu rulers used these pronunciations as markers of *amalala*-ness: "The amaLala were so called," a person named Dinya kaZokozwayo explained, "because they speak the *tekela* dialect and thereby speak with their tongues lying low (*lala*)."[113] Importantly, in the same way that the Zulu rulers used derogatory terms for tributaries, they slandered the latter's speaking practices. Thus, Döhne explained that *ukutekeza* referred to the speaking practices of the *amalala*, who were considered "neglectful in their pronunciation as they were sleepy in speaking."[114] Colenso added that *ukutekeza* referred to "speak[ing] roughly, as the *amaLala*."[115] As the phrases "neglectful in their pronunciation" and "speaking roughly" suggest, the Zulu rulers characterized *ukutekeza* as an inferior mode of speech. Statements from African informants make this particularly clear. "We were laughed at by the Zulus," one explained, "because of our [*ukutekeza*] dialect."[116] Another one, a convert of Qadi background and, thus, of the same background as many of the American Board missionaries' intermediaries, explained similarly: "[Shaka] said that we were Lala because our tongues lay [*lala*] flat in our mouths, and we did not speak in the Ntungwa fashion."[117]

The Zulu state thus promoted a discourse of collective identity that represented a significant innovation from the type of collective identity discourses that had prevailed in South Africa's coastal belt in previous centuries. According to the latter, collective belonging depended not on language but on formal acts of submission or the assertion of real or fictive genealogical ties. The Zulu kingdom, however, introduced a language-based discourse of collective identity into South Africa's coastal belt. It classified as *amantungwa* the people who resided in the heartland of the Zulu state north of the Thukela River and spoke the "superior" speech pattern *ukukhuluma*, and it labeled as *amalala* the populations living on the state's margins to the south of the Thukela River and used the "inferior" mode of speech called *ukutekeza*.

The emergence of this innovation was made possible by a combination of factors—the militarization of circumcision schools (*amabutho*), the Ndwandwe threat to the emerging Zulu state, the need to support an expanding subject base, and the success of the Zulu regiments on the battlefield between 1817 and 1828. During the Zulu state's first expansion phase, the Ndwandwe threat encouraged the Zulu rulers to bind newly conquered polities more firmly to their rule by claiming that they were all *amantungwa*, unified by their "upcountry" origins and their shared speaking practice, *ukukhuluma*. During the next phase of expansion south of the Thukela River, the need to support their massive *amantungwa* motivated the Zulu rulers to permanently exclude newly conquered polities by claiming that they were *amalala*, unified by their general inferiority as well as their *ukutekeza* speech pattern. The resulting ideology defined *ukukhuluma* as the "official," "proper," or "best" language, while classifying *ukutekeza* as an inferior language and determining the Thukela River as the approximate dividing line between the two.

Old Rhetoric Becomes New Rhetoric

This preexisting ideology of language entered the American Board missionaries' understanding of language in the region at the turn of the 1850s, when they became more reliant on African language experts who had historical ties to the early Zulu state and whose own understanding of language had been shaped by this state's ideology of language. However, the missionaries did not simply adopt this preexisting ideology verbatim; rather, they reworked the Zulu state's rhetoric about *ukukhuluma* being superior to *ukutekeza* into their own argument about Zulu being superior to "Caffre."

This type of reworking is noticeable in Lewis Grout's *Zulu Grammar*, where the author argued that Zulu was purer than "any of the African languages or dialects," including "Caffre," because since "the days of Chaka" there "has been a steady refining elevating process, the language of the conquered being gradually fashioned to the higher standard and more fixed character of their superiors."[118] Jakob Döhne also reworked the old rhetoric into a new argument when he explained that Zulu was the "mother" or "foundation" of the "Caffre" language (that is, Zulu was superior to "Caffre") because "it is evident that the Zulu dialect, by Chaka's law regarding the *Ukukuluma*, has retained its originality with a precision and gravity of expression far beyond the other dialects, and this result has followed from that measure alone."[119]

The same conflation of argument occurred in Seth Stone's rejection letter of 1854, in which he claimed that Zulu should not be assimilated with "Caffre" into a single literary language because there existed an unparalleled "beauty in the (King's) Zulu." Consider again these excerpts of Stone's letter of rejection, which clearly illustrate the link between the old and new rhetoric:

> Is there a degree of affinity between the Kafir and the Zulu as would warrant the hope that one standard version of the Scriptures . . . would meet both languages and dialects? This question was decided in the negative. . . . The following are some of the reasons assigned for this decision. . . . The [American Board] Missionaries . . . when they had gained knowledge of this [Zulu dialect], as they had previously of the other [Kafir] dialect, thought they saw a smoothness and a beauty in the (King's) Zulu which they had not discovered in the other, and subsequent observations on other dialects have confirmed them in the belief that the Zulu is superior to all the kindred dialects in the vicinity.[120]

As revealed here, in the 1850s, the American Board missionaries began to construct arguments about the superiority of Zulu over "Caffre" by reworking the Zulu kingdom's preexisting ideology of language, which held that *ukukhuluma* (i.e., the King's Zulu) was the "best" speech pattern in the region. Importantly, this older ideology of language found its way into the American Board missionaries' ideas about the coastal belt's linguistic landscape in the 1850s only because this was the time when they began to rely more intensely on the African intermediaries—Davida, Nanise, Nembula, Hangu, Ntaba, and others—whose ideas about language had been shaped by the Zulu state.

The influence of these individuals on the American Board missionaries' understanding of the coastal belt's linguistic landscape was not radically dissimilar from the ways in which Diyani Tzatzoe, Noyi Gciniswa, Jantje Nooka, and others shaped the European missionaries' assessment of language in the region. What differed radically were the preexisting ideologies of language that these two groups of intermediaries communicated to their respective missionary patrons. The latter group had their most significant cultural roots in the métis (mixed) polities of the eastern Cape borderlands, including the Gonaqua, Gqunukhwebe, and Ntinde. These polities had long distrusted language as a useful marker of belonging because they had to forge meaningful polities out of people who spoke radically different languages—"Hottentot" (Khoesan) and "Caffre" (Nguni). Because these polities did not use language as a marker of belonging, people like Tzatzoe, Gciniswa, and Nooka were not culturally conditioned to perceive as significant the relatively small differences between the coastal belt's various (Nguni) speech forms even if they recognized them otherwise.

The situation was radically different in the Natal-Zululand region, where the Zulu conquest-state had for some time aggressively promoted a language-based discourse of collective identity. Because this discourse differentiated high-status subjects from low-status tributaries on the basis of "superior" and "inferior" speaking practices known as *ukukhuluma* and *ukutekeza*, people in this region were culturally conditioned to reperceive as very significant the relatively small differences between the speech forms north and south of the Thukela River. This preexisting ideology of language and belonging began to influence the American Board missionaries' views of local speaking practices at the turn of the 1850s because this was the time when they started to rely on the language expertise of Davida, Nanise, Nembula, Hangu, Ntaba, and others.

Consequently, African intermediaries and African ideologies contributed decisively to the missionaries' differing understandings of the coastal belt's linguistic landscape. By the early 1850s, European missionaries, notably William Shaw, were convinced that a single literary language could be developed for the entire coastal belt because they believed that no essential difference existed between the region's various forms of speech. The American Board missionaries rejected this single-language paradigm because they were convinced that Zulu was not only different from but also superior to the other speech forms in the coastal belt. When the ABM rebuffed Shaw's proposal in 1854, the opportunity to create a single Bible translation and, in doing so, form the basis for a single unifying literary language for all the African communities residing between the eastern Cape and Delagoa Bay slipped away. Henceforth, the American Board missionaries in Natal-Zululand and the European missionaries in the eastern Cape, with the help of their respective African language experts, promoted separate standardizing projects that eventually culminated in the emergence of distinct Zulu and Xhosa literary languages and language-based identities.

• 7 •

"Many People ... Explain This Identity Primarily in Terms of the Language They Speak"

*The Language-Based Zulu-Xhosa Divide
in South African Consciousness*

A language-based Zulu ethnic identity crystallized in the early twentieth century due to a convergence of factors, such as the collapse of the Zulu kingdom, the rise of a mission-educated Black elite (*amakholwa*), the implementation of oppressive colonial policies, and the widening experience of migrant labor.[1] Of pivotal importance was that African intellectuals from both sides of the Thukela River came together to found Zulu ethnic nationalist organizations that promoted the Zulu language as an important marker of Zuluness. This development began with the establishment of the Zulu Institute in 1917 and the Zulu National Association in 1919.[2] In 1924, African intellectuals founded *Inkatha ka Zulu*, an organization that defined "the Zulu nation ... as including all the Zulu-speaking people in the whole Province of Natal [i.e., on both side of the Thukela River]."[3] When *Inkatha ka Zulu* dissolved in 1930, other Zulu ethnic nationalist organizations picked up the torch. In 1937, the American Board mission–trained Albert Luthuli and the Natal Bantu Teachers Association founded "The Zulu Cultural and Language Society," whose object was to nurture the Zulu identity of younger generations by teaching them Zulu history, culture, and—crucially—*language*.[4] This practice only intensified when, with the support of the apartheid regime, Zulu ethnic nationalists such as Mangosutho Gatsha Buthelezi helped create the Zulu Territorial Authority in 1970 and the *Inkatha YaKwaZulu* in 1975 (which became the *Inkatha Freedom Party* in 1990).[5] As this brief overview makes

clear, a series of Zulu ethnic nationalist organizations more or less continuously fostered a broad, trans-Thukela language–based Zulu ethnic identity
in the twentieth century.

Africans in the eastern Cape region never established an organization that
promoted a broad, language-based Xhosa ethnic nationalism. Instead, they
created organizations that were either very narrow, such as *Intlanganiso Ye
Nqubelo Pambili Yama Ngqika* (est. 1885), which promoted primarily Ngqika-
Xhosa interests, or very broad, as in the case of *Imbumba Yama Nyama* (est.
1882), which sought to unify all Black people in South Africa.[6] In practice,
Imbumba Yama Nyama was not even able to resolve the gulf between the
eastern Cape's Xhosa and Mfengu communities, which only widened when
they established separate political organizations, newspapers, and annual
festivities in the late nineteenth and early twentieth centuries.[7] The apartheid state's creation of separate Transkei and Ciskei homelands in 1963 and
1972, presented other obstacles to the formation of a broad language-based
Xhosa identity in the eastern Cape.

But these factors did not prevent its eventual appearance. By the 1980s,
the populations of the Ciskei and Transkei protested against their division into two homelands by insisting they were "Xhosa speakers" and "one
people."[8] By 1992 even the Ciskei homeland ruler Joshua Oupa Gqozo
insisted that the Bhaca people of the Transkei were Xhosas because "we
consider all the Xhosa-speaking tribes to be Xhosas."[9] In the case of Xhosaness even more so perhaps than in the case of Zuluness, the emergence of a
broad, language-based identity was aided by the expansion of a vernacular
literature and press and the widening experience of migrant labor, urban
life, passbooks, and identity cards in the twentieth century.[10]

However, even after taking all of these factors into account, when it
comes to the history of South Africa's language-based Zulu and Xhosa identities, one foundational question remains: Why did Africans in the coastal
belt self-identify as Zulu or Xhosa speakers in the first place?

Put differently, why would a person from Natal or Zululand refer to
their vernaculars as the Zulu language if historically people distinguished
between *ukukhuluma* and *ukutekeza* in this region? Why would the Mfengu,
Thembu, Mpondomise, Mpondo, Bhaca, Bomvana, Xhesibe, and Hlubi
residents of the eastern Cape region recognize their vernaculars as part of
a common Xhosa language and on the basis of this recognition self-identify
as Xhosa speakers? Again, these languages were *not* already there, as the
previous chapters have made clear. What was there were Nguni vernaculars

that varied slightly from place to place. The languages that came to demarcate Zuluness and Xhosaness in the twentieth century, however, were not the same as these vernaculars but "standardized, written languages . . . fixed in time and space by grammars and orthographies."[11]

I argue that the origins of the Zulu and Xhosa languages that eventually came to demarcate two divergent identities date back to the year 1854, when the American Board missionaries rejected the proposal to produce a single "Caffre" language translation of the Bible for the entire region between the Cape Colony and Delagoa Bay. This rejection resulted in the bifurcation of what used to be considered a "Caffre" language continuum into distinct Zulu and "Caffre" (soon called Xhosa) languages. At first this bifurcation was purely theoretical, a mere fiction in the minds of the missionaries and their intermediaries. To turn it into reality, they and other stakeholders resorted to language standardization and language education. In Natal-Zululand, language standardization involved missionaries and Africans identifying the "King's Zulu" as the "purest" form of speech and elevating it to the standard of the Zulu language. In the eastern Cape region, missionaries and Africans developed standard Xhosa by harmonizing the region's diverse speech forms into a "more perfect" language.

Even though language standardization was a long and conflict-ridden process not fully completed until the early decades of the twentieth century, Africans and non-Africans in their capacity as lawmakers, superintendents of education, and schoolteachers started promoting standardized forms of Zulu and Xhosa as part of "mother-tongue" education in schools in the second half of the nineteenth century. As the availability of schooling and literacy increased in the twentieth century, more and more Africans came to accept their vernaculars (home dialects) as belonging to these standard languages, to recognize their vernaculars as inferior versions of these standards, and to shift gradually (and often imperfectly) from their vernaculars to these standard languages. The combined effect of this process was that pupils also moved from more local, non-language-based identity discourses (such as Thonga, Mpondo, or Hlubi, for instance) toward broader, language-based notions of Zuluness or Xhosaness.

Lest we exoticize the African experience, it is appropriate to point out that the same dynamics operated in Europe. I already discussed the German example in the introduction. France can serve as a second comparative example.[12]

Before 1300, the region that became modern France represented a patchwork of regional polities such as the county of Anjou, the duchy of Normandy, and the duchy of Aquitaine, some of which swore nominal fealty to the Capetian kings of France, who at times controlled no more than the city of Paris and its immediate environs (the Île-de-France). Although Latin functioned as the universal spoken and written language of the temporal and clerical elite in this period, each polity's subject population had its own regional vernacular (patois), which were slowly beginning to amalgamate into regional written vernaculars such as *langue d'oïl* and *langue d'oc*. *Langue d'oïl* became known as the king's French over time because it was based on the vernaculars of the Île-de-France, where the king had his power base. It achieved wider prominence as a result of the first (king's) French translation of the New Testament in 1523, and the introduction of limited (king's) French language education upon the foundation of the Collège de France in 1530.

Because reading and education were elite activities, these decisions did not lead to the widespread emergence of a language-based French identity. Indeed, when the Abbé Gregoire conducted the first comprehensive study of France's linguistic landscape in 1793, he reported that "six million French people, above all in the countryside, [were] in complete ignorance of the national language [i.e., the king's French]."[13] Inspired by the publication of Gregoire's report, the leaders of the French Revolution decided that instruction of standard French in public primary schools was needed to unify the nation linguistically and therefore politically. Widespread language-based education did not come to full fruition until the Third Republic, however, when, in the aftermath of the Franco-Prussian War (1870–71), education in standard French became both free and compulsory.[14] Designed to strengthen national identity, this program was so successful that, in 1923, the French linguist André Thérive proclaimed: "Our linguistic consciousness is nothing less than our national consciousness."[15]

The statement matches the situation in modern-day South Africa, where many people insist that the Zulu language defines Zuluness and the Xhosa language demarcates Xhosaness. The historical process that produced this outcome is also similar. It included human decision making about what constituted the Zulu and Xhosa languages and about who spoke, or rather was supposed to speak, these languages. It involved language standardization and language education. Language-based Zuluness and Xhosaness are therefore modern identities in the same way that language-based French and German identities are modern.

Zulu Language Standardization

The American Board missionaries' desire to standardize the Zulu language resulted from the recognition that what they considered the best vernacular in the Natal-Zululand region (i.e., *ukukhuluma* [the king's Zulu]) coexisted with a range of other vernaculars, notably *ukutekeza*. In 1854, Lewis Grout readily admitted that a lot of people in this region did not speak the king's Zulu but used "heterogeneous and diversified dialects."[16] Other individuals commented on the same phenomenon. In 1859, the Anglican bishop John Colenso explained that in Natal "there are also large bodies of the natives who speak other dialects, differing distinctly from the Zulu."[17] He identified one of these dialects as "*ukutekeza*," which was "understood with difficulty even by a Zulu, if unpracticed in it."[18]

In the face of this complex linguistic situation, the impulse of the missionaries was to engage in what Johannes Fabian has called "prescriptive imposition and control."[19] Much of this prescriptivism (as it is called in the field of sociolinguistics) occurred initially in the realm of discourse. Part and parcel of this discursive effort involved comparing the language situation in Natal-Zululand to familiar and already well-established language categories in Europe. For instance, Bishop Colenso claimed in 1855 that "the vernacular of different tribes [in Natal] may be expected to differ considerably from this [standard Zulu], just as the dialect of Yorkshire or Somersetshire differs from pure English."[20] Linguist Wilhelm Bleek deployed the same analogy, explaining in 1856 that *ukutekeza* "comprises a dialect or rather a number of dialects not less different from the proper Zulu language, as the proudest Scotch is from English."[21] Needless to say, neither Bleek nor Colenso reflected on the arbitrary process that had produced these dichotomies in Europe.

Some commentators tried to legitimize the concept of standard Zulu by tying it to the Zulu kingdom's practice of *ukukhuluma nje*. As Bleek explained in 1856, "In the whole of the Colony of Natal and in the Zulu Empire, one and the same language is now considered as the standard for all the different native tribes. This fact is of comparatively recent date, and finds its explanation in the former extension of the Zulu Empire over these parts, and in the peculiarity of the Zulu custom . . . *uku-Kuluma-nje*."[22] However, it was difficult to square this argument with evidence that suggested that many of the Africans in Natal had never been linguistically assimilated into the Zulu state. As Bleek himself explained in the same paragraph, "More generally this [*ukutekeza*] is known as the language of the Malala, i.e. those remnants of the subjugated tribes, who escaped an amalgamation with the Zulu nation, and lived hidden in the bushes or recesses of the mountains."[23] Lewis Grout avoided these contradictions by adopting a longer historical time frame. Although he admitted that a variety of dialects still coexisted in Natal-Zululand in the second half of the nineteenth century, he insisted that the imposition of standard Zulu remained sound because "it is evident . . . that the language of all these tribes, or clans, was substantially one, even before the days of Chaka."[24] For Lewis Grout this constituted a fact and a perfect rationale for prescribing the king's Zulu as the standard Zulu language for all the inhabitants of the region.

What helped with this effort were publications—schoolbooks, grammars, dictionaries, newspapers, and books—printed in standardized literary Zulu.[25] Particularly important were publications of the Bible. The New Testament in the Zulu language was first published in 1865. In the same manner in which Africans had been involved in the translation process at the turn of the 1850s, they continued to be involved in the succeeding decades. The ABM's work on the Old Testament, for instance, moved forward with the help of Talitha Hawes (the granddaughter of one of the first African members of Inanda Station), who translated the Song of Solomon.[26] John Nembula, the son of one of the first African members of Umlazi Station, helped American Board missionary Stephen Pixley produce the first complete Bible translation between 1879 and 1881. In the latter year, he also accompanied Pixley to Chicago, Illinois, in the United States to make sure that the manuscript made it correctly through the press.[27] Two years later, in 1883, the first copies of the complete Bible in the Zulu language—*Ibaible Eli Ingcwele. Eli Netestamente Elidala, Nelitya, Ku Kitywa Kuzo Izilimi Zokuqala, Ku Lotywa NgokwesiZulu*—arrived in Natal-Zululand.

The number of Zulu language Bibles sold in South Africa increased steadily thereafter, possibly aided by the American Board missionaries issuing revised versions in 1893 and 1924 and the Hermannsburger Evangelical-Lutheran Missionary Society releasing its own complete translation in 1924.[28] In 1911 alone, the American Bible Society supplied 6,766 Bibles in Zulu.[29] Four years later, the number was 20,005.[30] The British Foreign Bible Society also supplied the South African market. By the end of 1912, the BFBS had printed or purchased for distribution a cumulative 147,806 Bibles or portions of Bibles in the Zulu language.[31] By the end of 1929, this number had more than doubled to 304,571.[32]

After the turn of the twentieth century, a growing number of authors published in "standard" Zulu. James Stuart, the assistant magistrate of Durban, authored several histories of the people of the region in the Zulu language between 1923 and 1926.[33] Mission-trained African converts such as John Langalibalele Dube, Magema Fuze, and Sipetu (Petros) kaLutoluni Lamula also began to publish in "standard" Zulu. Starting in 1903, Dube issued the Zulu-language newspaper *Ilanga lase Natal* (The Natal Sun). Fuze published the monograph *Abantu Abamnyama Lapa Bavela Ngakona* (The Black People and Whence They Came) in 1922, and Lamula published his *UZulu kaMalandela* (Zulu the son of Mandela) in 1924. Three years later, in 1927, two African teachers, Alban Mbata and Garland Mdhladhla, authored a schoolbook of Zulu folk tales titled *UCakijana Bogcololo* (The Slender Mongoose).[34]

By 1928, these prescriptive efforts and publication activities had produced an important consensus among linguists about the language situation in Natal-Zululand. As the doyen of Bantu linguistics, Clement Doke explained at the time: "Zulu is the accepted language of Natal and Zululand."[35] In other words, Doke no longer acknowledged (or no longer recognized) the region's vernacular diversity. In his view, there was only one valid African language in the Natal-Zululand region, and that language was (standard) Zulu. These developments had parallels in the eastern Cape region. For as Doke made clear in 1928, the coastal belt consisted of "two major languages"—"Zulu *and* Xosa."[36]

Xhosa Language Standardization

The development of the Xhosa language began with the American Board missionaries' decision to reject Shaw's proposal in 1854. This rejection compelled the eastern Cape region's European missionaries and African intermediaries to reimagine the "Caffre" language continuum as extending only as far as the southern boundary of Natal. As part of this reimagination, missionaries and Africans gradually changed the name of this language continuum from "Caffre" to Xhosa (which prompts me to call this language Xhosa from this point forward—using Xhosa when direct quotes in English use "Caffre" or any of its derivatives). Moreover, the reimagining forced missionaries and Africans to revisit the question of how to best standardize this Xhosa language. This issue was pressing because the process of Bible translation was still ongoing and was supposed to render God's word accurately in the indigenous population's own language. Standardizing the Xhosa language in this context became a highly contentious issue when and where debates about language converged with other thorny issues, such as the Wesleyan-Presbyterian rivalry and the Xhosa-Mfengu animosity.

These issues first came to the fore in discussions about the Bible translation that Wesleyan missionary John Appleyard published in 1864. Appleyard's fellow Wesleyans and members of the Mfengu communities welcomed it. A Mfengu convert, Charles Pamla, for instance, noted that he had read the translation in the company of three friends, and they all had agreed that "this translation is quite correct."[37] Appleyard himself asked the Mfengu population of Mount Coke Station to comment on the quality of the translation and they allegedly "assured [him] it was perfect."[38]

The harshest criticisms came from Scottish Presbyterians who were connected to the region's Ngqika communities.[39] The leading voice among them was Tiyo Soga, who had strong ties to the Ngqika chiefdom because his father was a direct descendant of Jotello, who had been a leading councillor of Chief Ngqika himself. Perfectly bilingual in both English and the Ngqika vernacular, Soga had attended the Scottish mission school at Lovedale and was ordained a minister of the United Presbyterian Church while living in Scotland in the 1850s.[40] In 1866, he led the charge in criticizing the Appleyard Version: "It is not the language the Kaffirs [Xhosa] themselves speak.... Take any chapter from any book, or take any column from any page, and you will find challengeable unidiomatic sentences, that not only offend the ear, but make the book unpleasant to read—Do you tell me that such a Bible is in the vernacular of a people?"[41] Soga not only accused the translation of lacking idiomatic character, however. He added that the Appleyard Version was also faulty because the gospel of Matthew, chapter 27, verse 23 used "Kanangonolde," which "is not Kaffir [Xhosa]—but Fingo [Mfengu]."[42] This latter statement raises questions about exactly what Soga meant when he spoke of the Xhosa language. Although European missionaries and their African interpreters had long used a broad, inclusivist approach to defining the target language for translations in the coastal belt, Soga now argued that including Mfengu speech forms undermined the purity of the Xhosa language.

In 1868, the BFBS and a significant segment of the missionary and convert population agreed that it was best to prepare a new translation that addressed the concerns of the critics. They instructed the various denominations in the eastern Cape to appoint a board of revisers. The United

Presbyterian Church elected Soga as its representative.[43] The Free Church of Scotland sent Bryce Ross, who, as the son of Scottish missionary John Ross, had grown up among the Ngqika and spoke their vernacular fluently. Making up two of the seven board members allowed Scottish Presbyterians with Ngqika connections to exercise significant influence over the revising process, although it was never exclusively in their hands.

Similar to Appleyard's Version, this new edition functioned as a battleground on which various stakeholders fought over the character of the Xhosa language but also over denominational and ethnic influence in the region. The Wesleyans voiced their misgivings as soon as the New Testament of the revised version became available.[44] In 1879, Wesleyan missionary William S. Dewstoe reported that the Thembu converts of the Queenstown Native District disliked the new version because "instead of being pure Kaffir [Xhosa], it is full of Gaika [Ngqika] provincialisms."[45] The Thembu were not alone. Wesleyan missionaries most frequently mentioned the Mfengu population's negative reaction to the new translation as evidence of its failure to use the Xhosa language properly. They informed the BFBS repeatedly in the mid-1880s that "the Fingo Christians" under their care found "many expressions and phrases . . . objectionable."[46] So whereas the Appleyard Version had been accused of not being "pure" Xhosa because it included too many Mfengu terms, the revised version was criticized for not being "pure" Xhosa because it included too many Ngqika terms.

In order to break the stalemate, the BFBS commissioned a new revision and formed a new board of revisers in 1889. Initially composed of three European and two African reverends, the board came to consist of an African majority several years into the process.[47] When the BFBS published the complete rerevised version in 1905, the Wesleyan mission and its convert populations, notably those of Mfengu background, again voiced the harshest criticisms against it.[48] One of them, the aforementioned Charles Pamla, explained in 1908 that their chief grievance was that the new version was meant "to suit the Amanqika [Ngqika] only."[49] The testimony of John Tengo Jabavu, a Wesleyan of Mfengu descent who had briefly served on the board of revisers, voiced similar grievances: "The Kaffir [Xhosa] speaking people consist of two great divisions, the Fingos and the Xosa. The Fingos are more numerous than the Xosa and the dialects spoken by these peoples differ to some extent. . . . The rerevised version . . . contains certain expressions which would only be understood by the Xosas."[50] As these conflicts and testimonies reveal, the exact nature of the Xhosa language remained contested in the first decade of the twentieth century.

It is difficult to determine to what extent these conflicts were really about language or about other grievances. Some contemporary commentators argued that these disagreements were caused by a long-standing Wesleyan-Presbyterian rivalry in the region. A Lutheran missionary implied as much when he suggested in 1892 that the Wesleyans dismissed the revised version because it was the "Scotch Bible."[51] Similarly, in 1914, a member of the board of revisers explained that "the only people" who constantly agitated against the re-revised version were "the Wesleyan Missionaries. . . . Their whole idea is to perpetuate the Appleyard Version because he [Appleyard] was a Wesleyan."[52]

It was not uncommon for mission societies and their respective convert populations to view each other's actions with suspicion, and the tensions between English Wesleyans and Scottish Presbyterians in the eastern Cape were at times intense. As early as 1827, for instance, the Wesleyans had worried about the extent to which Presbyterian theology shaped Bible translations in the region.[53] Doctrinal tensions were made worse when, in 1837, the Wesleyans tried to erect a school among Chief Dodona's Mfengu community near the Debe Nek, only five miles from the Scottish-run Burnshill Station. When a Scottish missionary protested against the Wesleyan advance into his mission territory, his Wesleyan counterpart responded coldly: "In following the Fingoes as a nation I am only following a people with whom I have been connected for more than a quarter of a century."[54] In fact, the Wesleyans pursued Mfengu populations for the rest of the century. In 1866, the Scottish missionary Bryce Ross (still) complained about "a most determined attempt of the Wesleyans of the [Annshaw] Station to have us ousted from [three] Fingo villages or locations between this [Pirie] and Knox."[55]

It is very likely that this rivalry intensified the debates about "pure" Xhosa, as it encouraged Scottish and Wesleyan missionaries to insist that *their* perspective of the language captured its "true" nature. The Xhosa-Mfengu animosity had a similar effect on the contemporary debates over "pure" Xhosa.[56]

Although, as pointed out in chapter 3, the exact origin and identity of the Mfengu remains a subject of historical debate, there is good evidence that the term initially applied to Bantu-speaking refugees from the Natal-Zululand region who joined the Xhosa chiefdoms as clients in the early

1820s. The patron-client relationship dissolved during the Sixth Frontier War (1834–35), when, under the auspices of the colonial government and the Wesleyan missionary John Ayliff, some sixteen thousand Mfengu left their Xhosa patrons, swore an oath of loyalty to the British queen, and settled in the Cape Colony. The event turned a patron-client relationship into animosity because of how the two parties chose to interpret it. The Mfengu and their European supporters characterized it as a deliverance from Xhosa bondage, while the Xhosa chiefs and their followers viewed it as a violation of the Mfengu's oath of allegiance.[57]

This animosity was made worse when the Mfengu fought with British colonial forces against the Xhosa chiefdoms in the subsequent frontier wars and were rewarded with Xhosa land for their military service. The Mfengu also accepted Christianity and "Western" education more readily than the Xhosa did and, therefore, were able to secure "the bulk of elite positions as clerks, teachers, peasants, and petty traders that were available to blacks" in the expanding Cape Colony.[58] This economic power gave the Mfengu a political edge over the Xhosa because it enabled more of them to meet the property and wage qualifications necessary to get onto the colony's voter rolls. When members of the Xhosa communities (usually converts) gradually caught up with the Mfengu in terms of education, jobs, and voting rights, the animosity found expression in the formation of distinct political organizations, such as the Mfengu-dominated *Imbumba* (The Union, est. 1887) and the Xhosa and Thembu-dominated *Ingqungqutela* (The Congress, est. 1891).[59] It did not help that on 14 May 1907, Mfengu leaders organized "Fingo Emancipation Day," an annual celebration designed to commemorate their "deliverance" and the oath they had sworn to the British queen under the *umqwashu* (milkwood tree) at Mqwashini on the same date in 1835. Two years later, in 1909, Xhosa leaders responded with Ntsikana Day, celebrated in March at the New Brighton Location near Port Elizabeth and dedicated to the first local Xhosa prophet of Christianity, Ntsikana.[60]

Language and Bible translations operated as one important battleground on which the Xhosa and Mfengu fought out their animosity. In the 1880s, for instance, Mqhayi overheard a Ngqika-Xhosa man draw attention to the differences in pronunciation between the two speech patterns by exclaiming, "You Fingos, your faulty speech is detected by a little child."[61] Mqhayi added that the event occurred "at a time when it was maintained by the Xhosa that the Fingo teachers spoilt the language."[62] It is conceivable that the Mfengu responded in kind, notably by reading the rerevised version of the Xhosa Bible with a hypercritical eye only to find, as Jabavu did, that it "contains certain expressions which would only be understood by the Xosas."[63] During the second half of the nineteenth century, then, missionary rivalries and Xhosa-Mfengu animosity undermined acceptance of various Bible translations and thereby precluded the emergence of a widely accepted written standard for the Xhosa language as well.

Standardizing the Xhosa language became possible only when the conflicting parties revived the program of language "harmonization" the Wesleyans had first introduced in the late 1840s (see chapter 4). Jabavu was among the first to recommend this course of action when he explained that a unifying version of the Bible could be produced "by eliminating all words leaning too much to the Xosa side, or too much to the Fingo side, and by replacing these by words understood by both Fingos and Xosas."[64] The Anglican missionaries supported this approach. One of their leading members, Canon Cyril Wyche, explained in 1913 that "it is only by agreement that one version can be produced that will satisfy all sections of the community. More especially in the use of certain words that do not commend themselves in use to all the Xosa-speaking people, seeing that different meanings may be attended to them in different parts of the country."[65] The BFBS warmed up to this idea and, several months later, outlined a course of action that aimed at harmonizing the various speech variants in the coastal belt south of the Natal boundary. "What would most help the situation," the superintendent of the BFBS's translation department noted, "would be the formation of a list of those words in the Rerevised version which are said to be objectionable to Fingoes and others."[66] The outbreak of the First World War seems to have delayed this process until 1924, when the BFBS organized a new "Xosa Revision Board," which included an unprecedented number of Africans.[67] The fruit of their labor was published in 1927 as the "Union Version of the Xosa Bible." It bore this name because the revisers believed that this version successfully harmonized the speech variants of the Xhosa, Mfengu, Thembu, Mpondo, Mpondomise, and others into a unifying written language, which they now explicitly called "Xhosa" (rather than "Caffre").

Together with Albert Kropf's and Robert Godfrey's A *Kafir-English Dictionary* (1915) and Tiyo Soga's and John Henderson Soga's translation of John Bunyan's *The Pilgrim's Progress—Uhambo lomhambi* (1866, 1929), the "Union Version of the Xosa Bible" became the literary standard of all the speech variants south of Natal.[68] Importantly, by referring to this literary standard as the Xhosa language, the revisers effectively classified all the African inhabitants of this region as *Xhosa speakers*, in the same way as American Board missionaries classified all Africans in Natal-Zululand as *Zulu speakers*.

This language-based approach to classifying the two regions' African populations was made visible by linguist Clement Doke's assessment of the linguistic situation of South Africa's coastal region in 1928: "Xosa is established as the literary language of Kaffraria and the Transkei. The dialects of the Tembu, Pondo, Pondomisi, and so on, will never be anything but dialects [of this literary language]. . . . About 1,700,000 people speak Xosa. . . . Zulu is the accepted language of Natal and Zululand. . . . Zulus . . . number possibly as many as do the Xosas."[69] Doke's last sentence is particularly noteworthy because it suggests that he was not merely classifying Africans as Zulu or Xhosa speakers but was also equating Zulu speakers with Zulus and Xhosa speakers with Xhosas. In other words, Doke articulated language-based notions of Zuluness and Xhosaness that had no precedent in precolonial South Africa.

Education in Zulu and Xhosa

Although these language-based notions of Zuluness and Xhosaness had no precolonial antecedents, the wider African population of the coastal belt assimilated them over time. Language education was as foundational to this development as language standardization. After all, the officials responsible for education defined standard Zulu and Xhosa as the mother tongues of African pupils and designated them as the principal language subjects in African schools both in the coastal belt and the urban areas surrounding the diamond mines of Kimberley and the goldfields of the Rand.[70] Mother-tongue education set up standard Zulu and Xhosa languages as prestige languages, encouraging a growing number of Africans to conceptualize their vernaculars as part of these standardized languages and ultimately as markers of their Zuluness and Xhosaness. Although schooling and literacy rates expanded steadily over this nearly 150-year period (6.8 percent in 1911, 21.3 in 1946, and about 50 percent in 1981), education for African children varied immensely in accordance with the aims of a wide range of African and non-African actors.[71] It makes sense, therefore, to divide this long period into epochs beginning with 1854–1909.

1854–1909

The British colonial government had annexed Natal in 1844 and allowed it to become a separate colony in 1856. A decade later, this Natal colony annexed from the Mpondo chiefdom the region between the lower reaches of the Mzimkhulu and Mtamvuna Rivers as Alfred County. The colony's northeastern boundary also expanded when, following the defeat of the Zulu kingdom in 1879, it annexed the dispersed remnants of that kingdom as "Zululand" in 1887. Britain's Cape Colony expanded similarly. It annexed British Kaffraria in 1866 and Kaffraria (the Transkeian Territories) between 1877 and 1894. Through these annexations, Britain acquired some 1,300,000 additional African subjects by 1901, approximately 200,000 of whom became part of the Natal Colony, while 1,100,000 were incorporated into the Cape Colony.[72] Most importantly, these expansions created a direct boundary line between the Natal and Cape colonies—extending from the coast inland along the lower reaches of the Mtamvuna River and the upper reaches of the Mzimkhulu River to the Drakensberg Mountains (see map 5). This had a significant, long-term impact on the development of language-based Zulu and Xhosa identities because it divided the coastal belt into two school systems—that of Natal, in which Africans studied the Zulu language, and that of the Cape, where Africans studied the Xhosa language.

Because the British imperial government had implemented limited self-government in the Cape and Natal colonies on the basis of a nonracial franchise in 1853 and 1856, its representatives considered it important to provide Africans with a modicum of school education. In practice, however, this intention faced resistance from the white settler population, especially once both colonies attained full self-government in 1872 and 1893. Outnumbered approximately ten to one in the expanded Natal Colony and three to one in the expanded Cape Colony, the settler minorities desired to limit Africans' access to the vote.[73]

To safeguard white political dominance in Natal, they elaborated the colony's earlier forms of indirect rule (see chapter 5). In 1864, they set up the Natal Native Trust, which gave the governor and his executive council control over the land of the colony's locations.[74] They codified Africans' legal practices into a set of guidelines that became binding with the passage of the Natal Code of Native Law in 1891. This code excluded the majority of the colony's African population from the franchise by placing them directly under Natal's governor, who, acting as their "Supreme Chief," organized

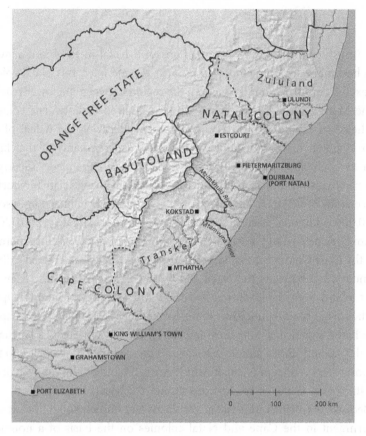

MAP 5. Boundary between Natal and Cape colonies, 1894.

them into individual tribes and kraals and subjected them to tribal chiefs, kraal heads, and "Native Law."[75] In theory the nonracial franchise was kept alive by allowing Africans to petition for individual exemption form "Native Law," which on its own involved several steps, including "furnishing proof of [one's] ability to read and write."[76] Once this exemption was granted, an applicant had to take additional steps to obtain the franchise itself. This made the entire process so onerous that by 1905, out of a total of about nine hundred thousand Africans, only about five thousand had obtained exemption from customary law and, of these, no more than three had acquired the vote.[77]

The situation was only marginally different in the Cape Colony. Theoretically, the Cape's Qualified Franchise Act of 1853 applied also to the annexed regions of British Kaffraria and the Transkeian Territories (hereafter referred to as Kaffraria-Transkei). However, the settler-dominated Cape legislature restricted the African vote by passing laws such as the Parliamentary Voters' Registration Act (1887) and the Franchise and Ballot Act (1892), which forced potential voters to pass education (literacy) tests to qualify for the vote.[78] The result of these exclusionary policies was that by 1909, Africans amounted to no more than 5 percent of the Cape Colony's electorate, in spite of their vast numerical superiority.[79]

Although school education alone was never enough for Africans to overcome these discriminatory policies, it did give them the tools to mount challenges. Africans in Natal, for instance, used education (notably literacy) as the basis for petitioning for exemption from customary law. In the Cape, Africans used school education to pass the required literacy tests but also to gain access to better-paying jobs and through these jobs the income or assets necessary to meet the property qualifications of the colony's franchise laws. Africans' use of education as a pathway to economic betterment and political influence incentivized the settler-dominated Natal and Cape legislatures to provide little funding for it and render it noncompulsory—education became compulsory for white children in 1904, while compulsory education for Africans began to be phased in gradually only in 1981.[80]

Between 1854 and 1909, therefore, African education in both regions depended primarily on missionary societies and Africans' voluntary engagement with mission schools. From the missionaries' viewpoint, the purpose of education was to "civilize" Africans in order to "Christianize" them.[81] As the LMS's Dr. John Philip explained in 1833, "The gospel never can have a permanent footing in a barbarous country, unless education and civilization go hand in hand with our religious instructions."[82] Mission-school education revolved primarily (though not exclusively) around mission day schools, which offered basic education to boys and girls whose parents lived on mission stations or in their vicinity. These schools struggled in the early decades of the missionary endeavor because African parents feared that education would alienate children from their culture and control. "Day schools are sustained at all of our stations," the American Board missionaries in Natal noted in 1856, "[but] none of the heathen send their children and, except for those living on the stations, none but those who work for us are instructed in reading."[83]

As the first mission school graduates became teachers and government interpreters, other Africans began to see that education opened doors to economic, social, and political advancement and a modicum of defense against the threats posed by British rule and settler interests.[84] These developments explain why more African parents sent their children to mission day schools over time. "At some of our stations the number of children attending our schools from heathen kraals has been larger than in former years," the American Board missionaries in Natal explained in 1862. "It is not so unpopular now for a heathen to read as it once was."[85] African interest in and support of education expanded steadily thereafter. By the early 1910s, Africans in Natal-Zululand shouldered 25 percent of the costs associated with the region's more than 230 mission schools.[86]

African attendance and support of mission schools in the Kaffraria-Transkei region expanded in similar ways.[87] In the 1870s, for instance, "The Mfengu contributed £5,600 of £7,000 needed to build Blythswood (sister school of Lovedale Seminary near Butterworth), and the Thembu contributed £1,000 of £1,500 needed to expand the Methodist school at Clarkebury (near the Mbashe River)."[88] The shift in attitude fueled an increase in the number of government-aided mission primary schools: in the Kaffraria section alone, it grew from 47 in 1864 to 541 in 1900.[89] To these numbers one must add the primary schools in Transkei section, which had some 190 schools in 1881.[90]

As to which languages were used and taught in these schools, the American Board missionaries are a good example for the Natal-Zululand region. Since they initially had complete control over their language curriculum, they simply mandated that African pupils acquire literacy in Zulu before adding English.[91] Little changed when an 1884 law brought "native" education more firmly under the control of the Natal Government Council of Education because the latter issued a directive that required schools to teach literacy in Zulu and English.[92] Generally speaking, schools appear to have promoted literacy in Zulu during the six years of primary education and literacy in English during advanced education.[93]

According to missionary reports of the time, African pupils experienced the process of acquiring literacy as an adversarial challenge known as "overcoming the book," "in which the simple spelling book . . . is arrayed on the one side, and the scholar, with all his zeal, pride, and ability to talk on the other."[94] A growing number of African primary school pupils—close to 1,683 in 1865 and 12,484 in 1909—engaged in this challenge in Natal-Zululand.[95] As they acquired basic literacy in Zulu, they also assimilated the idea that they were Zulu speakers and thus members of a language-based Zulu community.[96]

One of them was Petros Lamula. Born around 1880 north of the Thukela River, Lamula's school-based education began in 1898 when he entered the Norwegian Mission Society's Ekombe Station school and ended in 1914, when he graduated as a pastor from Oscarsberg Theological Seminary at Eshiyane (Rorke's Drift).[97] During these sixteen years, Lamula not only acquired literacy in standard Zulu, but he also taught others how to read and write Zulu.[98] Similar to school children in France and Germany, this process socialized Lamula into accepting language as a crucial marker of nationhood in general and Zulu as a crucial marker of *his* Zuluness in particular. Indeed, by 1920, Lamula was a Zulu cultural nationalist who feared that a loss of the Zulu language could bring about the death of the Zulu nation. In his book *UZulu kaMalandela* (1924), which is a compilation of African and Zulu history written in the Zulu language, Lamula explained to his readers, "Black people have no pride in their language. They think language is an insignificant thing. They do not realise that the death of the language is followed by the death of the nation. . . . [The English and Afrikaans] languages are preserved and enshrined in books used by their ancestors. With us that will happen when some wise men have appeared who are determined to preserve their nation and their language."[99] As Lamula's first two sentences suggest, few Africans in Natal-Zululand shared his concern for language as a marker of Zuluness in 1924. After all, while Africans in this region had used language as a marker of *amantungwa* and *amalala* identities since the rise of the Zulu kingdom in 1817, most Africans in the region were (as yet) unfamiliar with a language-based Zulu identity. Lamula had a different perspective because, unlike most of them, he had received a school-based education, as part of which he had assimilated that he was a Zulu speaker and that the Zulu language demarcated the Zulu nation and identity.

Although language education unfolded differently in the Cape Colony, it produced the same outcome. European missionaries working in this region agreed early on that literacy provided a crucial pathway to conversion.[100] They did not immediately agree on the language in which this literacy ought to be achieved, however. Wesleyan missionary John Ayliff insisted that Africans ought to learn how to read their own language first.[101] His colleague William Shrewsbury, however, believed that African pupils should acquire literacy in English only.[102] Neither won this debate, with the result that Africans who frequented Wesleyan primary schools learned reading and writing in English *and* the vernacular.[103] This was also broadly true for the mission schools that belonged to the Berlin and Scottish-Presbyterian missionaries in the eastern Cape region.[104]

The Cape Colony's Education Act of 1865 did not interfere with African pupils acquiring literacy in English *and* the vernacular. At the school of the Scottish-Presbyterian mission station of Cunningham in the Transkei region in 1873, for instance, African teacher Pato Mtshemla instructed fifty-six boys and twenty-nine girls in reading English and Xhosa.[105] In the same year, Charles Lwana, the African teacher of the school at the Wesleyan mission station of Butterworth, also taught seventy-three boys and eighty-six girls how to read English and Xhosa.[106] Government reports reveal that reading instruction in English and Xhosa continued for the rest of the century, including in the regions directly bordering on the Natal Colony. For example, for the Qumbu, Mount Frere, Mount Fletcher, Matatiele, Umzimkhulu, and Pondoland areas, the reports from mission schools whose pupils were of Thembu, Mfengu, Mpondomise, Mpondo, Bhaca, and Hlubi descent, invariably note that "all [pupils] read in both English and Kafir [i.e., Xhosa]."[107]

This meant that the majority of African pupils in the primary education programs of the Kaffraria-Transkei region acquired literacy in the Xhosa language (that was admittedly still undergoing a process of standardization at this time) and in so doing assimilated the idea that they were Xhosa speakers even if they belonged to Mfengu, Thembu, Mpondomise, Mpondo, Bhaca, or Hlubi communities. In other words, primary education opened the path for the development of language-based notions of Xhosaness that transcended the eastern Cape region's older, narrower, non-language-based identities. In Kaffraria alone, this process captured some two thousand pupils in 1864 and thirty-seven thousand in 1900.[108] The numbers in the Transkei region were at least as high, given that, in 1881, the government reported that the Transkei had about eight thousand pupils in mission day schools.[109]

1910–1947

The British victory in the Second Anglo-Boer War (1899–1902) brought all of South Africa under British imperial rule. Although large numbers of

Africans had supported the British war effort in the hope that their loyalty would be rewarded, the expansion of British rule did not improve their situation.[110] According to the new 1909 constitution, the former territories, including the Cape Colony (including the Kaffraria-Transkei region) and Natal Colony (i.e., the Natal-Zululand region), became the Cape and Natal provinces of a unitary state called the Union of South Africa, whose official languages were English and Dutch (Afrikaans). More significantly, it declared the Union's overall government to be limited to "British subject[s] of European descent," while allowing the Union's provincial governments to maintain their old franchise laws.[111]

It got worse. In 1913 and 1927, the white Union government implemented the Land and Native Administration Acts, both of which initiated the era of segregation in South Africa. The former distinguished between "White areas" and "Black areas," apportioned to Africans a mere 7 percent (later increased to roughly 12 percent) of the South African landmass and restricted their permanent residence to these rapidly overcrowding and predominantly rural areas. The Native Administration Act built on Natal's system of indirect rule by placing the populations of these Black areas under the Native Affairs Department and its administrative regime of white commissioners overseeing African chiefs and headmen ruling their populations according to codified customary laws.[112] Finally, the Union government used the already existing migrant labor system to channel healthy adult men from Black areas to White areas to provide cheap labor for the latter's mining and manufacturing industries on a temporary, contract basis.[113] This system worked imperfectly, however, as it could not prevent a growing number of African men, women, and children to leave the Black areas' overcrowded conditions and make their home in settlements known as "locations" or "townships" on the outskirts of the White area's cities and towns.[114]

The education of Africans had low priority in this context. For instance, the Union government levied an annual native general tax of one pound per adult male as early as 1925, but it apportioned only 20 percent of this tax revenue to "elementary education for Native children."[115] White inhabitants viewed even this funding as too much, fearing, "that improvement of the Natives' standard of civilization means a progressive loss of opportunities for Europeans."[116]

A crucial aspect of African education in the era of segregation was a focus on the vernacular both as a language subject (in addition to one of the official languages of English or Afrikaans) and as the medium of instruction. The general mandate was that in African primary schools throughout the Union's four provinces "every child is required . . . to take a Native language as a subject of study, and this subject be taught in every class." Furthermore, "The pupil's mother tongue shall be the medium of instruction in all subjects except the official language, for the following periods: in Natal, for the first six years . . . ; in the Cape . . . , for the first four years."[117] Thus, in the period between 1910 and 1947, the vast majority of African pupils enrolled in primary education in the Natal Province were supposed to study and receive instruction in the Zulu language, whereas the vast majority of African pupils in the Cape Province were supposed be instructed in the Xhosa language.[118]

In Natal some parents and pupils protested against this emphasis on Zulu, claiming that "Zulu can be taught at home, so that more school time may be devoted to English and Afrikaans for the sake of their economic and educational value."[119] Not everyone agreed, including John Langalibalele Dube, the publisher of the Zulu language newspaper *Ilanga lase Natal.*[120] Moreover, the provincial departments of education insisted that teachers abide by the government's language-oriented directives in spite of these protests. In 1929, Natal school inspector M. Prozesky warned his teachers, "If we want the natives to develop their national traits we must do this through the medium of the study of their own language."[121]

School inspectors operated similarly in the Cape Province's Transkeian region (which was inhabited by people who did not historically refer to themselves as Xhosa). In 1923, the inspector reminded the teachers of the Wesleyan mission school of Luzupu among the Mpondo people of the Lusikisiki district that "the instruction given with regard to Xosa reading, and oral Xosa, must be carried out."[122] He issued a similar admonition to the teachers of the Moravian mission school of Ezincuka among the Hlubi people of the Mount Fletcher district. "The work done in the official language [i.e., English] was, on the whole satisfactory, but in the native language [i.e., Xhosa] no work had been done and the staff is warned such serious omission must not be allowed to occur again."[123] According to Moravian missionaries, the Cape Province's (usually white) school inspectors and (usually Black) assistant inspectors were able to assess compliance with this directive because many of them spoke Xhosa.[124] Most inspector reports do not include critical comments, however, which suggests that most teachers taught Xhosa and the majority of pupils learned Xhosa in compliance with the government mandate. By 1932 this affected about 80,000 African pupils across some 1,130 mission schools in the Transkei alone.[125]

Perhaps most importantly, those in charge of African education made clear that the purpose of language education was to ensure that African children assimilated the standardized versions of these languages. In 1929, the Cape Province's Department of Public Education asked teachers to encourage African pupils to recognize and reproduce the standard version. The specific directive explained that "[the teacher] must set his face against the corruption of his language, and maintain it in its purity. . . . It is his duty to see that his pupils have before them a good example of what their speech ought to be."[126]

Education administrators in the Cape believed that the standard for Xhosa was set by the "Union Version of the Xosa Bible" as well as Soga's *Uhambo lomhambi* and Kropf and Godfrey's *A Kafir-English Dictionary*.[127] They used excerpts from these texts to produce language learning aids, such as the three-volume *Xosa Readers for Native Schools* and the six-volume *The Stewart Xosa Readers*.[128] Their counterparts in Natal argued that the standard for Zulu was set by works such as the Ebenezer Press's Zulu language primer, *Ukucatula* (Step by Step), the American Mission Board's *Incwadi Yabantwana* (Reader for Children), and James Stuart's translations of Aesop's fables, *uKwesukela* and *uVulingqondo*.[129]

At least theoretically, African pupils in Natal and the Cape provinces studied standard Zulu and Xhosa for eight years. Given that the number of African pupils and literacy rates increased steadily throughout the Union period (in Natal, specifically, the number of pupils increased from about 12,484 in 1909 to some 120,723 in 1945), more and more Africans assimilated the notion that they were Zulu or Xhosa speakers.[130] In so doing, primary education continued to foster language-based notions of Zuluness and Xhosaness.

Ashby Peter Solomzi Mda, the father of the South African novelist "Zakes" Mda, best illustrates this outcome for the Xhosa side of the process.[131] Born in April 1916 in the Cape Province's Herschel district, into "an Mpondomise clan called the ooJolinkomo, known as the royal tasters at traditional feasts," it was school-based education that helped socialize the young Mda into a broader language-based Xhosa identity in spite of his Mpondomise origins.[132] Educated at Catholic schools, he eventually obtained a teacher's certificate from the Catholic Teachers Training School at Mariazell, located northwest of Matatiele.[133] In all these years of schooling, he, like other African school-going children in the Cape Province, learned how to read and write standard Xhosa, coming to accept that standard Xhosa was *his* language and a crucial marker of *his* Xhosaness. Mda voiced his language-based Xhosa identity in an essay he published in 1935:

> Without doubt the Xhosa language [is] so rich in expression and ideas that to neglect it is almost a sin. It is a pity that the Xhosa people should have such an irresponsible attitude towards the improvement and development of their language. . . . . He who loves his country will surely love his nation will surely love the language of that nation. So be it, with ye Africans! Many complain that the capabilities of the Xhosa language are cramped and limited. I, for one, don't believe that for a second. Our language, if ever it was poor, we made it so, we were and are not willing to build and develop it, even as the English language was built and developed.[134]

As the excerpt suggests, A. P. Mda considered "the Xhosa language" an important marker of the "the Xhosa people" and "nation." And, in spite of his Mpondomise ancestry, he saw himself as a member of this Xhosa nation because he considered himself a speaker of "our language"—Xhosa.

1948–1990

The election of 1948 brought to power Daniel François Malan's (Reunited) National Party (NP) whose apartheid (apartness) platform addressed the white electorate's anxieties about Africans' demographic advantage, accelerating urbanization, and political radicalization. Following the victory, the NP implemented laws that not only separated the population into four racial camps (White, Colored, Indian, and African) but also combined white Afrikaans and English speakers into a single White nation (about 19 percent of the total population in 1950) while fragmenting the African majority (about 69 percent in 1950) into a plurality of distinct nations.[135]

The NP's Commission on Native Education played a crucial role in convincing the architects of apartheid that language could be used to circumscribe these distinct African nations. Chaired by Dr. Werner Willi Max Eiselen, a former anthropologist and chief inspector of native education in the Transvaal, the Eiselen Commission began its work in 1949 and issued its recommendations in 1951.[136] The theoretical point of departure of these recommendations was the assumption that Africans belonged to the "Bantu

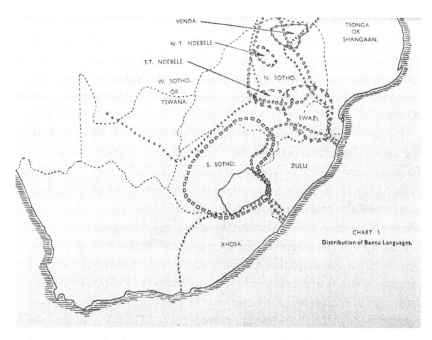

FIGURE 2. "Zulu" and "Xhosa" clusters, ca. 1950. Union of South Africa, *Report of the Commission on Native Education, 1949–1951* (Pretoria: Government Printer, 1951), chart no. 1.

race," which was made up of "tribes" such as the "Zulu, Xhosa, Tembu, Mpondo, Mpondomise, Swazi, Tonga and Ndebele."[137] Based on long-held ideas about the region's vernacular dialects and languages, the commission argued that these "tribes" could be grouped into mother-tongue clusters. For instance, all the "tribes" of the Natal Province formed part of the Zulu cluster because they all (allegedly) spoke dialects of the (standard) Zulu language, while the "tribes" of the Cape Province formed part of the Xhosa cluster because they supposedly all spoke dialects of the (standard) Xhosa language (see figure 2).[138]

Because Eiselen had studied for advanced degrees in phonetics and anthropology at the Universities of Hamburg and Berlin, his and the commission's thinking about these languages bore the imprint of German linguistic theory, notably the idea that language and ethnicity were naturally related phenomena.[139] This helps explain why the Eiselen Commission claimed that (standard) languages such as Zulu and Xhosa were the "bearer of the traditional heritage of the various ethnic groups," which was akin to saying that these languages captured the essence of these groups much more accurately than their asserted genealogical ties (lineages and clans) or their political affiliations (chiefdoms and kingdoms).[140] The corollary of this thinking was that it reinforced the ideas about the relationship between language and identity that linguist Clement Doke had articulated in 1928, notably that Zulu speakers were in effect Zulus and Xhosa speakers were Xhosas.

It is unclear if the Eiselen Commission was aware that, in spite of growing vernacular education over the course of the preceding century, these language-based identities were not yet fully entrenched in African consciousness. As late as the 1960s, for example, government ethnologists maintained that some Zulu speakers in Natal did not consider themselves Zulus.[141] Yet the Eiselen Commission helped make these language-based identities a growing reality by recommending the expansion of mother-tongue education. Specifically, it mandated that African children study their mother tongues as language subjects in primary education programs (in addition to the official languages of English and Afrikaans) and receive instruction in their mother tongues during all eight years of primary school.[142] The NP government followed the Eiselen Commission's logic and recommendations closely by way of the Bantu Education Act (No. 47) of 1953. When implemented in 1955, this act removed state subsidies from mission schools, thereby forcing most of these schools to either close or become government schools. It also transferred the control of African education from the provincial administrations to the Union Government—initially its Native Affairs Department and after 1958 a newly created Bantu Education Department.[143] Most significantly, it made African pupils' mother tongues compulsory both as subjects and the medium of instruction for all eight years of primary education (English and Afrikaans became mandatory as language subjects through primary school and mandatory as languages of instruction in secondary schools).

The government used its own publication, the *Bantu Education Journal*, to communicate this language curriculum to the principals and teachers on its payroll. In fact, "each issue was circulated around every school and the department required all teachers to sign that they had read and absorbed its contents," making it hard for anyone to avoid its messaging.[144] In 1955, the journal explained to its readership that the broad objective of the primary school curriculum was to show "how the Bantu child is bound to the people of his home through birth, marriage, izibongo, totem, [and] language." The journal advised that to reinforce the connection between language and identity, "strong emphasis must . . . still be laid on Bantu languages."[145] What the journal meant by "Bantu languages" was "the standardised form" of languages such as Zulu and Xhosa.[146]

The 1959 Promotion of Bantu Self-Government Act and the 1970 Bantu Homeland and Citizenship Act reinforced the link between language and identity in additional ways. These acts assigned to each African person a distinct national identity according to the Eiselen Commission's language clusters. Thus, for official purposes, members of the Zulu language cluster were classified as part of the Zulu nation and as belonging to the homeland of KwaZulu (which became self-governing in 1977), whereas members of the Xhosa language cluster were recognized as part of the Xhosa nation and as belonging to the homelands of the Ciskei (self-governing in 1972) or the Transkei (self-governing in 1963).[147] As government ethnologist A. O. Jackson explained in 1975, the 2,257,495 inhabitants of the Ciskei and Transkei are made up of various "divisions" and "subdivisions" such as the Xhosa, Thembu, Mpondomise, Mpondo, Xhesibe, Bomvana, Nhlangwini, Bhaca, Mfengu (including Hlubi, Zizi, Bhele, etc.).[148] He added that all these divisions and subdivisions were "*Xhosa speaking* . . . because Xhosa is, with minor dialectical variations, the language spoken by all."[149] Consequently, he explained, they all formed part of "the Xhosa national unit" as "recognised by virtue of the Promotion of Bantu Self-government Act."[150]

The apartheid-era expansion of mother-tongue education in African primary schools and the growing number of African children attending these school (by 1979, official records listed some 21.4 percent of the African population as attending school) played an important role in normalizing these language-based national identities.[151] This is not to say that there was no resistance against the apartheid regime's education policies. In white urban South Africa, that is, outside the "Black areas" and subsequently the newly created homelands, the resistance was complex. Urban Africans were dissatisfied with mother-tongue education because of its discriminatory intent (which, in the worst case, could mean forced removal to the homeland of one's mother tongue) but also because they lived in linguistically complex environments. Mark Mathabane recounts an episode from his childhood in Johannesburg's Alexandra township in the 1970s that exposes this disconnect. He was supposed to enroll in a Venda-language "tribal school" because the government classified his father as part of the Venda nation and language cluster. He eventually gained access to a Shangaan (Tsonga)–language school, however, because he also spoke Shangaan, which he had learned from his Shangaan mother.[152]

The issue that provoked most resistance in urban areas was the government demand in 1974 that all African secondary schools use Afrikaans as a medium of instruction. By May of 1976 and well into 1977, African pupils were engaged in major strikes through the country's urban areas, notably in Johannesburg's Soweto township in June 1976, when some 15,000 pupils confronted the police, resulting in the loss of 176 lives over the course of one week of protesting. In response to these protests, the apartheid government made reforms in 1978, notably allowing African schools to switch to English as the medium of instruction after the first four years of mother-tongue education.

In spite of this resistance and these reforms, mother tongues remained at the center of African education in South Africa's urban areas, ensuring that even if linguistic complexity was the norm in the streets of Alexandra, Soweto, and Katlehong, in the schools of these townships pupils would be pulled toward a specific African language and thus a specific African language–based identity. Unlike Mathabane, most township youth would study the language of their fathers' designated "tribe" and language cluster. Pupils whose fathers' tribal origins the government classified as part of the Zulu language cluster would study standard Zulu, while those whose father's tribal origins were deemed part of the Xhosa language cluster would study standard Xhosa.

The situation was not very different in the newly created national homelands, where some African parents and teachers also mounted resistance against mother-tongue education.[153] As in the pre-apartheid era, this resistance centered on the belief that English language skills provided better access to economic opportunities than skills in the mother tongues. The 1962 Transkeian government (the Cingo Commission), for instance, studied African views of "Bantu Education" policies and noted "the unanimous desire of the people that English should be learnt by all pupils and teachers in all schools."[154] It explained further that "many parents in the Transkei, and even some teachers, regard the learning of Xhosa and its use as a medium of instruction as entirely unnecessary as the child learns the language at home."[155] In 1963, the Transkeian Legislative Assembly responded by limiting the use of Xhosa as the medium of instruction to four years.[156] About a decade later, the Ciskei and KwaZulu homelands imposed similar limits on the use of Xhosa and Zulu as the medium of instruction.[157]

However, the homeland legislatures used these standard languages as their official languages and made them mandatory as language subjects in school.[158] This was especially the case in the homeland of KwaZulu, which was dominated by Chief Mangosuthu Buthelezi's Inkatha movement. In 1978, the Inkatha-affiliated Natal African teachers Union, the School Inspectors Association of KwaZulu and Inkatha-supporting academics at the University of Zululand came together to produce the Inkatha school syllabus known as *Ubuntu-botho*. In 1979 the KwaZulu legislature introduced the syllabus and, through the KwaZulu Department of Education and Culture, made it a compulsory subject in all KwaZulu schools in order "to dash Bantu Education in KwaZulu with a dose of Zulu nationalism."[159] The syllabus fostered Zulu nationalism in a variety of language-centric ways, including the singing of "Zulu war songs," the performing of Inkatha slogans such as *Sonqoba simunye* (United we conquer), and most importantly the reading of textbooks "written in Zulu."[160]

What did studying standard Zulu or Xhosa look like in practice for African pupils in South Africa's homelands of KwaZulu, Ciskei, and Transkei, and urban townships such as Alexandra, Soweto, and Katlehong? A *Handbook of Suggestions for Teachers in Native Primary Schools*, published in 1952, provides some clues.[161] First, the handbook asked teachers to impress on the minds of their pupils that there was a standard of "desirable—correct and pleasant speech."[162] Second, it instructed them to perform this standard speech in the classroom.[163] Finally, the text asked teachers to use "corrective work" to get pupils speaking nonstandard variants to assimilate the standard version of the language.[164] Two years later, the *Bantu Education Journal* gave the teachers similar directives: "Oral composition should form the basis of all language work in the Bantu language. Its aim should be both corrective and progressive. (a) Corrective.—To eliminate from the pupil's language dialectical forms and unwarranted words and expressions from European and other Bantu languages. . . . (b) Progressive.—To extend his vocabulary, to improve his pronunciation, to provide practice in correct forms of expression, and generally to increase his powers of expressing himself fluently in correct language."[165] The focus on the elimination of dialectical forms, and the performance of correct language meant that African pupils classified as Zulu speakers had to speak standard Zulu in school, whereas those identified as Xhosa speakers had to speak standard Xhosa. This established these standards as prestige languages and encouraged schoolchildren to feel embarrassed about the vernaculars (dialects) used at home and to replace them with the standard forms.[166] This process may not have succeeded in getting all pupils to speak standard Zulu or Xhosa perfectly, but it did get most of them to think of their vernaculars as belonging to these standards. In so doing, they internalized the latter as markers of new language-based Zulu or Xhosa identities.

This process would explain why Isaac Sibusiso Kubeka noticed as early as 1979 that most residents of KwaZulu "regard themselves as Zulus because they speak the Zulu language" and why, some fifteen years later, Mary de Haas and Paulus Zulu observed the same phenomenon in KwaZulu-Natal, notably that "many people describe themselves as Zulu, and explain this identity primarily in terms of the language they speak."[167]

It is important to note that this process also affected people who had only marginal affiliations with the historical Zulu kingdom. Consider the example of the Maputaland region, the historic home of the Thonga people, whose speech form is isiGonde (which is classified as a variant of the Thonga language). "Once KwaZulu was granted self-governing status by the apartheid government," Dingani Mthethwa explains, "The coherence of Thonga society . . . crumbled such that today many people in Maputaland speak isiZulu [i.e., the Zulu language] as their preferred language."[168] And the Thonga who adopted Zulu as *their* language experienced an identity shift from Thonganess toward Zuluness. Thus, David Webster explained in 1992, most men in Maputaland assume a Zulu rather than a Thonga identity because "for over thirty years Zulu has been the medium of instruction in the schools, while there is no written tradition in Thonga. It is also true that Zulu has become the prestige language and all people speak it. . . . For over fifty years, the people of this area have had access to Zulu identity books."[169] As Webster made clear, Thonga men assimilated a Zulu identity because they learned the Zulu language in school and because they carried identity cards that identified them as Zulus.

The same evidence is available for Xhosa. Mother-tongue education incentivized African pupils with Xhosa, Mfengu, Thembu, Mpondomise, Bomvana, Xhesibe, Bhaca, Nhlangwini, and Mpondo (or other) backgrounds to think of themselves as Xhosa speakers and, therefore, as members of a broader Xhosa nation. In this case, too, government-issued identity cards helped reinforce this identity by superimposing the Xhosa label on the older Thembu, Mfengu, Mpondo (etc.) affiliations (see figure 3).

This process offers a convincing explanation for Jeff Peires's observation that the inhabitants of Ciskei and Transkei saw themselves as "Xhosa-speakers" and as "one people" by the 1980s, if not earlier.[170] It would also explain why the Mpondo mine shaft steward Mlamli Botha explained in the

FIGURE 3. Apartheid-era "Mpondo-Xhosa" identity card. (David Turn-ley/Corbis Premium Historical via Getty Images)

aftermath of a faction fight among mine workers in the Northwest Province in the 1980s, "When I say Xhosa [were involved in the faction fight], I mean Xhosa-speaking people. It might be Pondos, Bacas, Bomvanas, Xhosas, but they are [all] Xhosas."[171]

Botha's testimony is noteworthy for additional reasons. On the one hand, it suggests that language-based identities such as Xhosa rarely achieved complete victories over the preexisting, more local identities such as Mpondo, Bhaca, or Bomvana. Instead, they coexisted with them.[172] On the other hand, Botha's testimony shows that the language-based identities that emerged with language standardization and education had developed critical mass by the 1980s at the latest, to the extent that they gained traction even among the relatively unschooled African migrant labor population. Indeed, although the similarity between their speech forms helps explain why the Mpondo, Bhaca, and Bomvana mine workers organized themselves into a faction, it does not explain why they self-identified as "Xhosa-speaking people" and "Xhosas." The appropriation of the Xhosa label by mine workers (and the Zulu label by others) suggests that they had assimilated these broader language-based identities because the latter had become part of South

Africa's mainstream discourse, popular culture, and administrative machinery. And once the language-equals-identity ideology had gone mainstream, individuals self-identified and were identified as Zulu or Xhosa speakers and therefore Zulus or Xhosas, even if they had only mastered the urban, rural, or regional variants of standard Zulu or Xhosa.

These identities had thoroughly entrenched themselves in South African discourse, culture, and consciousness by the early 1990s. Two foundational causes of this entrenchment were the overlapping processes of language standardization and language education. Both of these processes had their origins in the American missionaries' rejection of William Shaw's proposal in 1854, a rejection that resulted in the bifurcation of what used to be considered a single "Caffre" language community into distinct Zulu and Xhosa languages. Missionaries, Africans, and later government stakeholders resorted to language standardization and language education to turn this theoretical Zulu-Xhosa divide into practice. In Natal-Zululand, missionaries and Africans identified the king's Zulu as the "purest" form of speech and used it as the basis for the literary standard. In Kaffraria-Transkei, they developed standard "Xhosa" by harmonizing the region's diverse speech forms into a "more perfect" language. Once standardized, African and non-African educators promoted standard Zulu and Xhosa as part of "mother-tongue" education in schools. As schooling elevated the standards to prestige languages, pupils began to consider their home dialects inferior variants and shifted from the latter to standard Zulu or Xhosa. As part of this shift, they also moved from more local, non-language-based identity discourses (such as Thonga, Mpondo, or Hlubi, for instance) toward broader, language-based notions of Zuluness or Xhosaness.

The rapid expansion of the vernacular press and entertainment industry, and the widening experience of migrant labor and identity cards allowed these language-based identities to move from the classroom to the general culture as the twentieth century progressed. They rarely fully replaced pre-existing local identities but rather assembled them for comfort and protection as their bearers sought strength in numbers in the face of a South African state that became evermore dangerous to African men, women, and children. Although language standardization and language education were foundational to this development, it was the totality of these factors that had helped entrench a language-based Zulu-Xhosa divide into South African consciousness by the 1990s, ensuring that language also functioned as a key mechanism by which the participants of the Rand violence came to distinguish Zulu friend from Xhosa foe and vice versa. Even though the Rand violence's participants and observers liked to portray these language-based identities as "tribal" identities that connected them directly and unproblematically to South Africa's historical Zulu and Xhosa polities and clans, they were in fact modern identities—the products of the intense language mapping, standardization, and education activities European, American, and African-born actors had carried out since the early nineteenth century.

• EPILOGUE •

T he violence between 1990 and 1994 threatened but did not derail the transition process. Between 26 and 29 April 1994, South African citizens of all races participated in the country's general elections for the first time in history. The African-dominated African National Congress (ANC) carried 62 percent of the 19,726,579 valid votes, authorizing it to form a Government of National Unity with the white-dominated National Party (NP) and the Zulu-controlled Inkatha Freedom Party (IFP). The new National Assembly elected Nelson Mandela as president, making him the country's first African chief executive.

After its successful and much-celebrated birth, post-apartheid South Africa initiated numerous efforts to build a unified nation. Most of these initiatives were aimed at overcoming the stark racial divides the country had inherited from its colonial and apartheid predecessors. They included practical initiatives such as the Truth and Reconciliation Commission and more symbolic gestures such as the frequent mobilization of the image of a rainbow nation. However, the post-apartheid state made no significant efforts to engage critically with language-based ethnic divisions, even though they, too, represented the legacy of the political, legal, *and* linguistic interventions of colonial and apartheid-era rule.

This is not to say that these ethnic divisions have not been probed at all in the post-apartheid era. Academics have expended considerable time and effort questioning the notions of Zuluness (less so Xhosaness) that the new South Africa inherited from its predecessors.[1] Mbongiseni Buthelezi has been a particularly powerful voice in referring to the post-apartheid moment as "an appropriate time for isiZulu-speaking Africans and others who accept the language of unadulterated tribalism to interrogate their long-held views of pure Zuluness."[2]

However, scholars have not yet made the history of language and the history of the relationship between language and identity an important aspect of their critical analyses. This is problematic because without this critical engagement, it is impossible to understand why language has become a battleground in post-apartheid power and identity politics. Indeed, since 2007 activists who self-identify as Ndwandwe, Qwabe, Hlubi, and others have organized heritage associations, launched social media sites, and—crucially—initiated language development projects with a view to proclaiming and reviving identities that have hitherto been submerged within Zuluness and Xhosaness.[3]

Here I offer an initial explanation for this phenomenon by examining more closely the recent activism of people who identify as Hlubi and live predominantly in the western portions of the KwaZulu-Natal Province and the eastern sections of the Eastern Cape Province (see map 6). Since the end of apartheid rule, Hlubi individuals have engaged in activism that is best

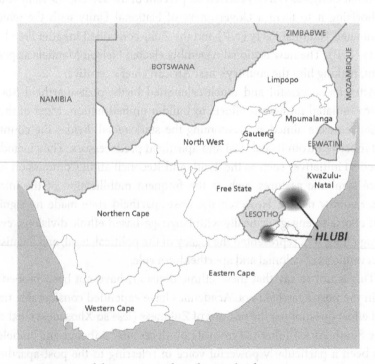

MAP 6. Main Hlubi areas in modern-day South Africa.

characterized as a mixture of power and identity politics. Hlubi power politics aim to reconstitute the Hlubi as an independent kingdom within what the post-apartheid constitution recognizes as "traditional leadership," and to use this status to improve access to communal land, notably in the KwaZulu-Natal Province. Hlubi identity politics aim to galvanize widespread support for the reconstitution of this independent kingship by promoting Hlubiness as a language-based identity distinct from Zuluness and Xhosaness.

This activism is entangled with the deeper history of the region. The Hlubi polity probably emerged as a small chiefdom near the upper Mzinyathi River in the northern region of modern-day KwaZulu-Natal in the sixteenth century. In the second half of the eighteenth century, this polity incorporated neighboring communities and, in so doing, evolved into a confederation of chiefdoms with a king as its ruler.[4] The confederation experienced important challenges in about 1800 when Hlubi king Bhungane died and succession disputes fragmented his polity into factions led by his principal son and heir, Mthimkhulu, and his two minor sons, Mpangazitha and Mahwanqa.[5] Shortly thereafter, Matiwane's Ngwane state collided with Mthimkhulu's and Mpangazitha's Hlubi factions in 1819 and 1825, killing both leaders and dispersing their followers throughout the region.[6] Hlubi lore remembers these events as *izwekufa*, "the destruction of the nation."[7]

In the aftermath of these disasters, minor chiefs reconstituted smaller Hlubi polities in the foothills of the Western Drakensberg, where, over the course of the second half of the nineteenth century, the expanding Cape Colony incorporated them into the separately administered Transkei region.[8] A more sizable Hlubi entity survived on the upper Mzinyathi River, where Mahwanqa provided refuge to Mthimkhulu's sons, Dlomo and Langalibalele. In 1848, Langalibalele, as the new ruler of this Hlubi community, led his people across the Thukela River into British-controlled Natal where, by 1850, they occupied locations at the sources of the Msuluzi (Bloucrans) River, west of today's town of Estcourt.[9] This history explains why when the first nonracial election ushered in the new South Africa in 1994, Hlubi communities were located in two separate provinces. Minor Hlubi chiefs and their followers resided in the Eastern Cape Province, which included the former Transkei, while the senior Hlubi ruler, Langalibalele II Muziwenkosi kaTataZela Johannes Radebe (1974–present), and his followers lived in the KwaZulu-Natal Province, which included the former Natal region.

The immediate post-apartheid situation posed some problems for the Hlubi in KwaZulu-Natal. The key reason for this was that just prior to the general election of 1994, the IFP-controlled KwaZulu (homeland) Legislative Assembly and the NP-controlled South African Parliament had passed the Ingonyama Trust Act, which made Zulu king Goodwill Zwelithini kaBhekuzulu the sole trustee of nearly all the land hitherto administered by the KwaZulu government (that is, some 2.8 million hectares), including sections claimed by Hlubi ruler Langalibalele II and his followers.[10] The situation worsened in the early 2000s. In 2003, the post-apartheid government passed the Traditional Leadership and Governance Framework Act, which provided the legal basis for reconstituting "traditional" kingships, chieftainships, and headmanships. Two years later, the legislature of the new KwaZulu-Natal Province used this act as the legal basis for passing the KwaZulu-Natal Traditional Leadership and Governance Act, which recognized King Zwelithini as "the [sole] Monarch for the Province of KwaZulu-Natal" and thus as the supreme ruler over all of the province's 296 senior traditional leaders and 3,372 headmen, including Hlubi ruler Langalibalele II.[11] By 2005, then, the senior Hlubi ruler Langalibalele II and his community fell politically and economically under the tutelage of the Zulu king.

However, the 2003 Framework Act also created opportunities to challenge this status quo. The act mandated that traditional leadership positions could be subject to legal dispute in front of the Commission on Traditional Leadership: Disputes and Claims (also known as the Nhlapo Commission, after Professor Thandabantu Nhlapo, its first chairperson).[12] Hlubi power brokers began to explore this legal option as early as 2004, when they organized the AmaHlubi National Coordinating Committee (later renamed AmaHlubi National Working Committee). The committee defined as its key mission to bring about "the recognition of one united Hlubi Nation in South Africa under one King" and to secure the "restitution as a result of loss suffered by Hlubi's [sic] under British rule, including land."[13]

Because this initiative represented a declaration of independence vis-à-vis the Zulu monarchy, supporters of the Zulu king accused the claimants of treason and threatened them with war.[14] The crisis only subsided when the Nhlapo Commission rejected the Hlubi claim in 2010 based on the argument that Hlubi ruler Langalibalele II did not "ruler over the entire traditional community" and that "Amahlubi do not share linguistic and cultural affinities" but "have been subsumed into traditional communities within which they reside."[15] Hlubi activists interpreted this verdict as politically motivated, designed to honor the agreements that had been negotiated just prior to the 1994 election. As the spokesperson of the AmaHlubi National Working Committee, Jobe Radebe, explained in 2017: "After the Commission had done its job with the Hlubi nation, . . . they presented their findings to the president and they couldn't agree on the verdict . . . because it would go against the agreement . . . about the Zulus; so it was supposed to be suppressed; that is why the truth did not come out from the Nhlapo Commission about the Hlubis; it was suppressed politically."[16] Not surprisingly, the verdict did not put an end to the committee's efforts to reconstitute the Hlubi as an independent kingdom. As a first step, the committee instructed its lawyers to file an appeal with the North Gauteng High Court in Pretoria in 2011 (which remains undecided by the time of this writing).[17]

More significantly, the committee revisited an issue that had first been raised in 2004: how to get ordinary people to embrace their "true identity, *yokuba ngamaHlubi* [of being Hlubi]" and defend this identity in the public realm.[18] Younger people responded with particular enthusiasm to this shift to Hlubi identity politics. In 2014, they established the "AmaHlubi National Youth Working Committee" to promote "the revival . . . of the rich history, culture and heritage of amaHlubi amongst the youth."[19] They also launched the Facebook page "AmaHlubi Amahle [The Beautiful Hlubi]," which encourages those who frequent the site to embrace their Hlubi identity.[20] One impassioned post showcases the ways in which the site has become an important platform for advancing Hlubi identity politics. "We didn't choose to be born amaHlubi," the post explains. "We were born amaHlubi and we shalt die as amaHlubi."[21] However, efforts to promote a strong sense of Hlubi identity are undermined by the persistence of the language-based notions of Zuluness and Xhosaness that emerged in the nineteenth and twentieth centuries.

Hlubi speech forms deviate from standard Zulu and standard Xhosa in a variety of small ways. Hlubi speech, for instance, uses "a fully nasalized" /ng'/ for the first-person prefix, whereas standard Zulu uses a "vocalized" /ng'/ and standard Xhosa uses /nd'/.[22] In terms of palatalization, Hlubi speech is also different; it employs /j/, whereas standard Zulu uses /tsh/ and standard Xhosa employs /ty/. Thus the Hlubi word for hill, for example, is *intajana*, whereas the Zulu and Xhosa languages use *intatshana* and *intatyana*.[23] There are also grammatical differences, notably in noun class 11 (/ulu-/) for which Hlubi speech uses /li/ as a prefix, while both

TABLE 4. Lexical Differences between Hlubi, Zulu, and Xhosa

HLUBI	ZULU	XHOSA
ilihlo (eye)	*iso, iliso*	*iliso*
uhlango (door)	*umnyango*	*ucango*
ukuqodzama (to kneel)	*ukuguqa*	*ukuguqa*
umniyane (mosquito)	*umiyane, unongxi*	*ingcongconi*

Source: Vuyokazi S. Nomlomo, "Language Variation in the Transkeian Xhosa Speech Community and Its Impact on Children's Education" (master's thesis, University of Cape Town, 1993), 57–58; Herbert W. Pahl, *IsiXhosa* (Johannesburg: Educum, 1983), 265, 208; Abner Nyamende, "Regional Variation in Xhosa," *Stellenbosch Papers in Linguistics Plus* 26 (1994): 207; Alfred T. Bryant, *A Zulu-English Dictionary* (Pinetown: Mariannhill Mission Press, 1905), 45, 209, 389, 594, 624.

standard Zulu and Xhosa use /lu/. This means that Hlubis say *inyawo lam* (my foot) whereas Zulus say *unyawo lwami* and Xhosas say *unyawo lwam*.[24] Finally, as table 4 shows, there are lexical differences between Hlubi speech and standard Zulu and Xhosa.

In spite of these differences, missionaries and intermediaries who promoted Zulu and Xhosa language mapping and standardization schemes in the nineteenth and twentieth centuries recognized Hlubi speech forms not as a distinct language but as a dialect of standard Zulu or standard Xhosa depending on where the speakers lived. This meant that they classified Hlubi-speaking populations in Natal as Zulu speakers and therefore Zulus, and Hlubi-speaking populations in the Transkei as Xhosa speakers and therefore Xhosas. As chapter 7 has shown, these new language-based identity discourses entrenched themselves firmly in people's consciousness through so-called mother-tongue education in the twentieth century with the result that a growing number of Hlubi self-identified as Zulu or Xhosa.

These language-based identity discourses largely survived South Africa's transition to nonracial democratic rule in 1994.[25] Moreover, they are continuously reinforced because the post-apartheid state recognizes standard Zulu and Xhosa as two of the country's nine official languages and uses these official languages as the basis for crafting policies.[26] The 1996 constitution, for example, argues that the focus on English and Afrikaans during the colonial and apartheid eras marginalized indigenous languages, and it mandates that the state "take practical and positive measures to elevate the status and advance the use of these [indigenous] languages."[27] This policy is problematic because the constitution defines "indigenous languages" as

"official standard languages" only and thus perpetuates the language policies of its predecessors, notably elevating standard Zulu and Xhosa above
nonstandard variants such as Hlubi.[28]

As in the colonial and apartheid era, this is most consequential in the
realm of education. In 1997, the government passed the Language in Education Policy of the National Education Policy Act, which declared as its
aim "to promote and develop" all the country's languages in primary and
secondary education.[29] The implementation of this policy required national
and provincial departments of education to record their student populations' "home language" (the language learners supposedly use at home)
and "language of learning and teaching" (the languages educational institutions should offer in order to meet learners' language education require-
ments). Both terms refer to official languages *only*, however, with the result
that Hlubi pupils are forced to identify themselves either as Zulu or Xhosa
speakers. One Hlubi person from the Eastern Cape explained: "If you are in
KwaZulu-Natal you tick under Zulu and if you are in the Eastern Cape you
tick under Xhosa because those are the official languages for that region and
those are the languages that are taught in school, regardless of what language
you speak at home, whether you speak isiHlubi, isiBhaca or whatever."[30]

As in the past, this has consequences. For one, Hlubi learners experience a language shift away from their home languages toward standard
Zulu and Xhosa because, by defining them as official languages, departments of education ascribe to them elevated prestige. Research in the Eastern Cape has shown that this context encourages schoolchildren to rank
their home variants below standard Xhosa and to shift toward the standard.[31] As in the past, some teachers contribute to this language shift by
ridiculing Hlubi-speaking pupils for their inability to speak standard Xhosa
"properly." One Hlubi individual explained that in some schools in the
Eastern Cape "you get mocked or ridiculed for speaking your own language in school. . . . You feel like an outcast. . . . Because you are human,
you want to fit in. . . . You start doubting yourself . . . [and] resenting your
language. . . . [You start] adopting this new language."[32] Finally, as in colonial and apartheid times, pupils shift not only from Hlubi to standard Zulu
or Xhosa but also adopt these languages as markers of their identities. One
interviewee explained the Hlubi-to-Zulu identity shift in these words: "A
Radebe can never be [of] another nation because we are in the kingship
lineage of the Hlubi nation, but you meet a Radebe and they say, 'I'm a

Zulu, a pure Zulu . . . [because] when I was growing up I was taught Zulu at school."[33] Hlubi-to-Xhosa shifts are equally common. One Hlubi person explained that "I . . . was under the illusion that I was Xhosa [because] I speak the [Xhosa] language."[34] Another individual added: "I have so many so called 'Xhosa' friends that are actually Hlubi but they don't know. . . . I am ashamed to say I am one of these Hlubi that has lost his true image . . . [because] I speak fluent Xhosa as my first language."[35]

The activists who are interested in reviving and strengthening the Hlubi identity in the post-apartheid era are aware of this problem. They have voiced frequently their frustrations about Hlubi self-identifying as Zulu or Xhosa on the basis of language, especially on the Facebook site "AmaHlubi Amahle." The site's moderator explained in 2014: "On a strong wording '*le nto ifana nomntana ongumgqakhwe' ozama uzifaka kwi* [This thing is like a child born out of wedlock who tries to force himself into the family that isn't his]. We as amaHlubi don't belong in those nations . . . we are not them. *SingamaHlubi* [we are Hlubi]."[36] The responses suggest that this frustration is widespread. One person responded by saying: "*thina mhlubi* [we, the Hlubi] should reject *intoyokuba sibizwe nje ngamaxhosa* [that we should be referred to as Xhosa] or *zulu* . . . we remain *amahlubi* . . . and *sizwe sakwahlubi* [the Hlubi nation] rise." Another person added: "It is our duty that if you are from the Eastern Cape, when you are referred to as *UmXhosa, baxele UliHlubi* [a Xhosa, tell them you are a Hlubi], *uma uphuma eKZN bethi Ungumzulu, batshele UyiHlubi* [if you come from KZN and they say you are a Zulu, tell them you are a Hlubi]. This can help emphasis [sic] to others that we [are] not Zulu and we are not Xhosa."[37]

This context also explains why the AmaHlubi National Working Committee declared as early as 2004 that reviving the Hlubi language had to be a cornerstone of their activism.[38] Ten years later, the AmaHlubi National Youth Working Committee made it its mission to revive the "Hlubi language amongst the youth and broader nation."[39] They appointed a "chief language research officer" tasked with "work[ing] with relevant stakeholders in the development and promotion of the Hlubi language."[40] They also established the "IsiHlubi Language Board" and charged it with finding ways to reverse the language-induced identity shift toward Zuluness and Xhosaness. Part and parcel of the board's strategy is to popularize the Hlubi speech by (among other things) getting it recognized as one of South Africa's official languages. Two members of the language board explained their efforts, stating:

The majority of youth do not even know that there is a language called isiHlubi . . . because one speaks this language that is taught in school [i.e., Zulu or Xhosa] . . . so we found there is a youth problem. . . . They don't know their heritage. . . . The main aim [therefore] is to actually collect all the youth . . . [by] promoting isiHlubi to the youth [so as to] make it popular so that they know who they are [and] they grow knowing who they are. . . . Our main battle is to get the language officially recognized as an official language, that's our struggle as the Language Board.[41]

If they are successful in this endeavor, the activists may yet be able to restore a strong sense of Hlubi identity and an independent Hlubi kingship in post-apartheid South Africa. Regardless of any future success or failure on their part, however, their activism illustrates the extent to which the language-based Zulu-Xhosa divide survived the transition to the new South Africa and to what extent this divide shapes post-apartheid power and identity politics. The new South Africa, it turns out, cannot be fully understood without coming to terms with the long history of the Zulu-Xhosa divide.

• NOTES •

INTRODUCTION

1. Gary Kynoch, *Township Violence and the End of Apartheid: War on the Reef* (Rochester, NY: James Currey, 2018); Gary Kynoch, "Reassessing Transition Violence: Voices from South Africa's Township Wars, 1990–4," *African Affairs* 112:447 (2013), 283–303; Philip Bonner and Vusi Ndima, "The Roots of Violence and Martial Zuluness on the East Rand," in *Zulu Identities: Being Zulu, Past and Present*, ed. Benedict Carton, John Laband, and Jabulani Sithole (New York: Columbia University Press, 2009), 363–82; Lauren Segal, "The Human Face of Violence: Hostel Dwellers Speak," *Journal of Southern African Studies* 18:1 (Mar. 1991): 190–231; Adam Ashforth, "Violence and Political Action in South Africa: Five Comrades Speak," in *Passages: A Chronicle of the African Humanities*, Program of African Studies, Northwestern University, no. 4 (1994), 1–3, 10–11, 13.
2. Jo-Anne Collinge, "Behind the Violence," *Weekly Mail*, 17 Aug. 1990; Segal, "The Human Face of Violence," 219; Kynoch, "Reassessing Transition Violence," 292–93.
3. Bonner and Ndima, "The Roots of Violence," 376.
4. Kynoch, *Township Violence*, 33.
5. Ashforth, "Violence and Political Action in South Africa."
6. Kynoch, *Township Violence*, 38.
7. Ibid., 94.
8. Segal, "The Human Face of Violence," 227.
9. Kynoch, "Reassessing Transition Violence," 293.
10. Segal, "The Human Face of Violence," 219.
11. Chris Lowe et al., "Talking about 'Tribe': Moving from Stereotypes to Analysis," *Africa Policy Information Center* (Washington, DC), Background Paper 10 (Nov. 1997), 1–8.

12. New York Times news service, "Tribal Strife Widens in S. Africa; 140 Dead," *Chicago Tribune*, 16 Aug. 1990.

13. Segal, "The Human Face of Violence," 231.

14. Jabulani Sithole, "Changing Meanings of the Battle of Ncome and Images of King Dingane in Twentieth-Century South Africa," in Carton, Laband, and Sithole, *Zulu Identities*, 328.

15. John B. Wright, "Making Identities in the Thukela-Mzimvubu Region c. 1770–c. 1940," in *Tribing and Untribing the Archive: Identity and the Material Record in Southern KwaZulu-Natal in the Late Independent and Colonial Periods*, 2 vols., ed. Carolyn Hamilton and Nessa Leibhammer (Pietermaritzburg: University of KwaZulu-Natal Press, 2016), 1:193.

16. Kynoch, "Reassessing Transition Violence," 293.

17. Segal, "Human Face of Violence," 217.

18. Kynoch, *Township Violence*, 144.

19. Mary de Haas and Paulus Zulu, "Ethnicity and Federalism: The Case of KwaZulu/Natal," in "Ethnicity and Identity in Southern Africa," special issue, ed. E. Wilmsen, S. Dubow, and J. Sharp, *Journal of Southern African Studies* 20:3 (Sept. 1994): 439.

20. Catherine Campbell, Gerhard Maré, and Cherryl Walker, "Evidence for an Ethnic Identity in the Life Histories of Zulu-Speaking Durban Township Residents," *Journal of Southern African Studies* 21:2 (June 1995): 295.

21. Sibusisiwe Nombuso Dlamini, *Youth and Identity Politics in South Africa, 1990–1994* (Toronto: University of Toronto Press, 2005), 80, 92, 116–18.

22. Ibid., 132–33.

23. Liz Sly, "Zulu King Picks a Bride, and Tongues Wag that She Is Not Really," *Chicago Tribune*, 28 July 1992.

24. T. Dunbar Moodie with Vivienne Ndatshe, *Going for Gold: Men, Mines, and Migration* (Berkeley: University of California Press, 1994), 206–7.

25. Trevor Noah, *Born a Crime: Stories from a South African Childhood* (London: John Murray, 2017), 15.

26. Ibid.

27. Mbongiseni Buthelezi, "The Empire Talks Back: Re-Examining the Legacies of Shaka and Zulu Power in Post-Apartheid South Africa," in Carton, Laband, and Sithole, *Zulu Identities*, 24.

28. Jabulani Sithole, "Preface: Zuluness in South Africa: From 'Struggle' Debate to Democratic Transformation," in Carton, Laband, and Sithole, *Zulu Identities*, xv.

29. Ibid., xvi.

30. Thomas R. Trautmann, *Languages and Nations: The Dravidian Proof in Colonial Madras* (Berkeley: University of California Press, 2006), 34,

38; Gottfried Wilhelm Leibnitz, "Nouveaux essais sur l'entendement humain," in *Oeuvres philosophiques latines et françoises de feu Mr. de Leibnitz,* ed. Rudolf Eric Raspe (Leipzig: Schreuder, 1765), 242; Johann Gottfried von Herder, *Briefe zur Beförderung der Humanität,* ed. Johann von Müller (Stuttgart: J. G. Gotta, 1829), 68. My translation.

31. Sara Pugach, *Africa in Translation: A History of Colonial Linguistics in Germany and Beyond, 1814–1945* (Ann Arbor: University of Michigan Press, 2012), 25–26.

32. For Bastian and Boas see Lawrence E. Cahoone, *Cultural Revolutions: Reason versus Culture in Philosophy, Politics, and Jihad* (University Park: Pennsylvania State University Press, 2005), 37.

33. For introductions to this complicated history, see Anthony B. Smith, *The Ethnic Origins of Nations* (Oxford: Basil Blackwell 1988); John A. Armstrong, *Nations before Nationalism* (Chapel Hill: University of North Carolina Press, 1982).

34. As quoted in Len Scales, *The Shaping of German Identity: Authority and Crisis, 1245–1414* (New York: Cambridge University Press, 2012), 500.

35. Ruth A. Sanders, *German: Biography of a Language* (New York: Oxford University Press, 2010), 137–38.

36. Ibid., 118, 138.

37. James R. Dow, "Germany," in *Handbook of Language and Ethnic Identity: Disciplinary and Regional Perspectives,* ed. Joshua A. Fishman and Ofelia García, 2nd ed., vol. 1 (New York: Oxford University Press, 2010), 224.

38. Winifred V. Davies, "Standard German in the Nineteenth Century," in *Landmarks in the History of the German Language,* ed. Geraldine Horan, Nils Langer, and Sheila Watts (New York: Peter Lang, 2009), 189–210.

39. Adolf Bach, *Geschichte der Deutschen Sprache* (Leipzig, 1938), as quoted in Dow, "Germany," 229.

40. Carton, Laband, and Sithole, *Zulu Identities;* Hamilton and Leibhammer, *Tribing and Untribing the Archive;* Jill E. Kelly, *To Swim with Crocodiles: Land, Violence, and Belonging in South Africa, 1800–1996* (East Lansing: Michigan State University Press, 2018).

41. Paul Landau, *Popular Politics in the History of South Africa, 1400–1948* (New York: Cambridge University Press, 2010), 109, 247.

42. Ibid., 246.

43. Leroy Vail, ed., *The Creation of Tribalism in Southern Africa* (Berkeley: University of California Press, 1989).

44. Vail, ibid., 3.

45. Ibid.

46. Ibid., 11.

47. Ibid.

48. Marie Louise Pratt, *Imperial Eyes: Travel Writing and Transculturation*, 2nd ed. (New York: Routledge, 2008), 28.

49. See also Johannes Fabian, "Missions and the Colonization of African Languages: Developments in the Former Belgian Congo," *Canadian Journal of African Studies* 17:2 (1983): 165–87; Terence Ranger, *The Invention of Tribalism in Zimbabwe* (Gweru: Mabo, 1985); William J. Samarin, "Protestant Missions and the History of Lingala," *Journal of Religion in Africa* 16:2 (June 1986): 138–63; Tore Janson and Joseph Tsonope, *Birth of a National Language: The History of Setswana* (Berkeley: University of California Press, 1991); Jean Comaroff and John Comaroff, *Of Revelation and Revolution: Christianity, Colonialism, and Consciousness in South Africa*, vol. 1 (Chicago: University of Chicago Press, 1991); Sinfree Makoni, "In the Beginning Was the Missionaries' Word: The European Invention of an African Language: The Case of Shona in Zimbabwe," in Kwesi Kwaa Prah, ed., *Between Distinction & Extinction: The Harmonisation and Standardisation of African Languages* (Johannesburg: Witwatersrand University Press, 1998), 157–64; Stephen Volz, "European Missionaries and the Development of Tswana Identity," *Le Fait Missionaire* 15 (2004): 97–128; Diana Jeater, *Law, Language, and Science: The Invention of the "Native Mind" in Southern Rhodesia, 1890–1930* (Portsmouth, NH: Heinemann, 2007); Tomasz Kamusella and Finex Ndhlovu, eds., *The Social and Political History of Southern Africa's Languages* (London: Palgrave, 2018).

50. Terence Ranger, "Missionaries, Migrants and the Manyika: The Invention of Ethnicity in Zimbabwe," in *The Creation of Tribalism in Southern Africa*, ed. Leroy Vail (Berkeley: University of California Press, 1989), 118–50; Patrick Harries, "Exclusion, Classification and Internal Colonialism: The Emergence of Ethnicity among the Tsonga-Speakers of South Africa," in ibid., 82–117.

51. For these conclusions see also Harries's earlier "The Roots of Ethnicity: Discourse and the Politics of Language Construction in South-East Africa," *African Affairs* 8 (Jan. 1988): 25–52, and his more comprehensive *Butterflies and Barbarians: Swiss Missionaries and Systems of Knowledge in South-East Africa* (Athens: Ohio University Press, 2007), notably chapter 6.

52. [Jeff Peires], "Ethnicity and Pseudo-Ethnicity in the Ciskei," in Vail, *The Creation of Tribalism*, 395.

53. Shula Marks, "Patriotism, Patriarchy and Purity: Natal and the Politics of Zulu Ethnic Consciousness," in Vail, *The Creation of Tribalism*, 217.

54. Ibid.

55. [Peires], "Ethnicity and Pseudo-Ethnicity," 395–96, 404.

56. Bernd Heine and Derek Nurse, introduction to *African Languages: An Introduction*, ed. Heine and Nurse (New York: Cambridge University Press, 2000), 1; Joseph H. Greenberg, *The Languages of Africa* (The Hague: Mouton, 1963).

57. Derek Nurse and Gérard Philippson, introduction to *The Bantu Languages*, ed. Nurse and Philippson (New York: Routledge 2003), 1–2.

58. Pali Lehohla, *Census 2011 Census Brief* (Pretoria: Statistics South Africa, 2012), 26, http://www.statssa.gov.za/census/census_2011/census _products/Census_2011_Census_in_brief.pdf.

59. William B. McGregor, *Linguistics: An Introduction*, 2nd ed. (New York: Bloomsbury, 2015), 383.

60. For some comments on this "mutual intelligibility," see Isaac W. Wauchope, "The Kafir Language," *Imvo*, 16 July 1891, 3, as quoted in *Isaac Williams Wauchope: Selected Writings, 1874–1916*, ed. and trans. Jeff Opland and Abner Nyamende (Cape Town: Van Riebeeck Society, 2008), 312; Jeff Opland, Wandile Kuse, and Pamela Maseko, eds. and trans., *William Wellington Gqoba: Isizwe esinembali, Xhosa histories and poetry (1873–1888)*, Publications of the Opland Collection of Xhosa Literature, vol. 1 (Pietermaritzburg: University of KwaZulu-Natal Press, 2015), 214.

61. See for instance Desmond T. Cole, "Doke's Classification of Bantu Languages," in *Contributions to the History of Bantu Linguistics*, ed. C. M. Doke and D. T. Cole (Johannesburg: Witwatersrand University Press, 1969), 81, 88.

62. Sinfree Makoni, "From Misinvention to Disinvention of Language: Multilinguism and the South African Constitution," in *Black Linguistics: Language, Society and Politics in Africa and the Americas*, ed. Sinfree Makoni, Geneva Smitherman, Arnetha F. Ball, and Arthur K. Spear (New York: Routledge, 2003), 134.

63. See for instance George Cory, *The Rise of South Africa*, 6 vols. (London: Longmans, 1910–40), and Alfred T. Bryant, *Olden Times in Zululand and Natal* (New York: Longman's, 1929).

64. In more recent times, this binary approach has leaned very heavily toward Zulu; see for instance the following pathbreaking edited collections: Carton, Laband, and Sithole, *Zulu Identities*; Hamilton and Leibhammer, *Tribing and Untribing the Archive*. A notable exception to this binary approach is Carolyn Hamilton, ed., *The Mfecane Aftermath: Reconstructive Debates in Southern African History* (Johannesburg: Witwatersrand University Press, 1995).

65. Rachel Gilmour, *Grammars of Colonialism: Representing Languages in Colonial South Africa* (New York: Palgrave, 2006), 5.

1. "WHAT DOES STICK TO PEOPLE—MORE THAN THEIR LANGUAGE—IS THEIR *ISIBONGO*"

1. Landau, *Popular Politics*, 47.
2. For a detailed discussion of these methods see Derek Nurse, "The Contributions of Linguistics to the Study of History in Africa," *Journal of African History* 38 (1997): 359–91; Lyle Campbell, *Historical Linguistics: An Introduction* (Cambridge, MA: MIT Press, 1998).
3. For a good overview, see Catherine Cymone Fourshey, Rhonda M. Gonzales, and Christine Saidi, *Bantu Africa, 3500 BCE to Present* (New York: Oxford University Press, 2018). For "slow expansion," see Nurse, "The Contributions of Linguistics," 379; Jan Vansina, *Paths in the Rainforest: Toward a History of Political Tradition in Equatorial Africa* (Madison: University of Wisconsin Press, 1990), 55.
4. Christopher Ehret, *An African Classical Age: Eastern and Southern Africa, 1000 B.C. to A.D. 400* (Charlottesville: University of Virginia Press, 2001), 105.
5. Fourshey, Gonzales, and Saidi, *Bantu Africa*, 7.
6. Fourshey, Gonzales, and Saidi, *Bantu Africa*, 155–56; Vansina, *Paths in the Rainforest*, 56.
7. Ehret, *Classical Age*, 47–51, 133, 271.
8. In addition to sources cited elsewhere, I have relied on Igor Kopytoff, "The Internal African Frontier: The Making of African Political Culture," in *The African Frontier: The Reproduction of Traditional African Societies*, ed. Kopytoff (Bloomington: Indiana University Press, 1987), 3–84; Kairn Klieman, *"The Pygmies Were Our Compass": Bantu and Batwa in the History of West and Central Africa, Early Times to c. 1900* (Portsmouth, NH: Heineman, 2003), chapter 3; Simon Hall, "Farming Communities of the Second Millennium: Internal Frontiers, Identity, Continuity and Change," in *The Cambridge History of South Africa*, vol. 1, *From Early Times to 1885*, ed. Carolyn Hamilton, Bernard Mbenga, and Robert Ross (New York: Cambridge University Press, 2012), 112–67.
9. The importance of migration is emphasized by Carolan Ownby, "Early Nguni History: The Linguistic Evidence and Its Correlation with Archeology and Oral Tradition" (PhD diss., University of California, Los Angeles, 1985); Thomas N. Huffman, "Ceramics, Settlements and Late Iron Age Migrations," *African Archeological Review* 7 (1989): 155–82. The importance of local innovation is highlighted by Raevin Jimenez, "Rites of Reproduction: Gender, Generation and Political Economic Transformation among Nguni-Speakers of Southern Africa, 8th–19th Century" (PhD diss., Northwestern University, 2017); Tim Maggs, "The Iron Age

Sequence South of the Vaal and Pongola Rivers: Some Historical Implications," *Journal of African History* 21 (1980): 1–15.

10. Ehret, *Classical Age*, 226–27.

11. Fourshey, Gonzales, and Saidi, *Bantu Africa*, 155–56.

12. Frans E. Prins and Hester Lewis, "Bushmen as Mediators in Nguni Cosmology," *Ethnography* 31 (1992): 133–47; Aron D. Mazel, "Hunter-Gatherers in the Thukela Basin during the last 1500 Years, with Special Reference to Hunter-Gatherer/Agriculturalist Relations," in *The Proceedings of the Khoisan Identities and Cultural Heritage Conference*, ed. Andrew Bank (Cape Town: Institute for Historical Research and Infosource, 1998), 94–101; Mdukiswa Tyabashe, "All the Land of the Mpondomise," in *The Tongue Is Fire: South African Storytellers and Apartheid*, ed. Harold Scheub (Madison: University of Wisconsin Press, 1996), 235.

13. Christopher Ehret, "Transformations in Southern Africa: Proposals for a Sweeping Overview of Change and Development, 6000 BC to the Present," *Ufahuma: A Journal of African Studies* 25:2 (1997): 65; Tyabashe, "All the Land," 235.

14. Tyabashe, "All the Land," 235–36; Landau, *Popular Politics*, 61.

15. For the complex relationship between Xhosa farmers and Thwa hunters in the eastern Cape, see Jeff Peires, *House of Phalo: A History of the Xhosa People in the Days of Their Independence* (Berkeley: University of California Press, 1982), 24; Ndumiso Bhotomane, "Origins of the Xhosa," 32.

16. Ehret, "Transformations in Southern Africa," 65.

17. Leonard W. Lanham, "The Proliferation and Extension of Bantu Phonemic System Influenced by Bushman and Hottentot," in *Proceedings of the Ninth International Congress of Linguistics, Cambridge 1962*, ed. Horace Gray Lunt (Paris: Mouton, 1964), 383–84.

18. Ehret, "Transformations in Southern Africa," 67–72. For "proto-Nguni" see Jimenez, "Rites of Reproduction," 67.

19. Gavin Whitelaw and Simon Hall, "Archeological Contexts and the Creation of Social Categories before the Zulu Kingdom," in Hamilton and Leibhammer, *Tribing and Untribing*, 1:157.

20. Ehret, "Transformations in Southern Africa," 68–72.

21. Whitelaw and Hall, "Archeological Contexts," 1:152.

22. Ownby, "Early Nguni History," 66, 139.

23. Richard Bailey, "Sociolinguistic Evidence of Nguni, Sotho, Tsonga and Venda Origins," in *Language and Social History; Studies in South African Sociolinguistics*, ed. Rajend Mesthrie (Cape Town: David Philip, 1995), 41–42; see also Ownby, "Early Nguni History," 66.

24. Jouni Filip Maho, comp., "NUGL Online: The Online Version of the New Updated Guthrie List, a Referential Classification of the Bantu

languages" (4 June 2009), 93, https://brill.com/fileasset/downloads_products/35125_Bantu-New-updated-Guthrie-List.pdf.

25. Peires, *House of Phalo*, 1.

26. Ibid., 10.

27. Ehret, *Classical Age*, 217–19.

28. The debate cannot be explored in detail here but see Richard Elphick, *Khoikhoi and the Founding of White South Africa* (Johannesburg: Ravan, 1985), 11–14, 30–42; Andrew B. Smith, "On Becoming Herders: Khoikhoi and San Ethnicity in Southern Africa," *African Studies* 49:2 (1990): 51–73.

29. Ehret, *Classical Age*, 217.

30. Ibid., 219–20.

31. Emile Boonzaier, Candy Malherbe, Penny Berens, and Andy Smith, *The Cape Herders: A History of the Khoikhoi of Southern Africa*, 2nd ed. (Athens: Ohio University Press, 2000), 1–2, 36.

32. Elphick, *Khoikhoi and the Founding*, 51; Susan Newton-King, *Masters and Servants on the Eastern Cape Frontier, 1760–1803* (New York: Cambridge University Press, 1999), 28.

33. Note, however, that some scholars argue that there existed significant differences between the Khoesan speech of the hunters and that of the herders. See Anthony Traill, "'!Khwa-ka Hhouiten,' 'The Rush of the Storm': The Linguistic Death of /Xam," in *Miscast: Negotiating the Presence of the Bushmen*, ed. Pippa Skotnes (Cape Town: University of Cape Town Press, 1996), 161–83.

34. For "*amaQèya*" see Albert Kropf, *A Kaffir-English Dictionary* (Lovedale: Lovedale Mission Press, 1899), 335.

35. Ehret, "Transformations in Southern Africa," 65; Landau, *Popular Politics*, 50.

36. Ehret, "Transformations in Southern Africa," 66.

37. Newton-King, *Masters and Servants*, 32–33, but see more on this in chapter 4.

38. Gerrit Harinck, "Interaction between Xhosa and Khoi; Emphasis on the Period 1620–1750," in *African Societies in Southern Africa*, ed. Leonard Thompson (London: Heinemann, 1969), especially 150–51; Ownby, "Early Nguni History," 71–73; and earlier works, notably Carl Meinhof, "Hottentotische Laute und Leihwörter im Kafir," *Zeitschrift der Deutschen Morgenländischen Gesellschaft* 58 (1904): 727–69, and 59 (1905): 36–89.

39. Harinck, "Interaction between Xhosa and Khoi," 153.

40. Boonzaier et al., *Cape Herders*, 49; London Missionary Society, *Transactions of the Missionary Society*, vol. 1 (London: Bye and Law, 1804), 397.

41. Robert K. Herbert, "The Sociohistory of Clicks in Southern Bantu," *Anthropological Linguistics* 32:3/4 (Fall–Winter 1990), 303–6.

42. Harinck, "Interaction between Xhosa and Khoi," 154–55.

43. For "violently incorporated" and "*//kosa*" see Peires, *House of Phalo*, 13, 19, 22–23.

44. Maho, "NUGL Online," 93.

45. Comaroff and Comaroff, *Of Revelation and Revolution*, 225.

46. Jakob L. Döhne, *A Zulu-Kafir Dictionary* (Cape Town: G. K. Pike's, 1857), 203; John Colenso, *Zulu-English Dictionary*, 2nd ed. (Natal: P. Davis, 1884), 300; William J. Davis, *A Dictionary of the Kaffir Language: Including Xosa and Zulu Dialects* (London: Wesleyan Mission House, 1872), 117.

47. Ranger, *Invention of Tribalism*, 4.

48. Elizabeth MacGonagle, *Crafting Identity in Zimbabwe and Mozambique* (Rochester, NY: University of Rochester Press, 2007), 16.

49. The meanings of these terms were neither monolithic nor static. For changes over time and alternative meanings, see John B. Wright, "Politics, Ideology and the Invention of the 'Nguni,'" in *Resistance and Ideology in Settler Societies*, Southern African Studies, vol. 4, ed. Tom Lodge (Johannesburg: Ravan, 1987), 96–118; Carolyn Hamilton and John B. Wright, "The Making of the AmaLala: Ethnicity, Ideology and Relations of Subordination in a Precolonial Context," *South African Historical Journal* 22 (1990): 3–23; Carolyn Hamilton, "Political Centralisation and the Making of Social Categories East of the Drakensberg in the Late Eighteenth and Early Nineteenth Centuries," *Journal of Southern African Studies* 38:2 (June 2012): 291–300; Carolyn Hamilton and John B. Wright, "Moving beyond Ethnic Framing: Political Differentiation in the Chiefdoms of KwaZulu-Natal Region before 1830," *Journal of Southern African Studies* 43:4 (2017): 663–79.

50. David W. Hedges, "Trade and Politics in Southern Mozambique and Zululand in the Eighteenth and Early Nineteenth Centuries" (PhD diss., University of London, 1978), 105.

51. Wright, "Politics, Ideology," 97.

52. Hedges, "Trade and Politics," 105.

53. Ibid.

54. Ibid., 106; Bhotomane, "Origins of the Xhosa," 45.

55. Opland, Kuse, and Maseko, *William Wellington Gqoba*, 356–57.

56. This usage is explained in Albert Kropf, *Das Volk der Xosa-Kaffern im östlichen Südafrika nach seiner Geschichte, Eigenart, Verfassung und Religion*, ed. Ulrich van der Heyden und Joachim Kundler (Bremen: Falkenberg, 2017), 46.

57. John B. Wright, "A. T. Bryant and the 'Lala,'" *Journal of Southern African Studies* 38:2 (June 2012): 361.

58. Ibid.

59. Fourshey, Gonzales, and Saidi, *Bantu Africa*, 57.

60. Richard T. Schaefer, ed., *Encyclopedia of Race, Ethnicity, and Society*, vol. 1 (Thousand Oaks, CA: Sage, 2008), 457. See also Harald Haarmann, *Language in Ethnicity: A View of Basic Ecological Relations* (New York: Mouton de Gruyter, 2010), 39; Jeffrey A. Ross, "Language and the Mobilization of Ethnic Identity," in *Language and Ethnic Relations*, ed. H. Giles and B. Saint-Jacques (New York: Pergamon, 1979), 12; René Appel and Pieter Muysken, *Language Contact and Bilingualism* (Amsterdam: Amsterdam University Press, 2005), 15.

61. Harald Haarmann, "Language Politics and the European Identity," in *A Language Policy for the European Community: Prospects and Quandaries*, ed. Florian Coulmans (New York: Mouton de Gruyter, 1991), 106.

62. Fourshey, Gonzales, and Saidi, *Bantu Africa*, 43.

63. Ibid., 59; Per Hage and Jeff Marck, "Proto-Bantu Descent Groups," in *Kinship, Language and Prehistory: Per Hage and the Renaissance in Kinship Studies*, ed. Doug Jones and Bojka Milicic (Salt Lake City: University of Utah Press, 2011), 75–78.

64. Fourshey, Gonzales, and Saidi, *Bantu Africa*, 64; Ehret, *Classical Age*, 149–50.

65. Jeff Peires, *The Dead Will Arise: Nongqawuse and the Great Xhosa Cattle-Killing Movement of 1856–7* (Johannesburg: Ravan, 1989), 131; Michael Mahoney, *The Other Zulus: The Spread of Zulu Ethnicity in Colonial South Africa* (Durham, NC: Duke University Press, 2012), 24.

66. This genealogical meaning is emphasized by Ehret, *Classical Age*, 150–54.

67. Max Gluckman, "The Kingdom of the Zulu of South Africa," in *African Political Systems*, ed. Myer Fortes and E. E. Evans-Pritchard (New York: Oxford University Press, 1940), 25–26, 28–29; John D. Omer-Cooper, "Aspects of Political Change in the Nineteenth-Century Mfecane," in *African Societies in Southern Africa*, ed. Leonard M. Thompson (London: Heinmann, 1969), 209–12; Monica Wilson, "The Nguni People," in *The Oxford History of South Africa*, vol. 1, ed. Wilson and Leonard Thompson (Oxford: University of Oxford Press, 1969), 75–130.

68. This process is known among anthropologists as the "segmentary lineage theory."

69. For "*isizwe*" see Colenso, *Zulu-English Dictionary*, 673; Peires, *House of Phalo*, 196n6.

70. Colin de B. Webb and John B. Wright, eds., *The James Stuart Archive of Recorded Oral Evidence Relating to the History of the Zulu and Neighbouring Peoples*, 6 vols. (Pietermaritzburg: University of Natal Press, 1976–2014), hereafter *JSA*, Ndukwana kaMbengwana (1897–1903), 4:297.

71. Vansina, *Paths in the Rainforest*, 75; Landau, *Popular Politics*, 49–50.

72. Ehret, *Classical Age*, 148.

73. Ehret, "Transformations in Southern Africa," 70–71.

74. For *"isizwe"* see Colenso, *Zulu-English Dictionary*, 673; Peires, *House of Phalo*, 196n6. Note that Colenso, like other Europeans at the time, uses the word "tribe" rather than "chiefdom" in his dictionary.

75. Nicolaas J. Van Warmelo, *A Preliminary Survey of the Bantu Tribes of South Africa* (Pretoria: Government Printer, 1935), 6.

76. *JSA*, Ndukwana kaMbengwana (1897–1903), 4:297.

77. Monica Wilson, "Strangers in Africa: Reflections on Nyakyusa, Nguni, and Sotho Evidence," in *Strangers in African Societies*, ed. William A. Shack and Elliott P. Skinner (Berkeley: University of California Press, 1979), 55.

78. Peires, *House of Phalo*, 16, 22–24.

79. Wilson, "Strangers in Africa," 52–54; Randolph Vigne, ed., *Guillaume Chenu de Chalezac, The "French Boy," the Narrative of his Experiences as a Huguenot Refugee, as a Castaway among the Xhosa, His Rescue with the Stavenisse Survivors by the Centaurus, His Service at the Cape and Return to Europe, 1686–9* (Cape Town: Van Riebeeck Society, 1993), 86, 90.

80. *JSA*, Ndukwana kaMbengwana (1897–1903), 4:297.

81. S. E. K. Mqhayi, "SoGqumahashe (N. C. Mhala)," in *Abantu besizwe: Historical and Biographical Writings, 1902–1944*, ed. and trans. Jeff Opland (Johannesburg: Wits University Press, 2009), 166.

82. Ibid.

83. Jimenez, "Rites of Reproduction," 386.

84. Mahoney, *Other Zulus*, 25.

85. Peires, *House of Phalo*, 19.

86. *JSA*, Ndukwana kaMbengwana (1897–1903), 4:299; ibid., Maziyana kaMahlabeni with Socwatsha kaPhaphu (1905), 2:280.

87. For a different view see William D. Hammond-Tooke, "Descent Groups, Chiefdoms and South African Historiography," *Journal of Southern African Studies* 11:2 (April, 1985): 311–12.

88. Ibid., 313.

89. Peires, *House of Phalo*, 27.

90. Ibid., 28, 30.

91. Ibid., 16, 31.

92. Ibid., 27.

93. Ibid., 20.

94. Wilson, "Strangers in Africa," 52.

95. Peires, *House of Phalo*, 19.

96. *JSA*, Ndukwana kaMbengwana (1897–1903), 4:299.

97. Opland, Kuse, and Maseko, *William Wellington Gqoba*, 231.

98. JSA, Maziyana kaMahlabeni with Socwatsha kaPhaphu (1905), 2:280.

99. Schaefer, *Encyclopedia of Race, Ethnicity, and Society*, 457.

100. Mahmood Mamdani, *Saviors and Survivors: Darfur, Politics, and the War on Terror* (New York: Doubleday, 2010), 24.

101. Landau, *Popular Politics*, 59.

102. Peires, *House of Phalo*, 15–16, 30.

103. Ibid., 36.

104. Ibid.

105. Kopytoff, "Internal African Frontier," 44, 48.

106. Peires, *House of Phalo*, 16.

107. As one oral tradition explains, "These nations stood alone and were ruling themselves long ago. They were abolished by fighting (*bagqugqiswa ngokulwa*) by Tshawe, they were overcome so that they became one nation." Quoted in ibid., 15.

108. Ibid., 14 note a, 15.

2. "SURROUNDED ON ALL SIDES BY PEOPLE THAT DIFFER FROM THEM IN EVERY POINT, IN COLOR . . . AND IN LANGUAGE"

1. For the sake of uniformity, the term "Caffre" is used except in direct quotations.

2. Penny Silva, Wendy Dore, Dorothea Mantzel, Colin Muller, and Madeleine Wright, eds., *Dictionary of South African English on Historical Principles* (New York: Oxford University Press, 1996), 342.

3. Mark Mathabane, *Kaffir Boy: The True Story of a Black Youth's Coming of Age in Apartheid South Africa* (New York: Free Press, 1986), xiii.

4. Peter Williams, "Hate Speech Is a Crime: Equality Court Rules in Favour of Domestic Worker," *De Rebus* 550 (Mar. 2015): 26–28.

5. Silva et al., *Dictionary*, 342; Gabeba Baderoon, "Ambiguous Visibility: Islam and the Making of a South African Landscape," *Arab World Geographer* 8:1–2 (2005): 92.

6. Robert C.-H. Shell, *Children of Bondage: A Social History of the Slave Society at the Cape of Good Hope, 1652–1838* (Johannesburg: Witwatersrand University Press, 1995), 189–90; Silva et al., *Dictionary*, 342; Baderoon, "Ambiguous," 91–92.

7. Silva et al., *Dictionary*, 342; Hazel Crampton, Jeff Peires, and Carl Vernon, eds., *Into the Hitherto Unknown: Ensign Beutler's Expedition to the Eastern Cape, 1752*, trans. Thea Toussaint van Hove and Michael Wilson (Cape Town: Van Riebeeck Society, 2013), xl.

8. John K. Thornton, *Africa and Africans in the Making of the Atlantic World, 1400–1800*, 2nd ed. (New York: Cambridge, 1998), 29–33.

9. Malyn D. D. Newitt, *A History of Mozambique* (Bloomington: Indiana University Press, 1995), 3–27.

10. James Sweet, "The Iberian Roots of American Racist Thought," *William and Mary Quarterly*, 3rd ser., 54:1 (Jan. 1997): 143–66.

11. Ibid., 148.

12. Gomes Eannes de Zurara, *Chronica do Descobrimento e Conquista de Guiné, escrita por Mandado de ElRei D. Affonso V*, ed. Visconde de Santarem (Paris: Aillaud, 1841), 158; Duarte Pacheco Pereira, *Esmeraldo de Situ Orbis*, ed. Augusto Epiphanio da Silva Dias (Lisbon: Typographia Universal, 1905), 80–81. For the Senegal River as the dividing line, see Zurara, *Chronica*, 278; Frederique Verrier, ed., *Voyages en Afrique Noire d'Alvise Cà da Mosto, 1455 & 1456*, 2nd ed. (Paris: Chandeigne, 2003), 25, 43, 54. My translations.

13. Álvaro Velho, *O Roteiro da Viagem de Vasco da Gama em 1497*, 2nd ed. (Lisbon: Imprensa Nacional, 1866), 6–7, 10–11, 18, 21. My translation.

14. *Documents on the Portuguese in Mozambique and Central Africa, 1497–1840* (*Documentos sobre os Portugueses em Moçambique e na África Central, 1497–1840*), 8 vols. (Lisbon: National Archives of Rhodesia and Nyasaland, Centro de Estudos Históricos Ultramarinos, 1962–75), 1:93.

15. Ibid., 1:367, 385, 507.

16. George McCall Theal, ed. and trans., *Records of South-Eastern Africa, Collected in Various Libraries and Archive Departments in Europe*, 6 vols. (London: W. Clowes, 1898–1900), 6:230; João de Barros, *Década Primeira: Da Asia de João de Barros* (Lisbon: Jorge Rodriguez, 1628), Livro 8, folio 160.

17. Louis-Marcel Devic, *Le pays des Zendjs: ou, La côte orientale d'Afrique au moyen-âge (géographie, moeurs, productions, animaux légendaires) d'après les écrivains arabes* (Paris: Hachette, 1888); Marina Tolmacheva, "Toward a Definition of the Term Zanj," *Azania* 21 (1986): 105–13; J. F. P. Hopkins and Nehemiah Levtzion, eds., *Corpus of Early Arabic Sources for West African History* (Cambridge: Cambridge University Press, 1981), 20–21, 332.

18. Devic, *Le pays*, 35, 125–26.

19. Ibn Battuta, *Ibn Battuta in Black Africa*, ed. and trans. Saïd Hamdun and Noël King (Princeton, NJ: Markus Wiener, 2003), 22. For the Arabic, see Michael A. Gomez, *African Dominion: A New History of Empire in Early and Medieval West Africa* (Princeton, NJ: Princeton University Press, 2018), 163.

20. Theal, *Records*, 6:230.

21. Ibid., 6:232.

22. Jan H. van Linschoten, *Itinerario: Voyage ofte Schipvaert van Jan Huygen van Linschoten naer Dost ofte Portugals Indien* (Amsterdam: C. Claesz, 1596), 60. My translation.

23. Paul E. H. Hair, "Portuguese Contacts with the Bantu Languages of the Transkei, Natal and Southern Mozambique, 1497–1650," *African Studies* 39:1 (1980): 14.

24. Charles Boxer, ed. and trans., *The Tragic History of the Sea, 1589–1622: Narratives of the Shipwrecks of the Portuguese East Indiamen São Thomé (1589), Santo Alberto (1593), São João Baptista (1622), and the Journeys of the Survivors in South East Africa* (New York: Cambridge University Press, 1959), 122, 200.

25. Mello d'Azevedo, ed., *Ethiopia Oriental por Fr. João dos Santos*, vol.1 (Lisbon: Bibliotheca de Classicos Portuguezes, 1891), 199, 224. My translation.

26. Boxer, *Tragic History*, 123.

27. *Documents on the Portuguese*, 7:425, 8:269, 271; Linschoten, *Itinerario*, 8, 60–61, 68; d'Azevedo, *Ethiopia Oriental*, 43–44, 100, 103, 136, 202–4, 251, 332.

28. See Theal, *Records*, 6:230; *Documents on the Portuguese*, 7:421, 425, 8:121; Boxer, *Tragic History*, 196.

29. J. (Giovanni) Botero Benes, *Relaciones universales del mundo*, trans. D. de Aguiar (Valladolid: Diego Fernandez de Cordova, 1603), 121–22; Nicolas Sanson d'Abbeville, *L'Afrique en plusieurs cartes nouvelles et exactes et en divers traicte's de géographie, et d'histoire* (Paris, 1656). See map entitled *Pays, et Coste des Cafres* and description.

30. Benes, *Relaciones*, 121–22; d'Abbeville, *L'Afrique*. See map entitled *Pays, et Coste des Cafres*.

31. Leonard Thompson, *A History of South Africa*, 4th ed. (Johannesburg: Jonathan Ball, 2014), 31–32.

32. Ibid., 33.

33. Ibid., 35.

34. Elphick, *Khoikhoi and the Founding*, 229–34; Newton-King, *Masters and Servants*, 36.

35. Thompson, *A History of South Africa*, 38.

36. Ibid., 36, 41.

37. Compare entries in Rowland Raven-Hart, *Before Van Riebeeck: Callers at South Africa from 1488 to 1652* (Cape Town: Struik, 1967); Albert H. Markham, ed., *The Voyages and Works of John Davis, the Navigator* (London: Hakluyt, 1880), 134–36, 162; William Foster, ed., *The Journal of John Jourdain, 1608–1617* (Cambridge: Hakluyt, 1905), 13–15; Edward Terry, *A Voyage to East-India* (London: J. Wilke, 1777), 14–18; Donald Moodie, ed., comp., and trans., *The Record; or, A Series of Official Papers Relative to the Condition and Treatment of the Native Tribes of South Africa*, part 1, *1649–1720* (Cape Town: A. S. Robertson, 1838), hereafter *Record 1*, Journal of Commander Van Riebeeck, 8 Apr. 1652, 10; 8 May

1652, 12; 19 June 1652, 12; 9 Oct. 1652, 16; 13 Nov. 1653, 24–26; 16 Dec. 1653, 24.

38. Moodie, *Record 1,* Memorandum left by Commander J. Van Riebeeck, for the information and guidance of his successor, Z. Wagenaar, 5 May 1662, 247–49. These names reflect how the Dutch heard and spelled the names. One aspect of Dutch misunderstanding was that they erroneously added an *s* to the endings "-qua" and "-na," for "people," in order to produce the plural.

39. The spelling varies in the sources between "Ottentoo," "Hottentoos," and "Hottentots." For the sake of uniformity the term "Hottentots" has been adopted. See Moodie, *Record 1,* 9, 224–25. For the use of a similar-sounding word in indigenous dance songs see Raven-Hart, *Before Van Riebeeck,* 101, 112.

40. John B. Wright, "Sonqua, Bosjesmans, Bushmen, abaThwa; Comment and Queries on Pre-Modern Identifications," *Suid-Afrikaanse Historiese Joernaal* 35 (1996): 22. Note that this issue relates to the long-standing debate about the historical relationship between herders and hunters mentioned in chapter 1.

41. Alexandre Chaumont (chevalier de), *Relation de l'ambasssade de Mr. le Chevalier de Chaumont a la Cour du Roy de Siam, Avec qui s'est passé de plus remarquable durant son voyage* (Amsterdam: Mortier, 1686), 7; Nicolas Louis de la Caille, *Journal Historique du Voyage fait au Cap de Bonne-Espérance* (Paris: Guillyn 1763), 259.

42. See for instance Moodie, *Record 1,* Journal of Commander Van Riebeeck, 8 Apr. 1652, 10; 19 June 1652, 12; 13 Nov. 1653, 24–26.

43. Olfert Dapper, "Kaffraria, or Land of the Kafirs, Otherwise Named the Hottentots (1668)," in Isaac Schapera and Benjamin Farrington, eds. and trans., *The Early Cape Hottentots Described in the Writings of Olfert Dapper (1668), Willem Ten Rhyne (1686) and Johannes Gulielmus de Grevenbroek (1695)* (Cape Town: Van Riebeeck Society, 1933), 7–77.

44. The spelling varies in the sources between "Choboquas," "Cobona" and "Chobonas." For the sake of uniformity the term "Choboquas" has been adopted. See Moodie, *Record 1,* 225.

45. Ibid., 248.

46. Ibid., 386, 347n2.

47. Otto F. Mentzel, *Vollständige und zuverläßige Geographische und Topographische Beschreibung des berühmten und in aller Betrachtung merkwürdigen Afrikanischen Vorgebirges der Guten Hofnung. Erster Theil* (Glogau: C. F. Günther, 1785), 103–4. My translation.

48. The spelling varies in the sources between "Magossa," "Magossche," "Macosses." For the sake of uniformity the term "Magossche" has been adopted. See Moodie, *Record 1,* 426–28.

49. Philip D. Curtin, *The Image of Africa: British Ideas and Action, 1780–1850*, vol. 1 (Madison: University of Wisconsin Press, 1964), 37.

50. Ibid., *Image*, 38; John S. Haller, *Outcasts from Evolution: Scientific Attitudes of Racial Inferiority, 1859–1900* (Carbondale: Southern Illinois University Press, 1995), 4–5.

51. Andrew S. Curran, *The Anatomy of Blackness: Science and Slavery in an Age of Enlightenment* (Baltimore: Johns Hopkins University Press, 2011), 12.

52. Peter Kolb, *Description du Cap de Bonne-Espérance*, Tome Premier (Amsterdam: J. Catuffe, 1742), 157. My translation.

53. Patrick Cullinan, *Robert Jacob Gordon, 1743–1795: The Man and His Travels at the Cape* (Cape Town: Struik, 1992), 68, 98, 112, 116. "Briqua" is a Nama compound term derived from "biri" for "goat" and "-qua" for "people"; see Louis Fernand Maingard, "The Brikwa and the Ethnic Origins of the Batlhaping," *South African Journal of Science* 30 (1933): 597–602.

54. Donald Moodie, ed., comp. and trans., *The Record; or, A Series of Official Papers Relative to the Condition and Treatment of the Native Tribes of South Africa*, part 5 (1808–19) (Cape Town: A. S. Robertson, 1838), hereafter *Record 5*, Colonel Collins, "Supplement to the Relations of Journey into the Country of the Bosjesman and Caffre People," 1809, 9.

55. E. C. Godée Molsbergen, ed., *Reizen in Zuid-Afrika in de Hollandse tijd. Deel III. Tochten langs de Z.O.-kust en naar het Oosten 1670–1752* (The Hague: Martinus Nijhoff, 1922), 273, 306, 311, hereafter *Reizen 3*.

56. Ibid., 321.

57. See introduction to this book, as well as Trautmann, *Languages and Nations*, 13, 15, 20.

58. Kolb, *Description*, 50.

59. Carl P. Thunberg, *Karl Peter Thunberg's Reise durch einen Theil von Europa, Afrika und Asien, hauptsächlich in Japan, in den Jahren 1770 bis 1779*, trans. C. H. Grosfurb, vol. 1, part 2, 61 (Berlin: Haude und Spener, 1792).

60. Kolb, *Description*, 156–57. My translation.

61. E. C. Godée Molsbergen, ed., *Reizen in Zuid-Afrika in de Hollandse tijd. Deel II. Tochten naar het Noorden 1686–1806* (The Hague: Martinus Nijhoff, 1916), 53; E. E. Mossop, ed., *The Journal of Hendrik Jacob Wikar (1779), The Journals of Jacobus Coetsé Jansz (1760) and Willem van Reenen (1791)*, trans. Mossop and A. W. Van der Horst (Cape Town: Van Riebeeck Society, 1935), 142–43n124.

62. Molsbergen, *Reizen 3*, 310.

63. Thunberg, *Reise*, 2:61–62. My translation. See also Anders Sparrman, *Voyage to the Cape of Good Hope*, 2 vols. (London: Robinson, 1785), 1:228.

64. Molsbergen, *Reizen 3*, 310. My translation. See also E. C. Godée Molsbergen, ed., *Reizen in Zuid-Afrika in de Hollandse tijd. Deel IV. Tochten in het*

Kafferland 1776–1805 (The Hague: Martinus Nijhoff, 1932), 63, hereafter *Reizen 4*; Heinrich Lichtenstein, *Foundation of the Cape and about the Bechuanas*, ed. and trans. O. H. Spohr (Cape Town: Balkema, 1973), 79; John Barrow, *An Account of Travels into the Interior of Southern Africa, in the Years 1797 and 1798*, 2 vols. (London: Cadell and Davies, 1801, 1804), 1:219.

65. Cullinan, *Gordon*, 68.

66. John Barrow, "An Account of a Journey to Leetakoo, the Residence of the Chief of the Booshuana Nation, Being the Remotest Point in the Interior of Southern Africa to Which Europeans have Hitherto Penetrated," in John Barrow, *A Voyage to Cochinchina in the Years 1792 and 1793* (London: Cadell and Davies, 1806), 401.

67. Heinrich Lichtenstein, *Travels in Southern Africa, in the Years 1803, 1804, 1805, and 1806*, 2 vols., trans. A. Plumptre (London: H. Colburn, 1812–15), 2:324.

68. Percival R. Kirby, ed., *Source Book on the Wreck of the Grosvenor East Indiaman* (Cape Town: Van Riebeeck Society, 1953), 33, 36, 38, 39, and 50n9.

69. Molsbergen, *Reizen 4*, 92. My translation.

70. Lichtenstein, *Travels*, 1:297–98; Ludwig Alberti, *Ludwig Alberti's Account of the Tribal Life & Customs of the Xhosa in 1807*, trans. William Fehr (Cape Town: Balkema, 1968), 6, 9 [Original German version: University of Cape Town Libraries, Manuscript BC 350, W. Fehr, MS Ludwig Alberti, *Nähere und ausgebreitetere Nachrichten von denen ein Theil der Südlichen Küste von Afrika bewohnenden Kaffern* (Im Haag, 1807), 7]. I thank Jeff Peires for pointing out to me that "Maduanas" most likely referred to the amaQwathi (i.e., Qwathi).

71. William Paterson, *Narrative of Four Journeys into the Country of the Hottentots, and Caffraria. In the Years 1777, 1778, and 1779* (London: J. Johnson, 1789), 93; Barrow, *Account*, 1:169, 205, 2:117; Alberti, *Account*, 20; Lichtenstein, *Travels*, 1:251.

72. Cullinan, *Gordon*, 116.

73. Lichtenstein, *Travels*, 1:298.

74. Ibid.

75. Moodie, *Record 5*, Colonel Collins, "Notes Made on a Journey to the Southern Branches of the River T'Ky, and through Kaffraria," 1809, 43.

76. Alberti, *Account*, 7.

77. Lichtenstein, *Travels*, vol. 1, appendix: "Remarks upon the Language of the Koossas."

78. Ibid.

79. Cullinan, *Gordon*, 111, 112.

80. Lichtenstein, *Travels*, 2:324.

81. Ibid.

82. Alberti, *Account*, 7, 9.

83. Lichtenstein, *Travels*, 1:244.

84. Barrow, *Account*, 1:283, 2:118–19.

85. Lichtenstein, *Travels*, 1:243.

86. Georges-Louis Leclerc, Comte de Buffon, *Histoire naturelle* (Paris: L'Imprimerie Royale, [1749] 1750), 3:480, 519. My translation.

87. Lichtenstein, *Travels*, 1:243.

88. Barrow, *Account*, 1:211–12.

89. Lichtenstein, *Travels*, 1:243.

90. Barrow, *Account*, 1:204–5.

91. Lichtenstein, *Travels*, 1:244 and appendix: "Remarks upon the Language of the Koossas."

92. Barrow, *Account*, 1:218.

93. Ibid., 1:212.

94. Lichtenstein, *Travels*, 1:245–46.

95. Edith R. Sanders, "The Hamitic Hypothesis: Its Origin and Functions in Time Perspective," *Journal of African History*, 10:4 (1969): 521–32; Michael F. Robinson, *The Lost White Tribe: Explorers, Scientists, and the Theory That Changed a Continent* (New York: Oxford, 2015), 8, 9, and especially chapter 8.

96. Charles Gabriel Seligman, *Races of Africa* (1930), quoted in Sanders, "The Hamitic Hypothesis," 521.

97. James C. Prichard, *Researches into the Physical History of Mankind*, 3rd ed., 2 vols. (London: Sherwood, 1836–37), 2:299.

98. Robert Knox, *The Races of Men: A Fragment* (Philadelphia: Lea and Blanchard, 1850), 160.

99. Petrus Johannes van der Merwe, *The Migrant Farmer in the History of the Cape Colony, 1657–1842*, trans. Roger Beck (Athens: Ohio University Press, 1995), 96, 107.

100. Molsbergen, *Reizen 3*, Journaal gehouden door den Adsistend Carel Albregt Haupt op de togt door den Vaandrig August Frederik Beutler, 5 Apr. 1752, 272; Donald Moodie, ed., *The Record; or, A Series of Official Papers Relative to the Condition and Treatment of the Native Tribes of South Africa*, part 3, *1769–1795* (Cape Town: A. S. Robertson, 1838), hereafter *Record 3*, Report Heemraden of Stellenbosch and Swellendam, 7 Feb. 1770, 2; ibid., Letter from Governor Tulbagh to the Landdrost of Swellendam, 5 June 1770, 7; ibid., Letter from the Landdrost of Swellendam to the Cape Government, 28 Oct. 1772, 17.

101. Ibid., Proclamation, Ryk Tulbagh, Governor of Cape of Good Hope, 26 Apr. 1770, 6; ibid., Resolution of Governor and Council, 5 Apr. 1774, 24.

102. Ibid., Resolution of Council 11 July 1775, 46–50.

103. Cullinan, *Gordon*, 40, 51.

104. Molsbergen, *Reizen 4*, Olof Godlieb de Wet, Dagverhaal van de landryse, door den Weledelen Gestrengen Heer Mr. Joachim Baron van Plettenberg, 15 Oct. 1778, 43–46; Cullinan, *Gordon*, 62; Moodie, *Record 5*, Statement of Abram Carel Greyling, 29 Dec. 1836, 9–10n1.

105. In the period under review, these hostilities broke out in 1779, 1789, 1799. See Noël Mostert, *Frontiers: The Epic of South Africa's Creation and the Tragedy of the Xhosa People* (New York: Alfred A. Knopf, 1992).

106. Alberti, *Account*, 13–14. See also Lichtenstein, *Travels*, 1:243.

107. François Le Vaillant, *Travels from the Cape of Good-Hope, into the Interior Parts of Africa*, 2 vols., trans. Elizabeth Helme (London: W. Lane, 1790), 1:354.

108. Barrow, *Account*, 1:196.

109. Clifton Crais, *White Supremacy and Black Resistance in Pre-Industrial South Africa: The Making of the Colonial Order in the Eastern Cape, 1770–1865* (New York: Cambridge University Press, 1992), 129; Jochen S. Arndt, "Treacherous Savages and Merciless Barbarians: Knowledge, Discourse and Violence during the Cape Frontier Wars, 1834–1853," *Journal of Military History* 74:3 (2010): 709–35.

110. Robert Godlonton, *A Narrative of the Irruption of the Kafir Hordes into the Eastern Province of the Cape of Good Hope, 1834–35* (Grahamstown: Meurant and Godlonton, 1836), 170.

111. George McCall Theal, ed., *Documents Relating to the Kaffir War of 1835* (London: Clowes and Sons, 1912), Smith to sister, Mrs. Sargant, 7 May 1835, 154.

3. "ALL SPEAK THE CAFFRE LANGUAGE"

1. London Missionary Society, *Transactions of the Missionary Society*, 372–431.

2. Timothy Keegan, *Colonial South Africa and the Origins of the Racial Order* (Charlottesville: University Press of Virginia, 1996), 42.

3. Thompson, *A History of South Africa*, 58, 60.

4. Ibid., 54–55.

5. Ben Maclennan, *A Proper Degree of Terror: John Graham and the Cape's Eastern Frontier* (Johannesburg: Ravan, 1986).

6. Thompson, *A History of South Africa*, 55–56; Crais, *White Supremacy*, 95.

7. Leonard Thompson, *The Political Mythology of Apartheid* (New Haven, CT: Yale University Press, 1985), 146–48.

8. Peires, *Dead Will Arise*, 7.

9. Ibid., 28.

10. Ibid., 319.

11. Ibid., 249.

12. Elizabeth Elbourne and Robert Ross, "Combating Spiritual and Social Bondage: Early Missions in the Cape Colony," in *Christianity in South Africa: A Political, Social, and Cultural History*, ed. Richard Elphick and Rodney Davenport (Berkeley: University of California Press, 1997), 31–50.

13. The history of the Scottish Presbyterian missionary societies in South Africa is complicated by the various secessions from the Church of Scotland that resulted in organizational and affiliation changes in South Africa. Because these missionaries cooperated closely with each other throughout these organizational changes, I use the acronym SPMS for all of them regardless of their specific affiliations.

14. W. Sigurd Nielsen, *The Twin Blossom of the Pear Tree Bears Fruit: The History of the Moravian Church Eastern Province in South Africa* (Port Shepstone: Baruk, 1999), 35–36.

15. For an overview of the BMS, see Gunther Pakendorf, "A Brief History of the Berlin Mission Society in South Africa," *History Compass* 9:2 (2011): 106–18.

16. Western Cape Archives and Records, Cape Town, South Africa (CA), Accessions (Acc.) A680, Short Biography of Johann Heinrich Albert Kropf (in English), 3.

17. *Wesleyan Missionary Magazine* (hereafter *WMM*), Feb. 1821, 151; William Shaw, *The Story of My Mission in South-Eastern Africa* (London: Hamilton, Adams, 1860), 327.

18. Shaw, *The Story of My Mission*, 337–38.

19. School of Oriental and African Studies, London, United Kingdom, Methodist Missionary Society Archives, Correspondence South Africa, microfiche (hereafter MMS/SA/mf) 301, William Shaw to the Committee of the Wesleyan Missionary Society, Wesleyville, 14 Oct. 1828.

20. London Missionary Society, *Transactions of the Missionary Society*, 442–58; Wilhelm Bleek, *The Library of His Excellency Sir George Grey, Philology*, vol. 1 (Leipzig: Brockhaus, 1858), 46.

21. *Report of the Glasgow Missionary Society*, hereafter *RGMS* (1825), 12.

22. Bleek, *Library*, 50; Cory Library for Historical Research, Rhodes University, Grahamstown, South Africa (hereafter CL), MS9037, Presbytery of Kaffraria Minutes (hereafter PKM), Monday, 9 Feb. 1824. Note that the original title translation in Bleek's work says, "The Book to begin in the speech of the Kafirs" rather than "of the Xhosa." However, since the original title in the language clearly uses the word "Xhosa," I substituted "Kafir" for "Xhosa." I apply the same rule with regard to title translations throughout.

23. Killie-Campbell Africana Library, Durban, South Africa, KCM47614, Rev. Robert Godfrey, "Rev. John Bennie, the Father of Kafir Literature" (1934), 124.

24. CL, MS15252, diary of William J. Shrewsbury (typescript), 29 Nov. 1826, 10.

25. William Boyce, *A Grammar of the Kafir Language* (Grahamstown: Wesleyan Mission Press, 1834).

26. *WMM*, Sept. 1832, W. Boyce, Letter, Buntingville, 4 Mar. 1832, 664.

27. Bleek, *Library*, 52; *Report of the Wesleyan-Methodist Missionary Society* (hereafter *RWM*), 1840, 61.

28. John Ayliff, *A Vocabulary of the Kafir Language* (London: Wesleyan Mission House, 1846); John Appleyard, *The Kafir Language: Comprising a Sketch of Its History; Which Includes a General Classification of South African Dialects, Ethnographical and Geographical: Remarks upon Its Nature: and a Grammar* (King William's Town: Wesleyan Missionary Society, 1850).

29. Bleek, *Library*, 79–80.

30. Ibid., 84–88.

31. Les Switzer, *Power and Resistance in an African Society: The Ciskei Xhosa and the Making of South Africa* (Madison: University of Wisconsin Press, 1993), 120.

32. Sandra Carolyn Teresa Rowoldt Shell, ed., "A Missionary Life among the amaXhosa: The Eastern Cape Journals of James Laing, 1830–1836" (master's thesis, University of Cape Town, 2006), hereafter JJL, 18 Jan. 1832, 262; *RGMS*, 1833, 14.

33. Bleek, *Library*, 60–61; *Caffrarian Messenger*, Apr. 1843, 194.

34. CL, MS9039, PKM, 6 July 1853; Bleek, *Library*, 61.

35. *RWM*, 1824, 54.

36. Bleek, *Library*, 61.

37. Ibid., 55; CL, MS9037, PKM, 6 Jan. 1825; CL, MS8091, John Ross to mother, Incehra, 23 Mar. 1825, no. 5; CL, MS9037, PKM, 11 May 1826; *RGMS*, 1826, 14.

38. MMS/SA/mf 301, William Shaw, Wesleyville, 31 Mar. 1827.

39. Ibid., William Shrewsbury, Wesleyville, 31 Dec. 1826; CL, MS15252, diary of Shrewsbury, 10 Dec. 1826, 13.

40. Bleek, *Library*, 56.

41. *RGMS*, 1825, 12.

42. Ibid.

43. Ibid., 1829, 18.

44. School of Oriental and African Studies, London, United Kingdom, Council for World Mission, London Missionary Society Archive, South Africa, Incoming Correspondence (hereafter CWM/LMSA/IC),

box10/2/E/no. 33, Brownlee, 3 Aug. 1827; Ibid., box12/1/A/no. 1, Kayser and Brownlee, 1 Jan. 1830; ibid., box12/1/C/no. 16, Kayser, 14 July 1830.

45. CL, MS15252, diary of Shrewsbury, 26 Sept. 1829, 42; ibid., 18 Sept. 1830, 46; ibid., 15 Dec. 1830, 47.

46. RGMS, 1831, 19.

47. Quarterly Papers of the Glasgow Missionary Society,, Mar. 1833, 5; RGMS, 1834, 23–24; JJL, 31 Jan. 1833, 320.

48. CWM/LMSA/IC/box12/4/D/no. 20, Kayser, 9 Dec. 1831; ibid., box13/2/A/no. 37, Kayser, 3 Dec. 1832; ibid., box13/4/B/no. 4, Brownlee, 16 Dec. 1833.

49. Shaw, Story, 548–49; CL, MS15252, diary of Shrewsbury, 27 Feb. 1831, 48; ibid., 20 Aug. 1831; ibid., 17 Oct. 1831, 54; ibid., 14 Jan. 1833, 63; ibid., 19 Feb. 1833, 63.

50. CL, MS9037, PKM, 5 Apr. 1836; RGMS, 1837, 18.

51. Bible Society Archive, D1/2, Records of the Secretaries, Foreign Correspondence Inwards (hereafter BSA/D1/2), Henry H. Dugmore, Mount Coke, 18 June 1842.

52. CL, MS9038, PKM, 1 Jan. 1840.

53. BSA/D1/2, Henry Dugmore, Mount Coke, 18 June 1842.

54. Ibid.

55. Abraham P. Smit, God Made It Grow: History of the Bible Society Movement in Southern Africa, 1820–1870, trans. Wouter P. De Vos (Cape Town: Bible Society of South Africa, 1970), 4.

56. Ibid., 11.

57. Ibid., 19.

58. BSA/D1/2, William Shrewsbury to Mr. Joseph Jowett, BFBS, Grahamstown, 18 July 1834.

59. Ibid., William Boyce, 25 Sept. 1844.

60. MMS/SA/mf 305, George Browne to Boyce, Bible Society House, 2 Dec. 1844.

61. BSA/D1/2, Henry Calderwood, Secretary, Minutes of Meeting respecting the Kaffer Scripture, Umxelo, 16 Apr. 1845.

62. Ibid., William Shaw to the Reverend Secretaries of the BFBS, Grahamstown, 4 July 1845.

63. Bleek, Library, 72–73.

64. Ibid., 74.

65. John W. Appleyard, An Apology for the Kafir Bible: Being a Reply to the Pamphlet Entitled, "Rev. J. W. Appleyard's Version Judged by Missionaries of Various Denominations and Others" (Mount Coke: Wesleyan Mission Press, 1867).

66. *Correspondence between the Committee of the South African Auxiliary Bible Society and Various Missionaries and Others, Relative to the Translation, Printing, and Circulation of the Scriptures in the Native Languages of South Africa, and More Especially in the Kafir Dialect; with the Resolutions of the Committee Thereupon* (Cape Town: Pike's 1857), W. R. Thomson to George Morgan, Balfour, 30 Aug. 1854, 74. I thank Jeff Peires for drawing my attention to this document.

67. Shaw, *Story*, 538.

68. Ibid.

69. *Correspondence between the Committee*, Thomson to Morgan, Balfour, 30 Aug. 1854, 74.

70. Shaw, *Story*, 539–40.

71. *Correspondence between the Committee*, John Appleyard to George Morgan, Mount Coke, 29 May 1854, 51.

72. Ibid., Appleyard to Morgan, Mount Coke, 25 May 1857, 105.

73. Ibid., R. B. Taylor to George Morgan, Cradock, 15 July 1853, 21.

74. Shaw, *Story*, 540.

75. *Quarterly Papers of the Glasgow Missionary Society*, Mar. 1833, 6.

76. CL, MS15252, diary of Shrewsbury, 27 Feb. 1831, 48.

77. MMS/SA/mf 305, Richard Haddy to Mr. Browne, 13 Apr. 1847.

78. *Correspondence between the Committee*, Taylor to Morgan, 15 July 1853, 21.

79. MMS/SA/mf 305, Haddy to Brown, secretary of the BFBS, Beaufort, 23 Dec. 1846; ibid., (no. 2) Copy of Letter to the Secretaries of the British and Foreign Bible Society, Grahamstown, South Africa, 12 Feb. 1847; *Correspondence between the Committee*, Richard Birt to George Morgan, Peelton, 10 Aug. 1853, 23; ibid., Birt to Morgan, Cape Town, 24 Mar. 1857, 97.

80. JJL, 417–18; *Wesleyan Missionary Notices* (hereafter *WMN*), 1 May 1821, 68; William Boyce, *Notes on South African Affairs from 1834 to 1838* (Grahamstown: Aldum and Harvey, 1838), iii–v.

81. *RGMS*, 1823, 18–19.

82. Lichtenstein, *Travels*, 2:324.

83. *WMM*, Apr. 1824, 277.

84. Alberti, *Account*, 7.

85. *WMM*, May 1833, 374.

86. It is beyond the scope of this work to explain this development. However, beyond the lack of mutual intelligibility mentioned by missionaries, it appears that it was driven in part by the growing number of missionary publications that helped circumscribe the Tswana language as a separate object of knowledge. See Robert Moffat, *Bechuana Spelling Book* (London: London Missionary Society, 1826); James Archbell, *A Grammar of*

the *Bechuana Language* (Grahamstown: Meurant and Godlonton, 1837); Eugène Casalis, *Études sur la Langue Séchuana* (Paris: L'Imprimerie Royale, 1841).

87. JJL, 27 Feb. 1832, 277.

88. William Boyce, introduction to Archbell, *Grammar*, xiii.

89. *WMM*, Sept. 1833, 661.

90. Boyce, introduction to Archbell, *Grammar*, xv.

91. BSA/D1/2, Boyce, "Answers to Certain Queries Respecting the Kaffer Translations Made by the Wesleyan Missionaries," 25 Sept. 1844.

92. *WMM*, Mar. 1849, 329.

93. *The Home and Foreign Missionary Record for the Free Church of Scotland* (hereafter *HFMR*), 1 Feb. 1848, 331.

94. The spelling of his names varies in the sources and includes "Yacob" and "Jackot" as well as "Sumbiti" and "Soembitchi."

95. Rajend Mesthrie, "Words across Worlds: Aspects of Language Contact and Language Learning in the Eastern Cape, 1800–1850," *African Studies* 57:1 (1998): 21.

96. William C. Holden, *History of the Colony of Natal, South Africa* (London: Alexander Heylin, 1855), 46; Joseph Shooter, *The Kafirs of Natal and the Zulu Country* (London: Stanford, 1857), 277; William Owen, *Narrative of Voyages to Explore the Shores of Africa, Arabia, and Madagascar; Performed by H. M. Ships Leven and Barracouta, under the Direction of Captain W. F. W. Owen, R.N.*, 2 vols. (London: Richard Bentley, 1833); Thomas Boteler, *A Narrative of a Voyage of Discovery to Africa and Arabia, Performed by His Majesty's Ships Leven and Barracouta, from 1821 to 1826, Under the Command of Capt. F. W. Owen, R.N.*, 2 vols. (London: Richard Bentley, 1835).

97. Ibid., 1:14.

98. Owen, *Narrative*, 1:79. For the presence of "Zoolos" (Zulus) at Delagoa Bay at this time, see Linell Chewins and Peter Delius, "The Northeastern Factor in South African History: Reevaluating the Volume of the Slave Trade out of Delagoa Bay and its Impact on Its Hinterland in the Early Nineteenth Century," *Journal of African History* 61:1 (Mar 2020): 89–110.

99. Owen, *Narrative*, 1:143.

100. Ibid., 1:82.

101. Ibid., 1:218.

102. *WMM*, Nov. 1823, 761.

103. Owen, *Narrative*, 1:253; Shooter, *Kafirs*, 277.

104. JSA, Mbovu kaMtshumayeli (1903), 3:25; ibid., Melapi kaMagaye (1905), 3:73.

105. Owen, *Narrative*, 2:222; Shooter, *Kafirs*, 278.

106. Owen, *Narrative*, 2:222. See also *JSA*, Melapi kaMagaye (1905), 3:73.

107. Nathaniel Isaacs, *Travels and Adventures in Eastern Africa, Descriptive of the Zoolus, Their Manners, Customs*, 2 vols. (London: Edward Churton, 1836), 1:46; Allen F. Gardiner, *Narrative of a Journey to the Zoolu Country, in South Africa. by Captain Allen F. Gardiner, R.N., Undertaken in 1835* (London: William Crofts, 1836), 37–38.

108. Isaacs, *Travels*, 1:258–59, 263; Shooter, *Kafirs*, 316–19.

109. MMS/SA/mf 301, William Shaw to the Committee of the WMS, Wesleyville, 11 Oct. 1828.

110. Percival R. Kirby, ed., *Andrew Smith and Natal: Documents Relating to the Early History of That Province* (Cape Town: Van Riebeeck Society, 1955), 70–71.

111. I thank the 1820 Settler Facebook community for supplying some of the information on George Cyrus. Special thanks to Beverly Young and Nolene Lossau Sproat.

112. MMS/SA/mf 301, W. Shaw to the Committee of the WMS, Wesleyville, 30 Sept. 1828. For "Aaron James Aldum" see *WMM*, July 1829, 492.

113. John Ayliff, *The Journal of John Ayliff*, vol. 1 *(1821–30)*, ed. Peter Hinchliff (Cape Town: Balkema, 1971), Somerset, 7 Apr. 1830, 93.

114. Bleek, *Library*, 61.

115. Gardiner, *Narrative*, 4.

116. Ibid., 5–6, 14, 24–26, 38, 42–44, 163, 174, 212–17, 253–54, 268, 398.

117. Ibid., 101.

118. John Cenlivres Chase, *The Cape of Good Hope and the Eastern Province of Algoa Bay, with Statistics of the Colony*, ed. Joseph S. Christophers (London: Richardson, 1848), 280, 282; BSA/D1/2, Henry Dugmore, Mount Coke, 18 June 1842; Appleyard, *An Apology for the Kafir Bible*, 10.

119. Notes Anne Clarkson, obtained in private correspondence from Marlene Hulley and Paul Tanner-Tremaine from the 1820 Settler Facebook community, 27 Mar. 2015.

120. George Cory, ed., *The Diary of the Rev. Francis Owen, M.A., Missionary with Dingaan in 1837–38. Together with Extracts from the Writings of the Interpreters in Zulu, Messrs. Hulley and Kirkman* (Cape Town: Van Riebeeck Society, 1926), Owen to D. Coates, 5 June 1837, 11n1.

121. For "Bhaca" people see ibid., "Account of the Rev. Owen's visit to Zululand in the year 1837, as Related by Mr. R. B. Hulley, the Interpreter for Mr. Owen," 172–73.

122. Ibid., "Owen's Diary," 11 Oct. 1837, 44; ibid., 20 Oct. 1837, 49.

123. Ibid., "Account of the Rev. Owen's Visit to Zululand in the year 1837, as Related by Mr. R. B. Hulley, the Interpreter for Mr. Owen," 173.

124. Ibid., 175.

125. Ibid., 179.

126. James Backhouse, *Extracts from the Letters of James Backhouse, Whilst Engaged in a Religious Visit to Van Dieman's Land, New South Wales, and South Africa, Accompanied by George Washington Walker,* vol. 2 (London: Harvey and Darton, 1842), 3 Apr. 1839, 59; J. W. Sauer and George M. Theal, eds., *Basutoland Records; Copies of Official Documents of Various Kinds,* vol. 3, *1862–68* (Cape Town: Richards and Sons, 1883), letter of Nehemiah Moshesh to the high commissioner, Bethesda, Basutoland, 8 June 1863, 212–13.

127. *Evangelical Magazine and Missionary Chronicle,* Aug. 1839, 409; D. J. Kotzé, ed., *Letters of the American Missionaries, 1835–1838* (Cape Town: Van Riebeeck Society, 1950), 92n9.

128. Charles P. Brownlee, *Reminiscences of Kaffir Life and History, and Other Papers* (Lovedale: Lovedale Mission Press, 1896), 28–47.

129. Kotzé, *Letters,* J. Monroe to A. Grout, Grahamstown, 30 Oct. 1835, 81.

130. Brownlee, *Reminiscences,* 23; Peires, *Dead Will Arise,* 66.

131. Kotzé, *Letters,* Newton Adams to A. Grout and G. Champion, Grahamstown, 20 Nov. 1835, 83; ibid., John Brownlee to A. Grout, Somerset, 21 Sept. 1835, 80.

132. *Missionary Herald,* hereafter *MH,* Apr. 1837, 141.

133. *Evangelical Magazine and Missionary Chronicle,* Aug. 1839, 409.

134. Edward C. Tabler, *Pioneers of Natal and Southeastern Africa, 1552–1878* (Cape Town: Balkema, 1977), 66; Killie-Campbell Africana Library, Durban, South Africa, KCM89/36/1/1, diary of Joseph Kirkman, 1826–40, 1.

135. Ibid., 2–3.

136. Kotzé, *Letters,* G. Champion to A. Grout, Umlazi, 8 Mar. 1838, 224; ibid., General Letter to Anderson, Port Elizabeth, 2 Apr. 1838, 237; Cory, *Diary,* "Owen's Diary," 6 Feb. 1838, 110; Brownlee, *Reminiscences,* 36, 57.

137. Tabler, *Pioneers,* 66; Kotzé, *Letters,* 81n2.

138. *Evangelical Magazine and Missionary Chronicle,* Aug. 1839, 409.

139. Quoted in Robert Ross, *The Borders of Race in Colonial South Africa: The Kat River Settlement, 1829–1856* (New York: Cambridge University Press, 2014), 241.

140. Backhouse, *Extracts,* 10 and 12 Feb. 1839, 7, 10; Brownlee, *Reminiscences,* 2–11.

141. Brownlee, *Reminiscences,* 387; *Correspondence between the Committee,* Charles Brownlee to Rev. G. Morgan, Döhne, 27 July 1853, 20.

142. *Correspondence between the Committee,* Brownlee to Morgan, Döhne, 8 Oct. 1855, 78–79.

143. On Shepstone's career as interpreter and colonial administrator, see Thomas McClendon, "Interpretation and Interpolation: Shepstone as Native Interpreter," in *Intermediaries, Interpreters, and Clerks: African Employees in the Making of Colonial Africa*, ed. Benjamin N. Lawrance, Emily N. Osborn, and Richard L. Roberts (University of Wisconsin Press, 2006), 77–93; and Thomas McClendon, *White Chief, Black Lords: Shepstone and the Colonial State in Natal, South Africa, 1845–1878* (Rochester, NY: University of Rochester Press, 2010).

144. Shaw, *Story*, 338.

145. *WMM*, Sept. 1833, 661.

146. Ibid., Sept. 1832, 664; Boyce, *Grammar*, preface; MMS/SA/mf 305, William Boyce to G. Browne, Bolton [?], 3 Dec. 1844.

147. *Copy of Minutes of Proceedings of the Court of Inquiry, Held at Fort Wilshire, in the Months of August and September, 1836, to Investigate and Report upon the Circumstances attendant on the Fate of the Caffer Chief Hintza* (Cape Town: Brand's, 1837), 91, 99; Bleek, *Library*, 84–85.

148. *Proceedings of the Commission Appointed to Inquire into the Past and Present State of the Kafirs in the District of Natal*, 6 parts (Natal: J. Archbell and Son, 1852–53), 1:58–59; McClendon, *White Chief*, 27.

149. John W. Appleyard, *The War of the Axe and the Xhosa Bible: The Journal of the Rev. J. W. Appleyard*, ed. John Frye (Cape Town: Struik, 1971), 17 Apr. 1842, 12; BSA/D1/2, William Boyce, 25 Sept. 1844; MMS/SA/mf 305, Boyce to Browne, Bolton [?], 3 Dec. 1844.

150. Holden, *History*, 160. See also *Proceedings of the Commission in Natal*, 1:61, 63.

151. *JSA*, Ngidi kaMcikaziswa (1904–5), 5:79.

152. John Colenso, *Ten Weeks in Natal: Journal of a First Tour of Visitation among the Colonists and Zulu Kafirs of Natal* (Cambridge: Macmillan, 1855), 147.

153. *Proceedings of the Commission in Natal*, 6:96.

154. *Correspondence between the Committee*, Shepstone to Morgan, Pietermaritzburg, Natal, 13 May 1854, 53.

155. Alberti, *Account*, 7.

156. Ibid.

157. Ibid., 9–10.

158. Philip, *Researches in South Africa; Illustrating the Civil, Moral, and Religious Condition of the Native Tribes*, 2 vols. (London: J. Duncan, 1828), 2:143–44.

159. Ibid., 2:143.

160. James Stuart and D. McK. Malcolm, eds., *The Diary of Henry Francis Fynn* (Pietermaritzburg: Shuter and Shooter, 1986), 58, 60.

161. John B. Wright, "Henry Francis Fynn," *Natalia* (4 Dec. 1974): 14–17; *Proceedings of the Commission in Natal*, 4:44.

162. John Ayliff and Joseph Whiteside, *History of the Abambo, Generally Known as the Fingos* (Butterworth: Transkei Gazette, 1912), 1–22; Richard T. Kawa, *Ibali lamaMfengu* (Lovedale: Lovedale, 1929), chapter 4; John H. Soga, *The South-Eastern Bantu* (Johannesburg: Witwatersrand University Press, 1930), 180; Bhotomane, "Origins of the Xhosa," 45–46; John D. Omer-Cooper, *The Zulu Aftermath: A Nineteenth-Century Revolution in Bantu Africa* (London: Longmans, 1966), 92, 164; Richard A. Moyer, "A History of the Mfengu of the Eastern Cape" (PhD diss., University of London, 1976), 10, 72–167; Colin Bundy, *The Rise and Fall of the South African Peasantry* (Berkeley: University of California Press, 1979), chapter 2, 32–42, esp. 33; Peires, *House of Phalo*, 86–89.

163. Julian Cobbing, "Mfecane as Alibi: Thoughts on Dithakong and Mbolompo," *Journal of African History* 29:3 (1988): 487–519.

164. Alan Webster, "Land Expropriation and Labour Extraction under Cape Colonial Rule: The War of 1835 and the 'Emancipation' of the Fingo" (master's thesis, Rhodes University, 1991); Alan Webster, "Unmasking the Fingo: The War of 1835 Revisited," in Hamilton, *Mfecane*, 241–76; Timothy Stapleton, "Oral Evidence of a Pseudo-Ethnicity; The Fingo Debate," *History in Africa* 22 (1995): 358–69; Timothy Stapleton, "The Expansion of a Pseudo-Ethnicity in the Eastern Cape: Reconsidering the Fingo 'Exodus' of 1865," *International Journal of African Historical Studies* 29:2 (1996): 240; Poppy Ann Fry, "Allies and Liabilities: Fingo Identity and British Imperialism in South Africa's Eastern Cape, 1800–1935" (PhD diss., Harvard University, 2007).

165. For this complex and complicated history, see Carolyn Hamilton, *Terrific Majesty: The Powers of Shaka Zulu and the Limits of Historical Invention* (Cambridge, MA: Harvard University Press, 1998).

166. On this issue, see also Moyer, "A History of the Mfengu," 125.

167. American Board of Commissioners for Foreign Missions Archives, Houghton Library, Harvard University, Cambridge, MA (hereafter ABC), 76, Personal Papers, Lewis Grout, folder 4: W. Posselt to L. Grout, new Germany, 11 Mar. 1852. See also Robert Edgar, *The Finger of God: Enoch Mgijima, the Israelites, and the Bulhoek Massacre in South Africa* (Charlottesville: University of Virginia Press, 2018), 176 n7.

168. Jeff Peires, "'Fellows with Big Holes in Their Ears': The Ethnic Origins of the amaMfengu," *Quarterly Bulletin of the National Library of South Africa* 65 (2011): 55–64.

169. George Thompson, *Travels and Adventures in Southern Africa*, vol. 1 (London: Genry Colburn, 1827), 370; CL, MS9037, PKM, W. Thomson,

5 Oct. 1826; ibid., 8 Aug. 1827; CWM/LMSA/IC/box10/1/B/no. 17, J. Brownlee, Chumie, 15 Apr. 1826; National Library of South Africa, Manuscript Collection, Cape Town, South Africa, hereafter NLSA, MSB435, William Shaw, journal (typescript), 4 Oct. 1829, 108; WMM, Dec. 1827, 844.

170. For the issues Mfengu faced among the Xhosa see WMM, Mar. 1834, 223–24; JJL, 19 Dec. 1831, 252; ibid., 26 Dec. 1831, 257; ibid., 29 June 1832, 292. For Mfengu movements into the Cape Colony see CL, MS9037, PKM, 5 Jan. 1832; JJL, 25 June 1832, 292; ibid., 29 June 1832, 292; ibid., 6 Sept. 1834, 373; ibid., 27 Sept. 1834, 375.

171. WMM, Dec. 1835, 960.

172. Edgar, Finger of God, 17; Bhotomane, "Origins of the Xhosa," 46–47.

173. Moyer, "A History of the Mfengu," 110; Bundy, Rise and Fall, 34–35.

174. CL, MS15252, diary of Shrewsbury, 10 Dec. 1826, 13–14. See also CWM/LMSA/IC/box10/1/B/no. 17, J. Brownlee, Chumie, 15 Apr. 1826; NLSA, MSB435, Shaw, journal, 31 Aug. 1827, 52; WMN, 1 Mar. 1828, 455; MMS/SA/mf 303, S. Young, Wesleyville, 1 May 1831; WMM, Mar. 1841, 251; ibid., Mar. 1849, 41, 46; HFMR, 1 Nov. 1848, 553–54.

175. Quarterly Intelligence of the Glasgow Missionary Society (hereafter QIGMS) no. X, 1841, 3.

176. Shaw, Story, 525–26.

177. WMN, 1 Sept. 1857, 6.

178. Opland, Kuse, and Maseko, William Wellington Gqoba, 472–75; Jeff Opland, Xhosa Literature: Spoken and Printed Words, Publications of the Opland Collection of Xhosa Literature, vol. 6 (Pietermaritzburg: University of KwaZulu-Natal Press, 2018), 138; CL, MS17038, George Cory Notebooks, George Pamla, Willovale, 29 Jan. 1910, 392–93. See also NLSA, MSC39, Methodist Church Collection, box 34.10, Charles Pamla, "The Early Life of the Rev. Chas. Pamla. Related by Himself," Methodist Churchman, 24 Dec. 1906, 13; JSA, John Kumalo (1900), 1:220.

179. CL, Lovedale collection, MS16369, Tiyo Burnside Soga, MS "Intlalo kaXhosa/The Original of Xhosa" (1917), 19.

180. WMM, Dec. 1827, 844.

181. Shaw, Story, 526.

182. Thompson, Travels, Rev. Thomson, letter, 3 July 1824, 376.

183. Brownlee as quoted in Shula Marks, "The Traditions of the Natal 'Nguni': A Second Look at the Work of A. T. Bryant," in African Societies in Southern Africa, ed. L. M. Thompson (London: Heinmann, 1969), 139.

184. Correspondence between the Committee, Laing to Morgan, Burnshill, 8 May 1855, 71.

185. Thompson, Travels, Rev. Thomson, letter, 3 July 1824, 376.

186. For Zizi origins, see Soga, *South-Eastern Bantu*, 425–26. For "Zizi and Baphuti," see Moyer, "A History of the Mfengu," 93, 100–101; Scott Rosenberg and Richard F. Weisfelder, *Historical Dictionary of Lesotho*, 2nd ed. (Lanham, MD: Scarecrow, 2013), 36–37, 46. For "Sotho-ized," see Rev. Brownlee, quoted in Marks, "Traditions," 139; CL, MS2642, Letters of Mrs. Ross, Apr. 1824; *Correspondence between the Committee*, Laing to Morgan, Burnshill, 8 May 1855, 71.

187. *WMM*, Aug. 1827, 563–64.

188. CL, MS1109, diary of John Ayliff (typescript), 6 Oct. 1830, 179.

189. CL, MS15252, diary of Shrewsbury, 14 Dec. 1828, 36; *WMN*, 1 Dec. 1830, 374; *WMM*, July 1831, 502–3.

190. CL, MS1109, diary of Ayliff, 19 Nov. 1830, 196; *WMM*, Jan. 1832, 60; ibid., Mar. 1834, 224; *JJL*, 2 Sept. 1833, 336; ibid., 4 June 1834, 363; ibid., 15 Dec. 1834, 386; NLSA, MSC39, Methodist Church Collection, box 34.10, Charles Pamla, "The Early Life."

191. *WMM*, 1 Dec. 1835, 960; ibid., Mar. 1841, 251, 253; ibid., 11 May 1850, 76.

192. *WMN*, 1 Dec. 1835, 194.

193. Ibid., 1 Jan. 1837, 398.

194. CL, MS15543.1, John Ayliff, "Sketch of Fingo History," 7 Nov. 1853. See also CL, MS15543.2, John Ayliff Papers, "Narrative of Fingo History."

195. *JJL*, 10 Dec. 1831; ibid., 15 June 1832, 289.

196. For "Mahlamene," see *JJL*, 18 Oct. 1832, 308; *HFMR*, 1 Nov. 1848, 553–54. For Fingoes as church attendees, see *JJL*, 15 Apr. 1833, 324; ibid., 27 May 1833, 328; ibid., 25 July 1833, 334.

197. Ibid., 27 Feb. 1832, 276–77, and 10 Sept. 1833, 338.

198. *QIGMS*, no. IV, 1839, 4; ibid., no. X, 1841, 3–4.

199. CL, MS9039, PKM, 5 Jan. 1848; *HFMR*, 1 Nov. 1848, 553–54; CL, MS9039, PKM, 5 July 1848.

200. Ibid., 5 Oct. 1853; ibid., 6 Feb. 1856; CL, MS9098, Mpambani Mzimba, Lovedale 4 Nov. 1869.

201. *HFMR*, 1 Nov. 1848, 553.

4. "THEIR LANGUAGE HAD AN AFFINITY WITH THAT OF BOTH OF THESE NATIONS"

1. Over the past two decades, in reaction to older claims that privileged non-African voices, historians have paid more attention to the ways in which newcomers to the African continent depended on indigenous intermediaries for the production of knowledge about Africa and Africans. I follow their lead here. See Jeff Guy, "Class, Imperialism and Literary Criticism: William Ngidi, John Colenso and Matthew Arbold," *Journal of Southern*

African Studies 23:2 (1997): 219–41; Lyn Schumaker, *Africanizing Anthro-pology: Fieldwork, Networks, and the Making of Cultural Knowledge in Central Africa* (Durham, NC: Duke University Press, 2001); Nancy J. Jacobs, "The Intimate Politics of Ornithology in Colonial Africa," *Comparative Studies in Society and History* 48 (2006): 564–603; Pugach, *Africa in Translation*, especially chapter 6; Andrew Bank and Leslie Bank, eds., *Inside African Anthropology: Monica Wilson and Her Interpreters* (Cambridge: Cambridge University Press, 2013); Andrew Bank and Nancy Jacobs, "Introduction: The Micro-Politics of Knowledge Production in Southern Africa," *Kronos: Southern African Histories* 41 (2015): 11–35.

2. For this older, hagiographic approach see Richard Lovett, *The History of the London Missionary Society, 1795–1895*, vol. 1 (London: Henry Frowde, 1899), 493; and Johannes Du Plessis, *A History of Christian Missions in South Africa* (London: Longmans, Green, 1911), 215. For a critical assess-ment, see Mesthrie, "Words across Worlds," 6–7.

3. Benjamin N. Lawrance, Emily Lynn Osborn, and Richard L. Roberts, "Introduction: African Intermediaries and the 'Bargain' of Collaboration," in *Intermediaries, Interpreters, and Clerks: African Employees in the Making of Colonial Africa*, ed. Lawrance, Osborn, and Roberts (Madison: Univer-sity of Wisconsin Press, 2006), 15; Ranger, "Missionaries," 128; Harries, *Butterflies and Barbarians*, 158.

4. For a groundbreaking study of one missionary-interpreter relationship, see Roger Levine, *A Living Man from Africa: Jan Tzatzoe, Xhosa Chief and Missionary, and the Making of Nineteenth-Century South Africa* (New Haven, CT: Yale University Press 2011), 5.

5. Comaroff and Comaroff, *Of Revelation and Revolution*, 218; Janet Hodg-son, "A Battle for Sacred Power: Christian Beginnings among the Xhosa," in *Christianity in South Africa: A Political, Social, and Cultural History*, ed. Richard Elphick and Rodney Davenport (Berkeley: University of Califor-nia Press, 1997), 77.

6. Derek Peterson, "Translating the Word: Dialogism and Debate in Two Gikuyu Dictionaries," *Journal of Religious History* 23:1 (Feb. 1999): 31–50; Jeater, *Law, Language, and Science*, 10–18; Landau, *Popular Politics*, chapter 3.

7. "Native-speaker" and "native-like speaker" or "near-native speaker" are used as linguistic terms and should not be read as meaning "African."

8. K. H. S. Kim, N. R. Relkin, N. R. de LaPaz, and K.-M. Lee, "Localiza-tion of Cortical Areas Activated by Native and Second Languages with Functional Magnetic Resonance Imaging (fMRI)," *Proceedings of the Inter-national Society for Magnetic Resonance Imaging* 1 (1996): 283; D. Perani et al., "The Bilingual Brain: Proficiency and Age of Acquisition of the Sec-ond Language," *Brain* 121 (1998): 1841–52; K. H. S. Kim, N. R. Relkin,

K.-M. Lee, and Joy Hirsch, "Distinct Cortical Areas Associated with Native and Second Languages," *Nature* 388 (10 July 1997): 171–74; John K. Thornton, *A Cultural History of the Atlantic World, 1250–1820* (New York: Cambridge University Press, 2012), 315.

9. [Tiyo Soga et al.], *The Kafir Bible: Rev. J. W. Appleyard's Version Judged by Missionaries of Various Denominations and Others* (Lovedale: Lovedale Mission Press, 1866), 30.

10. *QIGMS*, no. IV, 1839, 12.

11. The woman was Jane Soga, the wife of the (late) Xhosa minister Tiyo Soga. See National Library of Scotland, Edinburgh, Dep. 298, Church of Scotland Overseas Council, 64 United Presbyterian Church Mission Board, 28 Nov. 1871, 688.

12. *WMM*, Sept. 1832, 664. My emphasis.

13. The written Xhosa is taken verbatim from Mqhayi, "Hail, Busobengwe!" in Opland, *Abantu besizwe*, 456–57.

14. CWM/LMSA/IC/box11/3/C/no. 25, Kayser, Buffalo River, 4 June 1829.

15. CWM/LMSA/IC/box13/1/B/no. 16, Kayser, 15 July 1832.

16. CA, Acc, A558, Journal of Rev. William J. Davis, 3 Apr. 1832.

17. Ibid., 17 Apr. 1833.

18. Ibid., 18 Feb. 1834.

19. Ibid., 31 Dec. 1834.

20. Karl Wilhelm Posselt, *Wilhelm Posselt, der Kaffern-Missionar. Ein Lebensbild aus der Südafrikanischen Mission,* ed. E. Pfitzner and D. Wangemann, 4th ed. (Berlin: Berliner evangelische Missionsgesellschaft, 1891), 41.

21. Friedrich Gottlob Kayser, *Rev F. G. Kayser: Journal and Letters,* ed. Chris Hummel (Grahamstown: Maskew Miller Longman, 1990), 71.

22. CWM/LMSA/IC/box13/4/B/no. 4, Brownlee, 16 Dec. 1833.

23. Stephen Kay, *Travels and Researches in Caffraria* (New York: Harper, 1834), 40; CL, MS9037, PKM, 9 Oct. 1829; JJL, 6 Dec. 1834, 382.

24. Levine, *Living Man*, 75.

25. John Brownlee, Chumie, June 1820, as quoted in Philip, *Researches*, 2:189.

26. CWM/LMSA/IC/box10/2/E/no. 33, Brownlee, 3 Aug. 1827.

27. CWM/LMSA/IC/box12/1/A/no. 1, Kayser and Brownlee, Tzatzoo's Kraal, 1 Jan. 1830.

28. CWM/LMSA/IC/box10/3/C/no. 57, Brownlee, 31 Dec. 1827.

29. CWM/LMSA/IC/box11/2/C/no. 57, Kayser and Brownlee, Report, 26 Dec. 1828.

30. CWM/LMSA/IC/box13/3/C/no. 24, Kayser, 12 July 1833.

31. *London Christian Instructor or Congregational Magazine*, Feb. 1823, 110–11.

32. JJL, 31 July 1831, 215.

33. Ibid., 30 Sept. 1831, Laing to P. Falconer, esq., Glasgow, 227.

34. *QIGMS*, no. II, 1838, 3.

35. *RGMS*, 1831, 18.

36. Ibid., 1833, 17.

37. *QIGMS*, no. II, 1838, 3.

38. CL, MS15252, diary of Shrewsbury, 27 Oct. 1826, 6.

39. Ibid., 29 Nov. 1826, 10.

40. MMS/SA/mf 303, Shrewsbury, Mount Coke, 30 Sept. 1830.

41. CL, MS15252, diary of Shrewsbury, 23 June 1827, 20; ibid., 1 July 1827, 20; ibid., 20 Aug. 1827, 23; ibid., 12 Dec. 1827, 28; ibid., 21 Aug. 1828, 34; *WMM*, Jan. 1830, 56; ibid., Dec. 1830, 840.

42. CL, MS15252, diary of Shrewsbury, 10 Apr. 1829, 38.

43. *WMM*, Oct. 1829, 706.

44. CL, MS15252, diary of Shrewsbury, 15 Sept. 1831, 53; ibid., 19 Nov. 1831, 54; ibid., 12 Aug. 1832, 58.

45. Ibid., 11–17 Aug. 1832, 60.

46. BSA/D1/2, William J. Shrewsbury to Mr. Joseph Jowett, BFBS, Grahamstown, 18 July 1834. One of these youths was George Cyrus, whose services as Gardiner's interpreter have already been explored in chapter 3.

47. Samuel Young, *A Missionary Narrative of the Triumphs of Grace; as Seen in the Conversion of Kafirs, Hottentots, Fingoes, and Other Natives of South Africa* (London: Roche, 1842), 148. For details of this man and his identity, see also ibid., 114–15, 146–48; MMS/SA/mf 303, Young, Wesleyville, 4 Apr. 1832.

48. Bible Society Archive, E3/1/4, Records of the Editorial/Translation Department, Editorial Correspondence Inwards (hereafter BSA/E3/1/4), copybook 4, R. Lamplough to Appleyard, Annshaw, 17 Aug. 1866, 233.

49. [Tiyo Soga et al.], *The Kafir Bible: Rev. J. W. Appleyard's Version Judged by Missionaries*, 28.

50. Ibid., 27.

51. JJL, 30 Sept. 1831, letter to P. Falconer, esq., Glasgow, 227; ibid., 14 Nov. 1831, letter to Falconer, 231–32.

52. Ibid., 24 Jan. 1832, 265.

53. Ibid., 25 Jan. 1832, 265; ibid., 9 Feb. 1832, 270.

54. Ibid., 10 Sept. 1833, 338.

55. Ibid., 27 Feb. 1832, 276–77.

56. *QIGMS*, no. II, 1838, 4.

57. Ibid., no. XIII, 1841, 9–10.

58. Ibid., no. IV, 1839, 4–5; ibid., no. IX, 1840, 6.

59. CL, MS9039, PKM, 7 Apr. 1847.

60. *HFMR*, 1 Nov. 1848, 553.

61. *Correspondence between the Committee,* Laing to George Morgan, Lovedale, 9 Aug. 1854, 70.
62. Shaw, *Story,* 271–73; *WMM,* Feb. 1821, 150.
63. *WMM,* Mar. 1823, 186–92.
64. Ibid., Jan. 1824, 56–57; Shaw, *Story,* 341.
65. Young, *A Missionary Narrative,* 86; Shaw, *Story,* 351–52, 358.
66. *WMM,* Apr. 1824, 277.
67. CL, MS15252, diary of Shrewsbury, 26 Nov. 1826, 10.
68. Ibid., 10 Dec. 1826, 13; NLSA, MSB435, Shaw, journal, 21 May 1827, 48.
69. *WMM,* Dec. 1827, 844. See also CL, MS15252, diary of Shrewsbury, 10 Dec. 1826, 13–14.
70. *WMM,* Mar. 1829, 199; NLSA, MSB435, Shaw, journal, 12 Apr. 1828, 68; ibid., 21 May 1828, 72–73; *WMM,* Sept. 1829, 634; NLSA, MSB435, Shaw, journal, 17 Mar. 1829, 92; *WMM,* Jan. 1830, 56.
71. Ibid., Dec. 1830, 840.
72. NLSA, MSB435, Shaw, journal, 16 May 1829, 100. For these "conversations" see Shaw, *Story,* 512–14.
73. Ibid., 133–34.
74. William Boyce, *Memoir of the Rev. William Shaw, Late General Superintendent of the Wesleyan Missions in South-Eastern Africa* (London: Wesleyan Conference Office, 1874), 183, 192.
75. Ibid., 198.
76. *WMM,* Mar. 1849, William Shaw, Grahamstown, 8 Sept. 1848, 329.
77. CL, MS9039, PKM, 7 July 1847; ibid., 3 Apr. 1850; Natal Archives, Pietermaritzburg (PMB), Natal Colonial Publications, 6/1/1/6, *Natal Government Gazette,* 22 May 1855; Bleek, *Library,* 60.
78. Appleyard, *War of the Axe,* 7 Nov. 1848, 120.
79. Thornley Smith, *Memoir of the Rev. John Whittle Appleyard, Wesleyan Missionary in South Africa* (London: Wesleyan Missionary Society), 1881, 9 Nov. 1840, 50.
80. Appleyard, *War of the Axe,* 28 Apr. 1843, 19.
81. CL, MS15023, Minutes of the District Meeting, Grahamstown, 14 Jan. 1846.
82. John W. Appleyard, "The Kaffir Dialects," *South African Christian Watchman, and Missionary Magazine* (1847).
83. *Correspondence between the Committee,* Brownlee to Morgan, Döhne, 27 July 1853, 20; Appleyard, *War of the Axe,* 20 July 1846, 85.
84. BSA, E3/1/4, J. Appleyard to the secretary of BFBS, Mount Coke, 2 June 1859, 124–25.
85. Appleyard, *Kafir Language,* 36.

86. Ibid., appendix B, 377.

87. Comaroff and Comaroff, *Of Revelation and Revolution*, 216.

88. CL, MS9037, GMS Minutes, Chumie, 9 Mar. 1826.

89. *QIGMS*, no. II, 1838, 5; ibid., no. X, 1841, 11.

90. Zine Magubane, *Bringing the Empire Home: Race, Class, and Gender in Britain and Colonial South Africa* (Chicago: University of Chicago Press, 2004), 57.

91. National Library of Scotland, Acc.7548, Church of Scotland, D.80, Report of the Glasgow Committee acting on behalf of the Subscribers and Contributors toward the support of the Free Church Seminary at Lovedale, Kafirland, South Africa. Read at Annual Meeting, 19 Nov. 1850 (Glasgow: Robert Munsie, 1851), 12.

92. Donovan Williams, "Social and Economic Aspects of Christian Mission Stations in Caffraria 1816–1854," *Historia* 30:2 (1985): 33–48, and 31:1 (1986): 25–56, esp. (1985): 33.

93. Hodgson, "Battle for Sacred Power," 74; Peires, *House of Phalo*, 23, 197n12; Moodie, *Record 5*, Collins, "Notes," 53.

94. Anthony Traill, "The Khoesan Languages," in *Language in South Africa*, ed. Rajend Mesthrie (New York: Cambridge University Press, 2004), 30–31. Traill is citing Jane Sales, *Mission Stations and the Coloured Communities of the Eastern Cape, 1800–1852* (Cape Town: Balkema, 1975), 10, 29, 84.

95. Moodie, *Record 5*, Collins, "Notes," 53.

96. *Missionary Register*, 1 Jan. 1819, 8.

97. CL, MS15252, diary of Shrewsbury, 31 May 1829, 39.

98. *HFMR*, 1 Feb. 1848, 331; Robert Balfour (Noyi Gciniswa), "Appendix II. Ama-Xosa History by Robert Balfour Noyi: A Follower'," trans. John Bennie, in John Knox Bokwe, ed., *Ntsikana: The Story of an African Convert*, 2nd ed. (Lovedale: Mission, 1914), 36–39.

99. Kropf, *Das Volk der Xosa-Kaffern*, 41–46; Jeff Peires, "'He Wears Short Clothes!': Rethinking Rharhabe (c.1775–c.1782)," *Journal of Southern African Studies* 38:2 (June 2012): 336.

100. For "Gonaqua" see Hodgson, "Battle for Sacred Power," 74; Philip, *Researches*, 2:167–68.

101. *Report of the Glasgow African Missionary Society* (hereafter RGAMS), Mar. 1846, 13–14; Phyllis Ntantala, "Balfour, Noyi," in *Dictionary of African Christian Biography* (1995), https://dacb.org/stories/southafrica/balfour-noyi/.

102. John Brownlee, Chumie, June 1820, as quoted in Philip, *Researches*, 2:193.

103. CL, MS9037, PKM, 5 Feb. 1829.

104. *RGMS*, 1833, 17.

105. The information is pieced together from various sources, including JJL, 30 Sept. 1831, letter to P. Falconer esq., Glasgow, 227; ibid., 19 Jan. 1832, 261; ibid., 14 Nov. 1831, 230; QIGMS, no. XIII, 1841, 15; RGMS, 1841, 5–7. Note that Scottish missionary John Ross wrote that Anna had "suckled" his son Bryce, who was born circa 1824; see CL, MS3203, John Ross to Duff, Pirie, Apr. 1864.

106. QIGMS, No. XII, 1841, 11; RGMS, 1843, 13; CL, MS9038, PKM, 5 Jan. 1843.

107. Ibid., 5 Apr. 1843.

108. Ibid., 4 Oct. 1843; ibid., 3 Jan. 1844; ibid., 3 Apr. 1844.

109. Ibid., 2 Oct. 1844; CL, MS3170, John Ross to Macfarlane, Pirie, Oct. 1844.

110. HFMR, 1 Nov. 1845, 237; CL, MS9039, PKM, 1 Oct. 1845.

111. QIGMS, no. XIII, 1841, 15.

112. CL, MS3203, John Ross to Duff, Pirie, Apr. 1864.

113. QIGMS, no. XII, 1841, 11.

114. JJL, 30 Sept. 1831, Letter to P. Falconer esq., Glasgow, 227.

115. RGAMS, Mar. 1846, 13–14.

116. Ibid.

117. For "interpreter," see JJL, 28 Oct. 1831, 239. That Laing's interpreter Klaas was in fact Klaas Love emerges from JJL, 6 Sept. 1833, 336–37; ibid., 24 Oct. 1833, 345; CL, MS9037, PKM, 22 May 1834; JJL, 23 May 1834, 361; ibid., 6 Sept. 1834, 373–74.

118. Klaas Love appears to have been dissatisfied with his wages at this time; see JJL, 29 July 1834, 370; ibid., 2 Aug. 1834, 70. He was definitely a government interpreter in the 1840s when he served as the "government interpreter" attached to Charles Lennox Stretch, the diplomatic agent among the Ngqika-Xhosa. See Imperial Blue Book, No. 424. Copies of Extracts of Correspondence Relative to the Kafir Tribes, between the Years 1837 and 1845 (1851), enclosure no. 31, Statement of the Chief Tyali to Lieutenant-Governor, 14 Apr. 1842, 116; HFMR, 1 Apr. 1845, 62.

119. QIGMS, no. V, 1839, 1.

120. Ibid., 2.

121. Ibid.; JJL, 25 Jan. 1832, 266.

122. JJL, 4 July 1834, 367; ibid., 14 July 1834, 368.

123. Bleek, Library, 60–61.

124. CL, MS9038, PKM, 20 Sept. 1838; QIGMS, no. II, 1838, 5.

125. JJL, 29 July 1833, 334; QIGMS, no. V, 1839, 1–3.

126. "Tshetshe" was sometimes spelled "Tghetghe." For his last name being "Kleinveldt" (sometimes spelled "Kleinveld") see CL, MS9039, PKM, 4 Apr. 1855 and 4 July 1855.

127. CL, MS8116, J. Ross to H. Ross, 20 Dec. 1839.

128. *QIGMS*, no. XIII, 1841, 2–3; *RGMS*, 1843, 13–15.

129. Ibid., 13.

130. CL, MS9039, PKM, 21 July 1845 and 7 Apr. 1847.

131. Williams, "Social and Economic Aspects" (1986): 32–33.

132. CL, MS15252, diary of Shrewsbury, 4 Jan. 1829, 36; *WMM*, Oct. 1829, 705.

133. *WMM*, Oct. 1829, 705.

134. Ibid., Dec. 1830, 839–40.

135. Ibid., Sept. 1831, 645–46; ibid., Sept. 1832, 664.

136. Ibid., Oct. 1829, 705.

137. Ibid, Dec. 1830, 839–40; ibid., Sept. 1832, 664.

138. NLSA, MSB435, Shaw, journal, 11 Oct. 1829, 109.

139. *WMM*, Dec. 1825, 849; NLSA, MSB435, Shaw, journal, Apr. 1827, 46; *WMM*, Apr. 1831, 280.

140. MMS/SA/mf 301, W. Shaw, Wesleyville, 20 Sept. 1825. Note spellings of his name included Yosep, Yosef, and Joseph.

141. MMS/SA/mf 303, S. Young, Wesleyville, 10 Dec. 1830.

142. *WMM*, Dec. 1825, 851; Ayliff, *Journal of John Ayliff*, Wesleyville, 7 Dec. 1826, 65, and 8 Dec. 1826, 67; MMS/SA/mf 301, W. Shrewsbury, Wesleyville, 31 Mar. 1827; NLSA, MSB435, Shaw, journal, 10 Jan. 1828, 57; *WMM*, Sept. 1829, 634–35; Appleyard, *War of the Axe*, 20 July 1846, 85.

143. Compare with Williams, who says "Hottentot" or "Coloured." See Williams, "Social and Economic Aspects" (1986): 54.

144. NLSA, MSB435, Shaw, journal, 21 May 1827, 48. Spellings of the name include Boosak, Boozak, Boezak, etc.

145. MMS/SA/mf 303, S. Young, Wesleyville, 10 Dec. 1830.

146. Spelling of the name Jantje includes Hans, Joutie, Johannes, and Youtize. The spelling of "Nooka" also varies and includes Nookqa, Noeka, Nouka, Nucker, Noega, Nauka, Nquka, Noqwa, Guka, and Noqa.

147. Cullinan, *Gordon*, 53.

148. CWM/LMSA/IC/box6/3/D/32/J. Williams, 15 June 1816 to 7 Aug. 1817.

149. H. C. V. Leibbrandt, ed., *De Rebellie van 1815, algemeen bejan als Slachters Nek* (Cape Town: Juta, 1903), 11 Jan. 1816 and 13 Jan. 1816, 15–16. My translation.

150. Young, *A Missionary Narrative*, 86; Shaw, *Story*, 351–52; MMS/SA/mf 303, S. Young, Wesleyville, 10 Dec. 1830.

151. Backhouse, *Extracts*, 12 May 1839, 76; *Evangelical Magazine and Missionary Chronicle*, Aug. 1839, 409.

152. *Caffrarian Messenger*, Dec. 1845, 268.

153. For a definition of borderlands, see Landau, *Popular Politics*, 3. As he writes: "A borderlands, unlike a line of frontier, . . . suggests a space governed by interactive, overlapping, and incomplete authorities. In the borderlands, wildlife dwindled, trade thrived, and customs were violated and renewed."

154. Hermann Giliomee, "The Eastern Cape Frontier, 1770-1812," in *The Shaping of South African Society*, ed. Richard Elphick and Hermann Giliomee (Middleton: Wesleyan University Press, 1989), 424-29.

155. Peires, *House of Phalo*, 23, 197n12.

156. John Maclean, ed., *A Compendium of Kafir Laws and Customs: Including Genealogical Tables of Kafir Chiefs and Various Tribal Census Returns* (London: Frank Cass 1968), 18; Opland, Kuse, and Maseko, *William Wellington Gqoba*, 230; Kropf, *Das Volk der Xosa-Kaffern*, 40.

157. Kropf, *Das Volk der Xosa-Kaffern*, 40. My translation.

158. George McCall Theal, *History and Ethnography of Africa South of the Zambesi 1505-1795* (New York: Cambridge University Press, 2010), 3:86.

159. Crampton, Peires, and Vernon, *Into the Hitherto Unknown*, 95.

160. Moodie, *Record 5*, Collins, "Supplement," 9.

161. James Backhouse, *A Narrative of a Visit to the Mauritius and South Africa* (London: Hamilton, Adams, 1844), 238. Compare with Williams, "Social and Economic Aspects" (1986): 52.

162. They differ in detail. See Cowper Rose, *Four Years in Southern Africa* (London: Colburn and Bentley, 1829), 148-50; Maclean, *A Compendium of Kafir Laws and Customs*, 21-23.

163. Peires, *House of Phalo*, 25.

164. Ibid.

165. Ibid., 25-26.

166. Giliomee, "The Eastern Cape Frontier," 425.

167. Moodie, *Record 5*, Collins, "Supplement," 10; Peires, *House of Phalo*, 56.

168. Moodie, *Record 5*, Collins, "Supplement," 12.

169. Moodie, *Record 5*, Colonel Collins, "Letter of J. G. Cuyler to A. Barnard, Colonial Secretary, Algoa Bay 26 Sep 1807," 59.

170. Moodie, *Record 5*, Collins, "Notes," 54.

171. Peires, *House of Phalo*, 80.

172. Crampton, Peires, and Vernon, *Into the Hitherto Unknown*, xxxvii, note 85.

173. Moodie, *Record 1*, Journal kept by the Ensign Isaq Schreyver on his journey to the Inquahase Hottentots, beginning 4th January, and ending 10th April, 1689, 437. See also Newton-King, *Masters and Servants on the Cape Eastern Frontier*, 30-32.

174. *HFMR*, 1 Feb. 1848, 331; Balfour, "Appendix II. Ama-Xosa History," in Bokwe, *Ntsikana*, 36–39; Kropf, *Das Volk der Xosa-Kaffern*, 41–46; Harinck, "Interaction between the Xhosa and Khoi," 153–58; Peires, "'He Wears Short Clothes!,'" 336.

175. Kropf, *Das Volk der Xosa-Kaffern*, 44–45.

176. Moodie, *Record 5*, Collins, "Supplement," 12.

177. Kropf, *Das Volk der Xosa-Kaffern*, 45–46. My translation.

178. Newton-King, *Masters and Servants*, 32–33.

179. Willem Adriaan van der Stel, *Korte deductie van Willem Adriaen van der Stel, gewesene extraordinaris Raat van India en Gouverneur aen Cabo de bon Esperance; Tot destructie ende wederlegginge van alle de klaghten, die enige vry-luyden vande voorfz. Cabo, aen de Edele Achtbare Heren Bewinthebberen van de Oost Indische Compagnie over hem hadden gedaen; onder verseeckeringe, dat van alle de stucken, daer by gementioneert, de originele, of copyen authentijcq onder hem van der Stel zijn berustende* (1706), 114–33; Elphick, *Khoikhoi and the Founding*, 228; Newton-King, *Masters and Servants*, 36.

180. Crampton, Peires, and Vernon, *Into the Hitherto Unknown*, xxxviii.

181. Ibid., "Journal Haupt," 2 July 1752, 121.

182. Cullinan, *Gordon*, 53.

183. Moodie, *Record 3*, Declaration of Field Corporal Johannes Hermanus Potgieter, 19 Dec. 1779, 92.

184. Elbourne and Ross, "Combating Spiritual and Social Bondage," 31.

185. London Missionary Society, *Transactions of the Missionary Society*, 415.

186. Moodie, *Record 5*, Collins, "Notes," 54; ibid., Collins, "Supplement," 12.

187. Elbourne and Ross, "Combating Spiritual and Social Bondage," 35–36, 42–43.

188. Molsbergen, *Reizen 3*, Journaal Haupt, 19 June 1752, 301; see also Crampton, Peires, and Vernon, *Into the Hitherto Unknown*, 101.

189. Paterson, *Narrative of Four Journeys*, 88.

190. Cullinan, *Gordon*, 51.

191. Sparrman, *Voyage to the Cape*, 2:6–7.

192. Le Vaillant, *Travels*, 2:2.

193. Ibid., 2:1–2. For a different interpretation of this evidence, see Newton-King, *Masters and Servants*, 33.

194. For the possibility of mixed languages, see Traill, "The Khoesan Languages," 29–30.

195. Lichtenstein, *Travels*, 1:218.

196. Elphick, *Khoikhoi and the Founding*, 211–12.

197. Traill, "The Khoesan Languages," 30–31.

198. Thornton, *Cultural History*, 315.

199. Kay McCormick, "Code-Switching, Code-Mixing and Convergence in Cape Town," in *Language in South Africa*, ed. Rajend Mesthrie (New York: Cambridge University Press, 2004), 219.

200. The inability to perceive small differences as significant can best be explained by recalling Michel Foucault's argument about the relationship between discourse and meaning, notably that we construct meaning about the world's phenomena by way of discourse, with the corollary that in the absence of discourse our ability to ascribe meaning to these phenomena is greatly diminished. See Stuart Hall, "Foucault: Power, Knowledge and Discourse," in *Discourse Theory and Practice: A Reader*, ed. Margaret Wetherell, Stephanie Taylor, and Simeon J. Yates (London: Sage, 2011), 73.

201. Alberti, *Account*, 7.

202. Ibid.

203. *Correspondence between the Committee*, W. Shaw to G. Morgan, Grahamstown, 2 June 1854, 52.

204. Appleyard, *Kafir Language*, 7–8.

205. Ibid., 50.

206. Ibid., 44.

207. *WMM*, Sept. 1840, 785.

208. Ibid.

209. *QIGMS*, no. X, 1841, 3–4.

210. *RGMS*, 1841, 13.

211. Appleyard, *Kafir Language*, 47.

212. *Correspondence between the Committee*, Rev. Bryce Ross to Morgan, Lovedale, 15 Feb. 1856, 73.

213. Ibid., Laing to Morgan, Lovedale, 9 Aug. 1854, 70.

214. Bodleian Library of Commonwealth and African Studies, Rhodes House, Oxford, Papers of the United Society for the Propagation of the Gospel (USPG), E Series Missionaries' Reports (E)/23a, H. R. Woodrooffe, 4 Apr. 1867; Isaac W. Wauchope, "U Mr. Malgas Kunene," *Imvo*, 24 Feb. 1886, 3, as quoted in Opland and Nyamende, *Isaac Williams Wauchope*, 85, 87.

215. *Correspondence between the Committee*, Pearse to George Morgan, Pietermaritzburg, 5 Dec. 1853, 34. My emphasis.

216. Ibid., 35.

217. Ibid., Appleyard to George Morgan, King William's Town, 12 July 1853, 14.

218. Bleek, *Library*, 61–62.

219. Ibid., 52, 54.

220. Ibid., 56–58.

5. "THE NATIVES. IN WHAT RESPECTS, IF ANY, DO THEY DIFFER FROM THE SOUTHERN CAFFRES?"

1. *Correspondence between the Committee*, Circular, Cape Town, 15 June 1853, 1.
2. Ibid., William Shaw to George Morgan, Grahamstown, 5 July 1853, 13.
3. Ibid., James Laing to Morgan, Lovedale, 9 Aug. 1854, 70.
4. Ibid., Charles Brownlee to Morgan, Döhne, 8 Oct. 1855, 78–79.
5. Ibid., Theophilus Shepstone to Morgan, Pietermaritzburg, 13 May 1854, 53.
6. Ibid., John Appleyard to Morgan, Mount Coke, 29 May 1854, 50.
7. BSA/E3/1/4, John Appleyard to Mr. H. Knolleke, Mount Coke, 8 Sept. 1859, 204–8.
8. *Correspondence between the Committee*, Seth Stone to Morgan, Ifafa, 17 July 1854, 59–61.
9. Robert J. Houle, *Making African Christianity: Africans Re-Imagining Their Faith in Colonial Southern Africa* (Bethlehem, PA: Lehigh University Press, 2011), 8.
10. Joseph Tracy, *History of the American Board of Commissioners for Foreign Missions. Compiled Chiefly from the Published and Unpublished Documents of the Board*, 2nd ed. (New York: M. W. Dodd, 1842), 26–27; Judson Smith, *A History of the American Board Missions in Africa* (Boston: American Board of Commissioners for Foreign Missions, 1905), 7.
11. Kotzé, *Letters*, J. B. Purney to Dr. John Philip, New Jersey, 16 Mar. 1832, 22.
12. Smith, *A History*, 7–8.
13. David W. Kling, "The New Divinity and the Origins of the American Board of Commissioners for Foreign Missions," in *North American Foreign Missions, 1810–1914*, ed. Wilbert R. Shenk (Grand Rapids, MI: Eerdmans, 2004), 15.
14. Kling, "The New Divinity," 20.
15. As quoted in Tracy, *History*, 28.
16. Houle, *Making African Christianity*, 10.
17. *The National Preacher* 4:5 (October 1829), Archibald Alexander to the American Board of Foreign Missions, Albany, NY, 7 Oct. 1829, 258.
18. *MH*, Nov. 1833, 415–16. The spelling of the term "Zulu" varied significantly until 1837, when the ABM decided to adopt the current spelling. For the sake of uniformity, I will use "Zulu" throughout the text. See *MH*, Feb. 1838, 66; S. J. R. Martin, "British Images of the Zulu, c. 1820–1879" (PhD diss., University of Cambridge, 1982), 80.
19. Kotzé, *Letters*, Dr. R. Anderson to A. Grout, Champion, and Adams, Boston, 18 Dec. 1835, 85.
20. Ibid., Instructions of the Prudential Committee to the Rev. Daniel Lindley, Rev. Aldin Grout, Rev. Alexander E. Wilson, M.D., Rev. George

Champion, Rev. Henry I. Venable, and Newton Adams, MD, and their Wives, Boston, 22 Nov. 1834, 47; *MH*, Jan. 1835, 5.

21. Kotzé, *Letters,* Joint Letter to Anderson, Mosega, 18 Aug. 1836, 124–26.

22. Ibid., Adams to A. Grout and Champion, Grahamstown, 29 May 1835, 71–73; ibid., A. Grout to Champion and Adams, Grahamstown, 18 Sept. 1835, 78–79.

23. Ibid., Venable to Anderson, Mhlatuzi, 5 Dec. 1837, 218–19.

24. Ibid., A. Grout to Anderson, Bethelsdorp, 12 Feb. 1836, 97–103.

25. Ibid., joint letter, Champion, Grout, and Adams to Anderson, Port Natal, 11 Aug. 1836, 122–23.

26. Ibid., A. Grout to Anderson, Bethelsdorp, 12 Feb. 1836, 100.

27. Ibid., Wilson to Anderson, Grahamstown, 17 Apr. 1837, 151–55; *MH*, Oct. 1837, 416.

28. Kotzé, *Letters,* Champion to A. Grout, Port Elizabeth, 3 Apr. 1838, 228–31.

29. *MH*, Feb. 1839, 49.

30. Kotzé, *Letters,* Anderson to "The Brethren of the S. African Mission," Boston, 11 Apr. 1838, 250.

31. The return to the Zulu kingdom occurred in early 1841; see *MH*, Apr. 1842, 131.

32. Ibid., Feb. 1843, 77–78.

33. Ibid., Apr. 1843, 155. See also William F. van Altena, ed., "Mission to the Zulus (1834–1866): Journal of the Reverend Aldin B. Grout," unpublished MS (Mar. 2017), hereafter JAG, 105–6. Note that this MS is currently being edited for publication by Robert J. Houle.

34. Special Collections and University Archives, University of Massachusetts Amherst Libraries, Massachusetts (hereafter UMass), Aldin Grout Papers, MS 797, box 1:17, A. Grout to Elizabeth Bailey, Umgeni, 29 Apr. 1844.

35. Edwin W. Smith, *The Life and Times of Daniel Lindley (1801–1880)* (London: Epworth, 1949), 250–51.

36. David Welsh, *The Roots of Segregation: Native Policy in Colonial Natal, 1845–1910* (New York: Oxford University Press, 1971), 11.

37. Arthur Fridjof Christofersen, *Adventuring with God: The Story of the American Board Mission in South Africa,* ed. Richard W. Sales (Durban: Robinson, 1967), 67.

38. Norman Etherington, *Preachers, Peasants and Politics in Southeast Africa, 1835–1880: African Christian Communities in Natal, Pondoland and Zululand* (London: Royal Historical Society, 1978), 27–40.

39. ABC, microfilm reel 175, picture 347 (hereafter ABC 175/347), Annual Tabular View, Mission to the Zulus of Southern Africa, 1849.

40. ABC 175/447, A General Letter from the American Mission at Natal, Amahlongwa, 11 Sept. 1851; PMB, American Board Mission Collection (ABMC), A608, A/1/1, Minutes of Committee Meetings, 1837–1883, vol. 2, 1846–1853, General Meeting, Amahlongwa, 11 Sept. 1851.

41. ABC 176/867–68, H. Wilder to Anderson, Umtwalume, 17 Nov. 1851; PMB, ABMC, A608, A/1/1, Minutes of Committee Meetings, 1837–1883, vol. 2, 1846–1853, D'Urban, 25 May 1852; ABC 175/356, Annual Tabular View for 1853, American Zulu Mission; PMB, ABMC, A608, A/1/1, Minutes of Committee Meetings, 1837–1883, vol. 3, 1854–1860, Amanzimtoti (Umlazi), 7 June 1854; ABC 175/497, General Letter of the American Zulu Mission, Umvoti, 20 June 1855.

42. PMB, ABMC, A608, A/1/1, Minutes of Committee Meetings, 1837–1883, vol. 3, 1854–1860, Amanzimtoti (Umlazi), 7 June 1854.

43. *Correspondence between the Committee*, Lewis Grout on behalf of the Government Commission for Preparing a Dictionary and Grammar of the Zulu Languages, to Rev. G. Morgan, Umsunduzi, Natal, 20 June 1854, 55.

44. Ibid., 54–55.

45. Ibid., Lewis Grout to Morgan, Umsunduzi, 15 Sept. 1854, 85.

46. BSA/D1/2, Rev. George Morgan to H. Knolleke, Cape Town, 7 Aug. 1854; *Correspondence between the Committee*, Appleyard to Morgan, Mount Coke, 29 May 1854, 51.

47. Lewis Grout, *The IsiZulu: A Grammar of the Zulu Language* (London: Trübner, 1859), 39.

48. *Correspondence between the Committee*, Appleyard to Morgan, Mount Coke, 25 May 1857, 104–5.

49. Ibid., 105–7.

50. Ibid., Lewis Grout to Morgan, Umsunduzi, 15 Sept. 1854, 85.

51. James Bryant, "The Zulu Language," *Journal of the American Oriental Society* 1:4 (1849): 395.

52. ABC 176/868, Hyman Wilder to Anderson, Umtwalume, 17 Nov. 1851.

53. ABC 176/678, Stone to Anderson, Durban, 6 Dec. 1852.

54. Ibid.

55. Bryant, "The Zulu Language," 395.

56. *Correspondence between the Committee*, Stone to Morgan, Ifafa, 17 July 1854, 59.

57. ABC 176/1003–4, Wilder to Anderson, Umtwalume, 2 Sept. 1856.

58. Kotzé, *Letters*, Champion to Collis, Cape Town, 2 Apr. 1835, 55. My emphasis.

59. Ibid., Instructions, Nov. 22, 1834, 46–50. My emphases.

60. Ibid., Champion to Anderson, Nginani, 21 Apr. 1837, 156; *MH,* Apr. 1838, 139; ibid., June 1838, 208; ibid., Oct. 1840, 387.

61. Ibid., Feb 1843, 79. For this immigration, see also ibid., June 1841, 247; ibid., Apr. 1843, 155; ibid., June 1844, 181; Keletso Atkins, *The Moon Is Dead! Give Us Our Money! The Cultural Origins of an African Work Ethic in Natal, South Africa, 1843–1900* (Portsmouth, NH: Heinemann, 1993), chapter 1.

62. *JSA,* John Kumalo (1900), 1:243; ibid., Mkando kaDhlova (1902), 3:158; ibid., Ndukwana kaMbengwana (1897–1903), 4:346; Hamilton, *Terrific Majesty,* 56; Atkins, *The Moon Is Dead!,* 12.

63. *MH,* June 1846, 191. Adams's statement is confirmed by *JSA,* Madikane kaMlomowetole (1903), 2:56; ibid., Magidigidi kaNobebe (1905), 2:85.

64. *MH,* May 1846, 158.

65. Patrick Harries, "Imagery, Symbolism and Tradition in a South African Bantustan: Mangosuthu Buthelezi, Inkatha, and Zulu History," *History and Theory* 32 (1993): 107.

66. Jeff Guy, *The Destruction of the Zulu Kingdom: The Civil War in Zululand, 1879–1884* (Johannesburg: Ravan Press, 1982), 11; Guy, "Ecological Factors in the Rise of Shaka and the Zulu Kingdom," in *Economy and Society in Pre-Industrial South Africa,* ed. Shula Marks and Anthony Atmore, 115–17 (Harlow: Longman, 1980).

67. The existing scholarship is not entirely clear as to who was subjected to these restrictive laws. See Atkins, *The Moon Is Dead!,* 31–34; Sean Hanretta, "Women, Marginality and the Zulu State: Women's Institutions and Power in the Early Nineteenth Century," *Journal of African History* 39:3 (1998): 402–3.

68. For "not the only ones" see John B. Wright and Carolyn Hamilton, "Traditions and Transformations: The Phongolo-Mzimkhulu Region in the Late Eighteenth and Early Nineteenth Centuries," in *Natal and Zululand from Earliest Times to 1910; A New History,* ed. Andrew Dumny and Bill Guest, 62–67 (Pietermaritzburg: University of Natal Press, 1989).

69. Isaacs, *Travels,* 1:114.

70. Gardiner, *Narrative,* 39.

71. For background on this phenomenon, see John Laband, "'Blood-stained Grandeur': Colonial and Imperial Stereotypes of Zulu Warriors and Zulu Warfare," in *Zulu Identities,* ed. Benedict Carton, Laband, and Jabulani Sithole, 168–76 (New York: Columbia University Press, 2009).

72. Stuart and Malcolm, *The Diary of Fynn,* 65n1. My emphasis.

73. As quoted in William Holden, *The Past and Future of the Kafir Races* (London: Nicholas, 1866), 22. My emphasis.
74. *MH*, Mar. 1837, 115; Crais, *White Supremacy*, 129.
75. Cory, *Diary*, "Owen's Diary," 22 Nov. 1837, 71.
76. *MH*, Apr. 1843, 155.
77. Ibid., Apr. 1837, *148*; ibid., Sept. 1836, 339. My emphasis.
78. Ibid., Aug. 1842, 337. My emphasis.
79. Ibid., Sept. 1836, 342. Also compare Kotzé, *Letters*, Wilson to Anderson, Kuruman, 21 Mar. 1836, 105, with ibid., Wilson to Anderson, Grahamstown, 17 Apr. 1837, 154.
80. *MH*, Nov. 1835, 413.
81. JAG, 28.
82. Stuart and Malcolm, *Diary of Fynn*, 60; Gardiner, *Narrative*, 101–2.
83. *MH*, Apr. 1837, 141.
84. JAG, 41.
85. Ibid., 31, 41; Kotzé, *Letters*, Adams to Champion, Port Natal, 4 Feb. 1836, 95 and note 4; John Bird, ed., *The Annals of Natal, 1495–1845*, 2 vols. (Pietermaritzburg: Davis, 1888), 1:197.
86. *Correspondence between the Committee*, Stone to Morgan, Ifafa, 17 July 1854, 61; Kotzé, *Letters*, Champion to A. Grout, Umlazi, 8 Mar. 1838, 224.
87. JAG, 93, 101; Tabler, *Pioneers*, 66.
88. ABC 175/860, A. Grout to Anderson, Umvoti, 1 Mar. 1847; ABC 175/895–96, A. Grout to Anderson, Ifumi, 15 Sept. 1849; ABC 175/899, A. Grout to Anderson, Umvoti, 17 Dec. 1849; ABC 176/187, L. Grout to Anderson, Umsunduzi, Sept. 1851.
89. Bryant, "The Zulu Language," 395.
90. ABC 76, Personal Papers, Lewis Grout, folder 1, L. Grout, J. C. Bryant, H. A. Wilder, N. Adams, J. L. Döhne, letter "To the Missionaries and Friends of Education among the Aborigines of Southern Africa," Port Natal, 6 Mar. 1850, 1–3.
91. Ibid., 2.
92. *MH*, June 1841, 246; ibid., Feb. 1843, 77.
93. ABC 175/52, A. Grout to Anderson, Umvoti, 2 Oct. 1845.
94. *MH*, May 1844, 151, 153; ibid., Nov. 1845, 369.
95. Ibid., Nov. 1845, 369.
96. Ibid., June 1846, 191.
97. Atkins, *The Moon Is Dead!*, 34–36.
98. Ibid.
99. *MH*, Mar. 1848, 100.

100. For the early 1850s, see ibid., Aug. 1852, 227; ibid., Feb. 1853, 35.

101. ABC 175/1191, Samuel Marsh to Anderson, Umlazi River, 5 Feb. 1848.

102. UMass, Aldin Grout Papers, MS 797, box 1:17, A. Grout to Elizabeth Bailey, Umgeni, 29 Apr. 1844.

103. Smith, *Daniel Lindley*, 263.

104. For these cases and their failures, see Welsh, *The Roots of Segregation*, 25 and 305; Government Notice, no. 64, 1852, in *Natal Government Gazette*, 25 Sept. 1852, as quoted in Smith, *Daniel Lindley*, 300; ABC 175/1158, Lindley to Anderson, 16 Nov. 1855; Sir G. Grey to the Colonial Secretary, 3 Dec. 1855, in Smith, *Daniel Lindley*, 305; ABC 175/971, A Grout to Anderson, Umvoti, 20 Nov. 1855.

105. ABC 76, Personal Papers, Lewis Grout, folder 5, "The History and Statistics of the Native Population of Natal," Port Natal, 10 Apr. 1852, 9, 11; *Proceedings of the Commission in Natal*, Evidence of L. Grout, 28 Dec. 1852, 4:28–29, 56.

106. ABC 175/51–52, A. Grout to Anderson, Umvoti, 2 Oct. 1845.

107. *MH*, Dec. 1849, 409.

108. ABC 175/485, Wilder to the Treasurer of the American Bible Society, Umwalume, 15 Feb. 1854; *Annual Report of the American Bible Society* 34 (1850), 80.

109. ABC 175/485, Wilder to the Treasurer of the American Bible Society, Umwalume, 15 Feb. 1854.

110. *Correspondence between the Committee*, A. Grout to Morgan, Umvoti Mission Station, 11 July 1853, 28.

111. *MH*, June 1851, 201; ibid., Jan. 1853, 2.

112. Ibid., Dec. 1854, 53; *Correspondence between the Committee*, Stone to Morgan, Ifafa, 2 Aug. 1853, 30.

113. *Correspondence between the Committee*, A. Grout to Morgan, Umvoti, 11 July 1853, 28; ibid., Stone to Morgan, Ifafa, 2 Aug. 1853, 30; *MH*, Dec. 1854, 53.

114. *MH*, Dec. 1854, 53.

115. PMB, ABMC, A608, A/1/1, Minutes of Committee Meetings, 1837–1883, vol. 2, 1846–1853, General Meeting, D'Urban, 17 Feb. 1852.

116. Colenso, *Ten Weeks*, 15.

117. PMB, Secretary of Native Affairs, I/8/5, Letter Book, 1851–55, 17 May 1853, 163.

118. Ibid.

119. ABC 176/905, Wilder to Anderson, D'Urban, 30 May 1853; ABC 176/918, Wilder to Anderson, Umtwalume, 1 Aug. 1853; Lewis Grout, "Announcement: Grammar and Dictionary of the Zulu Language," *Journal of the American Oriental Society* 4 (1854): 456.

120. PMB, ABMC, A608, A/1/1, Minutes of Committee Meetings, 1837–1883, vol. 2, 1846–1853, General Meeting, D'Urban, 12 Dec. 1849, and General Meeting, D'Urban, 17 Feb. 1852.
121. *MH*, Feb. 1843, 79.
122. *Proceedings of the Commission in Natal* (1852), 2:41; Keegan, *Colonial South Africa*, 207.
123. ABC 175/45, A. Grout to Anderson, Umvoti, 17 June 1845.
124. ABC, 175/58, A. Grout to Anderson, Umvoti, 10 Dec. 1845.
125. William C. Holden, *A Brief History of Methodism, and Methodism in South Africa* (London: Wesleyan-Methodist Book Room, 1887), 406.
126. ABC 176/42, L. Grout to Anderson, Umlazi, 7 Sept. 1847; ABC 175/722, J. Bryant to Anderson, Umlazi, 6 May 1848.
127. Kristin Fjelde Tjelle, *Missionary Masculinity, 1870–1930: Norwegian Missionaries in South-East Africa* (New York: Palgrave, 2013), 41.
128. ABC 175/61, A. Grout to Anderson, Umvoti, 22 June 1846; ABC 175/693, Bryant to Anderson, Umlazi, 20 Jan. 1847.
129. ABC 176/56, L. Grout to Anderson, Umsunduzi, 25 Dec. 1847.
130. ABC 176/56–7, L. Grout to Anderson, Umsunduzi, 25 Dec. 1847.
131. PMB, ABMC, A608, A/2/10, Correspondence Received, General, 1835–1900, Davis to the Brethren of the American Board of Missions, D'Urban, Port Natal, 9 Sept. 1846
132. ABC 175/693, Bryant to Anderson, Umlazi, 20 Jan. 1847.
133. PMB, ABMC, A608, A/3/34, Correspondence Dispatched, General, 1835–1930, Bryant to Davis, Amanzimtoti, 9 Feb. 1847.
134. ABC 175/695, Bryant to Anderson, Amanzimtoti, 30 Apr. 1847.
135. ABC 175/861, A. Grout to Anderson, Umvoti, 31 Mar. 1847.
136. ABC 175/56, L. Grout to Anderson, Umsunduzi, 25 Dec. 1847.
137. ABC 175/405–6, All to Anderson, Umbilo, 24 Apr. 1850; ABC 175/600, Abrahams to Anderson, Natal, 20 Mar. 1850.
138. Bleek, *Library*, 52, 54, 56–58, 61–62.
139. See, once more, *Correspondence between the Committee*, Grout on behalf of the Government Commission to Morgan, Umsunduzi, Natal, 20 June 1854, 54–55.
140. Colenso, *Ten Weeks*, 16.
141. *Correspondence between the Committee*, Stone to Morgan, Ifafa, 17 July 1854, 61. My emphasis.

6. "TO SPEAK PROPERLY AND CORRECTLY, VIZ. *UKU-KULUMA-NJE*"

1. *Correspondence between the Committee*, Stone to Morgan, Ifafa, 17 July 1854, 61.

2. UMass, Aldin Grout Papers, MS 797, box 1:10, A. Grout to Elnathan Davis, Cape Town, 12 Mar. 1835.

3. Ibid.

4. L. Grout, "The Zulu," 425.

5. Bryant, "The Zulu Language," 395.

6. *Correspondence between the Committee*, Döhne to Morgan, Table Mountain, 1 July 1854, 57.

7. Grout, *The IsiZulu*, xx.

8. *MH*, Mar. 1837, 121. My emphasis.

9. Kotzé, *Letters*, Champion to Anderson, Nginani, 21 Apr. 1837, 156. My emphasis.

10. Private conversation with Benedict Carton, 61st Annual Meeting of the African Studies Association in Atlanta, 2 Nov. 2018.

11. ABC 175/1091–92, William Ireland to Anderson, Ifumi, 30 June 1854; see also ABC 176/868, Hyman Wilder to Anderson, Umtwalume, 17 Nov. 1851.

12. *Correspondence between the Committee*, Stone to Morgan, Ifafa, 17 July 1854, 61.

13. Grout, *The IsiZulu*, xix–xx.

14. JAG, 53.

15. Ibid., 91.

16. *MH*, Jan. 1841, 36.

17. JAG, 93, 101.

18. UMass, Aldin Grout Papers, MS 797, box 1:14, A. Grout to James and Elizabeth Bailey, Umlazi, 5 Sept. 1841; JAG 92.

19. ABC 175/44–45, A. Grout to Anderson, Umvoti, 17 June 1845.

20. UMass, Aldin Grout Papers, MS 797, box 1:19, A. Grout and Charlotte Bailey to James Bailey, Umlazi, 13 Feb. 1846.

21. ABC 175/379, Bryant to Anderson, Ifumi, 10 May 1849.

22. ABC 176/369–370, L. Grout to Anderson, Umsunduzi, 26 Oct. 1852.

23. Benedict Carton, "Awaken *Nkulunkulu*, Zulu God of the Old Testament: Pioneering Missionaries during the Early Age of Racial Spectacle," in Carton, Laband, and Sithole, *Zulu Identities*, 136.

24. ABC 176/699, Stone to Anderson, Ifafa, 8 Dec. 1857.

25. ABC 175/1230–31, Silas McKinney to Anderson, Umlazi, 15 Aug. 1847.

26. ABC 175/1232, McKinney to Anderson, Umvoti, 9 Oct. 1847.

27. ABC 175/1241–42, McKinney to Anderson, Ifumi, 17 Oct. 1848.

28. ABC 175/1058, Ireland to Anderson, Umvoti, 31 May 1849.

29. ABC 175/1060–62, Ireland to Anderson, Umvoti, 1 Sept. 1849.

30. ABC 175/848, Döhne to Anderson, Table Mountain, 10 Jan. 1857.

31. Herman T. Wangemann, *Die Berliner Mission im Kafferlande* (Berlin: Ev. Missionshaus, 1873), 6, 28, 30–33, 97–100.
32. PMB, ABMC, A608, A/1/1, Minutes of Committee Meetings, 1837–1883, vol. 2, 1846–1853, General Meeting, D'Urban, 12 Dec. 1849.
33. ABC 175/1091–92, Ireland to Anderson, Ifumi, 30 June 1854. The case occurred in 1851. See ABC 176/868, Wilder to Anderson, Umtwalume, 17 Nov. 1851.
34. ABC 176/18, L. Grout to Anderson, Umvoti, 16 Apr. 1847.
35. ABC 175/865, A. Grout to Anderson, Umvoti, 27 Sept. 1847; ABC 176/28, L. Grout, journal, Umvoti, 2 May 1847.
36. ABC 176/187, 192–93, L. Grout to Anderson, Umsunduzi, Sept. 1851.
37. ABC 176/682, Stone to Anderson, Durban, 6 Dec. 1852.
38. ABC 180/28, Stone to Rev. N. G. Clark, Ifafa, 1 Dec. 1866. I thank Robert J. Houle for drawing my attention to this information.
39. ABC 180/31, Stone to Clark, Ifafa, 1 Dec. 1866.
40. ABC 176/683, Stone to Anderson, Durban, 6 Dec. 1852.
41. ABC 176/681, Stone to Anderson, Durban, 6 Dec. 1852; ABC 176/683, Stone to Anderson, Ifafa, 1 Aug. 1853.
42. Colenso, *Ten Weeks*, 234, 239.
43. PMB, ABMC, A608, A/1/1, Minutes of Committee Meetings, 1837–1883, Durban, 10 Jan. 1855.
44. Isaacs, *Travels*, 1:29, 146; Smith, *Life and Times*, 280.
45. Heather Hughes, *First President: A Life of John Dube, Founding President of the ANC* (Auckland Park: Jacana Media, 2011), 1–12.
46. JSA, Christian Cane (1907), 2:77; Smith, *Life and Times*, 280.
47. Ibid.
48. JSA, Rangu kaNotshiya (1899), 5:256; Eva Jackson, "The Economic Experimentation of Nembula Duze/Ira Adams Nembula, 1846–1886," *Journal of Natal and Zulu History* 28 (2010): 8.
49. The information on Nembula is compiled from several sources: ABC 175/650–53, Adams to Anderson, Umlazi, 1 Oct. 1847; JAG 84, 118–19; Christofersen, *Adventuring with God*, 28–29.
50. ABC 175/653, Adams to Anderson, Umlazi, 1 Oct. 1847.
51. ABC 175/1111–12, Lindley to Anderson, Umlazi, 4 Dec. 1847; *MH*, Mar. 1848, journal of J. Bryant, Jan.–July 1847.
52. ABC 175/1191, Marsh to Anderson, Umlazi River, 5 Feb. 1848.
53. In 1866, Stone referred to Nembula, who by then had adopted the name Ira Adams Nembula, as "our best native critic" for producing idiomatic Zulu translations. See ABC 180/28 and 30, Stone to Clark, Ifafa, 1 Dec. 1866.
54. Houle, *Making African Christianity*, 16.

55. ABC 175/893, A. Grout to Anderson, Umvoti, 11 Sept. 1849.

56. In 1844 A. Grout said that Hangu was sixteen years old, which means the approximate year of his birth was 1828. See UMass, Aldin Grout Papers, MS 797, box 1:18, A. Grout to James Bailey, Umvoti, 10 Nov. 1844.

57. Ibid.

58. UMass, Aldin Grout Papers, MS 797, box 1:19, A. Grout to Elizabeth Bailey, Umvoti River, 4 Mar. 1846; ABC 175/67, A. Grout to Anderson, Umvoti, 2 Dec. 1846; Christofersen, *Adventuring with God*, 30.

59. ABC 175/862, A. Grout to Anderson, Umvoti, 31 Mar. 1847.

60. ABC 175/862–63, A. Grout to Anderson, Umvoti, 31 Mar. 1847; ABC 175/870, A. Grout to Anderson, Umvoti, 29 Jan. 1848; Houle, *Making African Christianity*, 43.

61. ABC 175/409, All missionaries to Anderson, Port Natal, 23 Apr. 1850.

62. ABC 175/352, Annual Tabular View for 1851, Zulu Mission, South Africa.

63. Christofersen, *Adventuring with God*, 36.

64. ABC 175/882, A. Grout to Anderson, Report of the Umvoti Mission, 12 Sept. 1848; ABC 175/893–94, A. Grout to Anderson, Umvoti, 11 Sept. 1849.

65. Christofersen, *Adventuring with God*, 31; Smith, *Life and Times*, 283; Hughes, *First President*, 10.

66. Christofersen, *Adventuring with God*, 34.

67. Colenso, *Ten Weeks*, 250; ABC 176/92 and 95, L. Grout, journal extracts, 26 Dec. 1847 and 8 Jan. 1848.

68. *MH*, Apr. 1843, 155.

69. ABC 176/319, L. Grout to Anderson, 2 Sept. 1852.

70. Hughes, *First President*, 4. For the submission of the Qadi to Shaka's Zulu state, see also *JSA*, Madikane kaMlomowetole (1903), 2:47. For the longer history of the Qadi and the relationship of its members with the Zulu state and the American Board missionaries, see Heather Hughes, "Politics and Society in Inanda, Natal: The Qadi under Chief Mqhawe, c1840–1906" (PhD diss., University of London, 1995).

71. Hughes, *First President*, 1, 11.

72. Ibid., 2–12.

73. ABC 175/893, A. Grout to Anderson, Umvoti, 11 Sept. 1849; UMass, Aldin Grout Papers, MS 797, box 1:19, A. Grout to Elizabeth Bailey, Umvoti River, 4 Mar. 1846; ABC 175/67, A. Grout to Anderson, Umvoti, 2 Dec. 1846; Christofersen, *Adventuring with God*, 30.

74. For "Nembula" see note 49. For "Makhanya" see *JSA*, Jantshi kaNongila (1903), 1:186–87; ibid., Dinya kaZokozwayo (1905), 1:115–16; Elizabeth Eldredge, *The Creation of the Zulu Kingdom: War, Shaka, and the*

Consolidation of Power (New York: Cambridge University Press), 91, 110–12.

75. But they disagree on the causes for these transformations. Alfred T. Bryant considered the genius and ruthlessness of individuals, such as Shaka kaSenzangakhona, as the crucial engine of change. In contrast, John Omer-Cooper attributed the rise of conquest-states to population explosion and the resulting competition for scarce resources. Jeff Guy pursued this idea further and held that ecological changes promoted the rise of these states; David Shingirai Chanaiwa pushed back against the ecological argument by attributing the rise of states to the intensification of conflict between wealthy ruling elites and deprived royal princes. This contrasted with Alan Smith, who linked the rise of conquest states to external trade relations between the region's chiefdoms and the Portuguese at Delagoa Bay in southern Mozambique. Building on Smith, Henry Slater argued that the emergence of conquest states represented a major readjustment in the social formation that became necessary to resolve the complex social contradictions that arose when the region's polities came into contact with the emerging capitalist world economy. External trade was also at the center of Julian Cobbing's thesis, which posited that the rise of these conquest states should be seen as a defensive reaction against slave raiding and slave-export trading in the region at that time. See Bryant, *Olden Times;* Omer-Cooper, *Zulu Aftermath;* Guy, "Ecological Factors"; David S. Chanaiwa, "The Zulu Revolution: State Formation in a Pastoralist Society," *African Studies Review* 23 (Dec. 1980): 1–20; Alan Smith, "The Trade of Delagoa Bay as a Factor in Nguni Politics, 1750–1835," in *African Societies in Southern Africa,* ed. Leonard M. Thompson, 171–90 (London: Heinmann, 1969); Henry Slater, "Transitions in the Political Economy of South-East Africa before 1840" (PhD diss., University of Sussex, 1976); Cobbing, "Mfecane as Alibi."

76. John B. Wright, "Reflections on the Politics of Being 'Zulu,'" in Carton, Laband, and Sithole, *Zulu Identities,* 36.

77. Hamilton and Wright, "The Making of the AmaLala," 15–16.

78. Wright and Hamilton, "Traditions and Transformations," 69.

79. *JSA,* Ndukwana kaMbengwana (1897–1903), 4:326, 363.

80. Hamilton, "Political Centralisation," 293; *JSA,* Baleni kaSilvana (1914), 1:29; ibid., Madhlebe kaNjinjana (1905), 2:45–46; ibid., Stephen Mini (1899), 3:134; ibid., Madikane kaMlomowetole (1903), 2:57.

81. Hamilton "Political Centralisation," 293; *JSA,* Mkehlengana kaZulu, 3:212; ibid., Dinya kaZokozwayo (1905), 1:118.

82. *JSA,* Mkehlengana kaZulu (1905), 3:210.

83. Ibid., 3:214.

84. Hamilton, "Political Centralisation," 293–94; *JSA*, Ndhlovu kaSika-kana (1909), 4:217; ibid. Mkebeni kaDabulamanzi (1921), 3:195–96.

85. For the terms in quotation marks, see *Correspondence between the Committee*, Stone to Morgan, Ifafa, 17 July 1854, 61; Marks, "Traditions," 143; Hamilton, "Political Centralisation," 295; J. A. Louw, "The Development of Xhosa and Zulu as Languages," *Language Reform: History and Future 2* (1983): 373.

86. Döhne, *Zulu-Kafir Dictionary*, xv.

87. Ibid., xvi. Compare with *JSA*, Melapi kaMagaye (1905), 3:75, 87; ibid., Magidigidi kaNobebe (1905), 2:97; ibid., Mayinga kaMbekuzana (1905), 2:257; ibid., Mkondo kaDhlova (1902), 3:166–67; ibid., Mqayikana kaYenge (1916), 4:9.

88. See Bleek's quote in the next sentence. For context see also Alfred T. Bryant, *A Zulu-English Dictionary* (Pinetown: Mariannhill Mission Press, 1905), 27; Bryant, *Olden Times*, 233.

89. NLSA, MSC57/box 9/file 1, Wilhelm Bleek, "Preliminaries to a Grammar of the Zulu language," in "Zulu & Se-Tsuana" (1856). Note that the term Bleek used in the manuscript, *ukukhuluma nje*, differs significantly from the term he used in his diary, where he stated that *"nKukulumanje* mean[s] the slaughter of a language" (this latter derives from the verb *ukukhukhula*, "to sweep away," and the adverb *manje*, "now"). However, since Bleek's manuscript was written after his diary, it can be assumed that its version reflects the spelling and the meaning that he ascribed to the term after more thorough reflection. Furthermore, as I suggest below, it is quite possible that Bleek made the association between the term and the idea of "slaughter of a language" in his diary because he was speaking to "aMatonga" who, as *ukutekeza*-speakers, may have experienced *ukukhuluma nje* as akin to *ukukhukhula manje*, a "sweeping away" of their language; in other words, it is possible that his interlocutors engaged in a play of words. See Harries, "Imagery, Symbolism and Tradition,"107; Wright, "A. T. Bryant and the 'Lala,'" 356n9; Wilhelm Bleek, *The Natal Diaries of Dr. W. H. I. Bleek, 1855–1856*, ed. O. H. Spohr (Cape Town: Gothic, 1965), 76.

90. Döhne, *Zulu-Kafir Dictionary*, xv.

91. Kropf, *A Kaffir-English Dictionary*, 191. Note that toward the end of the nineteenth century, this meaning disappeared from editions produced in Natal, notably Colenso, *Zulu-English Dictionary*, 273; Bryant, *A Zulu-English Dictionary*, 328. These dictionaries no longer translated *ukukhuluma* as "speaking the official language" because they had already adopted the term "Zulu language" as a way of referring to all the speaking practices in the Natal-Zululand region and had already adopted what they called the "high Zulu

dialect" as the model for that language. Consequently, by the time of their writing, "khuluma" came to have only one meaning: "to speak."

92. *JSA*, Magidigidi kaNobebe (1905), 2:97.
93. Bryant, *Olden Times*, 58; *JSA*, Mabonza kaSidhlayi (1909), 2:24.
94. *JSA*, Mangati kaGodide (1918), 2:202–4.
95. Ibid., Lunguza kaMpukane (1909), 1:329.
96. Bleek, *Natal Diaries*, 76.
97. See note 89 above.
98. NLSA, MSC57/box 9/file 1, W. Bleek, "Preliminaries" (1856).
99. *JSA*, Kambi kaMatshobana (1903), 1:210. But see also ibid., Magidigidi kaNobebe (1905), 2:84; ibid., Mayinga kaMbekuzana (1905), 2:257.
100. John W Colenso, *First Steps in Zulu: Being an Elementary Grammar of the Zulu Language*, 4th ed. (Maritzburg: P. Davis, 1890), 4.
101. *JSA*, Lunguza kaMpukane (1909), 1:320. See also ibid., Jantshi kaNongila (1903), 1:195; ibid., Ngidi kaMcikaziswa (1904), 5:36; ibid., Sivivi kaMaqungo (1905), 5:378.
102. *JSA*, Baleni kaSilwana (1914), 1:46. See also NLSA, MSC57/box 9/file 1, W. Bleek, "Preliminaries" (1856).
103. Isaac Sibusiso Kubeka, "A Preliminary Survey of Zulu Dialects in Natal and Zululand" (master's thesis, University of Natal, 1979), 11.
104. NLSA, MSC57/box 9/file 1, W. Bleek, "Preliminaries" (1856). See also Shooter, *Kafirs*, 376.
105. For "1821," see Eldredge, *Creation of the Zulu Kingdom*, 120–21. But they were not fully destroyed until 1826; see John Laband, *Rise and Fall of the Zulu Nation* (London: Arms and Armour, 1998), 34.
106. Hamilton and Wright, "The Making of the AmaLala," 16–17.
107. Hamilton, "Political Centralisation," 295. But see also Shooter, *Kafirs*, 115; *JSA*, Mcotoyi kaMnini (1905), 3:65–66; Isaacs, *Travels*, 1:169. For a similar extractive relationship across the Phongolo River, see *JSA*, Bikwayo kaNoziwawa (1903), 1:63–68; ibid., John Kumalo (1900), 1:238.
108. Hamilton, "Political Centralisation," 295.
109. *JSA*, Dinya kaZokozwayo (1905), 1:118; ibid., Mahaya kaNongqabana (1905), 2:113; ibid., Mqayikana kaYenge (1916), 4:10; ibid., Singcofela kaMtshungu (1910), 5:341; ibid., Norman Nembula (1905), 5:13; ibid., Madikane kaMlomowetole (1903), 2:55
110. *JSA*, Mqayikana kaYenge (1916), 4:3, 14. See also ibid., Dinya kaZokozwayo (1905, 1908), 1:118; ibid., Madikane kaMlomowetole (1903), 2:55; ibid., Mageza kaKwefunga, 1905, 2:69, 70; ibid. Mkando kaDhlova (1902), 3:158.
111. Döhne, *Zulu-Kafir Dictionary*, xv.
112. Colenso, *First Steps*, 4; *JSA*, Mcotoyi kaMnini (1905), 3:57.

113. *JSA*, Dinya kaZokozwayo (1905, 1908), 1:118. See also ibid., Mmemi kaNguluzane (1904), 3:264.
114. Döhne, *Zulu-Kafir Dictionary*, 189.
115. Colenso, *Zulu-English Dictionary*, 543.
116. *JSA*, Mageza kaKwefunga (1905), 2:70.
117. Ibid., Madikane kaMlomowetole (1903), 2:55.
118. Grout, *The IsiZulu*, xix–xx.
119. *Correspondence between the Committee*, Döhne to Morgan, Table Mountain, 1 July 1854, 57; Döhne, *Zulu-Kafir Dictionary*, xxxviii, xv.
120. *Correspondence between the Committee*, Stone to Morgan, Ifafa, 17 July 1854, 59–61.

7. "MANY PEOPLE . . . EXPLAIN THIS IDENTITY PRIMARILY IN TERMS OF THE LANGUAGE THEY SPEAK"

1. These factors feature prominently in works such as Shula Marks, *The Ambiguities of Dependence in South Africa: Class, Nationalism, and the State in Twentieth-Century Natal, 1913–1933* (Baltimore: Johns Hopkins University Press, 1986); Nicholas Cope, *To Bind the Nation: Solomon kaDinuzulu and Zulu Nationalism, 1913–1933* (Pietermaritzburg: University of Natal Press, 1993); Paul la Hausse de Lalouvière, *Restless Identities: Signatures of Nationalism, Zulu Ethnicity and History in the Lives of Petros Lamula (c. 1881–1948) and Lymong Maling (1889–c. 1936)* (Pietermaritzburg: University of Natal Press, 2000); Wright, "Reflections on the Politics of Being 'Zulu,'" in Carton, Laband, and Sithole *Zulu Identities*, 35–43; Mahoney, *Other Zulus*.
2. La Hausse de Lalouvière, *Restless Identities*, 23, 24, 71, 104; La Hausse de Lalouvière, "'Death Is Not the End': Zulu Cosmopolitanism and the Politics of the Zulu Cultural Revival," in Carton, Laband, and Sithole, *Zulu Identities*, 264, 267.
3. Cope, *To Bind the Nation*, 113.
4. Robert Trent Vinson, *Albert Luthuli* (Athens: Ohio University Press, 2018), 20–21; Harries, "Imagery, Symbolism and Tradition," 112.
5. For the continued focus on "language" see Praisley Mdluli (a.k.a. Emmanuel Bonginkosi Nzimande), "Ubuntu-Botho: Inkatha's 'People's Education,'" *Transformation* 5 (1987): 61; Mangosuthu Buthelezi, King Shaka Day, Stanger, 24 Dec. 1985, as quoted in Harries, "Imagery, Symbolism and Tradition," 123.
6. André Odendaal, *The Founders: The Origins of the ANC and the Struggle for Democracy in South Africa* (Auckland Park: Jacana, 2012), 69, 75, 91, 92; Isaac W. Wauchope, "'Imbumba' Yomfo ka Gaba," *Isigidimi samaXosa*,

1 Nov. 1882, as quoted in Opland and Nyamende, *Isaac Williams Wauchope*, 170, 173.

7. Odendaal, *The Founders*, 152–53, 154–55, 314–15.

8. [Peires], "Ethnicity and Pseudo-Ethnicity," 395–96, 404.

9. Liz Sly, "Zulu King Picks a Bride, and Tongues Wag That She Is Not Really," *Chicago Tribune*, 28 July 1992.

10. Les Switzer, ed., *South Africa's Alternative Press: Voices of Protest and Resistance, 1880–1960* (New York: Cambridge University Press, 1997); Les Switzer and Mohamed Adhikari, eds., *South Africa's Resistance Press: Alternative Voices in the Last Generation under Apartheid* (Athens: Ohio University Press, 2000); Archibald C. Jordan, *Towards an African Literature: The Emergence of Literary Form in Xhosa* (Berkeley: University of California Press, 1973); B. E. N. Mahlasela, *A General Survey of Xhosa Literature from Its Early Beginnings in the 1800s to the Present* (Grahamstown: Dept. of African Languages, Rhodes University, 1973); Albert S. Gérard, *Four African Literatures: Xhosa, Sotho, Zulu, Amharic* (Berkeley: University of California Press, 1971); Patrick Harries, *Work, Culture, and Identity: Migrant Laborers on Mozambique and South Africa, c. 1860–1910* (Portsmouth, NH: Heinemann, 1994).

11. Harries, "Imagery, Symbolism and Tradition," 112.

12. I am basing the review on Leigh Oakes, *Language and National Identity: Comparing France and Sweden* (Philadelphia: John Benjamins, 2001).

13. As quoted in Oakes, *Language and National Identity*, 60.

14. Ibid., 62.

15. As quoted in ibid., 63.

16. Grout, *The IsiZulu*, xix–xx; *Correspondence between the Committee*, L. Grout to Morgan, Umsunduzi, Natal, 20 June 1854, 56.

17. Colenso, *First Steps*, 3.

18. Ibid., 4.

19. Fabian, "Missions," 173.

20. Colenso, *Ten Weeks*, 16–17.

21. NLSA, MSC57/box 9/file 1, W. Bleek, "Preliminaries" (1856).

22. Ibid.

23. Ibid.

24. Grout, *The IsiZulu*, xix.

25. Christofersen, *Adventuring with God*, 128; Welsh, *The Roots of Segregation*, 50.

26. Hughes, *First President*, 12.

27. R. A. Shiels, "John Mavuma Nembula, 1860–1897: First Black Physician in Southern Africa," *Journal of National Medical Association*, 80:11 (1988): 1256–58; Hughes, *First President*, 41–42.

28. Smit, *God Made It Grow*, 215–17; Clement M. Doke, "Scripture Translation into Bantu Languages," *African Studies* 17:2 (1958): 90; E. A. Hermanson, "A Brief Overview of Bible Translation in South Africa," *Acta Theologica Supplementum* 2 (2002): 15.

29. *Annual Report of the American Bible Society* 59 (1911).

30. *Story of the American Bible Society 1916* (New York: American Bible Society, 1916), 140.

31. *Report of the British Foreign Bible Society* (1913), appendix, 31.

32. Ibid., 1930, appendix A, 19.

33. Marks, *The Ambiguities of Dependence in South Africa*, 112.

34. C. M. Doke, "The Linguistic Situation in South Africa," *Africa: Journal of the International African Institute* 1:4 (Oct. 1928): 480. On Fuze's work see especially Hlonipha Mokoena, *Magema Fuze: The Making of a Kholwa Intellectual* (Pietermaritzburg: University of KwaZulu-Natal Press, 2011).

35. Doke, "The Linguistic Situation," 479.

36. Ibid. My emphasis.

37. BSA/E3/1/4, Copybook 4, Rev. R. Lamplough to Appleyard, 17 Aug. 1866, 233.

38. BSA/E3/1/4, Copybook 5, Appleyard to Bergne, Mount Coke, 11 Dec. 1866, 14.

39. Multiple testimonies in [Tiyo Soga et al.], *The Kafir Bible: Rev. J. W. Appleyard's Version Judged by Missionaries*.

40. Donovan Williams, ed., *The Journal and Selected Writings of The Reverend Tiyo Soga* (Cape Town: Balkema, 1983), 1–5; Janet Hodgson, "Soga and Dukwana: The Christian Struggle for Liberation in Mid-19th Century South Africa," *Journal of Religion in Africa* 16:3 (Oct, 1986): 189–90.

41. [Tiyo Soga et al.], *The Kafir Bible: Rev. J. W. Appleyard's Version Judged by Missionaries*, 7–8.

42. Soga to Bryce Ross, 26 June 1870, as quoted in Joanne Ruth Davis, *Tiyo Soga: A Literary History* (Pretoria: University of South Africa Press, 2018), 181.

43. National Library of Scotland, Dep.298, Church of Scotland Overseas Council, 64. United Presbyterian Church Mission Board, 29 Dec. 1868, 256.

44. CL, Methodist Church of South Africa Archives, MS15192 Queenstown District, Minutes of the Native District Meeting, 10–16 Jan. 1879, 103.

45. WMM (Sept. 1879), 704.

46. BSA/E3/1/4, Copybook 18, A. E. Howse to W. Finch, 27 Nov. 1883, 272–74.

47. BSA/E3/1/4, Copybook 27, Albert Kropf, Stutterheim, 11 Dec. 1890, 98; and Copybook 29, Albert Kropf, Stutterheim, 13 July 1892, 256.

48. BSA/E3/1/4, E. J. Barrett to Mr. Curnick, Buntingville, 27 Nov. 1908.

49. BSA/E3/1/4, Charles Pamla to Rev. Theo R. Curnick, superintendent of the Wesleyan Native Training Institute at Emfundisweni, Pondoland, date unknown but probably 1908.

50. BSA/E3/3, Correspondence (Language Files), 614/1 Xhosa 1 (hereafter BSA/E3/3), Summary of interview with J. Tengo Jabavu, 24 Aug. 1909.

51. BSA/E3/1/4, Copybook 29, Albert Kropf, Stutterheim, 13 July 1892, 257.

52. BSA/E3/3, Rubusana to Rev. Van der Merwe, agent, BFBS Cape Town, East London, 16 Apr. 1914.

53. MMS/SA/mf 301, William Shaw, Wesleyville, 31 Mar. 1827.

54. CL, MS9039, PKM, Lovedale, 2 Apr. 1857.

55. CL, MS8082, Bryce Ross to Dr. Duff, Pirie, 11 Dec. 1866.

56. I borrow the terminology from Davidson Don Tengo Jabavu, who wrote about this "Xhosa-Fingo animosity" in 1935. See his article "The 'Fingo Slavery' Myth," *The South African Outlook* 65 (1 June 1935): 123.

57. [Peires], "Ethnicity and Pseudo-Ethnicity," 398.

58. Ibid.

59. Odendaal, *The Founders*, 145, 152–53; Stanley Trapido, "African Divisional Politics in the Cape Colony, 1884–1910," *Journal of African History* 9:1 (1968): 80–81.

60. Silwangangubo, "Isikumbuzo saba Mbo. Umbulelo ku Mhleli," *Imvo*, 10 June 1913, 3, as quoted in Opland and Nyamende, *Isaac Williams Wauchope*, 218; Edgar, *Finger of God*, 17; Odendaal, *The Founders*, 154–55.

61. CL, MS14760, Samuel E. K. Mqhayi, "A Short Autobiography," 18.

62. Ibid.

63. BSA/E3/3, summary of interview with J. Tengo Jabavu.

64. Ibid.

65. South African Bible Society Archive (Belleville), MIC 201.42.4 (Xhosa, 1913–14), Canon Cyril Wyche to Rev. Vernon Bird, 12 Apr. 1913.

66. Ibid., Rev. R. Kilgour, superintendent of the Translation Department of the BFBS, to Rev. D. B. Davies, 7 Aug. 1913.

67. BSA/E3/3, ESC Minutes, 2 July 1924, 14 (copy).

68. Department of Public Education, Cape of Good Hope, *The Native Primary School: Suggestions for the Consideration of Teachers* (Cape Town: Cape Times Limited, 1929), 147; Albert Kropf and Robert Godfrey, *A Kafir-English Dictionary*, 2nd ed. (Lovedale: Lovedale Mission Press, 1915); John Bunyan, *Uhambo lomhambi: Owesuka kweli lizwe, waye esinga kwelo lizayo*, trans. Tiyo Soga and John Henderson Soga (Lovedale: Lovedale Mission Press, 1866, 1929).

69. Doke, "The Linguistic Situation," 479.

70. Harries, *Work, Culture, and Identity*, 63.

71. Switzer, *South Africa's Alternative Press*, 1–2, 10; Donald L. Horowitz, *A Democratic South Africa? Constitutional Emergency in a Divided Society* (Berkeley: University of California Press, 1991), 232.

72. *Census of the British Empire 1901. Report with Summary and Detailed Tables* (London: Darling and Son, 1906), 147, 167.

73. Ibid.; Thompson, *A History of South Africa*, 148.

74. Mahmood Mamdani, *Citizen and Subject: Contemporary Africa and the Legacy of Late Colonialism* (Princeton, NJ: Princeton University Press, 2018), 63.

75. Ibid.

76. Odendaal, *The Founders*, 160.

77. Mamdani, *Citizen and Subject*, 70; Odendaal, *The Founders*, 160.

78. Richard Elphick, *The Equality of Believers: Protestant Missionaries and the Racial Politics of South Africa* (Charlottesville: University of Virginia Press, 2012), 202.

79. Thompson, *A History of South Africa*, 150.

80. Th. G. Renkewitz, *Mission-Schools: Their Difficulties, and How to Overcome Them*. Paper read at the Teachers' Conference in Cape Town (Genadendal, 1896), 3; USPG, E/59a, Rev. F. D. Binyon, St. Matthew's College, Keikammahoek, 1904; Thompson, *A History of South Africa*, 98–99; Welsh, *The Roots of Segregation*, 49, 268; Switzer, *Power and Resistance*, 131–33.

81. Michael Ashley, "African Education and Society in the Nineteenth-Century Eastern Cape," in Christopher Saunders and Robin Derricourt, eds., *Beyond the Cape Frontier: Studies in the History of the Transkei and Ciskei* (London: Longman, 1974), 201.

82. John Philip, *A Letter from the Rev. John Philip, D.D., Superintendent of the Missions of the London Society at the Cape of Good Hope to the Society of Inquiry on Missions in Theological Seminary, Princeton, New Jersey* (Princeton, NJ: John Gray, 1833), John Philip to J. B. Purney, Cape Town, 2 May 1833, 22.

83. As quoted in Christofersen, *Adventuring with God*, 38.

84. Ashley, "African Education and Society," 208–9.

85. Christofersen, *Adventuring with God*, 39.

86. Andrew John Moore, "Natal's 'Native' Education (1917–1953): Education for Segregation" (master's thesis, University of Natal, 1990), 34, 37.

87. Switzer, *Power and Resistance*, 132.

88. Ibid.

89. R. H. Davis, "Nineteenth-Century African Education in the Cape Colony: A Historical Analysis" (PhD diss., University of Wisconsin–Madison, 1969), as quoted in Switzer, *Power and Resistance*, 133.

90. Cape Parliamentary Papers, *Report and Proceedings with Appendices, of the Government Commission on Native Laws and Customs* (Cape Town: W. A. Richards and Sons, Government Printers, 1883), appendix H, Native Education, 391.

91. Hughes, *First President,* 27.

92. Moore, "Natal's 'Native' Education," 29.

93. Union of South Africa, *Report of the Interdepartmental Committee on Native Education, 1935-1936* (Pretoria: Government Printer, 1936), 19-20.

94. USPG, E/36, J. Blain, Durban, 31 Dec. 1881.

95. Welsh, *The Roots of Segregation,* 49, 268, 271.

96. Harries, "Imagery, Symbolism and Tradition," 111-12.

97. La Hausse de Lalouvière, *Restless Identities,* 37-40.

98. Ibid., 40.

99. Petrus Lamula, *UZulu kaMalandela: a Most Practical and Concise Compendium of African History Combined with Genealogy, Chronology, Geography and Biography* (Durban: Star Printing Works, 1924), ch. 16, 21, as quoted in La Hausse de Lalouvière, *Restless Identities,* 104.

100. *RGMS,* 1837, 26.

101. Ayliff, *Journal of John Ayliff,* Wesleyville, 8 Dec. 1826, 65.

102. CL, MS15252, diary of Shrewsbury, 23 Sept.1827, 25.

103. *RWM* (1831), 54.

104. BMW, 1/5163, Correspondenz mit den Missionaren (1852-1861), Statistik Bethel, 1857?; National Library of Scotland, Acc.7548, Church of Scotland, D.80, [handwritten] Report on the State of the African Mission of the Free Church, James Stuart, Dec. 1863, 4, 12.

105. CA, Superintendent General of Education (SGE), Miscellaneous Papers Received from Deputy Inspectors, 3.4 East Transkei, vol. 3 (1873-1878), O. H. Hogarth, deputy inspector, *Eastern Districts and Transkeian Territory: Report on Schools Inspected during the Quarter ended 30th June, 1873* (Cape Town: Saul Solomon, 1873), xi-xii.

106. Ibid., xiii-xiv.

107. CA, SGE, Inspectors' Reports, 2.5, Native Territories, vol. 5, 1893.

108. Davis, "Nineteenth-Century African Education," as quoted in Switzer, *Power and Resistance,* 133.

109. Cape Parliamentary Papers, *Report and Proceedings,* appendix H, Native Education, 391.

110. Odendaal, *The Founders,* 259-67.

111. John Scott Keltie and M. Epstein, *The Stateman's Yearbook: Statistical and Historical Annual of the States of the World for the Year 1918* (London: Macmillan, 1918), 202; Odendaal, *The Founders,* 355-63.

112. Mamdani, *Citizen and Subject,* 71-72.

113. Thompson, *A History of South Africa*, 163–64.

114. Ibid., 166; Tom Lodge, *Black Politics in South Africa since 1945* (Johannesburg: Ravan, 1983), 11–12.

115. J. E. Holloway, R. W. Anderson, F. A. W. Lucas, A. M. Mostert, A. W. Roberts, P. W. le Roux Van Niekerk, C. Faye, *Report of Native Economic Commission 1930–1932* (Pretoria: Government Printer, 1932), 87.

116. Ibid., 95. Also see Union of South Africa, *Report of the Interdepartmental Committee on Native Education, 1935–1936*, 87–89.

117. Ibid., 81.

118. Ibid., 38.

119. Moore, "Natal's 'Native' Education,"103.

120. Ibid., 114.

121. Ibid., 74.

122. CA, SGE, Inspectors' Reports, 2.599, Matatiele, 1923.

123. CA, SGE, Inspectors' Reports, 2.603, Mount Fletcher, 1923.

124. Samuel Baudert, "Die Kaffernschulen der Herrnhuter Mission," in *Die evangelischen Missionen: Illustriertes Familienblatt* 36 (Berlin: D. Julius Richter, 1930), 203; Walther Bourquin, *Bruder Mensch: 41 Jahre Herrnhuter Mission in Südafrika* (Hamburg: Ludwig Appel Verlag, 1967), 83.

125. J. T. Kenyon (accountant of the United Transkeian Territories General Council), "An Address on the General Council Administrative System of the Transkeian Territories at the University of Stellenbosch 12–14 Oct 1932," *Territorial News* (Umtata,1932), 20.

126. Department of Public Education, Cape of Good Hope, *The Native Primary School*, 149.

127. Ibid.; Doke, "Vernacular Text-Books in South African Native Schools," *Africa: Journal of the International African Institute*, 8:2 (Apr. 1935), 184–85.

128. Doke, "Vernacular Text-Books," 192.

129. Ibid., 193–94.

130. Welsh, *The Roots of Segregation*, 271; Moore, "Natal's 'Native' Education," 51, 99; Union of South Africa, *Report of the Interdepartmental Committee on Native Education, 1935–1936*, 139.

131. I thank Robert Edgar for bringing Mda's example to my attention.

132. Robert Edgar and Luyanda ka Msumza, eds., *Africa's Triumph: The Collected Writings of A. P. Mda* (Cape Town: Best Red, 2018), 6.

133. Ibid., 11–12.

134. Ibid., 99.

135. Charles H. Feinstein, *An Economic History of South Africa: Conquest, Discrimination and Development* (New York: Cambridge University Press, 2005), 259; National Party Minister of Native Affairs Hendrik F. Verwoerd

(1950), as quoted in John A. Williams, ed., *From the South African Past: Narratives, Documents, and Debates* (New York: Houghton Mifflin, 1997), 254.

136. Union of South Africa, *Report of the Commission on Native Education, 1949–1951* (Pretoria: Government Printer, 1951), 7. The commission members were Werner Willie M. Eiselen (chairman), P. A. W. Cook, Gustav Bernard Gerdener, Jan de W. Keyter, John Macleod, A. H. Murray, and Michael Daniel Christiaan de Wet Nel. See Cynthia Kros, *The Seeds of Separate Development: Origins of Bantu Education* (Pretoria: Unisa Press, 2010), 95–96.

137. Union of South Africa, *Report of the Commission on Native Education, 1949–1951*, 9.

138. Ibid.

139. Cynthia Kros, "W. W. M. Eiselen: Architect of Apartheid Education," in *The History of Education Under Apartheid, 1948–1994: The Doors of Learning and Culture Shall be Opened*, ed. Peter Kallaway (Cape Town: Pearson Education South Africa, 2002), 58; Pugach, *Africa in Translation*, 179–85.

140. Union of South Africa, *Report of the Commission on Native Education, 1949–1951*, 157.

141. For contemporary critiques of language-based Zulu identity see, for example, Ashley Parcells, "Ethnic Sovereignty and the Making of a Zulu Homeland in Apartheid South Africa" (PhD diss., Emory University, 2018), 98.

142. Union of South Africa, *Report of the Commission on Native Education, 1949–1951*, 146; Ken Hartshorne, "Language Policy in African Education: A Background to the Future," in *Language and Social History: Studies in South African Sociolinguistics*, ed. Rajend Mesthrie (Cape Town: David Philip, 1995), 310.

143. Brian Rose and Raymond Tunmer, eds., *Documents in South African Education* (Johannesburg: AD Donker Publisher, 1975), 258.

144. Moore, "Natal's 'Native' Education," 131.

145. *Bantu Education Journal* 1:8 (July 1955): 269, 272–73, 242, as quoted in Moore, "Natal's 'Native' Education," 134, 135, 132.

146. *Bantu Education Journal* 1:2 (Dec. 1954): 11.

147. Jason C. Myers, *Indirect Rule in South Africa: Tradition, Modernity, and the Costuming of Political Power* (Rochester, NY: University of Rochester Press, 2008), 32–33. The date reflects when KwaZulu was granted a legislative assembly.

148. A. O. Jackson, *The Ethnic Composition of the Ciskei and Transkei* (Pretoria: Government Printer, 1975), 1–2.

149. Ibid., 1.
150. Ibid., 3.
151. Feinstein, *An Economic History of South Africa*, 160; Thompson, *A History of South Africa*, 196.
152. Mathabane, *Kaffir Boy*, 126–29.
153. Hartshorne, "Language Policy in African Education," 311.
154. Rose and Tunmer, *Documents in South African Education*, 194.
155. Ibid., 197.
156. Ibid., 311.
157. Ibid.
158. Timothy G. Reagan, "The Politics of Linguistic Apartheid: Language Policies in Black Education in South Africa," *Journal of Negro Education* 56:3 (Summer 1987): 300. For "official homeland languages" see, for instance, Republic of South Africa, *Natal Government Gazette*, no. 5387, Proclamation no. R11, 28 Jan. 1977; and Republic of the Transkei Constitution Act no. 15 of 1976, chapter 3, 230, https://www.worldstatesmen.org/Transkei_Constitution.pdf.
159. Mdluli, "Ubuntu-Botho," 61.
160. Ibid., 62, 63, 64.
161. Wouter De Vos Malan, ed., *Handbook of Suggestions for Teachers in Native Primary Schools* (Cape Town: Department of Public Education, Cape of Good Hope, 1952).
162. Ibid., 71.
163. Ibid., 70.
164. Ibid.
165. *Bantu Education Journal* 1:2 (Dec. 1954): 12.
166. Vuyokazi S. Nomlomo, "Language Variation in the Transkeian Xhosa Speech Community and Its Impact on Children's Education" (master's thesis, University of Cape Town, 1993), 97, 109, 104.
167. Kubeka, "A Preliminary Survey of Zulu Dialects in Natal and Zululand," 34; De Haas and Zulu, "Ethnicity and Federalism," 439.
168. Dingani Mthethwa, "The Mobilization of History and the Tembe Chieftaincy in Maputaland, 1896–1997" (master's thesis, University of Natal-Durban, 2002), 132–33.
169. David Webster, "*Abafazi Bathonga Bafihlakala*: Ethnicity and Gender in a KwaZulu Border Community," in Andrew Spiegel and Patrick A. McAllister, eds., *Tradition and Transition in Southern Africa* (London: Transaction, 1992), 253–54.
170. [Peires], "Ethnicity and Pseudo-Ethnicity," 395–96, 404.
171. Moodie with Ndatshe, *Going for Gold*, 206–7.

172. Sithole, "Preface: Zuluness in South Africa," xvii; Patrick Harries, "History, Ethnicity and the Ngwavuma Land Deal: The Zulu Northern Frontier in the Nineteenth Century," *Journal of Natal and Zulu History* 6 (1983): 19.

EPILOGUE

1. Carton, Laband, and Sithole, *Zulu Identities*; Mahoney, *Other Zulus*; Hamilton and Leibhammer, *Tribing and Untribing the Archive*.
2. Buthelezi, "The Empire Talks Back," 24.
3. Sithole, "Preface: Zuluness in South Africa," xii–xx. See also Mbongiseni Buthelezi, "'*Sifuna umlando wethu*' (We are Looking for Our History): Oral Literature and the Meanings of the Past in Post-Apartheid South Africa" (PhD diss., Columbia University, 2012); Grant McNulty, "Custodianship on the Periphery: Archives, Power and Identity Politics in Post-Apartheid Umbumbulu, KwaZulu-Natal" (PhD diss., University of Cape Town, 2013).
4. John B. Wright and Andrew Manson, *The Hlubi Chiefdom in Zululand-Natal: A History* (Ladysmith, Natal: Ladysmith Historical Society, 1983), 4.
5. Ibid., 9.
6. Ibid., 13–20.
7. Ibid., 15.
8. Ibid., 20.
9. Ibid., 38.
10. Center for Law and Society, "Land Rights under the Ingonyama Trust" (Feb. 2015), 1, http://www.cls.uct.ac.za/usr/lrg/downloads/Factsheet Ingonyama_Final_Feb2015.pdf; Hilary Lynd, "Secret Details of the Land Deal That Brought the IFP into the 94 Poll," *Mail & Guardian* (7 Aug. 2019).
11. KwaZulu-Natal Traditional Leadership and Governance Act 5 (2005), section 17 (1); *Department of Traditional Affairs, Strategic Plan 2015–2020* (Pretoria: Department of Traditional Affairs, 2016), 24.
12. J. C. Bekker, "The Establishment of Kingdoms and the Identification of Kings and Queens in Terms of the Traditional Leadership and Governance Framework Act 41 of 2003," *Potchefstroomse Elektroniese Regsblad/ Potchefstroom Electronic Law Journal* 11:3 (2008): 27.
13. AmaHlubi National Coordinating Committee, "Program of Action to Revive and Strengthen the Hlubi Nation in South Africa" (2004), http://www.mkhangelingoma.co.za/heritage/POA.pdf.
14. A. Hlongwane, "Twelve Kings Saga Sparks KZN War Talk," *Independent Online*, 8 July 2007. Also Sithole, "Preface: Zuluness in South Africa," xvi.

15. *Nhlapo Commission Report (Reports for Paramountcies): Determination on the AmaHlubi Kingship Claim* (July 2010), 494, 500–502, https://static.pmg.org.za/docs/100729determination-chiefs.pdf.

16. Interview, Jobe Radebe, Spokesperson of the AmaHlubi National Working Committee, Johannesburg, 7 July 2017.

17. "Case No. 37875/2011, Inkosi Muziwenkosi Johannes Radebe vs. Commission on Traditional Leadership Disputes and Claims and 6 Others," in *Department of Traditional Affairs, Strategic Plan 2015–2020*, 18; Sandile Motha, "AmaHlubi Battle for Kingship Burns Bright," *Sunday World*, 26 Jan. 2021.

18. AmaHlubi National Coordinating Committee, "Program of Action to Revive and Strengthen the Hlubi Nation in South Africa" (2004).

19. AmaHlubi Amahle, "AmaHlubi National Youth Working Committee Constitution," Facebook, 11 July 2014, https://www.facebook.com/permalink.php?id=169290819757816&story_fbid=809061252447433.

20. AmaHlubi Amahle, "Story," Facebook, 23 Nov. 2010, https://www.facebook.com/pg/AmaHlubi-Amahle-169290819757816/about/?ref=page_internal.

21. AmaHlubi Amahle, Facebook, 11 Apr. 2014, https://www.facebook.com/permalink.php?story_fbid=756604674359758&id=169290819757816. I thank Dr. B. Mini for helping me with translating this and other passages in the article.

22. Abner Nyamende, "Regional Variation in Xhosa," *Stellenbosch Papers in Linguistics Plus* 26 (1994): 207; Herbert W. Pahl, *IsiXhosa* (Johannesburg: Educum, 1983), 263.

23. Nomlomo, "Language Variation," 55; Charles Roberts, *An English-Zulu Dictionary* (London: Paul, Trench, Truebner, 1904), xi.

24. Nyamende, "Regional Variation," 207; Archibald C. Jordan, "A Phonological and Literary Study of Literary Xhosa" (PhD diss., University of Cape Town, 1956), 192; Bryant, *A Zulu-English Dictionary*, 466; Nomlomo, "Language Variation," 54.

25. Robert Herbert and Richard Bailey, "The Bantu Languages: Sociohistorical Perspectives," in *Language in South Africa*, ed. Rajend Mesthrie (New York: Cambridge University Press, 2004), 67.

26. Makoni, "From Misinvention to Disinvention of Language," 134, 138; Nomlomo, "Language Variation," 6–7, 15–18.

27. Constitution of the Republic of South Africa (1996), chapter 1: Founding Provisions, Section 6 (2), https://www.gov.za/documents/constitution-republic-south-africa-1996.

28. Ibid., Section 6 (1).

29. Republic of South Africa, Language in Education Policy in Terms of Section 3(4)(m) of The National Education Policy Act, 1996 (Act 27 of 1996), https://www.education.gov.za/Portals/0/Documents/Policies/GET/LanguageEducationPolicy1997.pdf.

30. Interview, Sanele Godlo, member of the IsiHlubi Language Board, Johannesburg, 23 June 2017.

31. Nomlomo, "Language Variation," 91–92, 97, 104, 109.

32. Interview, Bandile Nodada, member of the IsiHlubi Language Board, Johannesburg, 23 June 2017 .

33. Interview, Jobe Radebe, spokesperson of the AmaHlubi National Working Committee, Johannesburg, 7 July 2017.

34. Lwazi Mntungwa, "The History of the Hlubi Nation," 30 Mar. 2016, http://www.vivmag.co.za/archives/3395.

35. Liviwe Lloydie Ntlola, AmaHlubi Amahle, Facebook, 5 Feb. 2014, https://www.facebook.com/permalink.php?story_fbid=720622794624613&id=169290819757816; ibid., 12 Apr. 2014, https://www.facebook.com/permalink.php?story_fbid=756604674359758&id=169290819757816.

36. AmaHlubi Amahle, Facebook, 11 Apr. 2014, https://www.facebook.com/permalink.php?story_fbid=756604674359758&id=169290819757816.

37. Mveliso Velida Mhlati Wolker and Nkosinathi Jozi, AmaHlubi Amahle, Facebook, 12 Apr. 2014, https://www.facebook.com/permalink.php?story_fbid=756604674359758&id=169290819757816.

38. AmaHlubi National Working Committee, AmaHlubi Royal Committee, and AmaHlubi King's Planning Committee, "*Isizwe SamaHlubi*," draft 1 (July 2004), https://pdf4pro.com/view/isizwe-samahlubi-mkhangeli-ngoma-194f95.html.

39. AmaHlubi Amahle, "AmaHlubi National Youth Working Committee Constitution," Facebook, 11 July 2014, https://www.facebook.com/permalink.php?id=169290819757816&story_fbid=809061252447433.

40. Ibid.

41. Interview, Sanele Godlo, member of the IsiHlubi Language Board, Johannesburg, 23 June 2017. As of 2021, the struggle for recognition of Hlubi as an official language is still ongoing. See Sandile Motha, "AmaHlubi Battle for Autonomy Gathers Steam," *Sunday World*, 8 June 2021.

• BIBLIOGRAPHY •

UNPUBLISHED MANUSCRIPTS AND ARCHIVAL SOURCES

American Board of Commissioners for Foreign Missions Archives, Houghton Library, Harvard University, Cambridge, Massachusetts (ABC)

76 Personal Papers: James C. Bryant and Lewis Grout

Papers of the Board of Commissioners for Foreign Missions, Microfilm, Reels 175, 176, 180

Berliner Missionswerk, Berlin (BMW)

1/5163, Correspondenz mit den Missionaren (1852–61)

Bible Society Archives, University of Cambridge (BSA)

D1/2, Records of the Secretaries, Foreign Correspondence Inwards

E3/1/4, Records of the Editorial/Translation Department, Editorial Correspondence Inwards

E3/3, Correspondence (Language Files), 614/1 Xhosa 1

Bodleian Library of Commonwealth and African Studies, Rhodes House, Oxford, Papers of the United Society for the Propagation of the Gospel (USPG)

E Series, Missionaries' Reports, 1867–1904

Cory Library for Historical Research, Rhodes University, Grahamstown, South Africa (CL)

MS1109, Diary of John Ayliff (1820–31)

MS2642, Letters of Mrs Ross (1824)

MS3203, 3170, 3572, 8091, 8116 John Ross Papers (1825–68)

MS9037–9039, Presbytery of Kaffraria Minutes (1824–53)

MS15023, Minutes of the District Meeting at Grahamstown (1846)

MS15192, Queenstown District, Minutes of Native & European Meetings (1876–86)
MS15543.1, John Ayliff, "Sketch of Fingo History"
MS15543.2, John Ayliff Papers, "Narrative of Fingo History" (typescript)
MS15252, Diary of William J. Shrewsbury, 1826–35 (typescript)
MS16369, T. B. Soga, MS "Intlalo KaXosa/The Origin of Xhosa" (1917)
MS17038, George Cory Notebooks

Killie-Campbell Africana Library, Durban, South Africa

KCM47614, Rev. Robert Godfrey, "Rev. John Bennie, the Father of Kafir Literature" (1934)
KCM89/36/1/1, Diary of Joseph Kirkman (1826–40)

Natal Archives, Pietermaritzburg, South Africa (PMB)
American Board Mission Collection (A), A608
A/1/1, Minutes of Committee Meetings, 1837–1860
A/2/10, Correspondence Received, general, 1835–1900
A/3/34, Correspondence Dispatched, general, 1835–1930
Natal Colonial Publications, 1845–1910
6/1/1/6, *The Natal Government Gazette*, 1855
Secretary of Native Affairs
I/8/5, Letter Book, 1851–55

National Library of Scotland, Edinburgh

Acc. 7548, Church of Scotland, D.80 (1853)
Dep. 298, Church of Scotland Overseas Council, 64 United Presbyterian Church Mission Board (1871)

National Library of South Africa, Manuscript Collection, Cape Town, South Africa (NLSA)

MSB435, Journal of William Shaw, 1820–29 (typescript)
MSC39, Methodist Church Collection
Box 28 (4), Henry H. Dugmore, Journal (1834–42)
Box 34 (10), Autobiographical Notes by Charles Pamla
MSC57, Wilhelm Bleek Collection
Box 9 (1), "Zulu & Se-Tsuana," includes "Preliminaries to a Grammar of the Zulu Language" (1856)

School of Oriental and African Studies, Special Collections, London

Council for World Mission, London Missionary Society Archive
Box 7–13, South Africa, Incoming Correspondence (1817–33)

Methodist Missionary Society Archives
Correspondence South Africa, Albany (1825–57), microfiches

Special Collections and University Archives,
University of Massachusetts Amherst Libraries

MS 797, Aldin Grout Papers

South African Bible Society Archive,
Belleville, South Africa

MIC 201.42.4 (Xhosa, 1913–14)

University of Cape Town Libraries,
Cape Town, South Africa

Manuscript BC 350, W. Fehr, MS Ludwig Alberti (1807)

Western Cape Archives and Records, Cape Town, South Africa (CA)

Accessions (Acc)

A558, Journal of Rev. William J. Davis
A680, Short Biography of Johann Heinrich Albert Kropf (in English)

Superintendent General of Education (SGE)

Miscellaneous Papers Received from Deputy Inspectors, 1872–1912
Inspectors' Reports, 1893–1923

INTERVIEWS BY AUTHOR

Godlo, Sanele. Member of the IsiHlubi Language Board. Johannesburg, 23 June 2017.
Nodada, Bandile. Member of the IsiHlubi Language Board. Johannesburg, 23 June 2017.
Radebe, Jobe. Spokesperson of the AmaHlubi National Working Committee. Johannesburg, 7 July 2017.

PUBLISHED PRIMARY SOURCES

Alberti, Ludwig. *Ludwig Alberti's Account of the Tribal Life & Customs of the Xhosa in 1807.* Translated by William Fehr. Cape Town: Balkema, 1968.
Appleyard, John. *An Apology for the Kafir Bible: Being a Reply to the Pamphlet Entitled, "Rev. J. W. Appleyard's Version Judged by Missionaries of Various Denominations and Others."* Mount Coke: Wesleyan Mission Press, 1867.
———. "The Kaffir Dialects." *South African Christian Watchman, and Missionary Magazine* (1847).

———. *The Kafir Language: Comprising a Sketch of Its History; Which Includes a General Classification of South African Dialects, Ethnographical and Geographical: Remarks upon Its Nature, and a Grammar.* King William's Town: Wesleyan Missionary Society, 1850.

———. *The War of the Axe and the Xhosa Bible: The Journal of the Rev. J. W. Appleyard.* Edited by John Frye. Cape Town: Struik, 1971.

Archbell, James. *A Grammar of the Bechuana Language.* Grahamstown: Meurant and Godlonton, 1837.

Ayliff, John. *A Vocabulary of the Kafir Language.* London: Wesleyan Mission House, 1846.

———. *The Journal of John Ayliff.* Vol. 1, *1821–30*, edited by Peter Hinchliff. Cape Town: Balkema, 1971.

Ayliff, John, and Joseph Whiteside. *History of the Abambo, Generally Known as the Fingos.* Butterworth: Transkei Gazette, 1912.

Backhouse, James. *Extracts from the Letters of James Backhouse, Whilst Engaged in a Religious Visit to Van Dieman's Land, New South Wales, and South Africa, Accompanied by George Washington Walker.* Vol. 2. London: Harvey and Darton, 1842.

———. *A Narrative of a Visit to the Mauritius and South Africa.* London: Hamilton, Adams, 1844.

Balfour, Robert (Noyi Gciniswa). "Appendix II. Ama-Xosa History by Robert Balfour Noyi: A Follower." Translated by John Bennie. In *Ntsikana: The Story of an African Convert,* edited by John Knox Bokwe, 2nd ed., 36–39. Lovedale: Mission Press, 1914.

Barros, João de. *Década Primeira: Da Asia de João de Barros.* Lisbon: Jorge Rodriguez, 1628.

Barrow, John. *An Account of Travels into the Interior of Southern Africa, in the Years 1797 and 1798.* 2 vols. London: Cadell and Davies, 1801, 1804.

———. *A Voyage to Cochinchina in the Years 1792 and 1793.* London: Cadell and Davies, 1806.

Battuta, Ibn. *Ibn Battuta in Black Africa.* Edited and translated by Saïd Hamdun and Noël King. Princeton, NJ: Markus Wiener, 2003.

Baudert, Samuel. "Die Kaffernschulen der Herrnhuter Mission." In *Die evangelischen Missionen: Illustriertes Familienblatt* 36 (Berlin: D. Julius Richter, 1930): 201–7.

Benes, J. (Giovanni) Botero. *Relaciones universales del mundo.* Translated by D. de Aguiar. Valladolid: Diego Fernandez de Cordova, 1603.

Bird, John, ed. *The Annals of Natal, 1495–1845.* 2 vols. Pietermaritzburg: Davis, 1888.

Bleek, Wilhelm E. *A Comparative Grammar of South African Languages.* London: Trübner, 1862.

———. *The Library of His Excellency Sir George Grey, Philology.* Vol. 1. Leipzig: Brockhaus, 1858.

———. *The Natal Diaries of Dr. W. H. I. Bleek, 1855–1856.* Edited by O. H. Spohr. Cape Town: Gothic, 1965.

Boteler, Thomas. *A Narrative of a Voyage of Discovery to Africa and Arabia, Performed by His Majesty's Ships* Leven *and* Barracouta, *from 1821 to 1826, under the Command of Capt. F. W. Owen, R.N.* 2 vols. London: Richard Bentley, 1835.

Bourquin, Walther. *Bruder Mensch: 41 Jahre Herrnhuter Mission in Südafrika.* Hamburg: Ludwig Appel Verlag, 1967.

Boxer, Charles, ed. and trans. *The Tragic History of the Sea, 1589–1622: Narratives of the Shipwrecks of the Portuguese East Indiamen* São Thomé *(1589),* Santo Alberto *(1593),* São João Baptista *(1622), and the Journeys of the Survivors in South East Africa.* New York: Cambridge University Press, 1959.

Boyce, William. *A Grammar of the Kafir Language.* Grahamstown: Wesleyan Mission Press, 1834.

———. *Memoir of the Rev. William Shaw, Late General Superintendent of the Wesleyan Missions in South-Eastern Africa.* London: Wesleyan Conference Office, 1874.

———. *Notes on South African Affairs from 1834 to 1838.* Grahamstown: Aldum and Harvey, 1838.

Brownlee, Charles P. *Reminiscences of Kaffir Life and History, and Other Papers.* Lovedale: Lovedale Mission Press, 1896.

Bryant, Alfred T. *A Zulu-English Dictionary.* Pinetown: Mariannhill Mission Press, 1905.

Bryant, James. "The Zulu Language." *Journal of the American Oriental Society* 1:4 (1849): 383, 385–96.

Buffon, Georges-Louis Leclerc, Comte de. *Histoire naturelle.* Vol. 3. Paris: L'Imprimerie Royale, 1750.

Bunyan, John. *Uhambo lomhambi: Owesuka kweli lizwe, waye esinga kwelo lizayo.* Translated by Tiyo Soga and John Henderson Soga. Lovedale: Lovedale Mission Press, 1866, 1929.

Caille, Nicolas Louis de la. *Journal Historique du Voyage fait au Cap de Bonne-Espérance.* Paris: Guillyn, 1763.

Cape Parliamentary Papers. *Report and Proceedings with Appendices, of the Government Commission on Native Laws and Customs.* Cape Town: W. A. Richards and Sons, Government Printers, 1883.

Casalis, Eugène. *Études sur la Langue Séchuana.* Paris: L'Imprimerie Royale, 1841.

Census of the British Empire 1901. Report with Summary and Detailed Tables. London: Darling and Son, 1906.

Chase, John Cenlivres. *The Cape of Good Hope and the Eastern Province of Algoa Bay, with Statistics of the Colony.* Edited by Joseph S. Christophers. London: Richardson, 1848.

Chaumont, Alexandre (chevalier de). *Relation de l'ambasssade de Mr. le Chevalier de Chaumont a la Cour du Roy de Siam, Avec qui s'est passé de plus remarquable durant son voyage.* Amsterdam: Mortier, 1686.

Colenso, John. *First Steps in Zulu: Being an Elementary Grammar of the Zulu Language.* 4th ed. Maritzburg: P. Davis, 1890.

———. *Ten Weeks in Natal: Journal of a First Tour of Visitation among the Colonists and Zulu Kafirs of Natal.* Cambridge: Macmillan, 1855.

———. *Zulu-English Dictionary.* 2nd ed. Natal: P. Davis, 1884.

Copy of Minutes of Proceedings of the Court of Inquiry, Held at Fort Wilshire, in the Months of August and September, 1836, to Investigate and Report upon the Circumstances Attendant on the Fate of the Caffer Chief Hintza. Cape Town: Brand's, 1837.

Correspondence between the Committee of the South African Auxiliary Bible Society and Various Missionaries and Others, Relative to the Translation, Printing, and Circulation of the Scriptures in the Native Languages of South Africa, and More Especially in the Kafir Dialect; with the Resolutions of the Committee Thereupon. Cape Town: Pike's, 1857.

Cory, George, ed. *The Diary of the Rev. Francis Owen, M.A., Missionary with Dingaan in 1837–38. Together with Extracts from the Writings of the Interpreters in Zulu, Messrs. Hulley and Kirkman.* Cape Town: Van Riebeeck Society, 1926.

———. *The Rise of South Africa.* 6 vols. London: Longmans, 1910–40.

Crampton, Hazel, Jeff Peires, and Carl Vernon, eds. *Into the Hitherto Unknown: Ensign Beutler's Expedition to the Eastern Cape, 1752.* Translated by Thea Toussaint van Hove and Michael Wilson. Cape Town: Van Riebeeck Society, 2013.

D'Abbeville, Nicolas Sanson. *L'Afrique en plusieurs cartes nouvelles et exactes et en divers traicte's de géographie, et d'histoire.* Paris, 1656.

Davis, William J. *A Dictionary of the Kaffir Language: Including Xosa and Zulu Dialects.* London: Wesleyan Mission House, 1872.

D'Azevedo, Mello, ed. *Ethiopia Oriental por Fr. João dos Santos.* Vol. 1. Lisbon: Bibliotheca de Classicos Portuguezes, 1891.

Department of Public Education, Cape of Good Hope. *The Native Primary School: Suggestions for the Consideration of Teachers.* Cape Town: Cape Times Limited, 1929.

Department of Traditional Affairs, Strategic Plan, 2015–2020. Pretoria: Department of Traditional Affairs, 2016.

Documents on the Portuguese in Mozambique and Central Africa, 1497–1840 (*Documentos sobre os Portugueses em Moçambique e em África Central, 1497–1840*). 8 vols. Lisbon: National Archives of Rhodesia and Nyasaland, Centro de Estudos Históricos Ultramarinos, 1962–75.

Döhne, Jakob L. *A Zulu-Kafir Dictionary*. Cape Town: G. K. Pike's, 1857.

Flacourt, Étienne de. *Relation de la Grande Isle Madagascar, contenant ce qui s'est passé entre les François & les Originaires de cette Isle, depuis l'an 1642 jusques en l'an 1655*. Paris: Lesselin, 1668.

Foster, William, ed. *The Journal of John Jourdain, 1608–1617*. Cambridge: Hakluyt, 1905.

Gardiner, Allen F. *Narrative of a Journey to the Zoolu Country, in South Africa. By Captain Allen F. Gardiner, R.N. Undertaken in 1835*. London: William Crofts, 1836.

Godlonton, Robert. *A Narrative of the Irruption of the Kafir Hordes into the Eastern Province of the Cape of Good Hope, 1834–35*. Grahamstown: Meurant and Godlonton, 1836.

Grout, Lewis. "Announcement: Grammar and Dictionary of the Zulu Language." *Journal of the American Oriental Society* 4 (1854): 456.

———. *The IsiZulu: A Grammar of the Zulu Language*. London: Trübner, 1859.

Herder, Johann Gottfried von. *Briefe zur Beförderung der Humanität*. Edited by Johann von Müller. Stuttgart: J. G. Gotta, 1829.

Holden, William C. *A Brief History of Methodism, and Methodism in South Africa*. London: Wesleyan-Methodist Book Room, 1887.

———. *History of the Colony of Natal, South Africa*. London: Alexander Heylin, 1855.

———. *The Past and Future of the Kafir Races*. London: Nicholas, 1866.

Holloway, J. E., R. W. Anderson, F. A. W. Lucas, A. M. Mostert, A. W. Roberts, P. W. le Roux Van Niekerk, C. Faye. *Report of Native Economic Commission, 1930–1932*. Pretoria: Government Printer, 1932.

Hopkins, J. F. P., and Nehemiah Levtzion, eds. *Corpus of Early Arabic Sources for West African History*. Cambridge: Cambridge University Press, 1981.

Imperial Blue Book No. 424. Copies of Extracts of Correspondence Relative to the Kafir Tribes, between the Years 1837 and 1845. London, 1851.

Isaacs, Nathaniel. *Travels and Adventures in Eastern Africa, Descriptive of the Zoolus, Their Manners, Customs*. 2 vols. London: Edward Churton, 1836.

Jackson, A. O. *The Ethnic Composition of the Ciskei and Transkei*. Pretoria: Government Printer, 1975.

Kay, Stephen. *Travels and Researches in Caffraria*. New York: Harper, 1834.

Kayser, Friedrich Gottlob. *Rev F. G. Kayser: Journal and Letters*. Edited by Chris Hummel. Grahamstown: Maskew Miller Longman, 1990.

Keltie, John Scott, and M. Epstein. *The Stateman's Yearbook: Statistical and Historical Annual of the States of the World for the Year 1918*. London: Macmillan, 1918.

Kirby, Percival R., ed. *Source Book on the Wreck of the Grosvenor East Indiaman*. Cape Town: Van Riebeeck Society, 1953.

———. *Andrew Smith and Natal: Documents Relating to the Early History of That Province*. Cape Town: Van Riebeeck Society, 1955.

Knox, Robert. *The Races of Men: A Fragment*. Philadelphia: Lea and Blanchard, 1850.

Kolb, Peter. *Description du Cap de Bonne-Espérance*. Tome Premier. Amsterdam: Jean Catuffe, 1742.

Kotzé, D. J., ed. *Letters of the American Missionaries, 1835–1838*. Cape Town: Van Riebeeck Society, 1950.

Kropf, Albert. *A Kaffir-English Dictionary*. Lovedale: Lovedale Mission Press, 1899.

———. *Das Volk der Xosa-Kaffern im östlichen Südafrika nach seiner Geschichte, Eigenart, Verfassung und Religion*. Edited by Ulrich van der Heyden and Joachim Kundler. Bremen: Falkenberg, 2017.

Kropf, Albert, and Robert Godfrey. *A Kafir-English Dictionary*. 2nd ed. Lovedale: Lovedale Mission Press, 1915.

Leibbrandt, H. C. V., ed. *De Rebellie van 1815, algemeen bejan als Slachters Nek*. Cape Town: Juta, 1903.

Leibnitz, Gottfried Wilhelm. "Nouveaux essais sur l'entendement humain." In *Oeuvres philosophiques latines et françoises de feu Mr. de Leibnitz*, edited by Rudolph Eric Raspe. Leipzig: Jean Schreuder, 1765.

Le Vaillant, François. *Travels from the Cape of Good-Hope, into the Interior Parts of Africa*. 2 vols. Translated by Elizabeth Helme. London: W. Lane, 1790.

Lichtenstein, Heinrich. *Foundation of the Cape and about the Bechuanas*. Edited and translated by O. H. Spohr. Cape Town: Balkema, 1973.

———. *Travels in Southern Africa, in the Years 1803, 1804, 1805, and 1806*. 2 vols. Translated by A. Plumptre. London: H. Colburn, 1812–15.

Linschoten, Jan H. van. *Itinerario: Voyage ofte Schipvaert van Jan Huygen van Linschoten naer Dost ofte Portugals Indien*. Amsterdam: Cornelis Claesz, 1596.

London Missionary Society. *Transactions of the Missionary Society*. Vol. 1. London: Bye and Law, 1804.

Maclean, John, ed. *A Compendium of Kafir Laws and Customs: Including Genealogical Tables of Kafir Chiefs and Various Tribal Census Returns*. London: Frank Cass, 1968.

Malan, Wouter De Vos, ed. *Handbook of Suggestions for Teachers in Native Primary Schools*. Cape Town: Department of Public Education, Cape of Good Hope, 1952.

Malte-Brun, Victor-Adolphe. *Carte itinéraire des explorations faites de 1849 à 1856, 7 ans l'Afrique australe, par le Rd David Livingstone*. Paris: Imp. de Bineteau, 1857.

Markham, Albert H., ed. *The Voyages and Works of John Davis, the Navigator.* London: Hakluyt, 1880.

Mathabane, Mark. *Kaffir Boy: The True Story of a Black Youth's Coming of Age in Apartheid South Africa*. New York: Free Press, 1986.

Mentzel, Otto F. *Vollständige und zuverläßige Geographische und Topographische Beschreibung des berühmten und in aller Betrachtung merkwürdigen Afrikanischen Vorgebirges der Guten Hofnung. Erster Theil*. Glogau: C. F. Günther, 1785.

Moffat, Robert. *Bechuana Spelling Book*. London: London Missionary Society, 1826.

Molsbergen, E. C. Godée, ed. *Reizen in Zuid-Afrika in de Hollandse tijd. Deel II. Tochten naar het Noorden 1686–1806*. The Hague: Martinus Nijhoff, 1916.

———. *Reizen in Zuid-Afrika in de Hollandse tijd. Deel III. Tochten langs de Z.O.-kust en naar het Oosten 1670–1752*. The Hague: Martinus Nijhoff, 1922.

———. *Reizen in Zuid-Afrika in de Hollandse tijd. Deel IV. Tochten in het Kafferland 1776–1805*. The Hague: Martinus Nijhoff, 1932.

Moodie, Donald, ed., comp., and trans. *The Record; or, A Series of Official Papers Relative to the Condition and Treatment of the Native Tribes of South Africa*. Part 1, *1649–1720*. Cape Town: A. S. Robertson, 1838.

———. *The Record; or, A Series of Official Papers Relative to the Condition and Treatment of the Native Tribes of South Africa*. Part 3, *1769–1795*. Cape Town: A. S. Robertson, 1838.

———. *The Record; or, A Series of Official Papers Relative to the Condition and Treatment of the Native Tribes of South Africa*. Part 5, *1808–1819*. Cape Town: A. S. Robertson, 1838.

Mossop, E. E., ed. *The Journal of Hendrik Jacob Wikar (1779), The Journals of Jacobus Coetsé Jansz (1760) and Willem van Reenen (1791)*. Translated by E. E. Mossop and A. W. Van der Horst. Cape Town: Van Riebeeck Society, 1935.

Mqhayi, S. E. K. *Abantu besizwe: Historiographical and Biographical Writings, 1902–1944*. Edited and translated by Jeff Opland. Johannesburg: Wits University Press, 2009.

Noah, Trevor. *Born a Crime: Stories from a South African Childhood*. London: John Murray, 2017.

Opland, Jeff. *Xhosa Literature: Spoken and Printed Words*. Publications of the Opland Collection of Xhosa Literature Volume 6. Pietermaritzburg: University of KwaZulu-Natal Press, 2018.

———. *Xhosa Oral Poetry: Aspects of a Black South Africa Tradition*. New York: Cambridge University Press, 1983.

Opland, Jeff, Wandile Kuse, and Pamela Maseko, eds. and trans. *William Wellington Gqoba: Isizwe esinembali, Xhosa Histories and Poetry (1873–1888)*. Publications of the Opland Collection of Xhosa Literature, vol. 1. Pietermaritzburg: University of KwaZulu-Natal Press, 2015.

Opland, Jeff, and Abner Nyamende, eds. and trans. *Isaac Williams Wauchope: Selected Writings, 1874–1916*. Cape Town: Van Riebeeck Society, 2008.

Owen, William. *Narrative of Voyages to Explore the Shores of Africa, Arabia, and Madagascar; Performed by H. M. Ships Leven and Barracouta, under the Direction of Captain W. F. W. Owen, R.N.* 2 vols. London: Richard Bentley, 1833.

Paterson, William. *Narrative of Four Journeys into the Country of the Hottentots, and Caffraria. In the Years 1777, 1778, and 1779.* London: J. Johnson, 1789.

Pereira, Duarte Pacheco. *Esmeraldo de Situ Orbis.* Edited by Augusto Epiphanio da Silva Dia. Lisbon: Typographia Universal, 1905.

Philip, John. *A Letter from the Rev. John Philip, D.D., Superintendent of the Missions of the London Society at the Cape of Good Hope to the Society of Inquiry on Missions in Theological Seminary, Princeton, New Jersey.* Princeton, NJ: John Gray, 1833.

———. *Researches in South Africa; Illustrating the Civil, Moral, and Religious Condition of the Native Tribes.* 2 vols. London: J. Duncan, 1828.

Posselt, Karl Wilhelm. *Wilhelm Posselt, der Kaffern-Missionar. Ein Lebensbild aus der Südafrikanischen Mission.* Edited by E. Pfitzner and D. Wangemann, 4th ed. Berlin: Berliner evangelische Missionsgesellschaft, 1891.

Prichard, James C. *Researches into the Physical History of Mankind.* 3rd ed, 2 vols. London: Sherwood, 1836–37.

Proceedings of the Commission Appointed to Inquire into the Past and Present State of the Kafirs in the District of Natal. 6 parts. Natal: J. Archbell and Son, 1852–53.

Raven-Hart, Rowland. *Before Van Riebeeck: Callers at South Africa from 1488 to 1652.* Cape Town: Struik, 1967.

Renkewitz, Th. G. *Mission-Schools: Their Difficulties, and How to Overcome Them.* Paper read at the Teachers' Conference in Cape Town. Genadendal, 1896.

Roberts, Charles. *An English-Zulu Dictionary.* London: Paul, Trench, Truebner, 1904.

Rose, Brian, and Raymond Tunmer, eds. *Documents in South African Education.* Johannesburg: AD Donker, 1975.

Rose, Cowper. *Four Years in Southern Africa.* London: Colburn and Bentley, 1829.

Sauer, J. W., and George M. Theal, eds. *Basutoland Records; Copies of Official Documents of Various Kinds.* vol. 3, 1862–68. Cape Town: Richards and Sons, 1883.

Schapera, Isaac, and Benjamin Farrington, eds. and trans. *The Early Cape Hottentots Described in the Writings of Olfert Dapper (1668), Willem Ten Rhyne (1686) and Johannes Gulielmus de Grevenbroek (1695).* Cape Town: Van Riebeeck Society, 1933.

Shaw, William. *The Story of My Mission in South-Eastern Africa.* London: Hamilton, Adams, 1860.

Shooter, Joseph. *The Kafirs of Natal and the Zulu Country.* London: Stanford, 1857.

Smith, Thornley. *Memoir of the Rev. John Whittle Appleyard, Wesleyan Missionary in South Africa.* London: Wesleyan Missionary Society, 1881.

[Soga, Tiyo, et al.]. *The Kafir Bible: Rev. J. W. Appleyard's Version Judged by Missionaries of Various Denominations.* Lovedale: Lovedale Mission Press, 1866.

Sparrman, Anders. *Voyage to the Cape of Good Hope.* 2 vols. London: Robinson, 1785.

Stel, Willem Adriaan van de. *Korte deductie van Willem Adriaen van der Stel, gewesene extraordinaris Raat van India en Gouverneur aen Cabo de bon Esperance; Tot destructie ende wederlegginge van alle de klaghten, die enige vryluyden vande voorfz. Cabo, aen de Edele Achtbare Heren Bewinthebberen van de Oost Indische Compagnie over hem hadden gedaen; onder verseeckeringe, dat van alle de stucken, daer by gementioneert, de originele, of copyen authentijcq onder hem van der Stel zijn berustende.* 1706.

Story of the American Bible Society 1916. New York: American Bible Society, 1916.

Stuart, James, and D. McK. Malcolm, eds. *The Diary of Henry Francis Fynn.* Pietermaritzburg: Shuter and Shooter, 1986.

Terry, Edward. *A Voyage to East-India.* London: J. Wilke, 1777.

Theal, George McCall, ed. *Documents Relating to the Kaffir War of 1835.* London: Clowes and Sons, 1912.

———. *History and Ethnography of Africa South of the Zambesi, 1505–1795.* Vol. 3. New York: Cambridge University Press, 2010.

———, ed. and trans. *Records of South-Eastern Africa, Collected in Various Libraries and Archive Departments in Europe.* 6 vols. London: William Clowes, 1898–1900.

Thompson, George. *Travels and Adventures in Southern Africa.* Vol. 1. London: Genry Colburn, 1827.

Thunberg, Carl Peter. *Karl Peter Thunberg's Reise durch einen Theil von Europa, Afrika und Asien, hauptsächlich in Japan, in den Jahren 1770 bis 1779.* Translated by Christian Heinrich Grosfurb, vol. 1, parts 1 and 2. Berlin: Haude und Spener, 1792.

Union of South Africa. *Report of the Commission on Native Education, 1949–1951.* Pretoria: Government Printer, 1951.

———. *Report of the Interdepartmental Committee on Native Education, 1935–1936.* Pretoria: Government Printer, 1936.

Velho, Álvaro. *O Roteiro da Viagem de Vasco da Gama em 1497.* 2nd ed. Lisbon: Imprensa Nacional, 1866.

Verrier, Frederique, ed. *Voyages en Afrique Noire d'Alvise Cadà Mosto, 1455 & 1456.* 2nd ed. Paris: Editions Chandeigne, 2003.

Vigne, Randolph, ed. *Guillaume Chenu de Chalezac, The "French Boy," the Narrative of His Experiences as a Huguenot Refugee, as a Castaway among the Xhosa, His Rescue with the Stavenisse Survivors by the Centaurus, His Service at the Cape and Return to Europe, 1686–9.* Cape Town: Van Riebeeck Society, 1993.

Webb, Colin de B., and John B. Wright, eds. *The James Stuart Archive of Recorded Oral Evidence Relating to the History of the Zulu and Neighbouring Peoples.* 6 vols. Pietermaritzburg: University of Natal Press, 1976–2014.

Young, Samuel. *A Missionary Narrative of the Triumphs of Grace; as Seen in the Conversion of Kafirs, Hottentots, Fingoes, and Other Natives of South Africa.* London: Roche, 1842.

Zurara, Gomes Eannes de. *Chronica do Descobrimento e Conquista de Guiné, escrita por Mandado de ElRei D. Affonso V.* Edited by Visconde de Santarem. Paris: J. P. Aillaud, 1841.

PERIODICALS

Annual Report of the American Bible Society (1850)

Bantu Education Journal (1954–55)

Caffrarian Messenger (1841–45)

Chicago Tribune (1990–92)

Evangelical Magazine and Missionary Chronicle (1839)

Home and Foreign Missionary Record for the Free Church of Scotland (1843–50)

Independent Online (2007)

London Christian Instructor or Congregational Magazine (1823)

Mail & Guardian (2019)

Methodist Churchman (1906)

Missionary Herald (1833–61)

Missionary Register (1819)

The National Preacher (1829)

Quarterly Intelligence of the Glasgow Missionary Society (1838–43)

Quarterly Papers of the Glasgow Missionary Society (1828–37)

Report of the British Foreign Bible Society (1913–30)

Report of the Glasgow African Missionary Society (1838–47)

Report of the Glasgow Missionary Society (1823–36, 1837–43)

Report of the Wesleyan-Methodist Missionary Society (1824–40)

Sunday World (2021)

Territorial News (1932)

Weekly Mail (1990)
Wesleyan Missionary Magazine (1821–35)
Wesleyan Missionary Notices (1821–57)

SECONDARY SOURCES

Books and Book Chapters

Álvarez, Román, and M. Carmen-África Vidal. "Translating: A Political Act." In *Translation, Power, Subversion,* edited by Álvarez and Carmen-África Vidal, 1–9. Bristol, PA: Multilingual Matters, 1996.

Appel, René, and Pieter Muysken. *Language Contact and Bilingualism.* Amsterdam: Amsterdam University Press, 2005.

Armstrong, John A. *Nations before Nationalism.* Chapel Hill: University of North Carolina Press, 1982.

Ashley, Michael. "African Education and Society in the Nineteenth-Century Eastern Cape." In *Beyond the Cape Frontier: Studies in the History of the Transkei and Ciskei,* edited by Christopher Saunders and Robin Derricourt, 119–211. London: Longman, 1974.

Atkins, Keletso. *The Moon Is Dead! Give Us Our Money! The Cultural Origins of an African Work Ethic in Natal, South Africa, 1843–1900.* Portsmouth, NH: Heinemann, 1993.

Bank, Andrew, and Leslie Bank, eds. *Inside African Anthropology: Monica Wilson and Her Interpreters.* Cambridge: Cambridge University Press, 2013.

Bhotomane, Ndumiso. "Origins of the Xhosa." In *The Tongue Is Fire: South African Storytellers and Apartheid,* edited by Harold Scheub, 31–47. Madison: University of Wisconsin Press, 1996.

Bonner, Philip, and Vusi Ndima. "The Roots of Violence and Martial Zuluness on the East Rand." In *Zulu Identities: Being Zulu, Past and Present,* edited by Benedict Carton, John Laband, and Jabulani Sithole, 363–82. New York: Columbia University Press, 2009.

Boonzaier, Emile, Candy Malherbe, Penny Berens, and Andy Smith. *The Cape Herders: A History of the Khoikhoi of Southern Africa.* 2nd ed. Athens: Ohio University Press, 2000.

Bryant, Alfred T. *Olden Times in Zululand and Natal.* New York: Longmans, 1929.

Bundy, Colin. *The Rise and Fall of the South African Peasantry.* Berkeley: University of California Press, 1979.

Buthelezi, Mbongiseni. "The Empire Talks Back: Re-examining the Legacies of Shaka and Zulu Power in Post-apartheid South Africa." In *Zulu Identities: Being Zulu, Past and Present,* edited by Benedict Carton, John Laband, and Jabulani Sithole, 23–34. New York: Columbia University Press, 2009.

Cahoone, Lawrence E. *Cultural Revolutions: Reason versus Culture in Philosophy, Politics, and Jihad.* University Park: Pennsylvania State University Press, 2005.

Campbell, Lyle. *Historical Linguistics: An Introduction.* Cambridge, MA: MIT Press, 1998.

Carton, Benedict. "Awaken *Nkulunkulu*, Zulu God of the Old Testament: Pioneering Missionaries during the Early Age of Racial Spectacle." In *Zulu Identities: Being Zulu, Past and Present*, edited by Benedict Carton, John Laband, and Jabulani Sithole, 133–52. New York: Columbia University Press, 2009.

Carton, Benedict, John Laband, and Jabulani Sithole, eds. *Zulu Identities: Being Zulu, Past and Present.* New York: Columbia University Press, 2009.

Christofersen, Arthur Fridjof. *Adventuring with God: The Story of the American Board Mission in South Africa.* Edited by Richard W. Sales. Durban: Robinson, 1967.

Cole, Desmond T. "Doke's Classification of Bantu Languages." In. *Contributions to the History of Bantu Linguistics*, edited by C. M. Doke and D. T. Cole, 80–96. Johannesburg: Witwatersrand University Press, 1969.

Comaroff, Jean, and John Comaroff. *Of Revelation and Revolution: Christianity, Colonialism, and Consciousness in South Africa.* Vol. 1. Chicago: University of Chicago Press, 1991.

Cope, Nicholas. *To Bind the Nation: Solomon kaDinuzulu and Zulu Nationalism, 1913–1933.* Pietermaritzburg: University of Natal Press, 1993.

Crais, Clifton. *White Supremacy and Black Resistance in Pre-Industrial South Africa: The Making of the Colonial Order in the Eastern Cape, 1770–1865.* New York: Cambridge University Press, 1992.

Cullinan, Patrick. *Robert Jacob Gordon, 1743–1795: The Man and His Travels at the Cape.* Cape Town: Struik, 1992.

Curran, Andrew S. *The Anatomy of Blackness: Science and Slavery in an Age of Enlightenment* Baltimore: Johns Hopkins University Press, 2011.

Curtin, Philip D. *The Image of Africa: British Ideas and Action, 1780–1850.* Vol. 1. Madison: University of Wisconsin Press, 1964.

Davies, Winifred V. "Standard German in the Nineteenth Century." In *Landmarks in the History of the German Language*, ed. Geraldine Horan, Nils Langer, and Sheila Watts, 189–210. New York: Peter Lang, 2009.

Davis, Joanne R. *Tiyo Soga: A Literary History.* Pretoria: University of South Africa Press, 2018.

Devic, Louis-Marcel. *Le pays des Zendjs: ou, La côte orientale d'Afrique au moyen-âge (géographie, moeurs, productions, animaux légendaires) d'après les écrivains arabes.* Paris: Hachette, 1888.

Dlamini, Sibusisiwe Nombuso. *Youth and Identity Politics in South Africa, 1990–1994.* Toronto: University of Toronto Press, 2005.

Dow, James R. "Germany." In *Handbook of Language and Ethnic Identity: Disciplinary and Regional Perspectives,* edited by Joshua A. Fishman and Ofelia García, 2nd ed., vol. 1, 221–36. New York: Oxford University Press, 2010.

Du Plessis, Johannes. *A History of Christian Missions in South Africa.* London: Longmans, Green, 1911.

Dwight, Henry Otis. *The Centennial History of the American Bible Society.* Vol. 1. New York: Macmillan, 1916.

Edgar, Robert. *The Finger of God: Enoch Mgijima, the Israelites, and the Bulhoek Massacre in South Africa.* Charlottesville: University of Virginia Press, 2018.

Edgar, Robert, and Luyanda ka Msumza, eds. *Africa's Triumph: The Collected Writings of A. P. Mda.* Cape Town: Best Red, 2018.

Ehret, Christopher. *An African Classical Age: Eastern and Southern Africa, 1000 B.C. to A.D. 400.* Charlottesville: University of Virginia Press, 2001.

Elbourne, Elizabeth, and Robert Ross. "Combating Spiritual and Social Bondage: Early Missions in the Cape Colony." In *Christianity in South Africa: A Political, Social, and Cultural History,* edited by Richard Elphick and Rodney Davenport, 31–50. Berkeley: University of California Press, 1997.

Eldredge, Elizabeth. *The Creation of the Zulu Kingdom: War, Shaka, and the Consolidation of Power.* New York: Cambridge University Press, 2014.

Elphick, Richard. *Khoikhoi and the Founding of White South Africa.* Johannesburg: Ravan, 1985.

———. *The Equality of Believers: Protestant Missionaries and the Racial Politics of South Africa.* Charlottesville: University of Virginia Press, 2012.

Elphick, Richard, and Rodney Davenport, eds. *Christianity in South Africa: A Political, Social, and Cultural History.* Berkeley: University of California Press, 1997.

Etherington, Norman. *Preachers, Peasants and Politics in Southeast Africa, 1835–1880: African Christian Communities in Natal, Pondoland and Zululand.* London: Royal Historical Society, 1978.

Feinstein, Charles H. *An Economic History of South Africa: Conquest, Discrimination and Development.* New York: Cambridge University Press, 2005.

Finlayson, Rosalie, and Sarah Slabbert. "'I'll Meet You Halfway with Language': Code-Switching within a South African Urban Context." In *Language Choices: Conditions, Constraints and Consequences,* edited by Martin Pütz, 381–421. Philadelphia: John Benjamins, 1997.

Fourshey, Catherine Cymone, Rhonda M. Gonzales, and Christine Saidi. *Bantu Africa, 3500 BCE to Present.* New York: Oxford University Press, 2018.

Gérard, Albert S. *Four African Literatures: Xhosa, Sotho, Zulu, Amharic.* Berkeley: University of California Press, 1971.

Giliomee, Hermann. "The Eastern Cape Frontier, 1770–1812." In *The Shaping of South African Society,* edited by Richard Elphick and Giliomee, 421–70. Middleton, CT: Wesleyan University Press, 1989.

Gilmour, Rachel. *Grammars of Colonialism: Representing Languages in Colonial South Africa.* New York: Palgrave, 2006.

Gluckman, Max. "The Kingdom of the Zulu of South Africa." In *African Political Systems,* edited by Meyer Fortes and E. E. Evans-Pritchard, 25–55. New York: Oxford University Press, 1940.

Gomez, Michael A. *African Dominion: A New History of Empire in Early and Medieval West Africa.* Princeton, NJ: Princeton University Press, 2018.

Greenberg, Joseph H. *The Languages of Africa.* The Hague: Mouton, 1963.

Guy, Jeff. *The Destruction of the Zulu Kingdom: The Civil War in Zululand, 1879–1884.* Johannesburg: Ravan, 1982.

———. "Ecological Factors in the Rise of Shaka and the Zulu Kingdom." In *Economy and Society in Pre-Industrial South Africa,* edited by Shula Marks and Anthony Atmore, 102–19. Harlow: Longman, 1980.

Haarmann, Harald. *Language in Ethnicity: A View of Basic Ecological Relations.* New York: Mouton de Gruyter, 2010.

———. "Language Politics and the European Identity." In *A Language Policy for the European Community: Prospects and Quandaries,* edited by Florian Coulmans, 103–20. New York: Mouton de Gruyter, 1991.

Hage, Per, and Jeff Marck. "Proto-Bantu Descent Groups." In *Kinship, Language and Prehistory: Per Hage and the Renaissance in Kinship Studies,* edited by Doug Jones and Bojka Milicic, 75–78. Salt Lake City: The University of Utah Press, 2011.

Hall, Simon. "Farming Communities of the Second Millennium: Internal Frontiers, Identity, Continuity and Change." In *The Cambridge History of South Africa,* vol. 1, *From Early Times to 1885,* edited by Carolyn Hamilton, Bernard Mbenga, and Robert Ross, 112–67. New York: Cambridge University Press, 2012.

Hall, Stuart. "Foucault: Power, Knowledge and Discourse." In *Discourse Theory and Practice: A Reader,* edited by Margaret Wetherell, Stephanie Taylor, and Simeon J. Yates., 72–81. London: Sage, 2011.

Haller, John S. *Outcasts from Evolution: Scientific Attitudes of Racial Inferiority, 1859–1900.* 2nd ed. Carbondale: Southern Illinois University Press, 1995.

Hamilton, Carolyn. *The Mfecane Aftermath: Reconstructive Debates in Southern African History.* Johannesburg: Witwatersrand University Press, 1995.

———. *Terrific Majesty: The Powers of Shaka Zulu and the Limits of Historical Invention.* Cambridge, MA: Harvard University Press, 1998.

Hamilton, Carolyn, and Nessa Leibhammer, eds. *Tribing and Untribing the Archive: Identity and the Material Record in Southern KwaZulu-Natal in the Late Independent and Colonial Periods.* 2 vols. Pietermaritzburg: University of KwaZulu-Natal Press, 2016.

Harinck, Gerrit. "Interaction between Xhosa and Khoi; Emphasis on the Period 1620–1750." In *African Societies in Southern Africa,* edited by Leonard Thompson, 145–70. London: Heinmann, 1969.

Harries, Patrick. *Butterflies and Barbarians: Swiss Missionaries and Systems of Knowledge in South-East Africa.* Athens: Ohio University Press, 2007.

———. "Exclusion, Classification and Internal Colonialism: The Emergence of Ethnicity among the Tsonga-Speakers of South Africa." In *The Creation of Tribalism in Southern Africa,* edited by Leroy Vail, 82–117. Berkeley: University of California Press, 1989.

———. *Work, Culture, and Identity: Migrant Laborers on Mozambique and South Africa, c. 1860–1910.* Portsmouth, NH: Heinemann, 1994.

Hartshorne, Ken. "Language Policy in African Education: A Background to the Future." In *Language and Social History: Studies in South African Sociolinguistics, edited by* Rajend Mesthrie, 306–18. Cape Town: David Philip, 1995.

Heine, Bernd, and Derek Nurse. Introduction to *African Languages: An Introduction,* edited by Bernd Heine and Derek Nurse, 1–10. New York: Cambridge University Press, 2000.

Herbert, Robert, and Richard Bailey. "The Bantu Languages: Sociohistorical Perspectives." In *Language in South Africa,* edited by Rajend Mesthrie, 50–78. New York: Cambridge University Press, 2004.

Hodgson, Janet. "A Battle for Sacred Power: Christian Beginnings among the Xhosa." In *Christianity in South Africa: A Political, Social, and Cultural History,* edited by Richard Elphick and Rodney Davenport, 68–88. Berkeley: University of California Press, 1997.

Horowitz, Donald L. *A Democratic South Africa? Constitutional Emergency in a Divided Society.* Berkeley: University of California Press, 1991.

Houle, Robert J. *Making African Christianity: Africans Re-Imagining Their Faith in Colonial Southern Africa.* Bethlehem, PA: Lehigh University Press, 2011.

Hughes, Heather. *First President: A Life of John Dube, Founding President of the ANC.* Auckland Park: Jacana Media, 2011.

Janson, Tore, and Joseph Tsonope. *Birth of a National Language: The History of Setswana.* Berkeley: University of California Press, 1991.

Jeater, Diana. *Law, Language, and Science: The Invention of the "Native Mind" in Southern Rhodesia, 1890–1930.* Portsmouth, NH: Heinemann, 2007.

Jordan, Archibald C. *Towards an African Literature: The Emergence of Literary Form in Xhosa.* Berkeley: University of California Press, 1973.

Kamawangamalu, Nkonko M. "The Language Planning Situation in South Africa." In *Language Planning and Policy in Africa*, vol. 1, *Botswana, Malawi, Mozambique and South Africa*, edited by Richard B. Baldauf and Robert B. Kaplan, 197–281. Tonawanda, NY: Multilingual Matters, 2004.

Kamusella, Tomasz, and Finex Ndhlovu, eds. *The Social and Political History of Southern Africa's Languages*. London: Palgrave, 2018.

Karttunen, Frances. *Between Worlds: Interpreters, Guides, and Survivors*. New Brunswick, NJ: Rutgers University Press, 1994.

Keegan, Timothy. *Colonial South Africa and the Origins of the Racial Order*. Charlottesville: University Press of Virginia, 1996.

Kelly, Jill E. *To Swim with Crocodiles: Land, Violence, and Belonging in South Africa, 1800–1996*. East Lansing: Michigan State University Press, 2018.

Klieman, Kairn. *"The Pygmies Were Our Compass": Bantu and Batwa in the History of West and Central Africa, Early Times to c. 1900*. Portsmouth, NH: Heineman, 2003.

Kling, David W. "The New Divinity and the Origins of the American Board of Commissioners for Foreign Missions." In *North American Foreign Missions, 1810–1914*, edited by Wilbert R. Shenk, 27–38. Grand Rapids, MI: Eerdmans, 2004.

Kopytoff, Igor. "The Internal African Frontier: The Making of African Political Culture." In *The African Frontier: The Reproduction of Traditional African Societies*, edited by Kopytoff, 3–84. Bloomington: Indiana University Press, 1987.

Kros, Cynthia. *The Seeds of Separate Development: Origins of Bantu Education*. Pretoria: Unisa, 2010.

———. "W. W. M. Eiselen: Architect of Apartheid Education." In *The History of Education Under Apartheid, 1948–1994: The Doors of Learning and Culture Shall be Opened*, edited by Peter Kallaway, 53–73. Cape Town: Pearson Education South Africa, 2002.

Kynoch, Gary. *Township Violence and the End of Apartheid: War on the Reef*. Rochester, NY: James Currey, 2018.

Laband, John. "'Bloodstained Grandeur': Colonial and Imperial Stereotypes of Zulu Warriors and Zulu Warfare." In *Zulu Identities: Being Zulu, Past and Present*, edited by Benedict Carton, Laband, and Jabulani Sithole, 168–76. New York: Columbia University Press, 2009.

———. *Rise and Fall of the Zulu Nation*. London: Arms and Armour, 1998.

———. *Historical Dictionary of the Zulu Wars*. Lanham, MD: Scarecrow, 2009.

La Hausse de Lalouvière, Paul. *Restless Identities: Signatures of Nationalism, Zulu Ethnicity and History in the Lives of Petros Lamula (c. 1881–1948) and Lymong Maling (1889–c. 1936)*. Pietermaritzburg: University of Natal Press, 2000.

Landau, Paul. *Popular Politics in the History of South Africa, 1400–1948.* New York: Cambridge University Press, 2010.

Lawrance, Benjamin N., Emily Lynn Osborn, and Richard L. Roberts. "Introduction: African Intermediaries and the 'Bargain' of Collaboration." In *Intermediaries, Interpreters, and Clerks: African Employees in the Making of Colonial Africa,* edited by Benjamin N. Lawrance, Emily Lynn Osborn, and Richard L. Roberts, 3–34. Madison: University of Wisconsin Press, 2006.

Levine, Roger. *A Living Man from Africa: Jan Tzatzoe, Xhosa Chief and Missionary, and the Making of Nineteenth-Century South Africa.* New Haven, CT: Yale University Press, 2011.

Lodge, Tom. *Black Politics in South Africa since 1945.* Johannesburg: Ravan, 1983.

Lovett, Richard. *The History of the London Missionary Society, 1795–1895.* Vol. 1. London: Henry Frowde, 1899.

MacGonagle, Elizabeth. *Crafting Identity in Zimbabwe and Mozambique.* Rochester, NY: University of Rochester Press, 2007.

Maclennan, Ben. *A Proper Degree of Terror: John Graham and the Cape's Eastern Frontier.* Johannesburg: Ravan, 1986.

Magubane, Zine. *Bringing the Empire Home: Race, Class, and Gender in Britain and Colonial South Africa.* Chicago: University of Chicago Press, 2004.

Mahlasela, B. E. N. *A General Survey of Xhosa Literature from Its Early Beginnings in the 1800s to the Present.* Grahamstown: Dept. of African Languages, Rhodes University, 1973.

Mahoney, Michael. *The Other Zulus: The Spread of Zulu Ethnicity in Colonial South Africa.* Durham, NC: Duke University Press, 2012.

Makoni, Sinfree. "From Misinvention to Disinvention of Language: Multilingualism and the South African Constitution." In *Black Linguistics: Language, Society and Politics in Africa and the Americas,* edited by Sinfree Makoni, Geneva Smitherman, Arnetha F. Ball, and Arthur K. Spear, 132–51. New York: Routledge, 2003.

———. "In the Beginning Was the Missionaries' Word: The European Invention of an African Language: The Case of Shona in Zimbabwe." In *Between Distinction & Extinction: The Harmonisation and Standardisation of African Languages,* edited by Kwesi Kwaa Prah, 157–64. Johannesburg: Witwatersrand University Press, 1998.

Makoni, Sinfree, and Pedzisai Mashiri. "Critical Historiography: Does Language Planning in Africa Need a Construct of Language as Part of Its Theoretical Apparatus?" In *Disinventing and Reconstituting Languages,* edited by Makoni and Alastair Pennycook, 62–89. Tonawanda, NY: Multilingual Matters, 2006.

Mamdani, Mahmood. *Citizen and Subject: Contemporary Africa and the Legacy of Late Colonialism.* Princeton, NJ: Princeton University Press, 2018.

———. *Saviors and Survivors: Darfur, Politics, and the War on Terror.* New York: Doubleday, 2010.

Marks, Shula. *The Ambiguities of Dependence in South Africa: Class, Nationalism, and the State in Twentieth-Century Natal, 1913–1933.* Baltimore: Johns Hopkins University Press, 1986.

———. "Patriotism, Patriarchy and Purity: Natal and the Politics of Zulu Ethnic Consciousness." In *The Creation of Tribalism in Southern Africa,* edited by Leroy Vail, 215–40. Berkeley: University of California Press, 1989.

———. "The Traditions of the Natal 'Nguni': A Second Look at the Work of A. T. Bryant." In *African Societies in Southern Africa,* edited by L. M. Thompson, 126–44. London: Heinmann, 1969.

McClendon, Thomas. "Interpretation and Interpolation: Shepstone as Native Interpreter." In *Intermediaries, Interpreters, and Clerks: African Employees in the Making of Colonial Africa,* edited by Benjamin N. Lawrance, Emily Lynn Osborn, and Richard L. Roberts, 77–93. Madison: University of Wisconsin Press, 2006.

———. *White Chief, Black Lords: Shepstone and the Colonial State in Natal, South Africa, 1845–1878.* Rochester, NY: University of Rochester Press, 2010.

McCormick, Kay. "Code-Switching, Code-Mixing and Convergence in Cape Town." In *Language in South Africa,* edited by Rajend Mesthrie, 216–34. New York: Cambridge University Press, 2004.

McGregor, William B. *Linguistics: An Introduction.* 2nd ed. New York: Bloomsbury, 2015.

Mesthrie, Rajend, ed. *Language and Social History; Studies in South African Sociolinguistics.* Cape Town: David Philip, 1995.

———, ed. *Language in South Africa.* New York: Cambridge University Press, 2004.

Mokoena, Hlonipha. *Magema Fuze: The Making of a Kholwa Intellectual.* Pietermaritzburg: University of KwaZulu-Natal Press, 2011.

Moodie, T. Dunbar, with Vivienne Ndatshe. *Going for Gold: Men, Mines, and Migration.* Berkeley: University of California Press, 1994.

Mostert, Noël. *Frontiers: The Epic of South Africa's Creation and the Tragedy of the Xhosa People.* New York: Alfred A. Knopf, 1992.

Myers, Jason C. *Indirect Rule in South Africa: Tradition, Modernity, and the Costuming of Political Power.* Rochester, NY: University of Rochester Press, 2008.

Newitt, Malyin D. D. *A History of Mozambique.* Bloomington: Indiana University Press, 1995.

Newton-King, Susan. *Masters and Servants on the Cape Eastern Frontier, 1760–1803*. New York: Cambridge University Press, 1999.

Nielsen, W. Sigurd. *The Twin Blossom of the Pear Tree: The History of the Moravian Church in the Eastern Province in South Africa*. Port Shepstone: Baruk, 1999.

Nurse, Derek, and Gérard Philippson. Introduction to *The Bantu Languages*, edited by Nurse and Philippson, 1–12. New York: Routledge, 2003.

Oakes, Leigh. *Language and National Identity: Comparing France and Sweden*. Philadelphia: John Benjamins, 2001.

Odendaal, André. *The Founders: The Origins of the ANC and the Struggle for Democracy in South Africa*. Auckland Park: Jacana, 2012.

Omer-Cooper, John D. "Aspects of Political Change in the Nineteenth-Century Mfecane." In *African Societies in Southern Africa*, edited by L. M. Thompson, 207–29. London: Heinmann, 1969.

———. *The Zulu Aftermath: A Nineteenth-Century Revolution in Bantu Africa*. London: Longmans, 1966.

Pahl, Herbert W. *IsiXhosa*. Johannesburg: Educum, 1983.

Peires, Jeff. *The Dead Will Arise: Nongqawuse and the Great Xhosa Cattle-Killing Movement of 1856-7*. Johannesburg: Ravan, 1989.

[———]. "Ethnicity and Pseudo-Ethnicity in the Ciskei." In *The Creation of Tribalism in Southern Africa*, edited by Leroy Vail, 395–413. Berkeley: University of California Press, 1989.

———. *House of Phalo: A History of the Xhosa People in the Days of Their Independence*. Berkeley: University of California Press, 1982.

Pratt, Marie Louise. *Imperial Eyes: Travel Writing and Transculturation*. 2nd ed. New York: Routledge, 2008.

Pugach, Sara. *Africa in Translation: A History of Colonial Linguistics in Germany and Beyond, 1814–1945*. Ann Arbor: University of Michigan Press, 2012.

Ranger, Terence. *The Invention of Tribalism in Zimbabwe*. Gweru: Mabo, 1985.

———. "Missionaries, Migrants and the Manyika: The Invention of Ethnicity in Zimbabwe." In *The Creation of Tribalism in Southern Africa*, edited by Leroy Vail, 118–50. Berkeley: University of California Press, 1989.

Robinson, Michael F. *The Lost White Tribe: Explorers, Scientists, and the Theory That Changed a Continent*. New York: Oxford, 2015.

Rosenberg, Scott, and Richard F. Weisfelder, eds. *Historical Dictionary of Lesotho*. 2nd ed. Lanham, MD: Scarecrow, 2013.

Ross, Jeffrey A. "Language and the Mobilization of Ethnic Identity." In *Language and Ethnic Relations*, edited by H. Giles and B. Saint-Jacques, 1–13. New York: Pergamon, 1979.

Ross, Robert. *The Borders of Race in Colonial South Africa: The Kat River Settlement, 1829–1856.* New York: Cambridge University Press, 2014.

Sales, Jane. *Mission Stations and the Coloured Communities of the Eastern Cape, 1800–1852.* Cape Town: Balkema, 1975.

Sanders, Ruth A. *German: Biography of a Language.* New York: Oxford University Press, 2010.

Saunders, Christopher, and Robin Derricourt, eds. *Beyond the Cape Frontier: Studies in the History of the Transkei and Ciskei.* London: Longman, 1974.

Scales, Len. *The Shaping of German Identity: Authority and Crisis, 1245–1414.* New York: Cambridge University Press, 2012.

Schaefer, Richard T., ed. *Encyclopedia of Race, Ethnicity, and Society.* Vol. 1. Thousand Oaks, CA: Sage, 2008.

Scheub, Harold. *The Tongue Is Fire: South African Storytellers and Apartheid.* Madison: University of Wisconsin Press, 1996.

Schumaker, Lyn. *Africanizing Anthropology: Fieldwork, Networks, and the Making of Cultural Knowledge in Central Africa.* Durham, NC: Duke University Press, 2001.

Shell, Robert C.-H. *Children of Bondage: A Social History of the Slave Society at the Cape of Good Hope, 1652–1838.* Johannesburg: Witwatersrand University Press, 1995.

Silva, Penny, Wendy Dore, Dorothea Mantzel, Colin Muller, and Madeleine Wright, eds. *Dictionary of South African English on Historical Principles.* New York: Oxford University Press, 1996.

Smit, Abraham Petrus. *God Made It Grow: History of the Bible Society Movement in Southern Africa, 1820–1870.* Translated by W. P. De Vos. Cape Town: Bible Society of South Africa, 1970.

Smith, Alan. "The Trade of Delagoa Bay as a Factor in Nguni Politics, 1750–1835." In *African Societies in Southern Africa,* edited by L. M. Thompson, 171–89. London: Heinmann, 1969.

Smith, Anthony B. *The Ethnic Origins of Nations.* Oxford: Basil Blackwell 1988.

Smith, Edwin W. *The Life and Times of Daniel Lindley (1801–1880).* London: Epworth, 1949.

Smith, Judson. *A History of the American Board Missions in Africa.* Boston: American Board of Commissioners for Foreign Missions, 1905.

Soga, John H. *The South-Eastern Bantu.* Johannesburg: Witwatersrand University Press, 1930.

———. *Ama-Xosa: Life and Customs.* New York: Cambridge University Press, 2014.

Switzer, Les. *Power and Resistance in an African Society: The Ciskei Xhosa and the Making of South Africa.* Madison: University of Wisconsin Press, 1993.

———, ed. *South Africa's Alternative Press: Voices of Protest and Resistance, 1880–1960.* New York: Cambridge University Press, 1997.

Switzer, Les, and Mohamed Adhikari, eds. *South Africa's Resistance Press: Alternative Voices in the Last Generation under Apartheid.* Athens: Ohio University Press, 2000.

Tabler, Edward C. *Pioneers of Natal and Southeastern Africa, 1552–1878.* Cape Town: Balkema, 1977.

Tjelle, Kristin Fjelde. *Missionary Masculinity, 1870–1930: Norwegian Missionaries in South-East Africa.* New York: Palgrave, 2013.

Thompson, Leonard. *A History of South Africa.* 4th ed. Johannesburg: Jonathan Ball, 2014.

———. *The Political Mythology of Apartheid.* New Haven, CT: Yale University Press, 1985.

Thornton, John K. *Africa and Africans in the Making of the Atlantic World, 1400–1800.* 2nd ed. New York: Cambridge University Press, 1998.

———. *A Cultural History of the Atlantic World, 1250–1820.* New York: Cambridge, 2012.

Traill, Anthony. "The Khoesan Languages." In *Language in South Africa,* edited by Rajend Mesthrie, 27–49. New York: Cambridge University Press, [2002] 2004.

———. "'!Khwa-ka Hhouiten,' 'The Rush of the Storm': The Linguistic Death of /Xam." In *Miscast: Negotiating the Presence of the Bushmen,* edited by Pippa Skotnes, 161–83. Cape Town: University of Cape Town Press, 1996.

Trautmann, Thomas R. *Languages and Nations: The Dravidian Proof in Colonial Madras.* Berkeley: University of California Press, 2006.

Tracy, Joseph. *History of the American Board of Commissioners for Foreign Missions. Compiled Chiefly from the Published and Unpublished Documents of the Board.* 2nd ed. New York: M. W. Dodd, 1842.

Tyabashe, Mdukiswa. "All the Land of the Mpondomise." In *The Tongue Is Fire: South African Storytellers and Apartheid,* edited by Harold Scheub. Madison: University of Wisconsin Press, 1996.

Vail, Leroy, ed. *The Creation of Tribalism in Southern Africa.* Berkeley: University of California Press, 1989.

Vansina, Jan. *Paths in the Rainforest: Toward a History of Political Tradition in Equatorial Africa.* Madison: University of Wisconsin Press, 1990.

Van Warmelo, Nicolaas J. *A Preliminary Survey of the Bantu Tribes of South Africa.* Pretoria: Government Printer, 1935.

Vinson, Robert Trent. *Albert Luthuli.* Athens: Ohio University Press, 2018.

Walter, Eugene Victor. *Terror and Resistance: A Study of Political Violence, with Case Studies of Some Primitive African Communities.* New York: Oxford University Press, 1969.

Wangemann, Herman T. *Die Berliner Mission im Kafferlande.* Berlin: Ev. Missionshaus, 1873.

Webster, Alan. "Unmasking the Fingo: The War of 1835 Revisited." In *The Mfe-cane Aftermath: Reconstructive Debates in Southern African History,* edited by Carolyn Hamilton, 241–76. Johannesburg: Witwatersrand University Press, 1995.

Webster, David. *"Abafazi Bathonga Bafihlakala:* Ethnicity and Gender in a Kwa-Zulu Border Community." In *Tradition and Transition in Southern Africa,* edited by Andrew Spiegel and Patrick A. McAllister, 243–71. London: Transaction, 1992.

Welsh, David. *The Roots of Segregation: Native Policy in Colonial Natal, 1845–1910.* New York: Oxford University Press, 1971.

Williams, Donovan, ed. *The Journal and Selected Writings of The Reverend Tiyo Soga.* Cape Town: Balkema, 1983.

Whitelaw, Gavin, and Simon Hall. "Archeological Contexts and the Creation of Social Categories before the Zulu Kingdom." In *Tribing and Untribing the Archive: Identity and the Material Record in Southern KwaZulu-Natal in the Late Independent and Colonial Periods,* edited by Carolyn Hamilton and Nessa Leibhammer, 1:147–81. Pietermaritzburg: University of KwaZulu-Natal Press, 2016.

Williams, John A., ed. *From the South African Past: Narratives, Documents, and Debates.* New York: Houghton Mifflin, 1997.

Wilson, Monica. "Changes in Social Structure in Southern Africa: The Relevance of Kinship Studies to the Historian." In *African Societies in Southern Africa,* edited by Leonard Thompson, 71–85. London: Heinemann, 1969.

——. "The Nguni People." In *The Oxford History of South Africa,* vol. 1, edited by Wilson and Leonard Thompson, 75–130. Oxford: University of Oxford Press, 1969.

——. "Strangers in Africa: Reflections on Nyakyusa, Nguni, and Sotho Evidence." In *Strangers in African Societies,* edited by William A. Shack and Elliott P. Skinner, 51–66. Berkeley: University of California Press, 1979.

Wright, John B. "Making Identities in the Thukela-Mzimvubu Region c. 1770–c. 1940." In *Tribing and Untribing the Archive: Identity and the Material Record in Southern KwaZulu-Natal in the Late Independent and Colonial Periods,* 2 vols., edited by Carolyn Hamilton and Nessa Leibhammer, 1:183–215. Pietermaritzburg: University of KwaZulu-Natal Press, 2016.

——. "Politics, Ideology and the Invention of the Nguni." In *Resistance and Ideology in Settler Societies,* edited by Tom Lodge, 96–118. Johannesburg: Ravan, 1986.

Wright, John B., and Andrew Manson. *The Hlubi Chiefdom in Zululand-Natal: A History.* Ladysmith, Natal: Ladysmith Historical Society, 1983.

Wright, John B., and Carolyn Hamilton. "Traditions and Transformations: The Phongolo-Mzimkhulu Region in the Late Eighteenth and Early Nineteenth

Centuries." In *Natal and Zululand from Earliest Times to 1910: A New History*, edited by Andrew Dumny and Bill Guest, 49–82. Pietermaritzburg: University of Natal Press, 1989.

Journal Articles

Arndt, Jochen S. "Treacherous Savages and Merciless Barbarians: Knowledge, Discourse and Violence during the Cape Frontier Wars, 1834–1853." *Journal of Military History* 74:3 (2010): 709–35.

Ashforth, Adam. "Violence and Political Action in South Africa: Five Comrades Speak." *Passages: A Chronicle of the African Humanities*, Program of African Studies, Northwestern University 4 (1994): 1–3, 10–11, 13.

Baderoon, Gabeba. "Ambiguous Visibility: Islam and the Making of a South African Landscape." *Arab World Geographer* 8:1–2 (2005): 90–103.

Bank, Andrew, and Nancy Jacobs. "Introduction: The Micro-Politics of Knowledge Production in Southern Africa." *Kronos: Southern African Histories* 41 (2015): 11–35.

Bekker, J. C. "The Establishment of Kingdoms and the Identification of Kings and Queens in Terms of the Traditional Leadership and Governance Framework Act 41 of 2003." *Potchefstroomse Elektroniese Regsblad/Potchefstroom Electronic Law Journal* 11:3 (2008): 27.

Campbell, Catherine, Gerhard Maré, and Cherryl Walker. "Evidence for an Ethnic Identity in the Life Histories of Zulu-Speaking Durban Township Residents." *Journal of Southern African Studies* 21:2 (June 1995): 287–301.

Chanaiwa, David S. "The Army and Politics in Pre-Industrial Africa: The Ndebele Nation, 1822–1893." *African Studies Review* 19:2 (Sept. 1976): 49–67.

———. "The Zulu Revolution: State Formation in a Pastoralist Society." *African Studies Review* 23 (Dec. 1980): 1–20.

Chewins, Linell, and Peter Delius. "The Northeastern Factor in South African History: Reevaluating the Volume of the Slave Trade Out of Delagoa Bay and Its Impact on Its Hinterland in the Early Nineteenth Century." *Journal of African History* 61:1 (Mar. 2020): 89–110.

Cobbing, Julian. "A Tainted Well: The Objectives, Historical Fantasies, and Working Methods of James Stuart, with Counter-Argument." *Journal of Natal and Zulu History* 11 (1988): 115–54.

———. "Mfecane as Alibi: Thoughts on Dithakong and Mbolompo." *Journal of African History* 29:3 (1988): 487–519.

Doke, Clement M. "Scripture Translation into Bantu Languages." *African Studies* 17:2 (1958): 82–99.

———. "The Linguistic Situation in South Africa." *Africa: Journal of the International African Institute* 1:4 (Oct. 1928): 478–85.

———. "Vernacular Text-Books in South African Native Schools." *Africa: Journal of the International African Institute* 8:2 (Apr. 1935): 183–209.

Ehret, Christopher. "Transformations in Southern Africa: Proposals for a Sweeping Overview of Change and Development, 6000 BC to the Present." *Ufahuma: A Journal of African Studies* 25:2 (1997): 54–80.

Fabian, Johannes. "Missions and the Colonization of African Languages: Developments in the Former Belgian Congo." *Canadian Journal of African Studies* 17:2 (1983): 165–87.

Guy, Jeff. "Class, Imperialism and Literary Criticism: William Ngidi, John Colenso and Matthew Arbold." *Journal of Southern African Studies* 23:2 (1997): 219–41.

Haas, Mary de, and Paulus Zulu. "Ethnicity and Federalism: The Case of Kwa-Zulu/Natal." In "Ethnicity and Identity in Southern Africa." Special issue, edited by E. Wilmsen, S. Dubow, and J. Sharp, *Journal of Southern African Studies* 20:3 (Sept. 1994): 433–46.

Hair, Paul E. H. "Portuguese Contacts with the Bantu Languages of the Transkei, Natal and Southern Mozambique, 1497–1650." *African Studies* 39:1 (1980): 3–46.

Hamilton, Carolyn. "Political Centralisation and the Making of Social Categories East of the Drakensberg in the Late Eighteenth and Early Nineteenth Centuries." *Journal of Southern African Studies* 38:2 (June 2012): 291–300.

Hamilton, Carolyn, and John B. Wright. "Ethnicity, Ideology and Relations of Subordination in a Precolonial Context." *South African Historical Journal* 22:1 (1990): 3–23.

———. "Moving beyond Ethnic Framing: Political Differentiation in the Chiefdoms of KwaZulu-Natal Region before 1830." *Journal of Southern African Studies* 43:4 (2017): 663–79.

———. "The Making of the *AmaLala*: Ethnicity, Ideology and Relations of Subordination in a Precolonial Context." *South African Historical Journal* 22 (1990): 3–23.

Hammond-Tooke, William D. "Descent Groups, Chiefdoms and South African Historiography." *Journal of Southern African Studies* 11:2 (April 1985): 305–19.

Hanretta, Sean. "Women, Marginality and the Zulu State: Women's Institutions and Power in the Early Nineteenth Century." *Journal of African History* 39:3 (1998): 389–415.

Harries, Patrick. "History, Ethnicity and the Ngwavuma Land Deal: The Zulu Northern Frontier in the Nineteenth Century." *Journal of Natal and Zulu History* 6 (1983): 1–27.

———. "Imagery, Symbolism and Tradition in a South African Bantustan: Mangosuthu Buthelezi, Inkatha, and Zulu History." *History and Theory* 32 (1993): 105–25.

——. "The Roots of Ethnicity: Discourse and the Politics of Language Construction in South-East Africa." *African Affairs* 8 (Jan. 1988): 25–52.

Herbert, Robert K. "The Sociohistory of Clicks in Southern Bantu." *Anthropological Linguistics* 32:3/4 (Fall–Winter 1990): 295–315.

Hermanson, E. A. "A Brief Overview of Bible Translation in South Africa." *Acta Theologica Supplementum* 2 (2002): 6–18.

Hodgson, Janet. "Soga and Dukwana: The Christian Struggle for Liberation in Mid-19th Century South Africa." *Journal of Religion in Africa* 16:3 (Oct. 1986): 187–208.

Huffman, Thomas N. "Ceramics, Settlements and Late Iron Age Migrations." *African Archeological Review* 7 (1989): 155–82.

Jabavu, Davidson Don Tengo. "The 'Fingo Slavery' Myth." *South African Outlook* 65 (1 June 1935): 123–24, 134–35.

Jackson, Eva. "The Economic Experimentation of Nembula Duze/Ira Adams Nembula, 1846–1886." *Journal of Natal and Zulu History* 28 (2010): 8–22.

Jacobs, Nancy J. "The Intimate Politics of Ornithology in Colonial Africa." *Comparative Studies in Society and History* 48 (2006): 564–603.

Kim, K. H. S., N. R. Relkin, K.-M. Lee, and Joy Hirsch. "Distinct Cortical Areas Associated with Native and Second Languages." *Nature* 388 (10 July 1997): 171–74.

Kynoch, Gary. "Reassessing Transition Violence: Voices from South Africa's Township Wars, 1990–4." *African Affairs* 112:447 (2013): 283–303.

Louw, J. A. "The Development of Xhosa and Zulu as Languages." *Language Reform; History and Future* 2 (1983): 371–92.

Lowe, Chris, Tunde Brimah, Pearl Alice Marsh, William Minter, and Monde Muyangwa. "Talking about 'Tribe': Moving from Stereotypes to Analysis." *Africa Policy Information Center* (Washington, DC), Background Paper 10 (Nov. 1997): 1–8.

Maggs, Tim. "The Iron Age Sequence South of the Vaal and Pongola Rivers: Some Historical Implications." *Journal of African History* 21 (1980): 1–15.

Maingard, Louis Fernand. "The Brikwa and the Ethnic Origins of the Bathlaping." *South African Journal of Science* 30 (1933): 597–602.

Mdluli, Praisley [Emmanuel Bonginkosi Nzimande]. "Ubuntu-Botho: Inkatha's 'People's Education.'" *Transformation* 5 (1987): 60–77.

Meinhof, Carl. "Hottentotische Laute und Leihwörter im Kafir." *Zeitschrift der Deutschen Morgenländischen Gesellschaft* 58 (1904): 727–69, and 59 (1905): 36–89.

Mesthrie, Rajend. "Words across Worlds: Aspects of Language Contact and Language Learning in the Eastern Cape, 1800–1850." *African Studies* 57:1 (1998): 5–26.

Nurse, Derek. "The Contributions of Linguistics to the Study of History in Africa." *Journal of African History* 38 (1997): 359–91.

Nyamende, Abner. "Regional Variation in Xhosa." *Stellenbosch Papers in Linguistics Plus* 26 (1994): 202–17.

Pakendorf, Gunther. "A Brief History of the Berlin Mission Society in South Africa." *History Compass* 9:2 (2011): 106–18.

Peires, Jeff. "'Fellows with Big Holes in Their Ears': The Ethnic Origins of the amaMfengu." *Quarterly Bulletin of the National Library of South Africa* 65 (2011): 55–64.

———. "'He Wears Short Clothes!': Rethinking Rharhabe (c.1775–c.1782)." *Journal of Southern African Studies* 38:2 (June 2012): 333–54.

Perani, D., et al. "The Bilingual Brain: Proficiency and Age of Acquisition of the Second Language." *Brain* 121 (1998): 1841–52.

Peterson, Derek. "Translating the Word: Dialogism and Debate in Two Gikuyu Dictionaries." *Journal of Religious History* 23:1 (Feb. 1999): 31–50.

Prins, Frans E., and Hester Lewis. "Bushmen as Mediators in Nguni Cosmology." *Ethnography* 31 (1992): 133–47.

Reagan, Timothy G. "The Politics of Linguistic Apartheid: Language Policies in Black Education in South Africa." *Journal of Negro Education* 56:3 (Summer 1987): 299–312.

Samarin, William J. "Protestant Missions and the History of Lingala." *Journal of Religion in Africa* 16:2 (June 1986): 138–63.

Sanders, Edith R. "The Hamitic Hypothesis: Its Origin and Functions in Time Perspective." *Journal of African History* 10:4 (1969): 521–32.

Segal, Lauren. "The Human Face of Violence: Hostel Dwellers Speak." *Journal of Southern African Studies* 18:1 (Mar. 1991): 190–231.

Shiels, R. A. "John Mavuma Nembula, 1860–1897: First Black Physician in Southern Africa." *Journal of National Medical Association,* 80:11 (1988): 1256–58.

Smith, Andrew B. "On Becoming Herders: Khoikhoi and San Ethnicity in Southern Africa." *African Studies* 49:2 (1990): 51–73.

Stapleton, Timothy. "The Expansion of a Pseudo-Ethnicity in the Eastern Cape: Reconsidering the Fingo 'Exodus' of 1865." *International Journal of African Historical Studies* 29:2 (1996): 233–50.

———. "Oral Evidence of a Pseudo-Ethnicity: The Fingo Debate." *History in Africa* 22 (1995): 358–69.

Sweet, James. "The Iberian Roots of American Racist Thought." *William and Mary Quarterly,* 3rd ser., 54:1 (Jan. 1997): 143–66.

Tolmacheva, Marina. "Toward a Definition of the Term Zanj." *Azania* 21 (1986): 105–13.

Trapido, Stanley. "African Divisional Politics in the Cape Colony, 1884–1910." *Journal of African History* 9:1 (1968): 79–98.

Volz, Stephen. "European Missionaries and the Development of Tswana Identity." *Le Fait Missionaire* 15 (2004): 97–128.

Williams, Donovan. "Social and Economic Aspects of Christian Mission Stations in Caffraria 1816–1854." *Historia* 30:2 (1985): 33–48, and 31:1 (1986): 25–56.

Williams, Peter. "Hate Speech Is a Crime: Equality Court Rules in Favour of Domestic Worker." *De Rebus* 550 (Mar. 2015): 26–28.

Wright, John B. "A. T. Bryant and the 'Lala.'" *Journal of Southern African Studies* 38:2 (June 2012): 355–68.

———. "Henry Francis Fynn." *Natalia* (4 Dec. 1974): 14–17.

———. "Sonqua, Bosjesmans, Bushmen, abaThwa: Comment and Queries on Pre-Modern Identifications." *Suid-Afrikaanse Historiese Joernaal* 35 (1996): 16–29.

Dissertations, Theses, and Conference Papers

Buthelezi, Mbongiseni. "'*Sifuna umlando wethu*' (We are Looking for Our History): Oral Literature and the Meanings of the Past in Post-Apartheid South Africa." PhD diss., Columbia University, 2012.

Fry, Poppy Ann. "Allies and Liabilities: Fingo Identity and British Imperialism in South Africa's Eastern Cape, 1800–1935." PhD diss., Harvard University, 2007.

Hedges, David W. "Trade and Politics in Southern Mozambique and Zululand in the Eighteenth and Early Nineteenth Centuries." PhD diss., University of London, 1978.

Hughes, Heather. "Politics and Society in Inanda, Natal: The Qadi under Chief Mqhawe, c1840–1906." PhD diss., University of London, 1995.

Jimenez, Raevin. "Rites of Reproduction: Gender, Generation and Political Economic Transformation among Nguni-Speakers of Southern Africa, 8th–19th Century." PhD diss., Northwestern University, 2017.

Jordan, Archibald C. "A Phonological and Literary Study of Literary Xhosa." PhD diss., University of Cape Town, 1956.

Kim, K. H. S., N. R. Relkin, N. R. de LaPaz, and K.-M. Lee. "Localization of Cortical Areas Activated by Native and Second Languages with Functional Magnetic Resonance Imaging (fMRI)." In *Proceedings of the International Society for Magnetic Resonance Imaging* 1 (1996): 283.

Kubeka, Isaac Sibusiso. "A Preliminary Survey of Zulu Dialects in Natal and Zululand." Master's thesis, University of Natal, 1979.

Lanham, Leonard W. "The Proliferation and Extension of Bantu Phonemic System Influenced by Bushman and Hottentot." In *Proceedings of the Ninth International Congress of Linguistics*, Cambridge, 1962, edited by Horace Gray Lunt, 382–91. Paris: Mouton, 1964.

Martin, S. J. R. "British Images of the Zulu, c. 1820–1879." PhD diss., Cambridge University, 1982.

Mazel, Aron D. "Hunter-Gatherers in the Thukela Basin during the Last 1500 Years, with Special Reference to Hunter-Gatherer/Agriculturalist Relations." In *The Proceedings of the Khoisan Identities and Cultural Heritage Conference*, edited by Andrew Bank, 94–101. Cape Town: Institute for Historical Research and Infosource, 1998.

McNulty, Grant. "Custodianship on the Periphery: Archives, Power and Identity Politics in Post-Apartheid Umbumbulu, KwaZulu-Natal." PhD diss., University of Cape Town, 2013.

More, Andrew John. "Natal's 'Native' Education (1917–1953): Education for Segregation." Master's thesis, University of Natal, 1990.

Moyer, Richard A. "A History of the Mfengu of the Eastern Cape." PhD diss., University of London, 1976.

Mthethwa, Dingani. "The Mobilization of History and the Tembe Chieftaincy in Maputaland, 1896–1997." Master's thesis, University of Natal-Durban, 2002.

Nomlomo, Vuyokazi S. "Language Variation in the Transkeian Xhosa Speech Community and Its Impact on Children's Education." Master's thesis, University of Cape Town, 1993.

Ownby, Carolan. "Early Nguni History: The Linguistic Evidence and Its Correlation with Archeology and Oral Tradition." PhD diss., University of California, Los Angeles, 1985.

Parcells, Ashley. "Ethnic Sovereignty and the Making of a Zulu Homeland in Apartheid South Africa." PhD diss., Emory University, 2018.

Shell, Sandra Carolyn Teresa Rowoldt, ed. "A Missionary Life among the amaXhosa: The Eastern Cape Journals of James Laing, 1830–1836." Master's thesis, University of Cape Town, 2006.

Slater, Henry. "Transitions in the Political Economy of South-East Africa before 1840." PhD diss., University of Sussex, 1976.

Webster, Alan. "Land Expropriation and Labour Extraction under Cape Colonial Rule: The War of 1835 and the 'Emancipation' of the Fingo." Master's thesis, Rhodes University, 1991.

Electronic Sources

AmaHlubi Amahle. Facebook (2010–14), https://m.facebook.com/AmaHlubi-Amahle-169290819757816/.

AmaHlubi National Coordinating Committee. "Program of Action to Revive and Strengthen the Hlubi Nation in South Africa" (2004), http://www.mkhangelingoma.co.za/heritage/POA.pdf.

AmaHlubi National Working Committee, AmaHlubi Royal Committee, and AmaHlubi King's Planning Committee. *"Isizwe SamaHlubi,"* draft 1 (July 2004), https://pdf4pro.com/view/isizwe-samahlubi-mkhangeli-ngoma -194f95.html.

Center for Law and Society. "Land Rights under the Ingonyama Trust" (Feb. 2015), http://www.cls.uct.ac.za/usr/lrg/downloads/FactsheetIngonyama _Final_Feb2015.pdf.

Constitution of the Republic of South Africa (1996), https://www.gov.za /documents/constitution-republic-south-africa-1996.

Lehohla, Pali. *Census 2011 Census Brief.* http://www.statssa.gov.za/census /census_2011/census_products/Census_2011_Census_in_brief.pdf. Pretoria: Statistics South Africa, 2012.

Maho, Jouni Filip, comp. *NUGL Online: The Online Version of the New Updated Guthrie List, a Referential Classification of the Bantu Languages* (4 June 2009), https://brill.com/fileasset/downloads_products/35125_Bantu-New -updated-Guthrie-List.pdf.

Mntungwa, Lwazi. "The History of the Hlubi Nation." 30 Mar. 2016, http:// www.vivmag.co.za/archives/3395.

Nhlapo Commission Report (Reports for Paramountcies): Determination on the AmaHlubi Kingship Claim. July 2010, https://static.pmg.org.za/docs/100729 determination-chiefs.pdf.

Ntantala, Phyllis. "Balfour, Noyi." In *Dictionary of African Christian Biography* 1995, https://dacb.org/stories/southafrica/balfour-noyi/.

Republic of South Africa, Language in Education Policy in Terms of Section 3(4)(m) of The National Education Policy Act. 1996 (Act 27 of 1996), https://www.education.gov.za/Portals/0/Documents/Policies/GET /LanguageEducationPolicy1997.pdf.

Republic of the Transkei Constitution Act no. 15 of 1976, https://www .worldstatesmen.org/Transkei_Constitution.pdf.

• INDEX •

Page numbers in italics indicate illustrations. Page numbers followed by "t" indicate tables.

abambo, 28–29
abenguni, 28–29
ABM. *See* American Board missionaries
Adams, Newton, 76, 125–26, 134, 136, 148, 150, 151, 154, 156, 161
adult versus childhood acquisition of language, 90–92, 95, 153
African language ideologies, 146–71; convert populations, interaction with, 158–60; expansion of Zulu state and language, 161–69, 265n75; exposure of American Board missionaries' African associates to Zulu culture, 159–61; interpreters introducing missionaries to, 89–90, 96, 120, 146–47, 149–50, 153–58; limitations on language skills of missionaries and, 89, 90–96, 149–55; migrant African populations with experience of Zulu language and culture, 159–61; reworked by American Board missionaries, 169–71; *ukukhuluma* and *ukukhuluma nje*, 146, 164–66, 167, 169, 170, 171, 173, 176, 266n89, 266–67n91; *ukutekeza*, 146, 166–69, 171, 176–77; *ukuthefula*, 165–66; Zulu sense of linguistic superiority, 144–45, 146–49, 161, 166–69

African National Congress (ANC), 1–3, 205
Afrikaans, 189, 191, 192, 194, 196, 198, 210
Afrikaners, 58–59, 76, 126–27, 134
Alberti, Ludwig, 50, 55, 69, 70, 80, 81, 115
Aldum, Aaron James, 74
Alexander, Archibald, 124–25
Allison, James, 141, 142
Almeida, Francisco de, 40
amabutho, 132, 160, 162, 167, 168
AmaHlubi National Coordinating Committee (later AmaHlubi National Working Committee), 208–9, 212
AmaHlubi National Youth Working Committee, 209
amalala identity, 28, 29, 37, 167, 169, 189
amantungwa identity, 27, 28t, 37, 163–67, 169, 189
American Bible Society, 123, 139, 177
American Board missionaries, 15, 121–45; ABM (American Board of Commissioners for Foreign Missions), establishment of, 124; African language ideologies influencing, 146–47 (*see also* African language ideologies); Bible

Magaye (of Cele confederation), 160
Magerman, Oerson, 76–78, 87, 134
Mahlamene (Mfengu), 86
Mahwanqa (son of Bhungane), 207
Makanya (teacher/preacher at ABM
    stations), 158
Makoni, Sinfree, 12–13
Malan, Daniel François, 194
Mambayendi (Natal chief), 75
Mamdani, Mahmood, 35
Mamuni (convert at Umvoti Station),
    158
Mande (of Cele confederation), 160
Mandela, Nelson, 1, 2, 205
maps: boundary between Natal and Cape
    colonies (1894), 186; "Caffraria" (early
    sixteenth century), 43; coastal belt of
    South Africa, 21; Hlubi areas in South
    Africa, 206; mission stations in coastal
    belt (ca. 1850), 61; "Zulu" and "Xhosa"
    clusters (1950), 195
Maqoma (Rharhabe-Xhosa chief), 93
Maré, Gerhard, 4
Marks, Shula, 11, 13
Marques, Lourenço, 40
massacre of Retief party, 76, 77, 126, 134
Matanda (teacher/preacher at ABM
    stations), 158
Mathabane, Mark, 38, 197
Matiwane (Ngwane ruler), 207
Matshaya, Charles Henry, 96, 97, 105
Matwa (interpreter), 105
Mavuma, John, 159, 160
Mbange (Ntinde chief), 110
Mbata, Alban, and Garland Mdhladhla,
    UCakijana Bogcololo, 178
Mbulazi Makhanya, 161
McKinney, Silas, 151–52
Mda, Ashby Peter Solomzi, 193–94
Mda, "Zakes," 193
Mdhladhla, Garland, and Alba Mbata,
    UCakijana Bogcololo, 178
meaning and discourse, relationship
    between, 254n200
Mehlwana (convert at Umsunduzi Sta-
    tion), 159, 160

Methodists. See Wesleyan (Methodist)
    Missionary Society
métis (mixed) chiefdoms, 103, 109,
    109–16, 116
Meyer, Heinrich, 95
Mfeka, Jonas, 159
Mfengu (Fingoes), 81–87, 97, 117–18, 122,
    173, 179–83
Mfisikazi (convert at Umvoti Station),
    158
Mhlongo, Patayi "George Champion," 159
migration: Afrikaner migration due to
    dissatisfaction with British rule, 126;
    coastal belt migrancy and mutual
    intelligibility, 71–87 (see also specific
    migrants); of Zulus into Natal (1840s),
    127, 132, 136–37, 145, 159–61. See also
    deeper past, language and collective
    identity in
millennialism, 60, 124
missionaries: arrival and establishment
    of, 14–15, 57–58, 60–62, 61, 90; British
    colonial government and, 62, 87;
    "Caffre" language paradigm reinforced
    by, 14–15; language skills, limitations
    of, 89, 90–96; linguistic education
    of children of, 91; Pentecost, Protes-
    tant interpretation of, 7, 124; tribal
    identities, historical development of,
    10; Wesleyan linguistic harmonization
    project, 117–19, 122, 183. See also Bible
    translation; interpreters; specific mis-
    sionaries and missionary societies
Mkehlengana (Qwabe), 163
Mlawu (convert at Umvoti Station), 158
Moravian Missionary Society (MMS), 60
Moset (interpreter), 97
mother-tongue education. See education
    in Zulu and Xhosa; language education
Mozambique, 10, 14, 20, 28, 42–43, 45,
    52, 57, 70, 71
Mozambique Island, 40, 43
Mpande (Zulu chief), 127, 132, 136, 166
Mpangazitha (son of Bhungane), 207
Mpholompo, Battle of (1828), 81
Mqayikana kaYenge, 167

Mqhayi, Samuel Edward Krune, 33,
182–83
Mqiko (teacher/preacher at ABM stations), 158
Msimbiti, Jacob, 72–74, 76, 87, 238n94
Msingaphansi (teacher/preacher at ABM
stations), 158
Mthethwa, Dingani, 200
Mthimkhulu (son of Bhungane), 207
Mtshemla, Pato, 190
Muslims: "Caffre" as term, use of, 38, 39,
41–42; "Caffres" distinguished from,
by European naturalists, 52; identified
as black by Portuguese, 40
mutual intelligibility of "Caffre" dialects,
51; discourse and meaning, Foucault
on relationship between, 254n200;
geographic extent of "Caffre" and,
42–43, 43, 51–52, 69–71, 96–101, 119–
22; interpreters influencing missionary
conclusions about, 96–103, 108–9,
115–16, 119–20, 134–35; migrancy in
coastal belt indicating, 71–87 (see also
specific migrants); of Zulu and Xhosa,
12, 71
Mzilikazi (ruler of Interior Zulus), 126,
132, 134
Mzimba, Ntibane, 86
Mzimba, Pambani, 86

Nanise (Nancy of Inanda), 146, 156, 170,
171
Napoleonic Wars, 8, 58, 60
Natal: British annexation, 127–28,
137–38, 143, 185; migrancy of Zulus
into Natal (1840s), 127, 132, 136–37,
145, 159–61; as province of Union of
South Africa, 191; as separate Colony,
185, 186
Natal Bantu Teachers Association, 172
Natal Code of Native Law (1891), 185–86
Natal Native Trust, 185
Natal-Zululand, defined, ix
National Education Policy Act, 211
national homelands, education in, 198–99
National Party (NP), 194, 196, 205

Ndau, 28
Ndlambe (Xhosa chief), 72
Ndlela kaSompisi, 165
Ndwandwe people, 160, 162, 166–69,
206
Nembula, John, 177
Nembula kaDuze (Ira Adams Nembula),
156–57, 160–61, 170, 171, 263n53
New York Times, 3
Ngangati (convert at Umvoti Station), 158
Ngqika (Rharhabe-Xhosa chief), 36, 50,
72, 80, 84, 105, 108, 115, 179
Nguni-speaking mixed farmers in
southern Africa: collective identity,
genealogy and political allegiance as
basis for, 36–37; insider perspective
on, 27–36; métis (mixed) chiefdoms,
development of, 109–10, 114; outsider
perspective on, 23–26
Nhlapo Commission (2010), 208
Noah, Trevor, 5
Nobuyiswa (Ntinde wife of Noyi
Gciniswa), 104
Nomantu (mother of Vimbe), 106
Nooka, Jantje, 98, 99, 107–8, 113,
251n146
Nooka (Nucker), Hendriek, 108
normalization of Zulu-Xhosa language
divide, 15–16, 172–203; in academic
studies, 11–13; ethnic identities,
Zulu and Xhosa viewed as, 172–73;
identity cards and, 173, 200, 201, 202;
language standardization and language
education as means of, 174–75, 202–3;
origins of/reasons for, 172–75; Xhosa
language standardization, 178–84;
Zulu language standardization,
176–78. See also education in Zulu and
Xhosa
Norwegian Missionary Society, 140
Nouka (Gonaqua chief), 108, 113
Noyi Gciniswa (Robert Balfour), 94, 95,
102, 103–4
NP (National Party), 194, 196, 205
Nqeno kaLanga (chief of the Mbalu-
Xhosa), 108

RECONSIDERATIONS IN SOUTHERN AFRICAN HISTORY

Violence and Solace: The Natal Civil War in Late-Apartheid South Africa
Mxolisi R. Mchunu

Masked Raiders: Irish Banditry in Southern Africa, 1880–1889
Charles van Onselen

Sol Plaatje: A Life of Solomon Tshekisho Plaatje, 1876–1932
Brian Willan

Bound for Work: Labor, Mobility, and Colonial Rule in Central Mozambique, 1940–1965
Zachary Kagan Guthrie

The Finger of God: Enoch Mgijima, the Israelites, and the Bulhoek Massacre in South Africa
Robert R. Edgar

The Cowboy Capitalist: John Hays Hammond, the American West, and the Jameson Raid in South Africa
Charles van Onselen

Historian: An Autobiography
Hermann Giliomee

Cradock: How Segregation and Apartheid Came to a South African Town
Jeffrey Butler, edited by Richard Elphick and Jeannette Hopkins

Imagining a Nation: History and Memory in Making Zimbabwe
Ruramisai Charumbira

A World of Their Own: A History of South African Women's Education
Meghan Healy-Clancy

The Last Afrikaner Leaders: A Supreme Test of Power
Hermann Giliomee

The Equality of Believers: Protestant Missionaries and the Racial Politics of South Africa
Richard Elphick